FINAL REPORT,

OF THE

COMMISSION ON
INDUSTRIAL RELATIONS

INCLUDING THE

REPORT OF BASIL M. MANLY
Director of Research and Investigation

AND THE

INDIVIDUAL REPORTS AND STATEMENTS OF
THE SEVERAL COMMISSIONERS

(Reprinted from Senate Doc. No. 415, 64th Congress)

WASHINGTON
GOVERNMENT PRINTING OFFICE
1916

AUTHORITY TO PRINT.

[Public Resolution No. 15, Sixty-fourth Congress, first session.]

Senate joint resolution No. 98.

Resolved by the Senate and House of Representatives of the United States of America in Congress assembled, That the final report of the United States Commission on Industrial Relations, including the report of Basil M. Manly, director of research and investigation, and the individual reports and statements of the several commissioners, together with all the testimony taken at its hearings, except exhibits submitted in printed form, which shall be appropriately referred to in said testimony, be printed as a Senate document under the direction of the Joint Committee on Printing; and that ten thousand additional copies be printed and bound in cloth, of which two thousand five hundred copies shall be for the use of the Senate and seven thousand five hundred copies for the use of the House of Representatives; and that of the final report of said commission one hundred thousand additional copies be printed, of which thirty thousand copies shall be for the use of the Senate and seventy thousand copies for the use of the House of Representatives: *Provided,* That the superintendent of documents is hereby authorized to reprint copies of the same for sale or distribution as provided by law.

Approved, April 28, 1916.

2

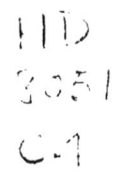

THE COMMISSION ON INDUSTRIAL RELATIONS.

FRANK P. WALSH, Missouri, *Chairman.*

JOHN R. COMMONS, Wisconsin.   S. THRUSTON BALLARD, Kentucky.
FLORENCE J. HARRIMAN, New York.   JOHN B. LENNON, Illinois.
RICHARD H. AISHTON, Illinois,[1]   JAMES O'CONNELL, District of Columbia.
HARRIS WEINSTOCK, California.   AUSTIN B. GARRETSON, Iowa.

LEWIS K. BROWN, *Secretary.*
WILLIAM O. THOMPSON, *Counsel.*
BASIL M. MANLY, *Director of Research and Investigation.*

EXTRACT FROM ACT OF CONGRESS OF AUGUST 23, 1912, CREATING AND DEFINING THE DUTIES OF THE COMMISSION ON INDUSTRIAL RELATIONS.

That a commission is hereby created to be called the Commission on Industrial Relations. Said commission shall be composed of nine persons, to be appointed by the President of the United States, by and with the advice and consent of the Senate, not less than three of whom shall be employers of labor and not less than three of whom shall be representatives of organized labor.

*   *   *   *   *   *

SEC. 4. That the commission shall inquire into the general condition of labor in the principal industries of the United States, including agriculture, and especially in those which are carried on in corporate forms; into existing relations between employers and employees; into the effect of industrial conditions on public welfare and into the rights and powers of the community to deal therewith; into the conditions of sanitation and safety of employees and the provisions for protecting the life, limb, and health of the employees; into the growth of associations of employers and of wage earners and the effect of such associations upon the relations between employers and employees; into the extent and results of methods of collective bargaining; into any methods which have been tried in any State or in foreign countries for maintaining mutually satisfactory relations between employees and employers; into methods for avoiding or adjusting labor disputes through peaceful and conciliatory mediation and negotiations; into the scope, methods, and resources of existing bureaus of labor and into possible ways of increasing their usefulness; into the question of smuggling or other illegal entry of Asiatics into the United States or its insular possessions, and of the methods by which such Asiatics have gained and are gaining such admission, and shall report to Congress as speedily as possible, with such recommendation as said commission may think proper to prevent such smuggling and illegal entry. The commission shall seek to discover the underlying causes of dissatisfaction in the industrial situation and report its conclusions thereon.

[1] Appointed commissioner Mar. 17, 1915, to serve the unexpired term of Hon. F. A. Delano, resigned.

TABLE OF CONTENTS.

5

II.

III.

IV.

LETTER OF TRANSMITTAL.

COMMISSION ON INDUSTRIAL RELATIONS,
Chicago, Ill., August 23, 1915.

To the Sixty-fourth Congress:

On behalf of the Commission on Industrial Relations, I have the honor to transmit herewith its final report.

The assembling of facts in the report of the staff from the records of our public hearings and the reports of investigators, under the direction of Mr. Basil M. Manly, might well be taken, in my opinion, as a model of efficiency and scientific treatment by governmental departments.

The plan of submitting none but undisputed facts in the final report of the commission has been faithfully adhered to.

No statement or conclusion of fact adverse to the attitude or interest of any person or group of persons is submitted, except as declared or assented to by the person or by the individuals comprising the group affected. Thus, for perhaps the first time in the history of our Government, the facts in relation to conditions in the industries examined and the relations inquired into are placed beyond the realm of controversy and established upon the solid and scientific basis of ascertained and indisputable fact.

It is believed that the work of the commission has been conducted in a spirit of social justice and an earnest desire to serve the public by bringing into the light the facts regarding the industrial relations of the country. For the creation of this spirit, as well as for an earnest insistence that the education of the public should be the keynote, I feel that full credit should be accorded Mr. George P. West, and that in addition thereto he should be credited with the inspiration and planning of many of the most effective public hearings of the commission.

Respectfully,

FRANK P. WALSH, *Chairman.*

9

I.

Report of Basil M. Manly

Director of Research and Investigation

Embodying the Findings of Fact, Conclusions, and Recommendations
of the Staff, based upon their Investigations and the
Testimony of Public Hearings

SIGNED BY

Commissioners Walsh, Lennon, O'Connell, and Garretson

TOGETHER WITH

Supplemental Statements by Chairman Walsh, Commissioners Garretson, Lennon, and O'Connell

LETTER OF SUBMITTAL.

CHICAGO, ILL., *August 9, 1915.*

To the COMMISSION ON INDUSTRIAL RELATIONS:

I have the honor to submit herewith my report, which has been prepared by direction of the commission as a summary and interpretation of the evidence contained in the public hearings of the commission and the reports of the staff, together with suggestions for action designed to remedy such evils and abuses as have been developed by investigation.

In the preparation of this report I have directed my attention primarily to the most important question placed before the commission by Congress, namely, "the underlying causes of dissatisfaction in the industrial situation." I have, however, attempted to cover as adequately as possible all the questions embodied in section 4 of the act.

A few words with regard to the method of preparation may be of value: The policy of the commission in intrusting certain important subjects to the members of the staff for investigation under the general supervision of the director has been continued throughout. The members of the staff who had charge of definite subjects have made their final reports embodying the results of their investigations and the pertinent parts of the testimony before the commission. These reports have, as far as possible, been accepted as the basis for the statements and recommendations contained in this report. It is only fair, however, to state that in certain respects they have been modified, largely as a result of the discussion which took place when these reports were presented to the commission in tentative form. Nevertheless, in every case the substance and essential ideas of each investigator's report have been retained.

The enormous mass of testimony heard by the commission has been drawn upon freely. In using this testimony I have been guided by the principle of quoting only statements made by the party to whom such evidence would be unfavorable or by persons who were clearly nonpartisan. For example, in the criticism of the attitude and actions of employers only the testimony given by employers or their agents has been quoted; the testimony of labor representatives being used only to show the attitude of the workers.

In addition, I have utilized to a very large extent the reports of other governmental agencies, not only as sources of original information but as a check upon the statements and conclusions contained herein. In relation to a few subjects, indeed, the information already collected made it unnecessary for the commission to conduct investigations of its own.

13

This report should properly be known as the report of the staff, except that, as noted above, I feel it necessary to assume personal responsibility for certain modifications which have been made from the original reports. I wish to state, however, that I have drawn most largely upon the following reports, which are submitted herewith, with the suggestion that Congress be requested to print them as supplements to this report:[1]

W. JETT LAUCK:
Analysis of Economic Causes of Unrest.
EDGAR SYDENSTRICKER:
Labor Conditions in American Industry.
CHRISTOPHER T. CHENERY:
The Telephone and Telegraph Industry.
Labor Conditions in Porto Rico.
MARIE L. OBENAUER:
Women in Industry.
Interstate Competition.
GERTRUDE BARNUM:
Enforcement of Laws Regulating Working Hours of Women in Wisconsin.
GEORGE P. WEST:
Labor Conditions in Colorado.
WILLIAM P. HARVEY:
Labor Conditions in the Black Hills.
Labor Conditions in Los Angeles.
CHARLES W. HOLMAN:
Preliminary Report on the Land Question.
JOHN L. COULTER:
Agricultural Labor and Tenancy.
WILLIAM M. LEISERSON:
Unemployment.
PETER A. SPEEK:
Conditions in Labor Camps.
Labor Complaints and Claims.
Migratory Workers.
GEORGE E. BARNETT:
Joint Agreements.
GEORGE E. BARNETT and D. A. McCABE:
Mediation and Arbitration.
LEO WOLMAN:
Extent and Growth of Labor Organizations.
J. WALLACE BRYAN:
Trade-Union Law.
EDWIN E. WITTE:
Injunctions in Labor Disputes.
ROBERT F. HOXIE:
Scientific Management and Labor.
B. S. WARREN:
Industrial Conditions and the Public Health.
LUKE GRANT:
Violence in Labor Disputes and the Policing of Industry.
The National Erectors' Association and the International Association of Bridge and Structural Iron Workers.
REDMOND S. BRENNAN and PATRICK F. GILL:
The Inferior Courts and Police of Paterson, N. J.
EDWARD A. FITZPATRICK:
Chinese Exclusion.

In addition to those named above, the following members of the staff, who have performed exceptional service and whose reports have to some extent been used directly, should be mentioned: Henry Winthrop Ballantine, Charles B. Barnes, Francis H. Bird, E. H.

---

[1] These reports have not been printed with this document, on the recommendation of Chairman Frank P. Walsh, as stated in his letter in Senate Report No. 143, Sixty-fourth Congress. The reports on Labor Conditions in Colorado and the National Erectors' Association were printed by the commission itself in 1915.

Busiek, W. J. Coyne, Nelle B. Curry, Alexander M. Daly, F. S. Deibler, Noel T. Dowling, H. E. Hoagland, Carl Hookstadt, B. F. Moore, Daniel T. O'Regan, M. O'Sullivan, Selig Perlman, Sumner Slichter, George L. Sprague, and Inis Weed.

Special mention should be made also of Charles J. Stowell and Elizabeth A. Hyde, whose work in research and in the digesting of testimony has been invaluable.

The success of the public hearings was due in large measure to the courage, tact, and good humor of Thomas J. Egan, who performed the difficult duties of sergeant at arms for the commission.

I wish to express my appreciation of the generous cooperation of the secretary, Mr. Lewis K. Brown, upon whose executive ability and tactful administration of the commission's affairs the work of the staff in large measure depended. I wish also to express to the commission my acknowledgment and appreciation of the unusual freedom which has been accorded me in the administration of the work of research and investigation, and in the conduct of the public hearings.

Respectfully,

BASIL M. MANLY, *Director.*

FINAL REPORT OF THE COMMISSION ON INDUSTRIAL RELATIONS.

REPORT OF BASIL M. MANLY, DIRECTOR OF RESEARCH AND INVESTIGATION.

INTRODUCTION.

The question of industrial relations assigned by Congress to the commission for investigation is more fundamental and of greater importance to the welfare of the Nation than any other question except the form of our government. The only hope for the solution of the tremendous problems created by industrial relationship lies in the effective use of our democratic institutions and in the rapid extension of the principles of democracy to industry.

The immediate effects of the form and character of industrial organization are, however, greater and closer to the lives and happiness of all classes of citizens than even the form and character of our political institutions. The ordinary man, whether employer or worker, has relatively little contact with the Government. If he and his family are well fed, well housed, and well clothed, and if he can pay for the education of his children, he can exist even under an autocratic monarchy with little concern, until some critical situation develops in which his own liberty is interfered with or until he is deprived of life or property by the overwhelming power of his tyrannical ruler. But his industrial relations determine every day what he and his family shall eat, what they shall wear, how many hours of his life he shall labor and in what surroundings. Under certain conditions where his individual or corporate employer owns or controls the community in which he lives, the education of his children, the character and prices of his food, clothing, and house, his own actions, speech, and opinions, and in some cases even his religion, are controlled and determined, in so far as the interests of the employer make it desirable for him to exercise such control. Such conditions are established and maintained not only through the dictation of all working conditions by the employer, but by his usurpation or control of the functions and machinery of political government in such communities.

In the available time it has been impossible to ascertain how general such conditions are, but it is clearly indicated by the investigations that in isolated industrial, mining, or agricultural communities, which are owned or controlled by single individuals or corporations, and in which the employees are unorganized, industrial feudalism is the rule rather than the exception.

In such communities democratic government does not, as a rule, exist, except in name or form, and as a consequence there now exist within the body of our Republic industrial communities which are virtually principalities, oppressive to those dependent upon them for a livelihood and a dreadful menace to the peace and welfare of the Nation.

Such conditions as these are the direct and inevitable consequence of the industrial relations which exist in such communities. Political freedom can exist only where there is industrial freedom; political democracy only where there is industrial democracy.

Such industrial democracy has been established in a greater or less degree in certain American industries or for certain classes of employees. But between conditions of industrial democracy and industrial feudalism there are almost infinite gradations marking the stages of evolution which have been reached. In every case, however, investigation has shown that the degree of political freedom and democracy which exists is conditioned by the industrial status of the citizens who form the majority of the community.

The problems of industrial relations, therefore, demand the attention of Congress, not only because they determine the life, security, and happiness of the 25,000,000 citizens of the United States who occupy the position of wage earners but because they affect for good or evil the government of localities and States and to a smaller degree that of the Nation itself. What each of these wage earners shall eat, what he shall wear, where he shall live, and how long and under what conditions he shall labor are determined by his industrial status and by his relation, individually or collectively, to the person or corporation employing him. Similarly and almost as directly, this relationship determines whether the machinery of government shall be used for or against his welfare; whether his vote shall count for or against his own interest; whether he shall be tried by a jury of his peers or a jury selected in collusion with the employing company, or, under conditions of so-called martial law, by no jury whatever; whether, in fact, he shall be a free man or be deprived of every right guaranteed by Federal and State constitutions, imprisoned without warrant for the commission of crimes of which he may be innocent or forcibly deported from the community or State in which he has made his home. For these reasons it seems desirable at the outset to suggest a recommendation to Congress that these problems of industrial relationship should occupy their due prominence in the deliberations of that honorable body, and that the entire machinery of the Federal Government should be utilized to the greatest possible degree for the correction of such deplorable conditions as have been found to exist.

The lack of a proper industrial relationship and the existence of bad labor conditions is a matter of the most serious moment during times of peace, but the events of the past year have demonstrated how enormously their menace to the welfare of a nation is increased during a period of war. The present European war is being fought on the farms and in the factories as much as in the trenches. The effective mobilization of our industrial resources is as important, simply from the standpoint of war, as is the mobilization of our military and naval forces.

It is equally important that action should be taken now, and not after war is a reality.

An attempt has been made in the succeeding pages of this report to suggest some of the measures which should be adopted, with a full realization, however, that no action will be effective which does not come through an understanding by the American people of the essential facts regarding industrial conditions. Practically there are only two alternatives for effective action: First, the creation of a huge system of bureaucratic paternalism such as has been developed in Germany; second, action which removes the many existing obstacles which prevent effective organization and cooperation, reserving for performance by the Government only those services which can not be effectively conducted by voluntary organizations and those which are of such vital importance to the entire Nation that they should not be left to the hazard of private enterprise.

In closing this introductory statement it is proper to append a quotation from Carlyle, the great Scotch historian, which contains in a few eloquent sentences the very heart of the situation in American industry:

With the working people, again, it is not so well. Unlucky! For there are from twenty to twenty-five millions of them. Whom, however, we lump together into a kind of dim compendious unity, * * *, as "the masses." Masses indeed; and yet, singular to say, the masses consist of units, * * *, every unit of whom has his own heart and sorrows; stands covered there with his own skin, and if you prick him he will bleed. Every unit of these masses is a miraculous man, even as thou thyself art; struggling with vision or with blindness for his infinite kingdom (this life which he has got once only in the middle of eternities); with a spark of the divinity, what thou callest an immortal soul, in him!

Clearly a difficult "point" for government, that of dealing with these masses; if indeed it be not rather the sole point and problem of government, and all other points mere accidental crotchets, superficialities, and beatings of the wind! For let charter chests, use and wont, law common and special, say what they will, the masses count to so many millions of units, made, to all appearance, by God, whose earth this is declared to be.

METHOD AND CHARACTER OF INVESTIGATION.

In the investigation of questions so intimately affecting the lives of a large part of the American people the ordinary methods of compiling facts and drawing deductions would have been utterly insufficient, not only because the ground to be covered was too extensive, but because the situation was too largely the result of the opinions, beliefs, and convictions of employers and employees to be susceptible of ascertainment by such a method. Furthermore, it became clear very early in the investigation that the problems which were presented could be solved only by the will and conscience of the American people acting either directly or through their representatives in the State and Federal Governments.

The commission has therefore called before it witnesses representing persons drawn from almost every walk of life, whose knowledge and opinions were believed to be of value. In order that the information developed by these hearings should reach the people they were not only held in public, but, through the newspapers, the facts developed by them have been carried throughout the Nation.

These hearings have occupied in all 154 days, or rather more than the equivalent of 6 months of the commission's time. One or more hearings were held in each of the following cities: Washington, New York, Paterson, Philadelphia, Boston, Chicago, Lead (S. Dak.), Butte, Seattle, Portland, San Francisco, Los Angeles, Denver, and Dallas. The witnesses, however, were by no means limited to these localities, but in every case the best-informed persons were brought to the centers at which the hearings were held.

The representative character of the witnesses may best be shown by the statement on the following page.

Classification of witnesses upon industrial subjects.

Affiliated with employers:
Employers, managers, foremen, etc	134
Representatives of employers' organizations	37
Attorneys	15
Efficiency engineers	10
Employment agents	14
Capitalists, bankers, directors, etc	20
	230

Affiliated with labor:
Trades-union officials	135
Workingmen and working women	90
Attorneys	6
Industrial Workers of the World	8
Representatives of the Socialist Party	6
	245

Not affiliated with either group:
Agriculturists	22
Attorneys	15
Public officials	69
Representatives of civic organizations	24
Educators	22
Economists and sociologists	20
Investigators	11
Representatives of the press	14
Clergy	10
Physicians	7
Unclassified	17
On Chinese exclusion	34
	265

Total	740

These witnesses were not arbitrarily selected by the commission, but were chosen only after careful investigation by agents of the commission, who consulted the persons best informed regarding the industry, locality, or question under consideration. Every opportunity was given employers and employees to suggest the names of witnesses who could best present their side of the case, and the persons thus suggested were without exception heard with absolute freedom not only as regards time, but without regard to the technical rules of evidence.

It seems desirable also to call attention to the fact that in this report, except for citations from admittedly nonpartisan official bodies, there are no statements of fact affecting any person or group of persons which have not been submitted to the parties directly concerned, or which have not been quoted from documents submitted by them or from their public testimony. The submission of the facts developed by preliminary investigation to the parties affected for verification or correction at public hearings is believed to be the best means of ascertaining the truth and avoiding evasion. The same is true of the recommendations and conclusions contained in the report, a very large number of which were submitted for criticism at public hearings or by correspondence.

SUMMARY OF CONCLUSIONS AND RECOMMENDATIONS.

In the act of Congress creating the commission, section 4 named 11 questions into which inquiry was specifically directed. Of these questions three, relating to industrial conditions, industrial relations, and the causes of industrial unrest, were fundamental in character and of broad scope, while eight were specific and dealt more largely with matters of detail. Leaving these eight specific questions for detailed consideration in the body of the report, it seems desirable to present briefly at this point the findings and conclusions with regard to these general questions.

LABOR CONDITIONS IN THE PRINCIPAL INDUSTRIES, INCLUDING AGRICULTURE.

In considering the conditions of labor in American industries, it has seemed that they could be judged or appraised only by comparing conditions as they actually exist with what knowledge and experience shows that they might easily be made during the immediate future if proper action were taken to utilize the resources of our Nation efficiently and distribute the products equitably.

As against this view there has been an attempt by some persons to urge the judgment of all things by comparison with the past. Much stress has been laid by certain witnesses upon the alleged improvement of the condition of the workers during the past quarter century.

This point, however, is regarded as generally immaterial. The crux of the question rather is, Have the workers received a fair share of the enormous increase in wealth which has taken place in this country, during the period, as a result largely of their labors? The answer is emphatically, No!

The wealth of the country between 1890 and 1912 increased from sixty-five to one hundred and eighty-seven billions, or 188 per cent, whereas the aggregate income of wage earners in manufacturing, mining, and transportation has risen between 1889 and 1909 only 95 per cent, from two thousand five hundred and sixteen millions in 1889 to four thousand nine hundred and sixteen millions in 1909. Furthermore, the wage earners' share of the net product[1] of industry in the case of manufactures was only 40.2 per cent in 1909, as compared with 44.9 per cent in 1889.

Similarly, the attempt to dismiss deplorable labor conditions in the United States by arguments that they are better than in European countries is repugnant. To say that conditions are better than in Great Britain, for example, is simply to say that somewhat less than one-third of the population is in a state of absolute poverty, for that was the condition reported by the latest British commission It should be a matter of shame also to boast that the condition of

---

[1] The net product is the value that remains after subtracting the cost of materials from the total value.

American laborers is better than that of laborers in the " black bread belt " of Germany.

That conditions are, as a matter of fact, but little better is proved conclusively by the almost complete cessation of immigration from Germany, England, and France. No better proof of the miserable condition of the mass of American workers need be sought than the fact that in recent years laborers in large numbers have come to this country only from Russia, Italy, Austria-Hungary, and the backward and impoverished nations of southern and eastern Europe.

With the inexhaustible natural resources of the United States, her tremendous mechanical achievements, and the genius of her people for organization and industry, there can be no natural reason to prevent every able-bodied man of our present population from being well fed, well housed, comfortably clothed, and from rearing a family of moderate size in comfort, health, and security. How far this ideal is actually achieved is discussed in some detail in the following pages.

It is evident both from the investigations of this commission and from the reports of all recent governmental bodies that a large part of our industrial population are, as a result of the combination of low wages and unemployment, living in a condition of actual poverty. How large this proportion is can not be exactly determined, but it is certain that at least one-third and possibly one-half of the families of wage earners employed in manufacturing and mining earn in the course of the year less than enough to support them in anything like a comfortable and decent condition. The detailed evidence is presented in a separate report which is submitted for transmittal to Congress.[1] At this point it is sufficient to call attention to the results of the most exhaustive and sweeping official investigation of recent years, that of the Immigration Commission, which reported to Congress in 1909. This investigation secured detailed information regarding the daily or weekly earnings of 619,595 employees of all classes in our basic manufacturing industries and in coal mining, and information regarding income and living conditions for 15,726 families.

It was found that the incomes of almost two-thirds of these families (64 per cent) were less than $750 per year and of almost one-third (31 per cent) were less than $500, the average for all being $721. The average size of these families was 5.6 members. Elaborate studies of the cost of living made in all parts of the country at the same time have shown that the very least that a family of five persons can live upon in anything approaching decency is $700. It is probable that, owing to the fact that the families investigated by the Immigration Commission were, to a large extent, foreign born, the incomes reported are lower than the average for the entire working population; nevertheless, even when every allowance is made for that fact, the figures show conclusively that between one-half and two-thirds of these families were living below the standards of decent subsistence, while about one-third were living in a state which can be described only as abject poverty.

American society was founded and for a long period existed upon the theory that the family should derive its support from the earn-

---

[1] Report of Edgar Sydenstricker: Labor Conditions in American Industries.

ings of the father. How far we have departed from this condition is shown by the fact that 79 per cent of the fathers of these families earned less than $700 per year. In brief, only one-fourth of these fathers could have supported their families on the barest subsistence level without the earnings of other members of the family or income from outside sources.

Other facts collected in this investigation show conclusively that a very large proportion of these families did not live in decency and comfort. Thirty per cent kept boarders and lodgers, a condition repugnant to every ideal of American family life, especially in the crowded tenements or tiny cottages in which the wage, earners of America characteristically live. Furthermore, in 77 per cent of the families two or more persons occupied each sleeping room, in 37 per cent three or more persons, and in 15 per cent four or more persons.

The most striking evidence of poverty is the proportion of pauper burials. Th repugnance of all classes of wage earners of all races to pauper burial is such that everything will be sacrificed and heavy debts incurred rather than permit any member of the family to lie in the " potter's field "; nevertheless in New York City 1 out of every 12 corpses is buried at the expense of the city or turned over to physicians for dissection.[1]

The terrible effects of such poverty may be outlined in a few paragraphs, but their far-reaching consequences could not be adequately shown in a volume.

Children are the basis of the State; as they live or die, as they thrive or are ill nourished, as they are intelligent or ignorant, so fares the State. How do the children of American workers fare?

It has been proved by studies here and abroad that there is a direct relation between poverty and the death rate of babies; but the frightful rate at which poverty kills was not known, at least for this country, until very recently, when through a study made in Johnstown, Pa., by the Federal Children's Bureau, it was shown that the babies whose fathers earned less than $10 per week died during the first year at the appalling rate of 256 per 1,000. On the other hand, those whose fathers earned $25 per week or more died at the rate of only 84 per 1,000. The babies of the poor died at three times the rate of those who were in fairly well-to-do families. The tremendous significance of these figures will be appreciated when it is known that one-third of all the adult workmen reported by the Immigration Commission earned less than $10 per week, even exclusive of time lost. On the showing of Johnstown these workmen may expect one out of four of their babies to die during the first year of life.

The last of the family to go hungry are the children, yet statistics show that in six of our largest cities from 12 to 20 per cent of the children are noticeably underfed and ill nourished.

The minimum amount of education which any child should receive is certainly the grammar school course, yet statistics show that only one-third of the children in our public schools complete the grammar school course, and less than 10 per cent finish high school.[2] Those

---

[1] Statistics for New York are the only ones available which are reasonably complete. Even there not all are included who die in a state of extreme poverty, as it is well known that national societies and sympathetic individuals claim a large number of bodies of persons absolutely unknown to them.
[2] Elimination of Pupils from School. Edward L. Thorndike. Bull. 379, U. S. Bureau of Education.

who leave are almost entirely the children of the workers, who, as soon as they reach working age, are thrown, immature, ill trained, and will no practical knowledge, into the complexities of industrial life.   In each of four industrial towns studied by the Bureau of Labor Statistics, more than 75 per cent of the children quit school before reaching the seventh grade.[1]

The great seriousness of this condition is even more acutely realized when it is known that in the families of the workers 37 per cent of the mothers are at work[2] and consequently unable to give the children more than scant attention. Of these mothers 30 per cent keep boarders and lodgers and 7 per cent work outside the home.

As a final statement of the far-reaching effects of the economic condition of American wage earners, it seems proper to quote the following statement of the Chicago Commission on Crime, which after thorough investigation, has reported during the past year:

> The pressure of economic conditions has an enormous influence in producing certain types of crime. Insanitary housing and working conditions, unemployment, wages inadequate to maintain a human standard of living, inevitably produce the crushed or distorted bodies and minds from which the army of crime is recruited. The crime problem is not merely a question of police and courts; it leads to the broader problems of public sanitation, education, home care, a living wage, and industrial democracy.[3]

The other factors in the conditions under which labor is employed in American industry, such as working hours, regularity of employment, safety, and sanitation, are left for later discussion. Suffice it to say in this connection that while in certain fields great improvements have been made, the general situation is such that they accentuate rather than relieve the deplorable effects of inadequate income which have been pointed out.

As a picture of American industry, this presentation is undeniably gloomy and depressing, but as a diagnosis of what is wrong with American labor conditions, it is true and exact.   There are, of course, many bright spots in American industry, where workmen are well paid and regularly employed under good working conditions in the determination of which they have some share.   But, even as the physician pays little attention to the good eyes and sound teeth of a patient whose vital organs are diseased, so impressive is the urgent need for attention to the diseased spots in industry, it is felt to be unnecessary to waste time in word pictures of conditions which are all right or which may be depended upon to right themselves.

In agriculture there is no array of exact figures which can be quoted to show the condition of labor. But, speaking generally, the available evidence indicates clearly that while in some sections agricultural laborers are well paid and fairly treated, the condition of the mass is very much like that of the industrial workers.

Moreover, there is a peculiar condition in agriculture which merits a brief but strong statement at this point as a preface to a more detailed discussion later. The most alarming fact in American agriculture is the rapid growth of tenancy. In 1910 there were 37 tenant-

---

[1] Conditions Under Which Children Leave School to Go to Work. Vol. VII of Report on Conditions of Woman and Child Wage Earners in the United States. S. Doc. No. 645, 61st Cong., 2d sess.
[2] Summary Report on Immigrants in Manufacturing and Mining. Vols. 19 and 20 of Reports of the Immigration Commission. S. Doc. No. 633, 61st Cong., 2d sess.
[3] Report of the City Council Committee on Crime, Chicago, Summary of Findings, sec. 14, p. 12.

operated farms in each 100 farms in the United States, as compared
with 28 in 1890, an increase of 32 per cent during 20 years. No
nation-wide investigation of the condition of tenant farmers has ever
been made, but in Texas, where the investigations of this commission
were thorough and conclusive, it was found not only that the economic
condition of the tenant was extremely bad but that he was far from
being free, while his future was regarded as hopeless. Badly housed,
ill nourished, uneducated, and hopeless, these tenants continue year
after year to eke out a bare living, moving frequently from one farm
to another in the hope that something will turn up. Without a large
family the tenant can not hope to succeed or break even, so in each
tenant family numerous children are being reared to a future which
under present conditions will be no better than that of their parents,
if as good. The wife of a typical tenant farmer, the mother of 11
children, stated in her testimony before the commission that in addition to the rearing of children, making their clothes, and doing the
work of the house, she always helped with the crops, working up to
within three or four months before children were born, and that
during all the years of her married life she had had no ready-made
dresses and only three hats. The investigations of this commission
in that rich and generally prosperous section of the country only confirm and accentuate the statements of the Federal Industrial Commission which reported in 1902:

> The result of this system [share tenancy] is that the renters rarely if ever
> succeed in laying by a surplus. On the contrary, their experiences are so dis-
> couraging that they seldom remain on the same farm for more than a year.
> They are not only unable to lay by any money, but their children remain un-
> educated and half clothed. The system is apparently one of the most undesira-
> ble, so far as its effect on the community is concerned.[1]

Similarly, the Public Lands Commission reported in 1905:

> There exists and is spreading in the West a tenant or hired labor system
> which not only represents a relatively low industrial development, but whose
> further development carries with it a most serious threat. Politically, socially,
> and economically this system is indefensible.

The condition of agricultural laborers can not, however, be dismissed without referring to the development of huge estates which
are operated by managers with hired labor on what may properly
be called a "factory system." The conditions upon such estates are
deplorable, not only because of the extremely low wages paid (80
cents per day in the case of one which was carefully investigated),
but even more because these estates, embracing within their boundaries entire counties and towns, are a law unto themselves and the
absolute dictators of the lives, liberties, and happiness of their employees. It is industrial feudalism in an extreme form. Such estates
are, as a rule, the property of absentee landlords, who are for the
most part millionaires, resident in the eastern States or in Europe.

EXISTING RELATIONS BETWEEN EMPLOYERS AND EMPLOYEES.

Considering the whole field of American industry, there are almost
infinite variations of relationship between employers and employees,
ranging from the individual worker hired by a single employer, as

---

[1] Reports of the Industrial Commission, Vol. XIX, 1902, p. 98.

in domestic service and agriculture, to the huge corporation with a hundred thousand stockholders and a quarter of a million employees. Relationship varies from that of direct contact to a situation where the employee, together with thousands of his fellow workers, is separated by hundreds of miles from the individuals who finally control his employment and of whose existence he is usually entirely ignorant.

A thorough discussion of the relationships which exist under these various forms of industrial organization would be not only tedious, but useless for all practical purposes. The typical form of industrial organization is the corporation. In transportation approximately 100 per cent of the wage earners are employed by corporations; in mining, 90 per cent; and in manufacturing, 75 per cent. Moreover, it is under this form that the great problems of industrial relations have developed.

The actual relationship which exists between employers and employees under the artificial conditions which characterize the corporate form of organization can not be understood without an analysis of the powers, functions, and responsibilities of the different elements which go to make up the typical corporation. The actual ownership of a corporation is vested in the stockholders and bondholders, whose only interest in the industry is represented by certificates upon the basis of which they expect the payment of interest or dividends at stated intervals.

The control of the property, as far as operation is concerned, rests finally with the stockholders, or with some particular class of stockholders whose shares entitle them to vote. The stockholders, however, act through the board of directors, who are usually elected in such a way that they represent only the dominant interest.[1] As far as the organization of the corporation is concerned, the principal function of the board of directors is to select the executive officials. These executive officials, either directly or indirectly, select the numerous superintendents, foremen, and petty bosses by whom the direct operation of the enterprise is managed and through whom all the workers are hired, discharged, and disciplined.

This is a skeleton of corporate organization. To understand its operations it is necessary to examine the functions and responsibilities of the different parts of the organization.

Theoretically and legally, the final control and responsibility rests with the stockholders, but in actual practice a very different situation is found. The relationship of stockholders to a corporation is anything but permanent; in a busy week on Wall Street the number of shares bought and sold in one of the great corporations will greatly exceed the total number of shares that are in existence. The stockholders as a class, therefore, have no guiding interests in the permanent efficiency of the corporation as regards either the preservation of its physical property or the maintenance of an efficient productive organization. Stocks are bought either as a speculation or as an investment, and in case either the physical property deteriorates or the productive organization tends to become inefficient, the well-informed stockholder generally takes no steps to correct the

[1] See the testimony of Mr. Jacob H. Schiff, Mr. Samuel Untermyer, and others upon this point.

condition, but merely throws his stock upon the market. This marks a very real and definite distinction from the actual ownership of a property or business which must be kept in good condition by its owner as regards both plant and organization. If all industries were owned and operated by individuals, there might be some reason to hope that generally satisfactory wages and physical conditions might be attained through the education of the owner to a realization that permanent success depended absolutely upon the maintenance of the plant in the best condition and the permanent satisfaction of the legitimate demands of the workers, but with the impersonal, remote, and irresponsible status of control by stock ownership, such a hope must be purely illusory. The ordinary stockholder in a large corporation actually occupies a less direct relationship to the corporation in which he is interested, has less knowledge of its actual operations, and less control over its management than the ordinary citizen has over local, State, and National Governments.

Boards of directors in theory are responsible for and would naturally be expected to maintain supervision over every phase of the corporation's management, but, as a matter of fact, we know that such supervision is maintained only over the financial phase of the business, controlling the acquisition of money to operate the business and distributing the profits. Actual direction generally exists only through the removal of executive officials who fail to deliver the expected profits, and through the appointment of their successors.[1]

Upon the testimony of financiers representing, as directors, hundreds of corporations, the typical director of large corporations is not only totally ignorant of the actual operations of such corporations, whose properties he seldom, if ever, visits, but feels and exercises no responsibility for anything beyond the financial condition and the selection of executive officials. Upon their own statements, these directors know nothing and care nothing about the quality of the product, the condition and treatment of the workers from whose labor they derive their income, nor the general management of the business.[2]

As far as operation and actual management are concerned, the executive officials are practically supreme. Upon their orders production is increased or decreased, plants are operated or shut down, and upon their recommendations wages are raised or lowered. But even they have little direct contact with the actual establishment of working conditions, and no relation at all with the rank and file of the workers. They act upon the recommendations of superintendents, whose information comes from their assistants and foremen, and from the elaborate statistics of modern business, which account for every piece of material and product, show the disposition of every penny that comes and goes, but ignore as though they did not exist the men and women whose labor drives the whole mechanism of business.

Here, then, is the field of industrial relations: Masses of workers on the one side dealing in some manner with foremen and superintendents on the other, behind whom is an organization of execu-

---

[1] See especially the testimony of Messrs. J. P. Morgan, John D. Rockefeller, jr., and August Belmont upon this point.
[2] See the testimony of Messrs. Jacob H. Schiff, Daniel Guggenheim, Roger W. Babson, and John D. Rockefeller, jr.

tive officials, representing in turn the board of directors, who are the chosen representatives of the stockholders.

The crux of the whole question of industrial relations is: Shall the workers for the protection of their interests be organized and represented collectively by their chosen delegates, even as the stockholders are represented by their directors and by the various grades of executive officials and bosses?

In considering this issue the first question that presents itself is, Why should such representation be demanded as a necessity? Not only are the executive officials, superintendents and bosses, some witnesses have urged before the commission, for the most part humane and well-intentioned men, but they know that the interests of the business depend upon the welfare of the workers and, if unhindered, will pay the best wages and create the best working conditions that the business can afford. Organization and representation are therefore argued to be unnecessary and tending only to promote friction and interfere with the management of the business.

Let us grant the high character and good intentions of officials and consider the statement of the workers in reply.

They say that in modern corporate business the actions of officials are governed not by their personal intentions, but by the inexorable demands for interest and dividends, and are driven not by their desire to create a permanently successful business with a contented labor force, but by the never-relaxed spur of the comparative cost sheet. The constant demand is for high production at low cost, not through improvements and good conditions which might give them next year, but this very month. In the high pressure of business every superintendent knows that if his plant is at the bottom of the comparative scale for two months his position topples, and if for three months it is virtually gone. He can not afford to experiment with changes that will not give immediate results. If he were his own master he might take a chance, knowing that the loss of this year would be compensated by gains under better conditions next year, but the monthly cost sheet does not wait for next year; it demands results now.

But it may be said that if he can not improve conditions himself he can at least recommend them to his superiors, to be transmitted to the board of directors for approval. This might indeed be done, and with the extension of an understanding among managers that low-production costs may be secured with high wages, probably would be to an increasing extent, except that boards of directors scorn such abstractions as the high-wage-low-cost theory and habitually insist that managers shall buy labor, as they buy material, in the cheapest market. Moreover, raising wages is traditionally unpopular among stockholders and directors, and recommendations for better conditions, particularly if they involve new capital, are frowned upon.[1] Neither the stockholders nor the directors have to live on wages or work in the existing surroundings, and profits deferred are considered profits lost.

The workers, therefore, deny the potency of even good intentions on the part of managers and point to labor history, which they

---

[1] See the discussion in the 1915 stockholders' meeting of the United States Steel Corporation which was devoted almost exclusively to the question whether the corporation, at an expense of a few thousand dollars, should continue to send a copy of the annual report to each stockholder of record.

allege shows that at best only isolated cases can be pointed out where marked improvements have taken place except in response to repeated demands from the workers or to forestall the growth of threatened organization. They point also to such facts as that children of 12 years or younger were not only employed in the factories (as they still are in some States where there has been little aggressive agitation), but almost without exception were insisted upon by the employers as a necessity.

The evidence of this character, which is summarized elsewhere, seems to be conclusive of the necessity for organization and representation under modern business conditions. But even if it were not necessary it is difficult to see any reason why what is demanded and required by stockholders should be denied to workers. It would be as illogical for stockholders individually to attempt to deal with the representatives of the unions as it is for the individual worker to attempt to deal with executive officials representing the organized stockholders.

CAUSES OF INDUSTRIAL UNREST.

It is presumed that Congress had in mind, in directing the commission to inquire into the "causes of dissatisfaction in the industrial situation," something far different from that "dissatisfaction with the present which is the hope of the future," that desire for better things which drives men forever forward. Such dissatisfaction is the mainspring of all progress and is to be desired in every nation in all walks of life.

It is believed that Congress intended the inquiry to be directed to that unrest and dissatisfaction which grows out of the existence of intolerable industrial conditions and which, if unrelieved, will in the natural course of events rise into active revolt or, if forcibly suppressed, sink into sullen hatred.

Of the existence of such unrest ample evidence has been found. It is the basis of the establishment and growth of the I. W. W., whose card-carrying members number only a few thousands, but which as "a spirit and a vocabulary" permeates to a large extent enormous masses of workers, particularly among the unskilled and migratory laborers. But entirely apart from those who accept its philosophy and creed, there are numberless thousands of workers, skilled and unskilled, organized and unorganized, who feel bitterly that they and their fellows are being denied justice, economically, politically, and legally. Just how widespread this feeling is or whether there is imminent danger of a quickening into active, nation-wide revolt, none can say. But no one who reads the papers from which the workers get their ideas and inspiration; no one who has studied with care the history of such strikes as those at Lawrence and Paterson, in West Virginia and Colorado, and has understood the temper of the strikers; no one who has associated with large numbers of workers in any part of the country, can fail to be impressed by the gravity of the situation.

This sense of tension and impending danger has been expressed by numerous witnesses before the commission, but by none more forcibly than by Mr. Daniel Guggenheim, a capitalist whose interests in mines and industrial plants extend to every part of the country.

Chairman WALSH. What do you think has been accomplished by the philanthropic activities of the country in reducing suffering and want among the people?

Mr. GUGGENHEIM. There has a great deal been done. If it were not for what has been done and what is being done, we would have revolution in this country.

The sources from which this unrest springs are, when stated in full detail, almost numberless. But upon careful analysis of their real character they will be found to group themselves almost without exception under four main sources which include all the others. The four are:

1. Unjust distribution of wealth and income.
2. Unemployment and denial of an opportunity to earn a living.
3. Denial of justice in the creation, in the adjudication, and in the administration of law.
4. Denial of the right and opportunity to form effective organizations.

1. UNJUST DISTRIBUTION OF WEALTH AND INCOME.

The conviction that the wealth of the country and the income which is produced through the toil of the workers is distributed without regard to any standard of justice is as widespread as it is deep-seated. It is found among all classes of workers and takes every form from the dumb resentment of the day laborer, who, at the end of a week's back-breaking toil finds that he has less than enough to feed his family while others who have done nothing live in ease, to the elaborate philosophy of the " soap-box orator," who can quote statistics unendingly to demonstrate his contentions. At bottom, though, there is the one fundamental, controlling idea that income should be received for service and for service only, whereas, in fact, it bears no such relation, and he who serves least, or not at all, may receive most.

This idea has never been expressed more clearly than in the testimony of Mr. John H. Walker, president of the Illinois State Federation of Labor:

A workingman is not supposed to ask anything more than a fair day's wage for a fair day's work; he is supposed to work until he is pretty fairly tuckered out, say eight hours, and when he does a fair day's work he is not supposed to ask for any more wages than enough to support his family, while with the business man the amount of labor furnishes no criterion for the amount they receive. People accept it as all right if they do not do any work at all, and accept it as all right that they get as much money as they can; in fact, they are given credit for getting the greatest amount of money with the least amount of work; and those things that are being accepted by the other side as the things that govern in every-day life, and as being right, have brought about this condition, this being in my judgment absolutely unfair; that is, on the merits of the proposition in dealing with the workers.

The workers feel this, some unconsciously and some consciously, but all of them feel it, and it makes for unrest, in my judgment, and there can be no peace while that condition obtains.

In the highest paid occupations among wage earners, such as railroad engineers and conductors, glass blowers, certain steel-mill employees, and a few of the building trades, the incomes will range from $1,500 to $2,000 at best, ignoring a few exceptional men who are paid for personal qualities. Such an income means, under present-day conditions, a fair living for a family of moderate size, education of the children through high school, a small insurance policy, a bit put by for a rainy day—and nothing more. With unusual responsibilities or misfortunes, it is too little, and the pinch of necessity is keenly felt. To attain such wages, moreover, means that the worker must be far above the average, either in skill, physical strength, or reliability. He must also have served an apprenticeship equal in length to a professional course. Finally, and most important, he or his predecessors in the trade must have waged a long, aggressive fight for better wages, for there are other occupations whose demand for skill, strength, and reliability are almost as great as those mentioned, where the wages are very much less.

These occupations, however, include but a handful compared to the mass of the workers. What do the millions get for their toil, for their skill, for the risk of life and limb? That is the question to be faced in an industrial nation, for these millions are the backbone and sinew of the State, in peace or in war.

First, with regard to the adult workmen, the fathers and potential fathers, from whose earnings, according to the " American standard," the support of the family is supposed to be derived.

Between one-fourth and one-third of the male workers 18 years of age and over, in factories and mines, earn less than $10 per week; from two-thirds to three-fourths earn less than $15, and only about one-tenth earn more than $20 a week. This does not take into consideration lost working time for any cause.

Next are the women, the most portentously growing factor in the labor force, whose wages are important, not only for their own support or as the supplement of the meager earnings of their fathers and husbands, but because, through the force of competition in a rapidly extending field, they threaten the whole basis of the wage scale. From two-thirds to three-fourths of the women workers in factories, stores and laundries, and in industrial occupations generally, work at wages of less than $8 a week. Approximately one-fifth earn less than $4 and nearly one-half earn less than $6 a week.

Six dollars a week—what does it mean to many? Three theater tickets, gasoline for the week, or the price of a dinner for two; a pair of shoes, three pairs of gloves, or the cost of an evening at bridge. To the girl it means that every penny must be counted, every normal desire stifled, and each basic necessity of life barely satisfied by the sacrifice of some other necessity. If more food must be had than is given with 15-cent dinners, it must be bought with what should go for clothes; if there is need for a new waist to replace the old one at which the forewoman has glanced reproachfully or at which the girls have giggled, there can be no lunches for a week and dinners must cost 5 cents less each day. Always too the room must be paid for, and back of it lies the certainty that with slack seasons will come lay-offs and discharges. If the breaking point has come, and she must have some amusement, where can it come from? Surely not out of $6 a week.

Last of all are the children, for whose petty addition to the stream of production the Nation is paying a heavy toll in ignorance, deformity of body or mind, and premature old age. After all, does it matter much what they are paid? For all experience has shown that in the end the father's wages are reduced by about the amount that the children earn. This is the so-called " family wage," and examination of the wages in different industries corroborates the theory that in those industries, such as textiles, where women and children can be largely utilized, the wages of men are extremely low.

The competitive effect of the employment of women and children upon the wages of men, can scarcely be overestimated. Surely it is hard enough to be forced to put children to work, without having to see the wages of men held down by their employment.

This is the condition at one end of the social scale. What is at the other?

Massed in millions, at the other end of the social scale, are fortunes of a size never before dreamed of, whose very owners do not know the extent nor, without the aid of an intelligent clerk, even the sources of their incomes. Incapable of being spent in any legitimate manner, these fortunes are burdens, which can only be squandered, hoarded, put into so-called "benefactions" which, for the most part, constitute a menace to the State, or put back into the industrial machine to pile up ever-increasing mountains of gold.

In many cases, no doubt, these huge fortunes have come, in whole or in part, as the rich reward of exceptional service. None would deny or envy him who has performed such service the richest of rewards, although one may question the ideals of a Nation which rewards exceptional service only by burdensome fortunes. But such reward can be claimed as a right only by those who have performed service, not by those who through relationship or mere parasitism chance to be designated as heirs. Legal right, of course, they have by virtue of the law of inheritance, which, however, runs counter to the whole theory of American society, and which was adopted, with important variations, from the English law, without any conception of its ultimate results and apparently with the idea that it would prevent exactly the condition which has arisen. In effect the American law of inheritance is as efficient for the establishment and maintenance of families as is the English law, which has bulwarked the British aristocracy through the centuries. Every year, indeed, sees this tendency increase, as the creation of "estates in trust" secures the ends which might be more simply reached if there were no prohibition of "entail." According to the income-tax returns for 10 months of 1914, there are in the United States 1,598 fortunes yielding an income of $100,000 or more per year. Practically all of these fortunes are so invested and hedged about with restrictions upon expenditure that they are, to all intents and purposes, perpetuities.

An analysis of 50 of the largest American fortunes shows that nearly one-half have already passed to the control of heirs or to trustees (their vice regents) and that the remainder will pass to the control of heirs within 20 years, upon the deaths of the "founders." Already, indeed, these founders have almost without exception retired from active service, leaving the management ostensibly to their heirs but actually to executive officials upon salary.

We have, according to the income-tax returns, 44 families with incomes of $1,000,000 or more,[1] whose members perform little or no useful service, but whose aggregate incomes, totaling at the very least $50,000,000 per year, are equivalent to the earnings of 100,000 wage earners at the average rate of $500.

The ownership of wealth in the United States has become concentrated to a degree which is difficult to grasp. The recently published

---

[1] The income tax statistics, as a matter of fact, cover only a period of 10 months in 1914.

researches of a statistician of conservative views[1] have shown that as nearly as can be estimated the distribution of wealth in the United States is as follows:

The "rich," 2 per cent of the people, own 60 per cent of the wealth.

The "middle class," 33 per cent of the people, own 35 per cent of the wealth.

The "poor," 65 per cent of the people, own 5 per cent of the wealth.

This means in brief that a little less than 2,000,000 people, who would make up a city smaller than Chicago, own 20 per cent more of the Nation's wealth than all the other 90,000,000.

The figures also show that with a reasonably equitable division of wealth, the entire population should occupy the position of comfort and security which we characterize as middle class.

The actual concentration has, however, been carried very much further than these figures indicate. The largest private fortune in the United States, estimated at $1,000,000,000, is equivalent to the aggregate wealth of 2,500,000 of those who are classed as "poor," who are shown in the studies cited to own on the average about $400 each.

Between the two extremes of superfluity and poverty is the large middle class—farmers, manufacturers, merchants, professional men, skilled artisans, and salaried officials—whose incomes are more or less adequate for their legitimate needs and desires, and who are rewarded more or less exactly in proportion to service. They have problems to meet in adjusting expenses to income, but the pinch of want and hunger is not felt, nor is there the deadening, devitalizing effect of superfluous, unearned wealth.

From top to bottom of society, however, in all grades of incomes, are innumerable number of parasites of every conceivable type. They perform no useful service, but drain off from the income of the producers a sum whose total can not be estimated.

This whole situation has never been more accurately described than by Hon. David Lloyd-George in an address on "Social waste":

I have recently had to pay some attention to the affairs of the Sudan, in connection with some projects that have been mooted for irrigation and development in that wonderful country. I will tell you what the problem is—you may know it already. Here you have a great, broad, rich river upon which both the Sudan and Egypt depend for their fertility. There is enough water in it to fertilize every part of both countries; but if, for some reason or other, the water is wasted in the upper regions, the whole land suffers sterility and famine. There is a large region in the upper Sudan where the water has been absorbed by one tract of country, which, by this process, has been converted into a morass, breeding nothing but pestilence. Properly and fairly husbanded, distributed, and used, there is enough to fertilize the most barren valley and make the whole wilderness blossom like the rose.

That represents the problem of civilization, not merely in this country but in all lands. Some men get their fair share of wealth in a land and no more—sometimes even the streams of wealth overflow to waste over some favored regions, often producing a morass, which poisons the social atmosphere. Many have to depend on a little trickling runlet, which quickly evaporates with every commercial or industrial drought; sometimes you have masses of men and women whom the flood at its height barely reaches, and then you witness parched specimens of humanity, withered, hardened in misery, living in a desert where even the well of tears has long ago run dry.

---

[1] Prof. Willard I. King, The Wealth and Income of the People of the United States.

Besides the economic significance of these great inequalities of wealth and income, there is a social aspect which equally merits the attention of Congress. It has been shown that the great fortunes of those who have profited by the enormous expansion of American industry have already passed, or will pass in a few years, by right of inheritance to the control of heirs or to trustees who act as their "vice regents." They are frequently styled by our newspapers "monarchs of industry," and indeed occupy within our Republic a position almost exactly analogous to that of feudal lords.

These heirs, owners only by virtue of the accident of birth, control the livelihood and have the power to dictate the happiness of more human beings than populated England in the Middle Ages. Their principalities, it is true, are scattered and, through the medium of stock ownership, shared in part with others; but they are none the less real. In fact, such scattered invisible industrial principalities are a greater menace to the welfare of the Nation than would be equal power consolidated into numerous petty kingdoms in different parts of the country. They might then be visualized and guarded against; now their influence invisibly permeates and controls every phase of life and industry.

"The king can do no wrong," not only because he is above the law but because every function is performed or responsibility assumed by his ministers and agents. Similarly our Rockefellers, Morgans, Fricks, Vanderbilts, and Astors can do no industrial wrong, because all effective action and direct responsibility is shifted from them to the executive officials who manage American industry. As a basis for this conclusion we have the testimony of many, among which, however, the following statements stand out most clearly:

Mr. John D. Rockefeller, jr.:[1]

* * * Those of us who are in charge there elect the ablest and most upright and competent men whom we can find, in so far as our interests give us the opportunity to select, to have the responsibility for the conduct of the business in which we are interested as investors. We can not pretend to follow the business ourselves.

Mr. J. Pierpont Morgan:

Chairman WALSH. In your opinion, to what extent are the directors of corporations responsible for the labor conditions existing in the industries in which they are the directing power?
Mr. MORGAN. Not at all I should say.

The similitude, indeed, runs even to mental attitude and phrase. Compare these two statements:

Mr. John D. Rockefeller, jr.:

My appreciation of the conditions surrounding wage earners and my sympathy with every endeavor to better these conditions are as strong as those of any man.

Louis XVI:

There is none but you and me that has the people's interest at heart. ("Il n'y a que vous et moi aimions le peuple.")

The families of these industrial princes are already well established and are knit together not only by commercial alliances but by a network of intermarriages which assures harmonious action whenever their common interest is threatened.

---

[1] Before congressional investigating committee.

Effective action by Congress is required, therefore, not only to readjust on a basis of compensation approximating the service actually performed, the existing inequalities in the distribution of wealth and income, but to check the growth of an hereditary aristocracy, which is foreign to every conception of American Government and menacing to the welfare of the people and the existence of the Nation as a democracy.

The objects to be attained in making this readjustment are: To reduce the swollen, unearned fortunes of those who have a superfluity; to raise the underpaid masses to a level of decent and comfortable living; and at the same time to accomplish this on a basis which will, in some measure, approximate the just standard of income proportional to service.

The discussion of how this can best be accomplished forms the greater part of the remainder of this report, but at this point it seems proper to indicate one of the most immediate steps which need to be taken.

It is suggested that the commission recommend to Congress the enactment of an inheritance tax, so graded that, while making generous provision for the support of dependents and the education of minor children, it shall leave no large accumulation of wealth to pass into hands which had no share in its production.[1] The revenue from this tax, which we are informed would be very great, should be reserved by the Federal Government for three principal purposes:

1. The extension of education.

2. The development of other important social services which should properly be performed by the Nation, which are discussed in detail elsewhere.

3. The development, in cooperation with States and municipalities, of great constructive works, such as road building, irrigation, and reforestation, which would materially increase the efficiency and welfare of the entire Nation.

We are informed by counsel not only that such a tax is clearly within the power of Congress, but that upon two occasions, namely, during the Civil War and in 1898, such graded inheritance taxes were enacted with scarcely any opposition and were sustained by the Supreme Court, which held that the inheritance tax was not a direct tax within the meaning of the Constitution. We are aware that similar taxes are levied in the various States, but the conflict with such State taxes seems to have presented little difficulty during the period in which the tax of 1898 was in effect. Under any circumstances this need cause no great complication, as the matter could be readily adjusted by having the Federal Government collect the entire tax and refund a part to the States on an equitable basis.

There is no legislation which could be passed by Congress the immediate and ultimate efforts of which would be more salutary or would more greatly assist in tempering the existing spirit of unrest.

2. UNEMPLOYMENT AND DENIAL OF OPPORTUNITY TO EARN A LIVING.

As a prime cause of a burning resentment and a rising feeling of unrest among the workers, unemployment and the denial of an op-

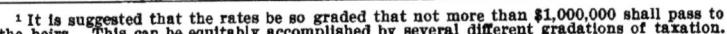

---

[1] It is suggested that the rates be so graded that not more than $1,000,000 shall pass to the heirs. This can be equitably accomplished by several different gradations of taxation.

portunity to earn a living is on a parity with the unjust distribution of wealth. They may on final analysis prove to be simply the two sides of the same shield, but that is a matter which need not be discussed at this point. They differ in this, however, that while unjust distribution of wealth is a matter of degree, unemployment is an absolute actuality, from which there is no relief but soul-killing crime and soul-killing charity.

To be forced to accept employment on conditions which are insufficient to maintain a decent livelihood is indeed a hardship, but to be unable to get work on any terms whatever is a position of black despair.

A careful analysis of all available statistics shows that in our great basic industries the workers are unemployed for an average of at least one-fifth of the year, and that at all times during any normal year there is an army of men, who can be numbered only by hundreds of thousands, who are unable to find work or who have so far degenerated that they can not or will not work. Can any nation boast of industrial efficiency when the workers, the source of her productive wealth, are employed to so small a fraction of their total capacity?

Fundamentally, this unemployment seems to rise from two great causes, although many others are contributory. First, the inequality of the distribution of income which leaves the great masses of the population (the true ultimate consumers) unable to purchase the products of industry which they create, while a few have such a superfluity that it can not be normally consumed but must be invested in new machinery for production or in the further monopolization of land and natural resources. The result is that in mining and other basic industries we have an equipment in plant and developed property far in excess of the demands of any normal year, the excess being, in all probability, at least 25 per cent. Each of these mines and industrial plants keeps around it a labor force which, on the average, can get work for only four-fifths of the year, while at the same time the people have never had enough of the products of those very industries—have never been adequately fed, clothed, housed, nor warmed—for the very simple reason that they have never been paid enough to permit their purchase.

The second principal cause lies in the denial of access to land and natural resources even when they are unused and unproductive, except at a price and under conditions which are practically prohibitive. This situation, while bound up with the land and taxation policies of our States and Nation, also rests fundamentally upon the unjust distribution of wealth. Land or mineral resources in the hands of persons of average income must and will be used either by their original owners or by some more enterprising person. By the overwhelming forces of economic pressure, taxation, and competition they can not be permitted to lie idle if they will produce anything which the people need. Only in the hands of large owners—free from economic pressure, able to evade or minimize the effects of taxation and to await the ripening of the fruits of unearned increment—can land be held out of use if its products are needed.

There can be no more complete evidence of the truth of this statement than the condition of the farms of 1,000 acres and over, which, valued at two and one-third billion dollars, comprise 19 per cent of all the farm land of the country and are held by less than 1 per cent

of the farm owners. The United States census returns show that
in these 1,000-acre farms only 18.7 per cent of the land is cultivated
as compared with 60 to 70 per cent in farms of from 50 to 499 acres.
Furthermore, it is well known that the greater part of these smaller
farms which are left uncultivated are held by real estate men, bankers, and others who have independent sources of income. More than
four-fifths of the area of the large holdings is being held out of active
use by their 50,000 owners, while 2,250,000 farmers are struggling
for a bare existence on farms of less than 50 acres, and an untold
number who would willingly work these lands are swelling the
armies of the unemployed in the cities and towns.

A basic theory of our Government, which found expression in the
homestead acts, was that every man should have opportunity to secure
land enough to support a family. If this theory had been carried
out and homesteads had either gone to those who would use them
productively or remained in the hands of the Government, we should
not yet have a problem of such a character. But these acts were
evaded; land was stolen outright by wholesale, and fraudulent en-
tries were consolidated into enormous tracts which are now held by
wealthy individuals and corporations.

The Public Lands Commission, after an exhaustive inquiry, reported in 1905:

Detailed study of the practical operation of the present land laws shows that
their tendency far too often is to bring about land monopoly rather than to
multiply small holdings by actual settlers.

* * * Not infrequently their effect is to put a premium on perjury and
dishonest methods in the acquisition of land. It is apparent, in consequence,
that in very many localities, and perhaps in general, a larger proportion of the
public land is passing into the hands of speculators than into those of actual
settlers making homes. * * * Nearly everywhere the large landowner
has succeeded in monopolizing the best tracts, whether of timber or agricultural lands.

To one who has not read the preceding statements carefully there
may seem to be a contradiction in proposing to prevent great capitalists from creating an excess of productive machinery and over-
developing mineral resources while pointing out the necessity of
forcing land and other natural resources into full and effective use
by the people. The two propositions are, as a matter of fact, as
fundamentally distinct as monopoly and freedom. The capitalist
increases his holdings in productive machinery and resources only
because through monopolization and maintenance of prices he hopes
to reap rewards for himself or increase his power, while the aim
in desiring the full development of land and other resources by the
people is that they, producing for themselves, may enjoy a sufficiency
of good things and exchange them for the products of others, and
thus reduce to a minimum the condition of unemployment.

There are, of course, many other causes of unemployment than the
inequality of wealth and the monopolization of land which there is
no desire to minimize. Chief among these are immigration, the inadequate organization of the labor market, the seasonal character of
many industries, and the personal deficiencies of a very large number of the unemployed. It can not be denied that a considerable
proportion of the men who fill the city lodging houses in winter are
virtually unemployables as a result of weakness of character, lack

---

[1] S. Doc. 154, 58th Cong., 3d sess., p. 14.

of training, the debasing effects of lodging-house living and city dissipation, and, last but not least, the conditions under which they are forced to work in the harvest fields and lumber, railroad, and construction camps. The seasonal fluctuations of our industries are enormous, employing hundreds of thousands during the busy season and throwing them out on the community during the dull season, and almost nothing has been done to remedy this condition. It would be difficult to imagine anything more chaotic and demoralizing than the existing methods of bringing workmen and jobs together. Certain measures for dealing with these conditions, which are discussed elsewhere in the report, need to be pushed forward with all possible vigor. But it may be confidently predicted that the unemployment situation will not be appreciably relieved until great advances have been made in the removal of the two prime causes—unjust distribution of wealth and monopolization of land and natural resources.

The most direct methods of dealing with the inequality of wealth have already been briefly discussed and will be considered elsewhere in the report. With respect to the land question, however, the following basic suggestions are submitted:

1. Vigorous and unrelenting prosecutions to regain all land, water power, and mineral rights secured from the Government by fraud.

2. A general revision of our land laws, so as to apply to all future land grants the doctrine of "superior use," as in the case of water rights in California, and provision for forfeiture in case of actual nonuse. In its simplest form the doctrine of "superior use" implies merely that at the time of making the lease the purpose for which the land will be used must be taken into consideration, and the use which is of greatest social value shall be given preference.

3. The forcing of all unused land into use by making the tax on nonproductive land the same as on productive land of the same kind and exempting all improvements.

Other measures for dealing with unemployment are discussed under that head on page —.

The unemployed have aptly been called "the shifting sands beneath the State." Surely there is no condition which more immediately demands the attention of Congress than that of unemployment, which is annually driving hundreds of thousands of otherwise productive citizens into poverty and bitter despair, sapping the very basis of our national efficiency, and germinating the seeds of revolution.

3. DENIAL OF JUSTICE.

No testimony presented to the commission has left a deeper impression than the evidence that there exists among the workers an almost universal conviction that they, both as individuals and as a class, are denied justice in the enactment, adjudication, and administration of law, that the very instruments of democracy are often used to oppress them and to place obstacles in the way of their movement toward economic, industrial, and political freedom and justice. Many witnesses, speaking for millions of workers as well as for themselves, have asserted with the greatest earnestness that the mass of the workers are convinced that laws necessary for their protection against the most grievous wrongs can not be passed except after long and exhausting struggles; that such beneficent measures as become laws are largely nullified by the unwarranted decisions of the courts; that the laws which stand upon the statute books are not equally enforced; and that the whole machinery of Government has frequently been placed at the disposal of the employers for the oppression of the workers; that the Constitution itself has been ignored in the interests of the employers; and that constitutional guaranties erected primarily for the protection of the workers have been denied to them and used as a cloak for the misdeeds of corporations.

If it be true that these statements represent the opinions of the mass of American workers, there is reason for grave concern, for there are 25,000,000 of them, of whom 3,000,000 are welded together into compact organizations.

But if it be true that these charges are justified; if, in fact, our legislators, our judges, and executives, do not afford equal consideration to the workers and are concerned with protecting the rights of property rather than the rights of men, and at times even become the instruments for the oppression of the poor and humble, then the situation demands and must receive the prompt and decisive action of every right-thinking man in order that these evils may be eradicated and justice and liberty established in the place of injustice and oppression.

Before examining the evidence, it should be understood that it is not charged that such acts of injustice are universal, but that they occur so frequently and in such diverse parts of the country that any man may reasonably fear that he himself or those with whom he is associated may at any time be the victim of injustice or discrimination. It has been urged, and perhaps properly, that the charges would be sustained if it were found that such acts of injustice had been committed only upon rare occasions, if it should also be established that such injustices were allowed to stand without redress, and if those who were guilty of their commission were left unimpeached and unpunished.

An enormous mass of evidence bearing upon these charges has been presented to the commission by witnesses or collected by its staff. This material is presented in some detail in another part of the report, but the summary which follows may be regarded as reasonably full and exact.

First, with regard to the enactment of laws, it is charged that the workers have been unable to secure legislation to protect them against grievous wrongs, except after exhausting struggles against overwhelming odds and against insidious influences.

The evidence bearing upon this question has dealt with the history of three principal lines of legislation in which the evils sought to be remedies are now universally admitted to have been very great, involving wanton destruction of life, the exploitation of women and children, and the practical enslavement of American seamen. A careful examination has been made of the history of attempts to secure adequate legislation to prevent child labor, to protect women against extreme hours of labor and night work, to secure the safety of factories, railroads, and mines, and to provide for the safety, comfort, and liberty of seamen.

The history of child-labor legislation shows that although agitation for the protection and education of children began during the early part of the nineteenth century in Massachusetts, Rhode Island, Connecticut, New York, and Pennsylvania; no adequate legislation was obtained until nearly the end of the century. Time after time in each of these industrial States the sentiment of the public was aroused, organization was effected, and well-drafted bills were introduced only to be killed in committee, emasculated or killed on the floor of the legislature, or passed with exceptions which rendered them entirely ineffective. Even the attempt to reduce the hours of children below 12 per day. was bitterly contested and met by every known trick of legislative chicanery. The whole history of the contest for adequate child-labor legislation is even now being repeated in some of the Southern States, where laws prohibiting the employment of children are bitterly contested and beaten session after session by legislators, unsympathetic or controlled by the cotton-mill interests.

Similarly, although the movement to restrict the working hours of women and to prohibit night work began in Massachusetts and Pennsylvania as early as 1840, the first legislation limiting the hours was the 10-hour bill passed in Massachusetts in 1874, and night work went unregulated until the passage of the act of 1899 in Nebraska.[1]

The movement for safety of life and limb in the factories and workshops, although pushed with great vigor in almost every session of the State legislatures after 1880, secured only a few acts providing for such obvious matters as the guarding of set screws and gears, but made practically no provision for their enforcement. No really effective action to promote safety took place until, after many years of hard fighting, the first workmen's compensation acts were passed between 1900 and 1910, which for the first time made the unsafe condition of factories directly expensive.

Even upon the railroads, where the safety of the public as well as of the workers was involved, at least 10 years of constant agitation on the part of the railroad brotherhoods and various interested citizens was necessary before the first Federal act providing for safety appliances was passed in 1893.

In the case of the movement to secure the safety, comfort, and liberty of seamen, it is a matter of record that Andrew Furuseth, president of the seamen's union, backed not only by all the members of his own organization but by the entire American labor movement, attended each session of Congress and devoted his whole energies to securing legislation upon this subject for the entire period of 22 years from 1893 to 1915, when the seamen's bill finally became a law.

Other evidence has been presented covering the long fights to secure legislation to remove the evils of company stores, payment in scrip, prison labor, arbitrary deductions from wages, "sweating," tenement houses, and a number of other matters upon which ade-

---

[1] It is worthy of note that although the decision on the Massachusetts law was favorable and thus established a precedent (Commonwealth v. Hamilton Mfg. Co., 120 Mass., 383), it was thrown aside by the Illinois court in 1895 in holding unconstitutional a law of that State prescribing an 8-hour day for women (Ritchie v. People, 155 Ill., 98), and it was not until 1910 that the same court accepted a 10-hour law as constitutional (Ritchie v. Wyman, 244 Ill., 509). The Nebraska statute limited the hours of women to 10 a day and prohibited night work between the hours of 10 p. m. and 6 a. m., but the first case did not raise the question of night work (Wenham v. State, 65 Neb., 394). In New York, however, a statute regulating night work was held unconstitutional in 1907 (People v. Williams, 189 N. Y., 131, and it was not until the present year that a similar law was sustained (People v. Schweinler Press, 214 N. Y., 395).

quate legislation has not yet been secured, except perhaps in a few States, although there has been unremitting agitation upon these questions for more than half a century. This evidence shows clearly that the workers have just grounds for the charge that the legislatures have been criminally slow in acting for the relief of grievous wrongs and have used every subterfuge to escape adequate and aggressive action, even while thousands of men, women, and children were being killed, maimed, or deformed as a result of their negligence.

Evidence has further been presented to show that such a condition has not been the result entirely of the complacency or slothfulness of legislators, but that powerful influences have been at work to prevent such remedial legislation. The most convincing evidence presented upon this phase of the question is the record of the National Association of Manufacturers and its allied organizations, as contained in the testimony and findings before congressional committees,[1] in the printed reports of that association and in the testimony before the commission of the representatives of various State employers' associations. The substance of this evidence is so well known to Congress and to the public that it is necessary here to call attention only to the fact that the efforts of such associations in preventing the enactment of practically all legislation intended to improve the condition or advance the interests of workers were not confined to Congress, but were even more effective in the State legislatures.

The persistent and bitter manner in which the railroads fought the laws providing for safety appliances, although the measures were moderate and necessary, not only for the safety of the traveling public, but for the efficient operation of the roads, is well known to Congress.

Perhaps the most significant statement regarding the insidious influences of this character is contained in a letter from Mr. L. M. Bowers, chairman of the board of directors of the Colorado Fuel & Iron Co., to the Secretary of Mr. John D. Rockefeller, jr., under date of May 13, 1913:

> The Colorado Fuel & Iron Co. for many years were accused of being the political dictator of southern Colorado, and, in fact, were a mighty power in the entire State. When I came here it was said that the C. F. & I. Co. voted every man and woman in their employ without any regard to their being naturalized or not, and even their mules, it used to be remarked, were registered if they were fortunate enough to possess names. Anyhow, a political department was maintained at a heavy expense. I had before me the contributions of the C. F. & I. Co. for the campaign of 1904, amounting to $80,605, paid out personally by President Hearne. All the vouchers and checks I have examined personally, all of which were payable to Albert A. Miller, upon which he drew the currency and, it is said, handed the money over to Mr. Hearne, who paid it out. So far as I can discover, not one particle of good was accomplished for the company, but Mr. Hearne was an aspirant for the position of United States Senator and devoted a vast amount of time and money with this end in view, I have no doubt.
>
> The company became notorious in many sections for their support of the liquor interests. They established saloons everywhere they possibly could.

---

[1] U. S. Senate Committee on Judiciary. Maintenance of a Lobby to Influence Legislation. Hearings before a subcommittee pursuant to S. Res. 92, 63d Cong.. 1st sess.
Charges Against Members of the House and Lobby Activities of the National Association of Manufacturers of the United States and Others. Hearings before select committee of House of Representatives appointed under H. Res. 198, 63d Cong., 1st sess.

This department was managed by one John Kebler, a brother of the one-time president of the company, who died about the time I came here, a victim of his own intemperate habits. A sheriff, elected by the votes of the C. F. & I. Co. employees, and who has been kept in office a great many years, established himself or became a partner in 16 liquor stores in our coal mines. To clean up the saloons and with them the gambling hells and houses of prostitution has been one of the things that Mr. Welborn and I have devoted an enormous amount of time to during the past five years. The decent newspapers everlastingly lampooned the C. F. & I. Co. at every election, and I am forced to say the company merited, from a moral standpoint, every shot that was fired into their camp.

Since I came here [1] not a nickel has been paid to any politician or political party. We have fought the saloons with all the power we possess. We have forbidden any politician from going into our camps, and every subordinate official connected with the company has been forbidden to influence our men to vote for any particular candidate. We have not lobbied in the legislature, but have gone directly to the governor and other able men and have demanded fair treatment.

Second, it is charged by the workers that after wholesome and necessary laws are passed they are in large part nullified by the courts either upon technicalities of a character which would not be held to invalidate legislation favorable to the interests of manufacturers, merchants, bankers, and other property owners, or thrown out on the broad ground of unconstitutionality, through strained or illogical construction of constitutional provisions. It is argued that such action is doubly evil, because the power to declare legislative acts unconstitutional has been assumed by the courts in the face of a complete absence of legal sanction, in complete disregard of early decisions denying the possession of such power, and in complete contrast to the practices of the courts in every other country of the civilized world. It is not within our province to decide whether or not this assumption of power by the courts was justified. It is sufficient here merely to examine the evidence bearing upon the allegations that laws necessary for the correction of grave industrial abuses are nullified by strained interpretations or for reasons which would be insufficient in other cases, and that they are held unconstitutional upon pretexts which in reality are the outgrowth of economic bias on the part of the judges.

A large number of decisions illustrating these points have been brought to the attention of the commission, but only a few need be cited here. It has been held, for example, even that statutes requiring dangerous machinery to be guarded may be disobeyed by the employer, and children employed about such unguarded machinery are held to have assumed the risk.[2] The same has been held regarding the employment of women.[3]

Many other cases might be cited on the question of strained interpretation,[4] bearing out the assertion made by Justice Lurton, of

---

[1] This statement of Mr. Bowers should be considered in conjunction with his testimony that the evil influences created by the Colorado Fuel & Iron Co. were still in power and his admission that the company was deeply interested in the last State election and that 150 men were put into the field from his office alone to work for the candidates favored by the company, which was deeply interested in the election of officials who would vigorously prosecute the strikers. His letters narrating how the governor of Colorado was whipped into line should also be considered, as well as the testimony of Dr. E. S. Gaddis, former head of the sociological department of the Colorado Fuel & Iron Co., that officials openly influenced elections.

[2] Higgins v. O'Keefe, 79 Fed., 900; White v. Wittemann Lith. Co., 131 N. Y., 631.

[3] Knisley v. Pratt, 148 N. Y., 372.

[4] Nappa v. Erie Ry. Co., 195 N. Y., 176, 184; Gallagher v. Newman, 190 N. Y., 444, 447–448; Cashman v. Chase, 156 Mass., 342; Quinlan v. Lackawanna Steel Co., 107 A. D. 176, affirmed 191 N. Y., 329; Finnigan v. N. Y. Contracting Co., 194 N. Y., 244.

the Federal Supreme Court, when, in a case not involving industrial relations, he says:

The judgment just rendered will have, as I think, the effect to defeat the clearly expressed will of the legislature by a construction of its words that can not be reconciled with their ordinary meaning.[1]

Probably there are no other cases which have created so much bitterness as those of personal injury in which the plaintiffs have been denied recovery of damages on the principles of "fellow servant," "assumption of risk," and "contributory negligence," and the obstacles which have been created by the courts to prevent the removal of these defenses for the employer have served only to intensify the feeling. The contrast in attitude of the judges can not better be shown than by considering that while they have held each employee of a corporation responsible under these three principles not only for his own involuntary acts but for the physical condition of the entire property and the conduct of each of his fellow workers, they have repeatedly absolved officials, directors, and stockholders from responsibility for accidents, even when the unsafe condition of the property had been published, or when orders had been issued which were directly responsible for the accidents. It would hardly be an exaggeration to say that, if the courts had held officials and directors to as great a degree of responsibility as employees for the condition of the property and the actions of their agents, there is hardly one who would have escaped punishment for criminal negligence. According to the best estimates, approximately 35,000 persons were killed last year in American industry, and at least one-half of these deaths were preventable.[2] What would be the situation if the courts, following the clear logic of their own decisions, should hold the stockholders, directors, and officials criminally responsible for each of the 17,500 preventable deaths to which attention has time after time been directed?

That the courts, including even the highest tribunal of the Nation, do allow their economic bias to influence them in holding laws unconstitutional is nowhere more clearly expressed than in the dissenting opinion of Mr. Justice Holmes in the case of Lochner v. New York,[3] wherein the right of the Legislature of New York to limit the hours of work in bakeries was involved. He said:

This case is decided upon an economic theory which a large part of the country does not entertain. If it were a question whether I agree with that theory [limiting the consecutive hours of labor in bakeries which may be required of an employee], I should desire to study it further and long before making up my mind. But I do not conceive that to be my duty, because I strongly believe that my agreement or disagreement has nothing to do with the right of a majority to embody their opinions in law.

* * * Some of these laws [referring to several which he has discussed] embody convictions or prejudices which judges are likely to share. Some may not, but a constitution is not intended to embody a particular economic theory, whether of paternalism and the organic relation of the citizen to the State, or of laissez faire. It is made for people of fundamentally differing views, and the accident of our finding certain opinions natural and familiar or novel, and even shocking, ought not to conclude our judgment upon the question whether statutes embodying them conflict with the Constitution of the United States.

---

[1] Thompson v. Thompson, 218 U. S., 611.
[2] Industrial Accident Statistics, Bul. Whole No. 157, U. S. Bureau of Labor Statistics, 1915.
[3] Lochner v. N. Y., 198 U. S., 45.

This statute of the State of New York, which had been sustained by the courts of New York, was thus held unconstitutional, we are assured by the highest possible authority, on the economic theories of five judges, whose bias is clearly reflected in the majority opinion. By that action not only were the bakers of New York deprived of all legal relief from the hardships of working long hours in underground bakeries, but the entire movement for relieving the condition of other workmen in similarly unhealthful occupations throughout the country was effectually checked for a decade. Can these judges, the workers ask, absolve themselves from responsibility for the thousands of lives which have been shortened as a result of their decisions, the ill health and suffering of other thousands who contracted disease as a result of unduly long exposure to bad conditions and a lack of sufficient fresh air and leisure? The provision of the Constitution which was held to be violated by this act was the fourteenth amendment, designed solely to protect the emancipated negroes.

The wide range of the labor laws declared unconstitutional may be seen from the following list, which includes only those cases which may be clearly understood from their titles:

LABOR LAWS DECLARED UNCONSTITUTIONAL.

Requiring statement of cause of discharge.[1]
Prohibiting blacklisting.[2]
Protecting workmen as members of labor unions.[3]
Restricting power of courts to grant injunctions, etc.[4]
Protecting employees as voters (Federal).[5]
Forbidding public employment office to furnish names of applicants to employers whose workmen were on strike.[6]
Fixing rates of wages on public works.[7]
Regulating weighing of coal at mines (four States).[8]
Providing for small attorneys' fees in successful actions to recover wage claims.[9]
Fixing the time of payment of wages.[10]
Prohibiting use of " scrip." [11]
Prohibiting or regulating company stores.[12]
Fixing hours of labor in private employment.[13]
Defining liability of employers for injuries.[14]

It is difficult to find parallel cases to illustrate the difference in the point of view assumed by the courts upon the same constitutional question according to economic or social results of the decisions in

---

[1] Wallace v. G. C. & N. R. Co., 94 Ga., 732.
[2] Wabash R. Co. v. Young, 162 Ind., 102.
[3] Gillespie v. People, 188 Ill., 176 ; Coffeeville Brick & Tile Co., v. Perry, 69 Kans., 297 ; State v. Julow, 129 Mo., 163 ; Goldfield Consolidated Mines Co. v. Goldfield Miners' Union. 159 Fed., 500 ; People v. Marcus, 185 N. Y., 257 ; State v. Kreutzberg, 114 Wis., 530 ; Adair v. United States, 208 U. S., 161.
[4] Pierce v. Stablemen's Union, 156 Cal., 70 ; State v. Shepherd, 177 Mo., 234 ; Cheadle v. State, 110 Ind., 301.
[5] United States v. Amsden, 1 Bissell, 283.
[6] Mathews v. People. 202 Ill., 389.
[7] Street v. Varney Electrical Supply Co., 160 Ind., 338.
[8] Harding v. People, 160 Ill., 459 ; In re Preston, 63 Ohio St., 428 ; Com. v. Brown, 8 Pa. Super. Ct., 339 ; In re House Bill No. 203, 21 Colo., 27.
[9] Randolph v. Builders' and Painters' Supply Co., 106 Ala., 501 ; Builders' Supply Depot v. O'Connor, 150 Cal., 265 ; Davidson v. Jennings, 27 Colo., 187 ; Manowsky v. Stephan, 233 Ill., 409.
[10] Republic Iron & Steel Co. v. State, 160 Ind., 379 ; Braceville Coal Co. v. People, 147 Ill., 66 ; Johnson v. Goodyear Mining Co., 127 Cal., 4.
[11] Godcharles v. Wigeman, 113 Pa. St., 431 ; Jordan v. State, 51 Texas Cr. App., 531.
[12] Frorer v. People, 141 Ill., 171 ; State v. Fire Creek Coal & Coke Co., 33 W. Va., 188.
[13] In re Morgan, 26 Colo., 415 ; Lochner v. New York, 198 U. S., 45 ; Low v. Rees Printing Co., 41 Nebr., 127 ; Ritchie v. People, 155 Ill., 98 ; People v. Williams, 189 N. Y., 131.
[14] Ballard v. Mississippi Cotton Oil Co., 81 Miss., 507 ; Baltimore & O. S. W. R. Co. v. Read, 158 Ind., 25.

different cases. There are a few clear-cut cases, however, in which the contrast is plainly shown, as, for example, in the inconsistency between the decisions in the Debs case,[1] wherein it is held that the control of Congress over interstate commerce is so complete that it may regulate the conduct of the employees engaged therein to the extent of enjoining them from going on a sympathetic strike, and the decision in the Adair case,[2] wherein it is held that Congress has so little power over the conduct of those engaged in interstate commerce that it can not constitutionally forbid employers engaged therein discharging their employees merely because of membership in a labor union.

In this same connection it is proper to contrast the almost uniform prohibition by the State and Federal courts of secondary boycotts in labor cases even to the extent of enjoining the publication of " unfair lists," with the decision in the case of Park Co. v. Druggists' Association (175 N. Y.). In this case the Park Co. charged that the Druggists' Association fixed prices of proprietary medicines; that they refused to sell to anyone who did not abide by the prices thus fixed; that the druggists combined in this association refused to sell to the Park Co.; and that they used spies to ascertain with whom the Park Co. did business with intent to compel such customers to cease doing business with the Park Co. The facts were admitted on demurrer, but the court refused to issue an injunction, holding that the boycott was caused by plaintiff himself and could be removed whenever he saw fit to abide by the association's rules; and, further, that there was no conspiracy. If the same line of reasoning were followed in labor cases, it is difficult to imagine any kind of boycott which would be illegal.

Finally, reference should be made to the history of the fight for the enactment of eight-hour legislation in Colorado, which illustrates the grounds upon which the workers not only of that State, but throughout the Nation, distrust legislatures, courts, and executive officials.

Although the 8-hour day was established in Colorado gold mines by agreement among the operators after the Cripple Creek strike of 1894, in the coal-mining industry a 20-year struggle followed the miners' first attempt at legislation.

The eight-hour bill presented to the general assembly in 1895, though supported by the Western Federation of Miners, the United Mine Workers of America, and labor organizations in general, was, upon reference to the Supreme Court for an advance opinion, reported as unconstitutional and failed of enactment.

A bill brought successfully to enactment in 1899, and which was substantially a copy of the Utah law upheld by State and Federal Supreme Courts, was declared by the Colorado Supreme Court to be unconstitutional.[3]

In 1901 the people adopted by an overwhelming vote an amendment to the constitution which provided for eight-hour legislation. This was followed by the introduction in the next general assembly (1903) of several bills, and by the inauguration of active opposition thereto on the part of corporations. No fewer than 11 anonymous bulletins were attributed to one officer of a smelting company.

[1] 158 U. S., 564.   [2] 208 U. S., 161.   [3] In re Morgan, 26 Colo., 415.

On account of disagreements in conference, none of the several bills passed; and so great was the public outcry that at the extra session in July, 1903, each house passed resolutions blaming the other for the failure.

In the session of 1904–5 a bill substantially the same as the present law, and favored by all political parties, was so amended by Mr. Guggenheim as to be "absolutely worthless." It remained on the statute books, a dead letter, until 1911.

In 1911, house bill No. 46 was passed. The operators succeeded in having it submitted to a referendum vote, and at the last moment they initiated a smelterman's eight-hour bill, the two came up on the same ballot, and in the succeeding confusion both were adopted by the people, because of their genuine interest in the passage of an eight-hour law.

The legislature of 1913 repealed both the laws so enacted in 1911, and reenacted house bill No. 46, the present law. By a decision of the Supreme Court, allowing a "safety clutch," this law may not be referred.

The essential injustice and stupidity of this long fight of the employers against eight-hour legislation is strikingly shown by a letter from Mr. L. M. Bowers, chairman of the board of directors of the Colorado Fuel & Iron Co., to Mr. J. D. Rockefeller, jr., stating that after they saw that such legislation was inevitable, they tried out the eight-hour day in their mines and found that it was economically profitable. The Colorado Fuel & Iron Co. thereby is shown to have stubbornly resisted by every conceivable device, for a period of 20 years, a just law which was not only necessary for the health and welfare of its 12,000 miners but was actually profitable for the company itself.

The reason for the effectiveness of the opposition of the Colorado Fuel & Iron Co. is also shown in the letter quoted on page 41 from Mr. Bowers to the secretary of Mr. Rockefeller, describing the complete and corrupt control which the company exercised over the State government during this period.

Third, it is alleged by the workers that in the administration of law, both common and statute, there is discrimination by the courts against the poor and in favor of the wealthy and powerful. It is further stated that this discrimination arises not only from the economic disabilities of the poor, which render them unable to employ equally skillful lawyers, to endure the law's delay, and to stand the expense of repeated appeals, but out of an actual bias on the part of the judges in favor of the wealthy and influential. It should arouse great concern if it be true that the courts do not resolve their doubts in favor of the poor and humble; how much graver then is the injustice if the judges do in fact lean toward the rich and mighty?

To establish this claim by the presentation of a sufficient number of cases would be a tedious task. Many such have been presented to the commission but can not be considered fully here. Instead, it would seem that in such cases we may safely rely upon the uncontradicted opinion of weighty authorities whose position removes from them any suspicion of bias.

Ex-President William H. Taft has said:

We must make it so that the poor man will have as nearly as possible an equal opportunity in litigating as the rich man; and under present conditions, ashamed as we may be of it, this is not the fact.

Prof. Henry R. Seager, of Columbia University, testified before the commission:

I don't see how any fair-minded person can question but what our judges have shown a decided bias in favor of the employers. I would not be inclined to ascribe this so much to a class bias, although I think this is a factor, as to the antecedent training of judges. Under our legal system the principal task of the lawyer is to protect property rights, and the property rights have come to be concentrated more and more into the hands of corporations, so that the successful lawyer of to-day, in a great majority of cases, is the corporation lawyer. His business is to protect the rights of employers and corporations. It is from the ranks of successful lawyers, for the most part, that our judges are selected, and from that results inevitably a certain angle on the part of a majority of our judges.

The bias of the courts is nowhere more clearly shown than in cases involving persons and organizations with whose economic and social views the court does not agree. An interesting example may be cited in the case of Warren v. United States, 183 Fed., 718, where the editor of Appeal to Reason, Fred D. Warren, was sentenced by the Federal district court to six months' imprisonment and a fine of $1,500 for the circulation through the mails of matter offering a reward to anyone who would kidnap a certain governor for whom extradition had been refused.[1]

The sentence was commuted by President Taft, against the protest of Warren, to a fine of $100 to be collected in a civil suit. In commenting on the sentence, President Taft is reported to have said:

The district court evidently looked beyond the record of the evidence in this case and found that Warren was the editor and publisher of a newspaper engaged in a crusade against society and government.

Moreover, this is not a prosecution for criminal libel; it is a prosecution for what at best is the violation of a regulation as to the use of the mails. To visit such an offense with a severe punishment is likely to appear to the public to be an effort to punish the defendant for something that could not be charged in the indictment.

This obviously was not intended as a reflection upon the court, but the attitude of a large part of the workers is that if President Taft was justified in making such an assertion it was a case demanding impeachment of the judges involved rather than a commutation of sentence for Warren.

Fourth, it is charged by the representatives of labor not only that courts have neglected or refused to protect workers in the rights guaranteed by the Constitution of the United States and of the several States, but that sections of the Constitution framed primarily to protect human rights have been perverted to protect property rights only and to deprive workers of the protection of rights secured to them by statutes.

First, with regard to the Federal courts, it is startling and alarming to citizens generally, and particularly to workers, to learn that the concensus of Federal decisions is to the effect that the sections of the Constitution defining the rights of citizens to trial by jury,

[1] It was alleged by Warren that this was done to call attention to the gross discrimination in the case of Haywood and Moyer, who were kidnaped and transported from one State to another.

security from unwarranted arrest and search, free speech, free assembly, writ of habeas corpus, bearing of arms, and protection from excessive bail and cruel and unusual punishments, apply only to Federal jurisdiction and in reality protect the citizen only against the action of the Federal Government. The only sections protecting the personal rights of citizens under ordinary circumstances are the thirteenth amendment, prohibiting involuntary servitude, the fifteenth, protecting the right to vote, and the fourteenth, providing that "No State shall make or enforce any law which shall abridge the privileges or immunities of citizens of the United States; nor shall any State deprive any person of life, liberty, or property, without due process of law, nor deny any person within its jurisdiction the equal protection of the laws."

We are, however, informed by counsel who has examined the cases involved that the fourteenth amendment has had no appreciable effect in protecting personal rights. According to the existing decisions, the due-process clause does not guarantee the right of trial by jury,[1] nor does it necessitate indictment by grand juries,[2] nor has it restrained arbitrary arrests and imprisonment on the part of State governments when men are kidnaped in one State and carried to another.[3]

Up to 1911 the United States Supreme Court intervened in 55 cases in which the fourteenth amendment was invoked. In 39 of these cases private corporations were the principal parties. Thirty-two statuates were affected by these decisions, and in only three, concerning the civil rights of negroes, were the personal rights of individual citizens involved. With the exceptions involving the rights of negroes in jury cases (e. g., Strauder v. West Virginia, 100 U. S., 303), the fourteenth amendment has not acted to secure or protect personal rights from State encroachment,[4] but only to prevent encroachment on property rights.[5] In all the other numerous cases in which the fourteenth amendment was invoked to protect personal rights, the attempt failed.

On the other hand there is abundant evidence of the great protection which it affords corporations and other forms of organized capital. On that point we may quote the statements of Mr. C. W. Collins, of the Alabama bar, who analyzed the decisions of the United States Supreme Court through the October, 1910, term.[6]

Private corporations are using it as a means to prevent the enforcement of State laws. Since 1891 a majority of cases under the amendment have involved a corporation as the principal party. * * * The increase of this kind of litigation runs parallel to the rise of the trust movement in America. At the 1909-10 term of the court, out of a total of 26 opinions rendered under the amendment 20 involved a corporation as the principal party.

* * * The fourteenth amendment is the easiest of all constitutional measures to invoke. In a country where economic activity is so intense and time so vital an element, it has been grasped as a sure measure of delay, with always the possibility of obtaining affirmative relief. The amendment, though intended primarily as a protection to the negro race, has in these latter days be-

[1] Maxwell v. Dow, 176 U. S., 581; Walker v. Sauvinet, 92 U. S., 90.
[2] Hurtado v. California, 110 U. S., 516.
[3] Re Pettibone, 12 Idaho, 264; 203 U. S., 192; Re Moyer, 35 Colo., 159; 140 F. R., 870; 203 U. S., 221; Re Boyle, 6 Idaho, 609.
[4] See for illustration: Virginia v. Rives, 100 U. S., 313; Plessy v. Ferguson, 163 U. S., 537; Twining v. New Jersey, 211 U. S., 78; Brown v. New Jersey, 175 U. S., 172.
[5] See for illustration: C. M. & St. P. Ry. v. Minnesota, 134 U. S., 418; Cotting v. K. C. Stockyards Co., 183 U. S., 79; G. C. & S. F. Ry. v. Ellis, 168 U. S., 150.
[6] The Fourteenth Amendment and the States, C. W. Collins.

come a constitutional guaranty to the corporations that no State action toward them can become effective until after years of litigation through the
State and Federal courts to the Supreme Court of the United States. The
course of the amendment is running away from its originally intended channel
(p. 145).

The fourteenth amendment, although a humanitarian measure in origin and
purpose, has been within recent years practically appropriated by the corporations. It was aimed at restraining and checking the powers of wealth and
privilege. It was to be a charter of liberty for human rights against property
rights. The transformation has been rapid and complete. It operates to-day
to protect the rights of property to the detriment of the rights of man. It has
become the Magna Charta of accumulated and organized capital (p. 137).

It is thus quite clear that the fourteenth amendment not only nas
failed to operate to protect personal rights but has operated almost
wholly for the protection of the property rights of corporations.
These facts taken in conjunction with the many decisions, such as
the Lochner case,[1] in which the fourteenth amendment has been
invoked to annul statutes designed to better conditions of life and
work, must constitute just ground for grave concern not only to the
workers but to every citizen who values his liberty.

With the "bills of rights" contained in the constitutions of the
several States, the situation, as far as the workers are concerned, is
somewhat different, since in many jurisdictions these have been used
upon numerous occasions to afford substantial protection to them in
their personal rights. The workers call attention particularly, however, to the long list of statutes, city ordinances, and military orders
abridging freedom of speech and press, which not only have not
been interfered with by the courts but whenever tested have almost
uniformly been upheld by the State and Federal courts.[2] They
point also to the grave injuries done to workers individually and
collectively by the thousands of arrests which have been made without just cause in labor disputes, without relief from either the courts
or the executive; to the denial of the right to the writ of habeas
corpus upon numerous occasions; to the fact that where, as for example, in Los Angeles, San Diego, and Fresno (Cal.), Spokane
(Wash.), Minot (N. Dak.), Paterson (N. J.), Little Falls (N. Y.),
Lawrence (Mass.), Idaho, Colorado, and West Virginia, workers
have been grievously injured, brutally treated, or interfered with in
the pursuit of their guaranteed rights by other classes of citizens or
by officials, the courts have not interfered and the perpetrators have
gone unpunished.

On the general question of martial law and habeas corpus a member of the staff has made an elaborate comparison of the cases arising from nonlabor disturbances with the cases arising from labor
disturbances. It is not necessary, and would require too much space,
to recite these cases in full, but among the former may be mentioned
the Milligan case, and other cases arising in the State courts of Indiana, Illinois, Kentucky, North Carolina, and Wisconsin[3] (all during
or immediately following the Civil War), and three cases in the
courts of Kentucky, Ohio, and Oklahoma since that time;[4] among

---

[1] Lochner v. N. Y., 198 U. S., 45.
[2] Fox v. Washington, 236 U. S., 273; Fitts v. Atlanta, 121 Ga., 267; Ex parte Thomas, 102 Pacific, 19.
[3] In re Milligan, 4 Wall. (U. S.), 2; Skeen v. Monkeimer, 21 Ind., 1; Johnson v. Jones, 44 Ill., 142; Corbin v. Marsh, 2 Dur., 193; Ex parte Moore, 64 N. C., 802; In re Kemp, 16 Wis., 382.
[4] Franks v. Smith, 142 Ky., 232; Ohio v. Coit, 8 Ohio, 62; Fluke v. Canton, 31 Okla., 718.

the latter, i. e., those arising from labor disturbances, are included the cases from Colorado, Idaho, Montana, Pennsylvania, and West Virginia.[1] The results of such comparison are summarized in part as follows:

Although uniformly held that the writ of habeas corpus can only be suspended by the legislature, in these labor disturbances the executive has in fact suspended or disregarded the writ. In the labor cases the judiciary either disregards the fact that the writ has been suspended by the executive or evades the issue. In nonlabor cases the courts have protested emphatically when the executive attempted to interfere with the writ of habeas corpus.

In many instances in which the military has been in active operation because of nonlabor disturbances, the judiciary has almost without exception protested against the exercise of any arbitrary power and has almost uniformly attempted to limit that power.

In cases arising from labor agitations, the judiciary has uniformly upheld the power exercised by the military, and in no case has there been any protest against the use of such power or any attempt to curtail it, except in Montana, where the conviction of a civilian by military commission was annulled.

Finally, it is impossible to imagine a more complete mockery of justice and travesty upon every conception of fair dealing than the innumerable decisions holding unconstitutional wise and salutary laws for the protection of workers, upon the ground that they violate the right of contract, even while the workers, whose rights are supposed to be affected, clamor for the maintenance of the statute. The appeal for the protection of the workers' rights in such cases comes invariably from the employers, and is urged against the protest of the workers, yet in almost unbroken succession the judges solemnly nullify the wisest acts of legislatures on just such specious, self-serving pleas. There are notable cases in which the judges have unmasked the mummery, as, for example, in Holden v. Hardy,[2] where it was said:

Although the prosecution in this case was against the employer of labor, who, apparently, under the statute, is the only one liable, his defense is not so much that his right to contract has been infringed upon, but that the act works a peculiar hardship to his employees, whose right to labor as long as they please is alleged to be thereby violated. The argument would certainly come with better grace and greater cogency from the latter class.

There appear to be no reported cases in which the workers have urged that their rights are violated by such restrictive legislation, which in fact invariably originates with them; but the courts continue to hand down decisions "protecting the sacred right of contract of the worker," when the only person benefited is the employer, who is thus able to "turn the very Constitution itself into an instrument of inequality."

This entire situation is fraught with such grave dangers not only to the workers but to all citizens who value their individual liberty, that the Nation can not be entirely secure until those fundamental rights are affirmatively guaranteed to every citizen of the United States by the Federal Government. It is therefore earnestly recommended that Congress forthwith initiate an amendment to the Constitution securing these rights against encroachment by Federal, State, or local governments or by private persons and corporations.

Fifth. It is charged that the ordinary legal machinery provides no adequate means whereby laborers and other poor men can secure

[1] In re Moyer, 35 Colo., 159; in re Boyle, 6 Idaho, 609; In re McDonald, 49 Mont., 455; Com. v. Shortall, 206 Pa., 165; Mays and Nance v. Brown, 71 W. Va., 519; Ex parte Jones, 71 W. Va., 567.
[2] 169 U. S., 366.

redress for wrongs inflicted upon them through the nonpayment of wages, through overcharges at company stores, through exorbitant hospital and other fees, fines, and deductions through fraud on the part of private employment offices, loan offices, and installment houses, and through the "grafting" of foremen and superintendents. The losses to wage earners from these sources are stated to amount each year to millions of dollars and to work untold hardship on a class of men who can ill afford to lose even a penny of their hard-won earnings.

These charges were thoroughly investigated in all parts of the country by an experienced member of the commission's staff.

He cites, for example, that in California, where the situation has been more completely uncovered than elsewhere and where remedies are beginning to be applied, during the year ending June, 1914, 9,621 claims were presented to the commissioner of labor alone. Of these, 7,330 were for nonpayment of wages, of which 4,904 were successfully settled and $110,912 of unpaid wages was collected. This is believed to have been only a small proportion of the total claims of laborers throughout the State, inasmuch as the number of claims was growing rapidly as the work of the bureau became better known, and because, during a period of only 10 months, over 2,200 claims were presented to the State commission on immigration and housing. The work of handling these claims and making its existence known to laborers throughout the State was just getting well under way, although with a small appropriation and inadequate force, when the collection of wage claims was suddenly checked by a decision of the State court of appeals[1] that the payment-of-wages law was unconstitutional on the ground that since it provided for fine or imprisonment where the wages of laborers were illegally retained, it was in effect a provision for imprisonment for debt.

The investigation in other States revealed equally bad or worse conditions, while in all except a few no efficient means existed by which these claims could be prosecuted. In conclusion, our investigator reported:

(a) The existing labor and life conditions of common laborers in this country produce immense numbers of justified labor complaints and claims, involving not only great sums of money in the aggregate but untold personal hardship and suffering.

(b) The existing public and private legal institutions are utterly inadequate to secure justice to the laborers in the matter of these complaints and claims.

(c) This situation has already created in the laborers distrust of the Government, of employers, and of the well-to-do classes generally, and is one of the contributory causes of the existing industrial unrest.

The measures recommended, which have to do largely with State and local administrations, are discussed on page 89. It is suggested, however, that the commission recommend to Congress that, inasmuch as the immigrant laborers, who suffer most largely from these injustices, are ethically and legally wards of the Nation until they become citizens, the Bureau of Immigration of the Federal Department of Labor should be given the authority and necessary

---

[1] Nov. 23, 1914.

appropriations to establish, wherever it may seem necessary, in connection with its existing offices in all parts of the country, legal aid divisions which would freely and aggressively prosecute these claims and complaints on behalf of the immigrant laborers, and, if there are no constitutional or statutory barriers, on behalf also of American citizens.

Sixth. It is charged by the workers that the courts, by the unwarranted extension of their powers in the issuance of injunctions, have not only grievously injured the workers individually and collectively upon innumerable occasions but have, by the contempt procedure consequent upon disobedience to such injunctions, deprived the workers of the right, fundamental to Anglo-Saxon institutions, to be tried by jury.

This charge is not limited to members of trades-unions, nor to workers, but is voiced also by many who have no reason for partisanship. For example, Mr. S. S. Gregory, former president of the American Bar Association, testified before the commission:

These injunctions are based upon the theory that the man carrying on a business has a certain sort of property right in the good will or the successful conduct of that business; and that when several hundred or several thousand excited men gather around his premises where he carries his business on and threaten everybody that comes in there to work, and possibly use violence, that that is such an unlawful interference with property right as may be the subject of protection in equity. And that view of the law has been sustained by the courts of practically all the States.

But the great difficulty about this was this, that having enjoined defendants, namely, striking workmen, perhaps from unlawful interference with the business of the employer, where that unlawful interference consisted in an attack or an assault and battery upon another man, to wit, perhaps a strikebreaker so-called, or one who was hired to take the place of one of the striking workmen, that thereafter the judge who had ordered the injunction and whose authority had been thus defied, was permitted to put the person charged with the breach of that injunction upon trial upon a charge of contempt, really for having committed an unlawful and criminal act.

Now the Constitution has thrown around the prosecution of criminals (the Constitutions, State and Federal) a number of securities. They are entitled to trial by jury; they are entitled to be confronted by the witnesses who are to testify against them; they are entitled to be heard by counsel.

But none of those guaranties except perhaps the right to be heard by counsel is secured in contempt proceedings; and the obvious wisdom of permitting 12 men drawn from the body of the people to pass on questions of fact—men who are supposed to be prejudiced neither for nor against the parties, who know nothing about the case until they are sworn in the jury box—has so far commended itself to the wisdom of legislators and jurists to such a degree that it has become a permanent feature of our jurisprudence; and to provide that the court may proceed against parties for contempt, where the conduct charged against them is criminal, is really an evasion of the constitutional guaranties and a plain attempt to commit to equity jurisdiction over matters which it has been decided over and over again by all the courts that it has no jurisdiction with respect to, namely, the administration of the criminal law.

For instance, I might receive, as I leave the room of this tribunal to-day, a threatening letter from somebody saying they were going to kill me for something I had said, or had not said, before the commission. Now, that involves personal loss possibly to my wife or those dependent upon me; but no court of equity would listen for a moment to a bill I should file saying "A B " or some other blackhand gentleman had threatened to kill me, or if filed by anybody dependent upon me, and therefore there should be an injunction to prevent him from killing me. That would be an absurdity—a legal absurdity; and none the less is it so where a man is enjoined from committing acts of violence in a strike to try him for contempt, without a trial by jury. And that has been an injustice that has rankled in the minds of everybody that has been a victim of it, and justly so.

Sir Charles Napier says, "People talk about agitators, but the only real agitator is injustice; and the only way is to correct the injustice and allay the agitation."

Judge Walter Clark, chief justice of the Supreme Court of North Carolina, also testified before the commission as follows:

Chairman WALSH. Have you studied the effect of the use of injunctions in labor disputes generally in the United States, as a student of economics and the law?

Judge CLARK. I do not think they can be justified, sir, * * * [Their effect] has been, of course, to irritate the men, because they feel that in an Anglo-Saxon community every man has a right to a trial by jury, and that to take him up and compel him to be tried by a judge is not in accordance with the principles of equality, liberty, and justice.

Chairman WALSH. Do you think that has been one of the causes of social unrest in the United States?

Judge CLARK. Yes, sir; and undoubtedly will be more so, unless it is remedied.

It is not within the province of the commission to attempt to decide the question of whether or not the issuance of such injunctions is an unwarranted extension upon the part of the courts; but the weighty opinions cited above are very impressive and are convincing that the workers have great reason for their attitude. It is known, however, from the evidence of witnesses and from the information collected by the staff, that such injunctions have in many cases inflicted grievous injury upon workmen engaged in disputes with their employers, and that their interests have been seriously prejudiced by the denial of jury trial, which every criminal is afforded, and by trial before the judge against whom the contempt was alleged.

It is felt to be a duty, therefore, to register a solemn protest against this condition, being convinced of its injustice not only by reason of the evil effects which have resulted from this procedure, but by virtue of a conviction that no person's liberty can safely be decided by any one man, particularly when that man is the object of the alleged contempt.

The Clayton Act undoubtedly contains many features which will relieve this situation as far as the Federal courts are concerned, but it seems clear that it does not contain anything like a complete solution of the existing injustices, even for the limited field of Federal jurisdiction.

Seventh, it is charged by the representatives of labor that laws designed for the protection of labor in workshops and mines and on railroads are not effectively enforced, except in a few States. This is a matter of considerable moment to labor, but it is, after all, regarded by the workers, since it concerns chiefly only their safety and comfort, as ranking far below the other matters discussed, which involve primarily their liberty and rights as freemen and, secondarily, their only means of bettering their condition. Moreover, it is almost entirely a matter of administration, which is discussed in detail elsewhere in the report. With the great attention which the method of administration is now receiving, not only from labor organizations but from civic organizations, and lately even from employers' associations, it is likely to reach a satisfactory stage before very long.

Eighth, it is charged that in cases involving industrial questions, the workers are liable to great injustice by reason of the fact that in many localities they are excluded from juries either by the qualifications prescribed (usually payment of property tax) or by the method of selection.

In California, for example, it was testified that grave injustice had been done in many cases because the juries (composed only of property owners, for the most part employers) were greatly prejudiced against the defendants, whose program, if successful, would directly or indirectly affect the interests of the jurors.

Similarly, in Cook County, Ill., which includes Chicago, it was found by a committee of the Lawyers' Association of Illinois that although the system of selection by commissioners was intended to produce an impartial selection from all classes of the community, out of probably 1,000 different occupations in Cook County the commissioners confine the selection of the great bulk of the jurors to the following 10 occupations: Managers, superintendents, foremen, presidents and owners of companies, secretaries of companies, merchants, agents, salesmen, clerks, and bookkeepers.

To quote from the report:

There are 76,000 mechanics affiliated with the Building Trades Council in Chicago, yet in the 3,440 jurors investigated by your committee there are only 200 mechanics drawn from the 76,000 in the Building Trades Council.

There are about 200,000 mechanics belonging to the different labor organizations in Chicago, yet there are only about 350 mechanics drawn as jurors by the commissions in the 3,440 investigated, or about 10 per cent, when the percentage ought to be about 70 per cent.

The report of the committee adds:

Another comparison will show that out of these 3,440 jurors the commission took only 314 jurors from 130 different occupations, or an average of less than 3 jurors from each occupation, while from the 10 favored occupations mentioned above, 1,723 jurors were picked, or the grossly excessive average of 172 from each of said 10 occupations.[1]

A similar situation was disclosed by the investigations of members of the staff in Paterson, N. J.

Finally, there is the very grave situation where, by putting aside the legal and customary methods, the jury is chosen by the sheriff or other officers, who may be unduly influenced by either party to the case. Such a situation, inimical in the extreme to the interests of the workers, has been conclusively proved to have existed in Colorado and in other mining districts.

In the belief that the right to trial by an impartial jury is necessary for the maintenance of justice, and that such impartiality can be secured only by including all classes of citizens, it is suggested that the commission recommend that Federal and States statutes should be passed providing for the creation of juries by drawing the names from a wheel, or other like device, which shall contain the name of every qualified voter in the district from which the jury is to be selected. The adoption of this method in Missouri and other States has resulted uniformly in securing impartial juries of much higher grade, and has also eliminated almost entirely the sources of corruption attending the selection of juries.

Ninth, it is charged by the workers that, during strikes, innocent men are in many cases arrested without just cause, charged with fictitious crimes, held under excessive bail, and treated frequently with unexampled brutality for the purpose of injuring the strikers and breaking the strike.

In support of this charge, the commission has been furnished with evidence showing that in a number of recent strikes large numbers

---

[1] Eternal Vigilance is the Price of Liberty. Report of committee to the Lawyers' Association of Illinois, 1914.

of strikers were arrested, but that only a small number were brought to trial and relatively few were convicted of any serious offense; that those arrested were, as a rule, required to give heavy bail, far beyond their means, or were detained without trial until their effectiveness as strikers was destroyed; and that in many cases strikers were brutally treated by the police or by special deputies in the pay of the companies. A number of these strikes have been investigated by public hearings of the commission, by members of its staff, or by other departments of the Federal Government. In each of the strikes investigated the charges as made were in essentials substantiated.

In Paterson, N. J., which was investigated with unusual thoroughness and which, because of its size and its location in the most densely populated section, might be considered likely to be free from such abuses, it was found that during the strike of the silk workers 2,238 arrests, charging unlawful assembly or disorderly conduct, were made, and that in all there were 300 convictions in the lower courts. Men arrested for unlawful assembly were held in bail of $500 to $5,000. The right of trial by jury was generally denied. Men were arrested for ridiculous reasons, as, for example, for standing on the opposite side of the street and beckoning to men in the mills to come out. This was the allegation on which the charge of unlawful assembly was placed against four men, and for which they were sent to jail in default of $500 bail, and, although never indicted, the charges still stand against them as a bar to their rights as citizens and voters. Men were fined arbitrarily, as in the case of one who was fined $10 for permitting strikers to sit on a bench in front of his house. Not more than $25 worth of damage was done during the entire strike, involving 25,000 workers, and there was no actual violence or attempt at violence on the part of the strikers during the entire strike. Under such conditions the editor of a local paper was arrested, charged with criminal libel, for comparing the conditions in Paterson with the rule of Cossacks; and four men who sold the paper on the streets also were arrested. The editor was tried and convicted in the lower court, but the verdict was set aside by the Supreme Court, while the four men, after being held several days in default of bail, were released without trial.

It is impossible to summarize the activities of the police and authorities during this strike better than by referring to the testimony of two of the leading citizens of Paterson, who said that they had resolved to get rid of the " agitators " and were ready to go beyond the law to accomplish their purpose.[1] A full appreciation of the

---

[1] In a letter recently received from one of these witnesses his position is reiterated with a striking illustration of inability to comprehend the fundamental principles of American Government and the limitations imposed upon the power of one class to oppress another:

" Another point which is only partially covered in my testimony is in regard to what Chairman Walsh endeavored to get me and various other citizens to admit would be an infraction of free speech and personal liberty if the agitators were prevented from coming into Paterson or not permitted to hold their meetings here. The United States Government puts up the bars at Ellis Island against certain classes of ' undesirable citizens,' and as far as I have been able to learn the Government's action in debarring from this country the immoral and criminal class and those who would become a charge on the country meets with the approval of the Americans generally. If it is proper and right for the United States Government to say who shall and who shall not enter this country I think it is equally proper for the city of Paterson to debar undesirable citizens who are coming here to sow discontent and cause trouble in the city. New York City has had a dead line at Fulton Street for a great many years and the police authorities have prevented certain persons from crossing that line, and this has been considered a proper exercise of the police powers of the city. I can see no difference between this action on the part of the New York authorities and similar action which was desired by many of our citizens in Paterson in regard to the I. W. W. agitators."

injustice committed during this strike can be secured only by reading the testimony taken at Paterson and the reports of the commission's investigators based upon the records of the police and the
courts.

In Los Angeles and Indianapolis essentially the same conditions
were found by the commission, while in McKees Rocks, Bethlehem,
and Westmoreland County, Pa., Lawrence, Mass., and Calumet,
Mich., investigated by the Federal Department of Labor, essentially
the same conditions of injustice were found to prevail. The conditions in West Virginia and Colorado, which were almost beyond
belief and had the additional feature of military rule, will be discussed elsewhere.

An examination of the entire mass of evidence is convincing that
such conditions are in fact typical of strikes which are serious enough
to arouse the authorities, especially where the workers are unorganized before the strike and therefore lacking in influence in the
community.

Tenth, it is asserted by the workers that in many localities during
strikes not only is one of the greatest functions of the State, that of
policing, virtually turned over to employers or arrogantly assumed
by them, but criminals employed by detective agencies and strike-
breaking agencies are clothed, by the process of deputization, with
arbitrary power and relieved of criminal liability for their acts.

Only three such cases are cited here, though the commission has in
its records evidence regarding a considerable number. At Roosevelt,
N. J., it was found by the commission's investigators and later confirmed in court that the office of sheriff was virtually turned over to
one Jerry O'Brien, the proprietor of a so-called detective agency;
that he imported a number of men of bad reputation and clothed
them with the authority of deputies; and that on January 19, 1915,
these criminals, without provocation, wantonly shot and killed 2
men and wounded 17 others who were on strike against the American
Agricultural Chemical Co., which paid and armed the deputies.

Similarly, during the Calumet, Mich., strike, about 230 men were
imported from detective agencies in eastern cities, 52 under pay from
the county board of supervisors, which was made up almost entirely of
copper company officials. The actions of these men were so wantonly
brutal that they were censured by the local judge, but they went
unchecked in their career of arrogant brutality, which culminated in
their shooting, without provocation, into a house in which women
and children were, killing two persons and wounding two others.

The recent strike in Bayonne, N. J., threw more light on these
armed guards. During this strike one of the New York detective
agencies furnished for the protection of the Tidewater Oil Co.'s
plant men who were so vicious and unreliable that the officials of
the company themselves say that their presence was sufficient to incite
a riot. These men shot without provocation at anyone or everyone
who came within sight, and the killing of at least three strikers in
Bayonne and the wounding of many more is directly chargeable to
these guards.

The character of the men who make a specialty of this kind of
employment has never been more frankly described than in the testimony of Mr. L. M. Bowers, chairman of the board of directors of

the Colorado Fuel & Iron Co., who repeatedly referred to those in the employ of that company as "cutthroats," against whose character, he stated, he had frequently protested.

According to the statement of Berghoff Bros. & Waddell, who style themselves "labor adjusters" and who do a business of strike breaking and strike policing, there are countless men who follow this business at all times. They say they can put 10,000 armed men into the field inside of 72 hours. The fact that these men may have a criminal record is no deterrent to their being employed, and no check can be made on the men sent out by these companies on hurry calls.

When the question of providing the bail for these men arose as a result of the killing of the strikers at Bayonne, the company attorney actually declined to furnish bail for them on the ground that they were thugs of whom the company knew nothing and that it would not be responsible for their appearance.

In view of the endless crimes [1] committed by the employees of the so-called detective agencies, who have been permitted to usurp a function that should belong only to the State, it is suggested that the commission recommend to Congress either that such of these agencies as may operate in more than one State, or may be employed by corporations engaged in interstate commerce, or may use the mails, shall be compelled to take out a Federal license, with regulations to insure the character of their employees and the limitation of their activities to the bona fide business of detecting crime, or that such agencies shall be utterly abolished through the operation of the taxing power or through denying them the use of the mails.

Eleventh. It is charged that in many localities the entire system of civil government is suspended during strikes and there is set up in its place a military despotism under so-called martial law.

In West Virginia, for example, during the strike of coal miners in 1912 martial law was declared and the writ of habeas corpus denied, in the face of a direct prohibition by the constitution of the State, in spite of the fact that the courts were open and unobstructed, and without reference to the protests of the strikers. Persons outside the military zone were arrested, dragged before military courts, tried and sentenced under so-called martial law. Upon appeal to the civil courts of the State the actions of the military authorities were upheld, in spite of the oath of the judges to support the constitution, which in terms provided "that no citizen, unless engaged in the military service of the State, shall be tried or punished by any military court for any offense that is cognizable by the civil courts of the State," and, further, "The privilege of the writ of habeas corpus shall not be suspended."

The decisions of the court stirred Hon. Edgar M. Cullen, a former chief judge of the Court of Appeals of New York—a witness before this commission and recognized as unusually conservative and careful in his utterances—to make the following statements:

Under these decisions the life and liberty of every man within the State would seem to be at the mercy of the governor. He may declare a state of war, whether the facts justify such a declaration or not, and that declaration is conclusive upon the courts.

---

[1] See the reports of congressional committees which investigated the Homestead strike, the Pullman strike, and the recent strikes in Colorado and West Virginia.

If he declares only a portion of the State to be in a state of war, under the decision in the second case a person in any other part of the State, however distant, may be arrested and delivered to the military authorities in the martial zone, and his fate, whether liberty or life, depends on the action of a military commission, for I know of no principle which authorizes a military commission to impose the punishment of imprisonment that would not equally authorize the imposition of the punishment of death. Under that doctrine, should armed resistance to the Federal authority justifying a suspension of the writ of habeas corpus occur in Arizona a citizen could, on a charge of aiding the insurrection, be dragged from his home in Maine and delivered to the military authorities in Arizona for trial and punishment.

The remedy suggested by the learned court, of impeachment by the legislature, would hardly seem of much efficacy. By impeachment the governor could only be removed from office. He could not be further punished, however flagrant his opposition may have been, except by a perversion of the criminal law, for if the doctrine of the courts is correct he would not have exceeded his legal power.

The governor might imprison or execute the members of the legislature, or even the learned judges of the supreme court themselves.[1]

The attention of the commission has also been directed by witnesses to the repeated occurrence of similar or, if possible, more extreme conditions in Colorado and Idaho, which testimony has been confirmed either by the investigations and hearings of the commission or by the reports of responsible officials of the Federal Government. In Colorado martial law has been in effect ten times since 1894. Similarly in Idaho martial law has been in effect on several occasions. In both of these States not only have strikers been imprisoned by military courts, but thousands have been held for long periods in "bull pens," hundreds have been forcibly deported from the State, and so arrogant have the troops become upon occasions that they have refused to obey the mandates of the civil courts, although the constitutions of both States provide that the military shall always be in strict subordination to the civil power.[2] In fact, on one occasion at least, when orders of the court for the production of prisoners had been ignored and the military officers were summoned before the court, they surrounded the courthouse with infantry and cavalry, came into court accompanied by soldiers with fixed bayonets, and stationed a gatling gun in a position commanding the courthouse.[2] During the recent strike in Colorado the military was supreme and wielded its arbitrary power despotically and at times brutally.

Twelfth, it is charged by the workers that in some localities the control by the employers of the entire machinery of government is so great that lawless acts on the part of agents of the employers go unheeded and unpunished, while vindictive action against the leaders of the strike is accomplished by methods unparalleled in civilized countries. It is seldom that evidence sufficient to substantiate such sweeping charges can be secured, even if the charges are true; but in the testimony and documents which have been gathered by the commission there seems to be conclusive proof that in one State at least, Colorado, such a condition of complete domination of the State government has prevailed and, it would seem, does still prevail.

---

[1] Address before New York State Bar Association, 1914.
[2] Constitution of Colorado I, 33. Constitution of Idaho I, 12.
[3] See report of U. S. Commissioner of Labor, Carroll D. Wright, on Labor Disturbances in Colorado for a detained history of events up to and including 1904.

First, Hon. Frederick Farrar, attorney general of Colorado, testified in substance as follows:

As a result of a personal investigation into conditions in Las Animas and Huerfano Counties, Colo., in the summer of 1913, a very perfect political machine was found to exist. The head of this political machine is the sheriff, and it is conducted along lines very similar to those maintained by corrupt political organizations. It has a system of relief in case of need, and a system of giving rewards to its people. It was difficult to determine which was cause and which effect, but there was undoubtedly some relationship between the political machine and the coal companies. Witness believes the machine existed through its power as a machine over the coal companies, but has no knowledge of any money being used. His investigation did not lead into question of whether the machine controlled coroners' juries in cases of death from accidents in mines, etc., or of whether mining laws were obeyed.

Second, Hon. Thomas M. Patterson, formerly United States Senator, testified:

The men employed by the large mining companies have been used to gain political power. There is no doubt that it is the deliberate purpose of these companies to control the officials of the counties in which they are operating, and to have a great influence in the selection of judges and in the constitution of the courts. In this purpose they have been successful. Election returns from the two or three counties in which the large companies operate show that in the precincts in which the mining camps are located the returns are nearly unanimous in favor of the men or measures approved by the companies, regardless of party. The companies know whom they want elected, and do not hesitate, judging from the results, to make it known.

Third, State Senator Helen Ring Robinson testified in substance as follows:

As a member of the committee of privileges and elections, which investigated conditions in Las Animas County, she listened for three weeks to the story of political conditions there. Long before the strike was ordered she realized that the industrial situation was hopeless because the political situation appeared hopeless.

" I found that while the counties of Las Animas and Huerfano are geographically a part of Colorado, yet industrially and politically they are a barony or a principality of the Colorado Fuel & Iron Co. Such situations, of course, must mean a knitting together of the industrial and political situation, and I don't wish to say that the Colorado Fuel & Iron Co. have limited their efforts to Las Animas and Huerfano Counties. If that were so, the situation in the State itself would not be so seriously affected by them; but they have in time past reached out beyond the boundaries of their principality and made and unmade governors; men who desire positions of high place in Colorado would be very loath to antagonize them whether they lived in Las Animas or Routt County, or in Denver, and it would not matter in that case to which political party they belonged."

Attention should be called to another aspect of the control of the machinery of government by one class for the oppression of another. The scales of justice have in the past swung far in one direction—legislatures, courts, and administrative officers under the domination of corporations have grievously wronged the workers. There is grave danger that, if the workers assert their collective power and secure the control of government by the massing of their numbers, the scales may swing equally far in the other direction and every act of injustice, every drop of blood, every moment of anguish, be repaid in full, not upon some obscure and humble worker, but upon those who now glory in the sense of boundless power and security.

In the few cases in which the workers have momentarily secured control of local situations, they have followed the examples that have been set and have in many instances used their power unjustly and oppressively. In Colorado, for example, during the strikes in the metal mines, where the Western Federation of Miners controlled a camp, they followed the example of the operators and deported persons whom they deemed to be obnoxious. Similarly, during the fight between two factions of the Western Federation of Miners in Butte, Mont., the dominant faction forced several persons to leave the city and set aside the ordinary processes of law. It is inevitable that this should be the case, and it is remarkable only that the masses of workers, even when acting as mobs, show greater self-restraint than do organizations made up of business men ordinarily regarded as upright, respectable, and admirable citizens.

For the security and honor of the Nation the scales of justice must be brought to a stable equilibrium. This can be accomplished only by a realization by every citizen that every act of injustice, whether done in far-off States or at one's very door, whether affecting a friend or an enemy, is in its consequences an invasion of one's own security and a menace to one's liberty.

There is reason, however, to expect that no sober and well-considered action for the removal of these abuses will be taken, and one may, without being an alarmist, share the fears expressed by Judge Seymour D. Thompson:[1]

The dangerous tendencies and extravagant pretensions of the courts which I have pointed out ought not to be minimized, but ought to be resisted. Their resistance ought not to take place as advised by Jefferson, by "meeting the invaders foot to foot," but it ought to take place under the wise and moderate guidance of the legal profession, but the danger is that the people do not always so act. In popular governments evils are often borne with stolid patience until a culminating point is reached, when the people burst into sudden frenzy and redress their grievances by violent and extreme measures, and even tear down the fabric of government itself. There is danger, real danger, that the people will see at one sweeping glance that all the powers of their Government, Federal and State, lie at the feet of us lawyers, that is to say, at the feet of a judicial oligarchy; that those powers are being steadily exercised in behalf of the wealthy and powerful classes, and to the prejudice of the scattered and segregated people; that the power thus seized includes the power of amending the Constitution; the power of superintending the action, not merely of Congress, but also of the State legislatures; the power of degrading the powers of the two Houses of Congress, in making those investigations which they may deem accessory to wise legislation, to the powers which an English court has ascribed to British colonial legislatures; * * * holding that a venal legislature, temporarily vested with power, may corruptly bargain away those essential attributes of sovereignty and for all time; that corporate franchises bought from corrupt legislatures are sanctified and placed forever beyond recall by the people; that great trusts and combinations may place their yokes upon the necks of the people of the United States, who must groan forever under the weight, without remedy and without hope; that trial by jury and the ordinary criminal justice of the States, which ought to be kept near the people, are to be set aside, and Federal court injunctions substituted therefor; that those injunctions extend to preventing laboring men quitting their employment, although they are liable to be discharged by their employers at any time, thus creating and perpetuating a state of slavery. There is danger that the people will see these things all at once; see their enrobed judges doing their thinking on the side of the rich and powerful; see them look with solemn cynicism upon the sufferings of the masses, nor heed the earthquake when it begins to rock beneath their feet; see them present a spectacle not unlike that of Nero fiddling while Rome burns. There is danger that the people will see all this at one sudden glance, and that the furies will then break loose and that all hell will ride on their wings.

---

[1] Address before State Bar Association of Texas, 1896.

It is true that Judge Thompson spoke 19 years ago, but the real danger lies in the fact that during that period we have done little to remove the evils cited by him, and that there is even reason to fear that we have simply moved nearer to the danger line instead of away from it.

In considering the action which needs to be taken it has been urged by some that the end to be achieved is to place personal rights on a parity with property rights. It is necessary to render a firm protest and warning against the acceptance of such an ideal. The establishment of property rights and personal rights on the same level can leave only a constant and ever-growing menace to our popular institutions. With the acceptance of such an ideal our democracy is doomed to ultimate destruction. Personal rights must be recognized as supreme and of unalterable ascendency over property rights.

Relief from these grave evils can not be secured by petty reforms. The action must be drastic and directed at the roots from which these evils spring.

With full recognition of the gravity of the suggestions, it seems necessary to urge the commission to make the following recommendations:

1. That Congress forthwith initiate an amendment to the Constitution providing in specific terms for the protection of the personal rights of every person in the United States from encroachment by the Federal and State Governments and by private individuals, associations, and corporations. The principal rights which should be thus specifically protected by the power of the Federal Government are the privilege of the writ of habeas corpus, the right to jury trial, to free speech, to peaceful assemblage, to keep and bear arms, to be free from unreasonable searches and seizures, to speedy public trial, and to freedom from excessive bail and from cruel and unusual punishments.

2. That Congress immediately enact a statute or, if deemed necessary, initiate a constitutional amendment, specifically prohibiting the courts from declaring legislative acts unconstitutional.

3. That Congress enact that in all Federal cases where the trial is by jury, all qualified voters in the district shall be included in the list from which jurors are selected, and that they shall be drawn by the use of a wheel or other device designed to promote absolute impartiality.

4. That Congress drastically regulate or prohibit private detective agencies doing business in more than one State, employed by a company doing an interstate business, or using the mails in connection with their business. Such regulation, if it is feasible, should include particularly the limitation of their activities to the bona fide functions of detecting crime, and adequate provision should be made for the rigid supervision of their organization and personnel.

4. DENIAL OF THE RIGHT OF ORGANIZATION.

The previous discussion of the causes of industrial unrest has dealt with the denial of certain fundamentals to which the workers believe they have natural and inalienable rights, namely, a fair distribution of the products of industry, the opportunity to earn a living, free access to unused land and natural resources, and just treatment by legislators, courts, and executive officials. A more serious and fundamental charge is, however, contained in the allegation by the workers that in spite of the nominal legal right which has been established by a century-long struggle, almost insurmountable obstacles are placed in the way of their using the only means by which economic and political justice can be secured, namely, combined action through voluntary organization. The workers insist that this right of organization is fundamental and necessary for their freedom, and that it is inherent in the general rights guaranteed every citizen of a democracy. They insist that "people can free themselves from oppression only by organized force. No people could gain or maintain their rights or liberties acting singly, and any class of citizens in the State subject to unjust burdens or oppression can gain relief only by combined action."

The demand for organization and collective action has been misunderstood, it is claimed, because of the belief among a large number of citizens that its purpose was simply to secure better wages and better physical conditions. It has been urged, however, by a large number of witnesses before the commission that this is a complete misconception of the purposes for which workers desire to form organizations. It has been pointed out with great force and logic that the struggle of labor for organization is not merely an attempt to secure an increased measure of the material comforts of life, but is a part of the age-long struggle for liberty; that this struggle is sharpened by the pinch of hunger and the exhaustion of body and mind by long hours and improper working conditions; but that even if men were well fed they would still struggle to be free. It is not denied that the exceptional individual can secure an economic sufficiency either by the sale of his unusual ability or talent or by sycophantic subservience to some person in authority, but it is insisted that no individual can achieve freedom by his own efforts. Similarly, while it is admitted that in some cases exceptional employers treat their employees with the greatest justice and liberality, it is held to be a social axiom that no group of workers can become free except by combined action, nor can the mass hope to achieve any material advance in their condition except by collective effort.

Furthermore, it is urged by the representatives of labor that the efforts of individuals who are bent upon bettering their own condition without reference to their health or to the interests of others directly injure each of their fellow workers and indirectly weaken the whole fabric of society.

It is also pointed out that the evolution of modern industry has greatly increased the necessity for organization on the part of wage earners. While it is not admitted that the employer who has only one employee is on an economic equality with the person who is employed by him, because of the fact that the employer controls the means of livelihood, which gives him an almost incalculable advantage in any bargain, nevertheless this condition of inequality is held to have been enormously increased by the development of corporations controlling the livelihood of hundreds of thousands of employees and by the growth of employers' associations whose members act as a unit in questions affecting their relations with employees.

There have been many able and convincing expositions of this belief by witnesses before the commission, but there is no other which seems to have so completely covered the entire field as the testimony of Mr. Louis D. Brandeis, who, as he stated, has studied this problem from the standpoint both of employers and of employees:

My observation leads me to believe that while there are many single things—single causes—contributing causes to unrest, that there is one cause which is fundamental, and it is the necessary conflict between—the contrast between—our political liberty and the industrial absolutism.

We are as free politically, perhaps, as it is possible for us to be. Every man has his voice and his vote, and the law has endeavored to enable, and has succeeded practically in enabling, him to exercise his political franchise without fear. He, therefore, has his part, and he certainly can secure an adequate part of the government of the country in all of its political relations—in all relations which are determined by legislation or governmental administration. On the other hand, in dealing with industrial problems the position of the ordinary worker is exactly the reverse. And the main objection, as I see it, to the large corporation is that it makes possible—and in many cases makes inevitable—the exercise of industrial absolutism. It is not merely the case of the individual worker against employer, which,. even if he is a reasonably sized employer, presents a serious situation calling for the interposition of a union to protect the individual. But we have the situation of an employer so potent, so well organized, with such concentrated forces and with such extraordinary powers of reserve and the ability to endure against strikes and other efforts of a union, that the relatively loosely organized masses of even strong unions are unable to cope with the situation.

We are dealing here with a question not of motive, but of condition. Now, the large corporations and the managers of the large corporations—of the powerful corporations—are probably, in a large part, actuated by motives just the same as an employer of one-tenth of their size. Neither of them, as a rule, wishes to have his liberty abridged; but the smaller concern usually comes to the conclusion that it is necessary that it should be where there is an important union found. But when you have created a great power, when there exist these powerful organizations who can afford—not only can successfully summon forces from all parts of the country—to use tremendous amounts of money in any conflict to carry out what they deem to be their business principles, you have necessarily a condition of inequality between the two contending forces. The result is that contests, doubtless undertaken with the best of motives and with strong convictions of what is for the bests interests not only of the company but of the community, leads to absolutism. In all cases of these large corporations the result has been to develop a benevolent absolutism—an absolutism all the same; and it is that which makes the great corporation so dangerous. It is because you have created within the State a state so powerful that the ordinary forces existing are insufficient to meet it.

Now, to my mind the situation of the worker that is involved—and I noted, Mr. Chairman, that when you put the question you put the question of physical condition—unrest, in my mind, never can be removed, and, fortunately never can be removed by the mere improvement of the physical and material conditions of the working man. If it were we should run great risk of improving their material conditions and reducing their manhood. We must bear in mind all the time that however much we may desire material improvement and must desire it for the comfort of the individual, we are a democracy; and that we must have above all things men; and it is the development of manhood to which any industrial and social system must be directed. We are committed not only to social justice in the sense of avoiding things which bring suffering and harm and unequal distribution of wealth, but we are committed primarily to democracy, and the social justice to which we are headed is an incident of our democracy, not an end itself. It is the result of democracy, but democracy we must have. And, therefore, the end to which we must move is a recognition of industrial democracy as the end to which we are to work, and that means this: It means that the problems are not any longer, or to be any longer, the problems of the employer. The problems of his business—it is not the employer's business. The union can not shift upon the employer the responsibility for the conditions, nor can the employer insist upon solving, according to his will, the conditions which shall exist; but the problems which exist are the problems of the trade; they are the problems of the employer and the employee.. No possible degree of profit sharing, however liberal, can meet the situation. That would be again merely dividing the proceeds of business. That might do harm or it might do good, dependent on how it is applied.

No mere liberality in the division of the proceeds of industry can meet this situation. There must be a division not only of the profits, but a division of the responsibilities; and the men must have the opportunity of deciding, in part, what shall be their condition and how the business shall be run. They also, as a part of that responsibility, must learn that they must bear the results, the fatal results, of grave mistakes, just as the employer. But the right to assist in producing the results, the right, if need be, the privilege of making mistakes, is a privilege which can not be denied to labor, just as we must insist on their sharing the responsibilities for the result of the business.

Now, to a certain extent we get that result—are gradually getting it—in smaller businesses. The grave objection to the large business is that almost inevitably, from its organization, through its absentee stockholdership, through its remote directorship, through the creation practically of stewards to take charge of the details of the operation of the business and coming into direct relation with labor, we lose that necessary cooperation which our own aspirations—American aspirations—of democracy demand. And it is in that, in my opinion, that we will find the very foundation of the unrest; and no matter what is done with the superstructure, no matter how it may be improved one way or the other, unless we reach that fundamental difficulty, the unrest will not only continue, but in my opinion will grow worse.

It is very significant that out of 230 representatives of the interests of employers, chosen largely on the recommendations of their own organizations, less than half a dozen have denied the propriety of collective action on the part of employees. A considerable number of these witnesses have, however, testified that they denied in practice what they admitted to be right in theory. A majority of such witnesses were employers who in the operation of their business maintained what they, in accordance with common terminology, called the "open shop." The theory of the "open shop," according to these witnesses, is that workers are employed without any reference to their membership or nonmembership in trade unions; while, as a matter of fact, it was found upon investigation that these employers did not, as a rule, willingly or knowingly employ union men. Nevertheless, this is deemed by the commission to be a minor point. The "open shop," even if union men are not discriminated against, is as much a denial of the right of collective action as is the "antiunion shop." In neither is the collective action of employees permitted for the purpose of negotiating with reference to labor conditions. Both in theory and in practice, in the absence of legislative regulation, the working conditions are fixed by the employer.

It is evident, therefore, that there can be at best only a benevolent despotism where collective action on the part of the employees does not exist.

A great deal of testimony has been introduced to show that employers who refuse to deal collectively with their workmen do in fact grant audiences at which the grievances of their workmen may be presented. One is repelled rather than impressed by the insistence with which this idea has been presented. Every tyrant in history has on stated days granted audiences to which his faithful subjects might bring their complaints against his officers and agents. At these audiences, in theory at least, even the poorest widow might be heard by her sovereign in her search for justice. That justice was never secured under such conditions, except at the whim of the tyrant, is sure. It is equally sure that in industry justice can never be attained by such a method.

The last point which needs to be considered in this connection is the attitude frequently assumed by employers that they are perfectly willing to deal with their own employees collectively, but will resist to the end dealing with any national organization, and resent the intrusion of any persons acting for their employees who are not members of their own labor force. In practice these statements have been generally found to be specious. Such employers as a rule oppose any effective form of organization among their own employees as bitterly as they fight the national unions. The underlying motive of such statements seems to be that as long as organizations are unsupported from outside they are ineffective and capable of being crushed with ease and impunity by discharging the ringleaders. Similarly, the opposition to the representation of their employees by persons outside their labor force seems to arise wholly from the knowledge that as long as the workers' representatives are on the pay roll they can be controlled, or, if they prove intractable they can be effectually disposed of by summary dismissal.

To suggest that labor unions can be effective if organized on less than a national scale seems to ignore entirely the facts and trend of present-day American business. There is no line of organized industry in which individual establishments can act independently. Ignoring for the time the centralization of control and ownership, and also the almost universal existence of employers' associations, the mere fact of competition would render totally ineffective any organization of employees which was limited to a single establishment. Advance in labor conditions must proceed with a fair degree of uniformity throughout any line of industry. This does not indeed require that all employees in an industry must belong to a national organization, for experience has shown that wherever even a considerable part are union members, the advances which they secure are almost invariably granted by competitors, even if they do not employ union men, in order to prevent their own employees from organizing.

The conclusions upon this question, however, are not based upon theory, but upon a thorough investigation of typical situations in which the contrast between organization and the denial of the right of organization could best be studied. The commission has held public hearings and has made thorough investigations in such industrial communities as Paterson, N. J., Los Angeles, Cal., Lead, S. Dak., and Colorado, where the right of collective action on the part of employees is denied. These investigations have shown that under the best possible conditions, and granting the most excellent motives on the part of employers, freedom does not exist either politically, industrially, or socially, and that the fiber of manhood will inevitably be destroyed by the continuance of the existing situation. Investigations have proved that although the physical and material conditions may be unusually good, as, for example, in Lead, S. Dak., they are the price paid for the absolute submission of the employees to the will of the employing corporation. Such conditions are, moreover, shown by the hearings of the commission and by the investigations of its staff to be unusual. Los Angeles, for example, although exceptionally endowed in location, climate, and natural resources, was sharply criticized for the labor conditions which had developed during its "open shop" régime even by Mr. Walter Drew, representing several of the largest associations which contend for the "open shop." It is significant that the only claim ordinarily made for the conditions in such establishments or localities is that "they are as good as are secured by the union." As a matter of fact, there are few establishments which make this boast, and in the majority the conditions were found to be far below any acceptable standards.

The commission has also, through public hearings and the investigations of its staff, made a thorough and searching investigation of the conditions in those industries and establishments where collective action, through the medium of trade unions and joint agreements, exists. It has not been found that the conditions in such industries are ideal, nor that friction between employers and the unions is unknown; nor has it been found that the employees in such industries have entirely achieved economic, political, and industrial freedom, for these ideals can not be gained until the fundamental changes in our political and economic structure, which have already been referred to, have in some way been accomplished. It has been found, however, that the material conditions of the workers in such industries and establishments are on a generally higher plane than where workers are unorganized; that important improvements in such conditions have been achieved as the direct result of organization; that the friction which exists in such industries and establishments has been reduced rather than increased by organization; and that the workers at least have secured a basis upon which their political and economic freedom may ultimately be established.

The evils of graft, "machine politics," factional fights, and false leadership, which have been found sometimes to exist in such organized industries, are those which are inevitable in any democratic form of organization. They are the same evils which have accompanied the development of the American Nation, and of its States and municipalities. Such evils as we have found to exist are indeed to be condemned, but a study of the history of these organizations seems to show clearly that there is a tendency to eradicate them as the organizations become stronger and as the membership becomes more familiar with the responsibilities and methods of democratic action. Furthermore, there is a fundamental principle which applies in this field as in all other lines of human activity. This principle is contained in the following contrast: In democratic organizations such evils and excesses as may arise tend to disrupt and destroy the organization and are therefore self-eradicating; while in an autocracy, evils and excesses tend inevitably to strengthen the existing autocrat and can be eradicated only in the event of a revolt on the part of those who suffer from such evils. This is the history not only of every form of artificial association, but of nations.

The fundamental question for the Nation to decide, for in the end public opinion will control here as elsewhere, is whether the workers shall have an effective means of adjusting their grievances, improving their condition, and securing their liberty, through negotiation with their employers, or whether they shall be driven by necessity and oppression to the extreme of revolt. Where men are well organized, and the power of employers and employees is fairly well balanced, agreements are nearly always reached by negotiation; but, even if this fails, the strikes or lockouts which follow are as a rule merely cessations of work until economic necessity forces the parties together again to adopt some form of compromise. With the unorganized there is no hope of achieving anything except by spontaneous revolt. Too often has it been found that during the delay of attempted negotiations the leaders are discharged and new men are found ready to take the place of those who protest against conditions. Without strike funds or other financial support the unorganized must achieve results at once; they can not afford to wait for reason and compromise to come into play. Lacking strong leaders and definite organization, such revolts can only be expected to change to mob action on the slightest provocation.

Looking back over the industrial history of the last quarter century, the industrial disputes which have attracted the attention of the country and which have been accompanied by bloodshed and violence have been revolutions against industrial oppression, and not mere strikes for the improvement of working conditions. Such revolutions in fact were the railway strikes of the late eighties, the Homestead strike, the bituminous coal strike of 1897, the anthracite strikes of 1900 and 1903, the strike at McKees Rocks in 1909, the Bethlehem strike of 1910, the strikes in the textile mills at Lawrence, Paterson, and Little Falls, many of the strikes in the mining camps of Idaho and Colorado, the garment workers' strikes in New York and other cities, and the recent strikes in the mining districts of West Virginia, Westmoreland County, Pa., and Calumet, Mich.

As a result, therefore, not only of fundamental considerations but of practical investigations, the results of which are described in detail hereinafter, it would appear that every means should be used to extend and strengthen organizations throughout the entire industrial field. Much attention has been devoted to the means by which this can best be accomplished, and a large number of suggestions have been received. As a result of careful consideration, it is suggested that the commission recommend the following action:

1. Incorporation among the rights guaranteed by the Constitution of the unlimited right of individuals to form associations, not for the sake of profit but for the advancement of their individual and collective interests.

2. Enactment of statutes specifically protecting this right and prohibiting the discharge of any person because of his membership in a labor organization.

3. Enactment of a statute providing that action on the part of an association of individuals not organized for profit shall not be held to be unlawful where such action would not be unlawful in the case of an individual.

4. That the Federal Trade Commission be specifically empowered and directed by Congress, in determining unfair methods of competition to take into account and specially investigate the unfair treatment of labor in all respects, with particular reference to the following points:

(a) Refusal to permit employees to become members of labor organizations.

(b) Refusal to meet or confer with the authorized representatives of employees.

5. That the Department of Labor, through the Secretary of Labor or any other authorized official, be empowered and directed to present to the Federal Trade Commission, and to prosecute before that body all cases of unfair competition arising out of the treatment of labor which may come to its attention.

6. That such cases, affecting as they do the lives of citizens in the humblest circumstances, as well as the profits of competitors and the peace of the community, be directed by Congress to have precedence over all other cases before the Federal Trade Commission.

CONCLUSIONS AND RECOMMENDATIONS.

The remainder of the report is devoted largely to the conclusions and recommendations with respect to specific questions propounded by Congress. The facts upon which these conclusions and recommendations are based are contained in the testimony taken by the commission and in the reports of its investigators. The complete corrected testimony is transmitted to Congress, as well as a carefully prepared digest of the evidence. The reports of the investigators have likewise been placed in the possession of Congress.[1]

I. INDUSTRIAL CONDITIONS OF ADULT WORKMEN IN GENERAL INDUSTRIES.

In this section only the conditions of adult workmen are considered, leaving the questions affecting women and children for separate consideration later. The problems involved are essentially different, and the position of women and children in relation to the State may be clearly distinguished from the position of adult workmen.

WAGES.

As a result of the investigations which have been made the following conclusions are justified:

1. The welfare of the State demands that the useful labor of every able-bodied workman should, as a minimum, be compensated by sufficient income to support in comfort himself, a wife, and at least three minor children, and in addition to provide for sickness, old age, and disability. Under no other conditions can a strong, contented, and efficient citizenship be developed.

2. Under existing conditions such an income is not received by fully one-half of the wage earners employed in industry.

3. The natural resources of the United States are such that an industrial population properly educated and efficiently organized can produce enough to achieve this standard of living.

4. It is probable that even at present the national agricultural and industrial output is sufficient to permit the establishment of such a standard.

5. The problem is therefore essentially one of distribution.

6. The fixing of the wages of adult workmen by legal enactment is not practicable nor desirable as a general policy, except for public employees.

7. A just standard of wages in any industry or occupation can best be reached by collective bargaining between employers and employees

---

[1] These reports have not been printed with this document, on the recommendation of Chairman Frank P. Walsh, as stated in his letter in Senate Report No. 143, Sixty-fourth Congress.

for the purpose of forming voluntary joint agreements. The success and justice of such joint agreements is, however, dependent upon the essential equality of the two parties and can not be attained unless effective organization exists.

It is suggested that the commission make the following recommendations:

1. In order that the public may be kept fully informed with regard to labor conditions, and that a proper basis of facts should exist for negotiation and arbitration, the Federal Government should enact the necessary legislation to provide for the collection, through the Bureau of Labor Statistics or otherwise, of the full and exact facts regarding wages, hours of labor, and extent of unemployment for every industry. Every employer should be required by law to file with the proper authority a sworn statement of these facts according to a prescribed form. These statistics should be published annually, and the full data regarding any industry or plant should be accessible to any mediator or any other responsible citizen.

2. Uniform statutes should be passed by the legislatures of all States requiring that wages be paid at least semimonthly and in cash, except where by joint agreement other methods are agreed upon.

HOURS OF LABOR.

As a result of investigation the following conclusions are justified:

1. The physical well-being, mental development, and recreational needs of every class of population demand that under normal circumstances the working day should not exceed eight hours.

2. A very large percentage of the workmen in manufactures, transportation, and mining work more than eight hours per day.

3. This is in marked contract to the condition of those whose economic position enables them to define the length of their own working day.

4. Practical experience has shown that the reduction of working hours is in the interest not only of the worker and the community generally, but of the employer.

5. The regulation by legal enactment of working hours of adult workmen is not generally practicable nor desirable, except for public employees.

It is suggested that the commission recommend:

1. That in the so-called continuous occupations, other than the movement of trains, requiring work during both the day and the night for six or seven days per week, the State and Federal Governments should directly intervene, so that the working hours should not exceed eight per day nor extend to more than six days per week.

SAFETY AND SANITATION.

The investigations which have been made warrant the following conclusions:

1. Great progress has been made during recent years in promoting safety and sanitation in manufacturing, mining, and transportation.

2. The progress has been most rapid in the direction of safeguarding workers from industrial accidents.

3. Progress in safety has been in part the result of continued agitation and education, but has proceeded most rapidly and satisfactorily since the enactment of workmen's compensation laws, which render unsafe working conditions expensive to the employer.

4. The movement has also been largely promoted by the formation of safety committees composed of officials and workmen, and by the creation of joint conferences of employers and employees to assist and advise State officials in the administration of the law and in the formulation of safety rules.

5. The campaign for safety needs, however, to be greatly extended as rapidly as possible. The annual list of accidents, approximately 35,000 fatalities and 700,000 injuries involving disability of over four weeks, can not be regarded complacently. From one-third to one-half of these accidents have been estimated by competent authorities to be preventable by proper safeguards, inspection, and control.

6. The advance in the sanitation of workshops has been less rapid, because not only are the dangers less obvious, but there is no financial liability for diseases or deaths occurring as the result of improper sanitation. Future progress in sanitation demands attention not only to cleanliness and ventilation but to occupational diseases.

7. The most direct incentive for the promotion of sanitation would be the adoption of a proper system of sickness insurance.

It is suggestion that the commission recommend:

1. The creation of a bureau of industrial safety (except that the section providing a museum of safety is not indorsed). Proper steps should be taken to provide for the coordination of the work of all Federal bureaus whose work is concerned with industrial safety.

2. The appropriations of the Public Health Service for the investigation and promotion of industrial sanitation should be increased.

HOUSING.

It has been found in the course of the commission's investigations:

1. The present provisions for the housing of workmen are generally bad, not only in the large cities but in industrial communities of every size and in rural districts.

2. Not only are the houses and tenements which are available for workers largely insanitary and unfit for habitation but they are inadequate, resulting in high rents, overcrowding, and congestion.

3. Such conditions make not only for discomfort and unhappiness, but for disease and degeneration.

4. The ordinary method of supplying houses through their erection by private capitalists for investment and speculation has rarely, if ever, been adequate.

5. Excellent plans for the housing of workmen have been put into effect by a number of firms and corporations, but such measures have not at all affected the general situation, and being dependent upon the volition of individuals can not be regarded as likely to greatly influence progress.

6. The tenement-house acts, as well as the health ordinances and building regulations of municipalities, while generally productive of good effects, are at best surface remedies and can never cure the evils of the present housing situation.

·7. In every important European country Government aid and direct intervention to curb speculation have proved to be necessary for the promotion of any real progress.

8. Governmental action in Europe has chiefly taken the following forms:

(a) Extension of credit to voluntary nonprofit-making associations.

(b) Construction by the Government of buildings which are leased for long periods on easy terms.

(c) Exemption from taxation and other subsidies for homes constructed for occupancy by their owners.

(d) Legislation designed to prevent the holding of land out of use and to secure for the Government a part of the "unearned increment."

It is suggested that the commission recommend:

1. The Federal and State Governments should institute investigations directed not so much to ascertaining existing housing conditions as to formulating constructive methods by which direct support and encouragement to the promotion of improved housing can be given. Actual experiment in the promotion of housing should proceed as rapidly as proper plans can be drafted.

2. Special attention should be given to taxation, in order that land should as far as possible be forced into use and the burden of taxation be removed from home owners.

3. The municipalities should be relieved from all State restrictions which now prevent them from undertaking the operation of adequate housing schemes and from engaging in other necessary municipal enterprises.

II. WOMEN AND CHILDREN IN INDUSTRY.

The investigations and hearings of the commission justify the conclusions:

1. As a result of their unprotected condition, women and children are exploited in industry, trade, domestic service, and agriculture to an extent which threatens their health and welfare and menaces the well-being of future generations.

2. The competition of women and children is a direct menace to the wage and salary standards of men.

3. Under present conditions, children are permitted by their parents to go to work largely because their earnings are necessary for the support of the rest of the family. The restrictive legislation of the past quarter century, although admirable in purpose and ultimate results, has thrown a heavy burden upon the fathers and mothers, who, at existing wages, have been barely able to support their families. The evidence shows that the burden of child-labor legislation has rested upon the wage earners rather than upon employers. It is the testimony of enlightened employers that the employment of children is unprofitable, and that the effect of excluding children from factories has been to increase rather than decrease profits. In the interests of society as a whole, further restrictions on the employment of immature children are necessary, but it is important that they should be made with an understanding that the burden will rest primarily upon the wage earners, whose self-sacrifice should be fully recognized.

4. The increasing employment of women has been due to two primary causes: First, the low wages of men, which have made the earnings of women necessary for the support of the family, and, second, the inducement to employers to substitute women for men because they will accept lower wages and are less likely to protest against conditions. The substitution of women for men has been greatly assisted by the introduction of improved machinery, which makes strength and technical skill unnecessary.

5. The increased employment of women under present working conditions is a serious menace to their own health and well-being, to the wages of their husbands and brothers, and to the ideals of family life upon which American civilization has been established.

6. The conditions under which women are employed in domestic service and in agriculture merit the attention of the Nation no less than does their employment in manufacturing and trade. Not only is the economic condition of women employed in agriculture and domestic service a matter of grave concern, but they are subject to overwork, unreasonable hours, and personal abuse of various kinds, from which they have been largely relieved in factories and stores through agitation and legislation.

7. The position of women in industry has been rendered doubly hard by reason of their lack of training for industrial work, by the oversupply of such labor and the consequent competition, by their traditional position of dependence, and by their disfranchisement.

8. A very thorough investigation in the New England States failed to show a single manufacturer who had left a State as a result of restrictive factory legislation. On the contrary, the majority of manufacturers expressed the opinion that the legislation regulating conditions for women and children had been advantageous to the industry as a whole, particularly because it placed all competitors upon the same footing. Similarly an investigation of the effects of minimum-wage legislation failed to show any calculable effects upon the cost of production or upon the employment of women after a sufficient period had elapsed to allow the necessary readjustments to be made.

9. Nevertheless, there is a strong and increasing demand on the part of manufacturers in the more progressive States that regulation of factory conditions should be undertaken by the Federal Government, in order that competitors in all parts of the country should be placed upon an equal footing in this respect. The same demand comes also from the representatives of labor not only because the argument of "interstate competition" is creating strong opposition to progressive legislation, but because of the great economy of effort which would result from having to make the fight for better legislation only at the National Capital instead of in 45 States.

It is suggested that the commission recommend:

1. The recognition both by public opinion and in such legislation as may be enacted of the principle that women should receive the same compensation as men for the same terms.

2. Until this principle is recognized and women are accorded equal political rights, the extension of State protection of women, through legislation regulating working conditions, hours of service, and minimum wages, is highly desirable.

3. The increased organization of working women for self-protection and the improvement of their industrial conditions.

4. The inclusion of all women working for wages, whether in industry, trade, domestic service, or agriculture, under future legislation regulating their wages, hours, or working conditions.

5. The extension of the principle of State protection of children and the rapid increase of facilities for their education as outlined elsewhere.

6. The enactment by Congress of legislation embodying the principles contained in the so-called Palmer-Owen bill, which was before Congress at the last session.

III. Industrial Conditions and Relations on Public Utilities.

GENERAL.

The investigations of the commission show:

1. The scope of the Newlands Act, which applies only to employees engaged in the operation of interstate railroads, is too narrow and leaves the public service in the transmission of intelligence and in the handling of interstate commerce likely to be interrupted by labor disputes without any adequate legal provision either for mediation and conciliation or for making the facts involved in the dispute known to the public.

2. Even as applied to train-service employees, the Newlands Act provides no means of bringing the facts before the public, except when both sides agree to arbitration.

3. The selection of impartial members of arbitration boards has almost without exception devolved upon the Board of Mediation and Conciliation, owing to the inability of the parties to agree. This not only imposes an unpleasant and burdensome task upon the Board of Mediation and Conciliation, but tends greatly to weaken its influence. The experience in Great Britain shows that agreement can be reached by joint conference of employers and employees during a period of industrial peace for the selection of a panel of impartial persons from which arbitrators can be selected when they are needed, and seems to indicate that in the United States the inability of the parties to agree upon impartial arbitrators is due in part at least to the fact that they are always selected during the heat of the conflict.

It is suggested that the commission recommend:

1. The extension of the Newlands Act to cover not only all classes of railroad employees, but all employees of public-service corporations which are engaged in interstate commerce.

2. The functions of the Board of Mediation and Conciliation under the Newlands Act should be extended to provide for the creation of boards of investigation, to be formed only by consent of both parties and to make a report of facts and recommendations which will not be binding upon either side.

3. The Board of Mediation and Conciliation should be authorized by Congress to create an advisory council, composed of equal numbers of employers and employees, for the purpose of creating a panel of names from which impartial arbitrators may be chosen by the Board of Mediation and Conciliation.

TELEGRAPH.

The investigations and hearings of the commission justify the following conclusions:

1. The workers employed by the two principal telegraph companies (the Western Union Telegraph and the Postal Telegraph-Cable) are not only underpaid, as admitted by the highest officials in their testimony before the commission, but subject to many abuses, such as the denial of proper periods of relief while on duty; the establishment of arbitrary speed rates, which frequently result in overstrain; the arbitrary discharge of employees without notice for any cause or no cause; the employment of young boys for messenger service under conditions which can result only in their moral corruption; and the employment of women for telegraph service at night.

2. Such conditions have existed practically without change at least since 1884, in spite of the facts having been made public by three Government investigations.

3. The workers are practically unable to improve their condition because these two companies, which control practically the entire industry, deny them the right of organization. The suppression of organization is effectively carried out by the discharge of all known to be union men or union sympathizers, by the use of spies who fraudulently secure the confidence of employees and report all known to be union members or sympathizers, by the use of an effective system of blacklisting, and by the control even of the personnel of the operators upon leased wires in the offices of brokers and other private individuals.

4. The two companies have a monopoly of the transmission of telegrams, and no effective competition exists between them. These companies are performing a service in the transmission of intelligence which has been held by the Federal Supreme Court to have been reserved by the Constitution specifically to the Federal Government.

5. The telegraph companies are enormously overcapitalized, and their rates, which are graded to pay dividends upon large amounts of stock which do not represent the investment of cash, are very much higher than the cost of service warrants.

6. Owing to the duplication of offices on the part of the two companies and the maintenance of branch offices which are idle for a large part of the time, this service is being performed inefficiently and at an unusually high cost in spite of the low wages paid the operators.

It is suggested that the commission recommend:

1. The property of the telegraph companies or such part of their equipment as may be necessary for the efficient operation of a national telegraph system should be purchased by the Federal Government after proper valuation and placed under the general jurisdiction of the Post Office Department for operation.[1] In transferring the service to the Federal Government all employees, including officials and other persons, necessary for successful operation should be retained, and those whom the elimination of the duplicate service of the two companies renders unnecessary for the national system

---

[1] The economic argument for the postalization of telegraphs and telephones is presented in the testimony of Hon. David J. Lewis before the commission.

should be absorbed into other branches of the Federal service as far as practicable.

2. At the time of the transfer to the Federal service a special commission should be appointed to revise the salary ratings and other working conditions and place them upon a proper basis.

TELEPHONE.

The investigations of the commission are the basis for the following statements:

1. The condition of the telephone operators in both interstate and local service is subject to grave criticism. The wages paid even in the cities having the highest standards are insufficient to provide decently for women who have no other means of support. The requirements and nervous strain incident to the service are so very severe that experienced physicians have testified that operators should work not more than five hours per day, whereas the regular working hours are from seven to nine per day. The operators, who are principally girls and young women, are required to work at night, going to and returning from their work at hours when they are subject to grave menace. The policy of the companies in general provides for sanitary and reasonably comfortable working places and for attention to the recreation and physical needs of the operators, but in a number of cities the conditions even in these respects are subject to severe criticism.

2. The telephone operators are unable to secure reasonable conditions for themselves because of their youth and the fact that they ordinarily remain in the service only a short time.

3. The organization of employees for their own protection is effectively resisted by the employing companies.

4. The American Telephone & Telegraph Co., with its subsidiary and affiliated corporations, controls more than 70 per cent of the total telephone business of the country. The American Telephone & Telegraph Co. has been enormously profitable and is well able to afford the necessary improvements in working conditions. The American Telephone & Telegraph Co. has increased its capitalization enormously without the investment of new capital.

5. The transaction by which the American Telephone & Telegraph Co., which had been a subsidiary of the American Bell Telephone Co., absorbed the parent company in 1899 was not only designed to evade the legal limitations contained in the Massachusetts charter of the American Bell Telephone Co., but resulted in the increase of the capitalization of the combination from $25,886,300 to $75,276,600 without the addition of any new capital.

6. The transmission of intelligence is a function which is specifically reserved by the Constitution to the Federal Government, but which in the telephone field has been permitted to become the practical monopoly of a single corporation.

It is suggested that the commission recommend:

1. The purchase by the Federal Government, after proper valuation, of the property of the interstate and local telephone companies, or such part of their equipment as may be necessary for the efficient operation of a national telephone system.

2. The transfer of all employees, including officials, necessary for the efficient operation of the national telephone system to the Federal service, as far as possible, and the absorption, as far as practicable, of all employees who are not necessary for the telephone system into other branches of the Federal service.

3. When such employees are transferred to the Federal service, the creation of a special commission to establish salary ratings and other working conditions on a proper basis.

4. In the meantime provision should be made by Congress for the creation of a minimum wage board to fix minimum wage standards for women employees who are engaged in the transmission of messages in interstate commerce. The board should be authorized to differentiate between localities in fixing minima, if on due consideration such differential rates should be deemed advisable.

5. The creation of minimum wage boards in the several States to fix minimum wages for all women employees engaged in service within the State.

THE PULLMAN CO.

The investigations and hearings of the commission developed the following facts:

1. The conductors and porters employed in the car service of the Pullman Co. are employed under conditions which seem to require radical readjustment. Both classes of employees are admitted by officials of the company to be underpaid.

The standard salary of the porters ($27.50 per month) is such that the porters are obliged to secure tips from the public in order to live. The Pullman Co. is admitted by the chairman of the board of directors to be the direct beneficiary of the tips from the public to the extent of the difference between a fair wage and that which is now paid.

The hours of service are extremely long, the regulations of the company allowing porters and conductors when in service only four hours' sleep per night and penalizing them severely if they sleep while on duty. Employees of the Pullman Co. are subject to many other abuses, among which may be mentioned the arbitrary deduction from their salaries for such time as they may not be needed for the actual service of the company, although they are required to report at the office each morning and are sometimes compelled to wait the greater part of the day without compensation; the requirement that porters shall furnish blacking, although they are not permitted to charge passengers for the service of shoe cleaning; the system of arbitrary penalties for the infraction of multitudinous rules; the requirement that all employees shall purchase their uniforms from one mercantile establishment, the owners of which are largely interested in the Pullman Co.; and the lack of proper provision of sleeping quarters for employees when away from their home stations.

2. The Pullman Co. has a bonus system by which employees who have a " clean record " for the year receive an extra month's salary. This system serves to increase the earnings of those who receive the bonus, and is unquestionably appreciated by them. Nevertheless it is inequitable in penalizing with extra severity any infractions of

rules which occur during the latter half of the year, and puts into the hands of officials and inspectors a means of discrimination which can be arbitrarily exercised.

3. The effect of the tipping system is not only to degrade those who are obliged by their economic conditions to accept tips but to promote discrimination in the service of the public.

4. The employees of the Pullman Co. are unable to improve their condition through organization, as employees known to be members of labor unions are discharged, and through the means of an effective system of espionage employees are deterred from affiliating with labor unions.

5. The company is tremendously overcapitalized, having increased its capitalization from $36,000,000 in 1893 to $120,000,000 in 1915, without the investment of a single dollar on the part of the stockholders. Upon the basis of actual cash paid in, the annual dividends of the company are not less than 29 per cent. During the history of the company the stockholders have received cash dividends amounting to at least $167,000,000 and special stock dividends of $64,000,000, making a total of $231,000,000 on an actual investment of $32,601,238.

6. The company enjoys a practical monopoly of the sleeping-car service.

It is suggested that the commission recommend:

1. The enactment by Congress of a statute prohibiting the tipping of any employee of a public-service corporation engaged in interstate commerce and providing a proper fine for both the giver and the recipient of the tip.

2. The amendment of the existing law regulating the hours of service of train employees to include the employees engaged in the Pullman service.

. 3. The extension of the Newlands Act, as already suggested, to cover the Pullman Co.

RAILROADS.

The investigations of the commission with regard to railroads have been too limited to permit of general findings or recommendations. Enough evidence has, however, come before the commission with regard to three points to warrant attention.

1. The railroad construction camps are largely insanitary, overcrowded, and improperly equipped for the health and comfort of the employees. In addition, there are many abuses, such as overcharging at the commissary and grafting by foremen.

2. The so-called voluntary benefit associations of a number of the railroads constitute, under the present system of management, a great injustice to employees. These funds, which are contributed almost entirely by the employees, the management as a rule paying only the cost of administration, until recently were generally used to relieve the companies from liability for accident, employees being required to sign a release in favor of the company at the time that they became members of the benefit association. In some cases, even, the membership is compulsory. Nevertheless, the employees have no voice in the management and receive no equity when they are discharged. Finally, such associations, under their present management, serve to

exert an undue influence over employees, since the members, if they quit the service for any period or for any cause, sacrifice to the company all that has been paid in.

3. Under the authority granted by the several States the railroads maintain a force of police, and some, at least, have established large arsenals of arms and ammunition. This armed force, when augmented by recruits from detective agencies and employment agencies, as seems to be the general practice during industrial disputes, constitutes a private army clothed with a degree of authority which should be exercised only by public officials; these armed bodies, usurping the supreme functions of the State and oftentimes encroaching on the rights of the citizens, are a distinct menace to public welfare.

It is suggested that the commission recommend:

1. Thorough investigation by the Public Health Service of railroad construction camps as well as other labor camps, and the preparation of definite plans for such camps and a standard code of sanitary regulations.

2. The enactment by Congress of a statute expressly prohibiting corporations engaged in interstate commerce from inducing or compelling their employees to sign releases of liability for accidents.

3. Congress should enact a statute prohibiting interstate employers from requiring their employees to contribute to benefit funds, and providing for the participation of employees engaged in interstate commerce in the management of all benefit funds and other funds to which they contribute.

4. The regulation by Federal statute of the employment of police on interstate railroads. The statute should not only provide for the organization, personnel, and powers of such police, but should definitely provide that during labor disputes such police should be subject to the proper civil authorities and paid out of the public treasury. The statute should also provide that such corporations should be permitted to have firearms only under license, requiring that a definite record be maintained showing the character of each firearm and to whom it is issued.

5. The assumption by the States of full responsibility and definite provision not only for protecting the property of railroads, but for preventing trespass upon their property.

IV. Industrial Conditions in Isolated Communities.

The investigations and hearings of the commission are the basis for the following statements:

1. The conditions existing in typical industrial communities which are either wholly or in large part owned or controlled by a single corporation or individual employer, present every aspect of a state of feudalism except the recognition of specific duties on the part of the employer. The employees in such communities are dependent on a single corporation, or employer, for their livelihood. Furthermore, the employer in many cases controls the social and political life of such communities, either by the complete absorption of local political powers or by domination of the local authorities.

2. The fundamental rights of citizens in such communities are, as a general rule, seriously abridged, if not actually denied. Among

the rights most seriously violated are the right of free speech and assemblage and the right of public highways.

In some cases, as, for example, in Colorado, employers in such communities have assumed to usurp the functions of the Federal Government itself in the issuance of money orders, and have not only denied employees access to the post office when located in their company stores but have opened and otherwise interfered with the mail directed to the employees.

Such feudalistic conditions tend to develop principally in connection with the private exploitation of natural resources, being most frequently found in mining camps, lumber camps (including turpentine camps), and large plantations. There are, however, striking examples even in the case of manufactures, as, for examples, the textile towns and steel towns.

3. The most extreme form of domination and control exists in what are known as "closed camps," where the employer owns all the land upon which such camps are located and, because of this private ownership, not only exercises control over the local government but dictates arbitrarily who shall be permitted to come into or pass through such communities. It has frequently been argued that such communities are simply the inevitable accompaniment of the development of new country and will be eliminated with time. This is not true, however, as the commission's investigations have disclosed a large number of "closed camps" which have been in existence for more than a generation.

It is suggested that the commission recommend:

1. The enactment of appropriate State legislation providing that where communities develop, even upon privately owned land, the powers of the civil government shall not be interfered with, nor shall the rights of access to the residence of any person be restricted, nor shall the rights of persons to come and go unmolested, to speak freely and to assemble peacefully, be interfered with or considered to stand upon a different basis from the rights of persons in other communities.

2. In the case of public lands containing timber or minerals, which are now or may hereafter come into the possession of the Federal Government, it should be provided by statute that neither the lands nor the mineral rights should under any circumstances be sold, but should be used only upon lease for a limited term, such lease to contain as a part of the contract the conditions with regard to the rights of inhabitants as recited above and such lease to be forfeitable without recourse in case of the infraction of said conditions.

3. The Post Office Department should be directed to report to Congress all communities in which the post office is in any company's store or other building operated by an employer or in which the postmaster is a private employer or the agent of an employer. The report should show the facts separately for those communities in which the employer or corporation operates an industry upon which any large number of inhabitants are dependent.

4. Congress and the State legislatures should enact statutes providing that any attempt on the part of an employer to influence his employees, either directly or indirectly, in connection with any Federal election, either for or against any particular candidate, shall

constitute intimidation; and further specifying that it shall constitute intimidation for any employer to give notice to his workmen that in the event of the election of any particular candidate the establishment will not be operated.

V. THE CONCENTRATION OF WEALTH AND INFLUENCE.

The evidence developed by the hearings and investigations of the commission is the basis for the following statements:

1. The control of manufacturing, mining, and transportation industries is to an increasing degree passing into the hands of great corporations through stock ownership, and control of credit is centralized in a comparatively small number of enormously powerful financial institutions. These financial institutions are in turn dominated by a single large corporation, and where this is not true the

2. The final control of American industry rests, therefore, in the hands of a small number of wealthy and powerful financiers.

3. The concentration of ownership and control is greatest in the basic industries upon which the welfare of the country must finally rest.

4. With few exceptions each of the great basic industries is dominated by a single large corporation, and where this is not true the control of the industry through stock ownership in supposedly independent corporations and through credit is almost, if not quite, as potent.

5. In such corporations, in spite of the large number of stockholders, the control through actual stock ownership rests with a very small number of persons. For example, in the United States Steel Corporation, which had in 1911 approximately 100,000 shareholders, 1.5 per cent of the stockholders held 57 per cent of the stock, while the final control rested with a single private banking house.

Similarly, in the American Tobacco Co., before the dissolution, 10 stockholders owned 60 per cent of the stock.

6. Almost without exception the employees of the large corporations are unorganized, as a result of the active and aggressive " nonunion " policy of the corporation managements.

Furthermore, the labor policy of the large corporations almost inevitably determines the labor policy of the entire industry.

7. A careful and conservative study shows that the corporations controlled by six financial groups and affiliated interests employ 2,651,684 wage earners and have a total capitalization of $19,875,-200,000. These six financial groups control 28 per cent of the total number of wage earners engaged in the industries covered by the report of our investigation. The Morgan-First National Bank group alone controls corporations employing 785,499 wage earners. That this control is effective is shown by the following telegram from J. P. Morgan to E. H. Gary:

AIX LES BAINS.

E. H. GARY, *New York:*

, Have received your cable of yesterday. My own views are in accordance with those of the financial committee in New York. Certainly until question of wages has been settled by the coal and railroads, which still in abeyance, but settlement seems imminent. Whole question wages should be settled simultaneously by all interests if possible. Going Paris Wednesday. Will see there

H. C. F., P. A. B. W., [1] and will cable you result of interview. If possible and meets your approval, think better wait until after interview. Perfectly delightful here. Weather superb.

J. P. M.[2]

8. The lives of millions of wage earners are therefore subject to the dictation of a relatively small number of men.

9. These industrial dictators for the most part are totally ignorant of every aspect of the industries which they control except the finances, and are totally unconcerned with regard to the working and living conditions of the employees in those industries. Even if they were deeply concerned, the position of the employees would be merely that of the subjects of benevolent industrial despots.

10. Except, perhaps, for improvements in safety and sanitation, the labor conditions of these corporation-controlled industries are subject to grave criticism and are a menace to the welfare of the Nation.

11. In order to prevent the organization of employees for the improvement of working conditions, elaborate systems of espionage are maintained by the large corporations which refuse to deal with labor unions, and employees suspected of union affiliation are discharged.

12. The domination by the men in whose hands the final control of a large part of American industry rests is not limited to their employees, but is being rapidly extended to control the education and "social service" of the Nation.

13. This control is being extended largely through the creation of enormous privately managed funds for indefinite purposes, hereinafter designated "foundations," by the endowment of colleges and universities, by the creation of funds for the pensioning of teachers, by contributions to private charities, as well as through controlling or influencing the public press.

14. Two groups of the "foundations," namely, the Rockefeller and Carnegie foundations, together have funds amounting to at least $250,000,000, yielding an annual revenue of at least $13,500,000, which is at least twice as great as the appropriations of the Federal Government for similar purposes, namely, education and social service.

15. The funds of these foundations are exempt from taxation, yet during the lives of the founders are subject to their dictation for any purpose other than commercial profit. In the case of the Rockefeller group of foundations, the absolute control of the funds and of the activties of the institutions now and in perpetuity rests with Mr. Rockefeller, his son, and whomsoever they may appoint as their successors.

16. The control of these funds has been widely published as being in the hands of eminent educators and public-spirited citizens. In the case of the Rockefeller foundations, however, not only is the control in the hands of Mr. John D. Rockefeller, jr., and two of the members of the personal staff of Mr. John D. Rockefeller, sr., who constitute the finance committee, but the majority of the trustees of the funds are salaried employees of Mr. Rockefeller or the founda-

---

[1] H. C. Frick and P. A. B. Widener.
[2] Read at meeting of finance committee, United States Steel Corporation, April 27, 1909.

tions, who are subject to personal dictation and may be removed at any moment.

17. The funds of these foundations are largely invested in securities of corporations dominant in American industry, whose position has been analyzed under the early headings of this section. The policies of these foundations must inevitably be colored, if not controlled, to conform to the policies of such corporations.

18. The funds of the foundations represent largely the results either of the exploitation of American workers through the payment of low wages or of the exploitation of the American public through the exaction of high prices. The funds, therefore, by every right belong to the American people.

19. The powers of these foundations are practically unlimited, except that they may not directly engage in business for profit. In the words of President Schurman, of Cornell, himself a trustee of the Carnegie foundation.

Under the terms of this broad charter there is scarcely anything which concerns the life and work of individuals or nations in which the Rockefeller foundation would not be authorized to participate. As the safety of the State is the supreme condition of national civilization the foundation might in time of war use its income or its entire principal for the defense of the Republic. In time of peace it might use its funds to effect economic and political reforms which the trustees deem essential to the vitality and efficiency of the Republic. The foundation might become the champion of free trade or protection, of trusts, or of the competing concerns out of which they grow, of socialism or individualism, of the program of the Republican Party or the program of the Democratic Party. It might endow the clergy of all religious denominations, or it might subsidize any existing or any new religous denomination. To-morrow it might be the champion of the Christian religion, and a hundred years hence furnish an endowment for the introduction of Buddhism into the United States. It might build tenement houses for the poor in New York City, or carry the results of science to enrich the exhausted soils of the East or the arid tracts of the West. It might set up an art gallery in every State of the United States or endow universities which would rival the great State universities of the West. With the consent of the legislature it might relieve any State of the care of its insane, pauper, and dependent classes or construct roads for the benefit of farmers and motorists. These may not be likely objects for the application of the funds of the Rockefeller foundation. I am not, however, attempting to forecast its work but to understand its charter.

And, so far as I can see, the proposed charter would authorize all these and a multitude of similar activities. If the object of the Rockefeller Foundation is to be coextensive with human civilization, then it may do anything and everything which its trustees think likely to effect reform or improvement in the material, economic, intellectual, artistic, religious, moral, and political conditions of the American people or of mankind.

20. The charters of these foundations, with their almost unlimited powers, were granted under conditions of such laxity that it has been testified by an eminent legal authority who made an extensive investigation that those granted by New York State are legally defective

and unconstitutional. Furthermore, evidence developed by the hearings of the commission showed that in increasing the number of its trustees without complying with the requirements of the law governing corporations the Rockefeller Foundation has already been guilty of a breach of the law.

21. These foundations are subject to no public control, and their powers can be curbed only by the difficult process of amending or revoking their charters. Past experience, as, for example, in the case of the insurance companies, indicates that the public can be aroused only when the abuses have become so great as to constitute a scandal.

22. The entrance of the foundations into the field of industrial relations, through the creation of a special division by the Rockefeller Foundation, constitutes a menace to the national welfare to which the attention not only of Congress but of the entire country should be directed. Backed by the $100,000,000 of the Rockefeller Foundation, this movement has the power to influence the entire country in the determination of its most vital policy.

23. The documentary evidence in the possession of the commission indicates:

(*a*) That the so-called "investigation of industrial relations" has not, as is claimed, either a scientific or a social basis, but originated to promote the industrial interests of Mr. Rockefeller. The original letter inviting Mr. W. L. Mackenzie King to associate himself with the Rockefellers stated that Mr. Rockefeller and Mr. Greene in "their purely corporate capacity as owners and directors of large industries" desired his aid.

(*b*) That the investigation forms part of what Mr. Rockefeller, in a letter to Mr. Ivy L. Lee (the press agent of the Colorado operators), called the "union educational campaign," which is referred to by Mr. Bowers as "the fight for the open shop," the results of which are clearly manifested in the conditions existing in the camps of the Colorado Fuel & Iron Co., conducted on the "open-shop" principle.

(*c*) That Mr. Rockefeller planned to utilize in this campaign literature containing statements which were known to him at the time to be untrue and misleading (as, for example, the numerous misstatements in the "Sermon to young men" of Dr. Newall Dwight Hillis, including the statement that the Colorado operators offered to recognize the miners' union), and also literature containing statements which constituted a malicious libel upon a large body of American citizens—for example, the following statement of Prof. John J. Stevenson:

Labor unions defy the law, but are ever ready to demand its protection; their principles are no better than those of the India thugs, who practiced robbery and murder in the name of the goddess Cali.

(*d*) That the investigation of industrial relations is not being made in good faith, inasmuch as its director states that he will not now nor hereafter make public his findings regarding a most important part of his investigation, namely, the investigation in Colorado.

24. The purpose of Mr. Rockefeller to influence the public press is clearly shown by the employment of an experienced publicity expert as a member of his personal staff, and is indicated by his evident interest in the ownership or control of a number of publications, of which we have records dating from the inquiry of his

secretary regarding the Pueblo Star Journal in May, 1913, to the extensive conferences regarding a loan of $125,000 to finance the Nation's Business, the organ of the National Chamber of Commerce, which was established and given a semiofficial status through the instrumentalities of the Secretary of Commerce and Labor, with the sanction of a former President of the United States.

25. The extent of the possible influence of these foundations and private endowments of institutions for education and public service is shown by a large amount of evidence in the possession of the commission. The following examples may be cited:

(a) The adoption of a definite line of policy by the Bureau of Municipal Research of New York to meet the conditions imposed by Mr. Rockefeller in connection with proposed contributions.

(b) The abandonment by several colleges and universities of sectarian affiliations and charter clauses relating to religion in order to secure endowments from the Carnegie Corporation and pensions for professors from the Carnegie Foundation for the Advancement of Teaching. It would seem conclusive that if an institution will willingly abandon its religious affiliations through the influence of these foundations, it will even more easily conform to their will any other part of its organization or teaching.

26. Apart from these foundations there is developing a degree of control over the teachings of professors in our colleges and universities which constitutes a most serious menace. In June of this year two professors, know throughout their professions as men of great talent and high character, were dropped from the positions they had occupied and no valid reason for such action was made public. Both were witnesses before the commission, and made statements based upon their own expert knowledge and experience which were given wide publicity. One was a professor of law in a State university, who had acted as counsel for the strikers in Colorado; the other a professor of economics, who had not only been active in fights in behalf of child-labor legislation and other progressive measures, but had recently published a work comparing the income paid for property ownership with the income paid for all classes of service.

In the case of the State university we know that the coal operators in conjunction with other business interests had gained the ascendancy and exercised a great degree of control over the former governor of the State, that the coal operators were bitterly opposed to the professor in question, and that the dismissal of the professor had been publicly urged by the operators upon numerous occasions, and we have the uncontroverted statement of the professor that he had been warned that if he testified before the commission he would not be reappointed. In the case of the professor in the other university (which, though privately endowed, receives large appropriations from the State) we know that its trustees are interested in corporations which have bitterly opposed progressive legislation, and are men whose incomes are derived from property ownership and not from service.

In the face of such an enormous problem one can only frankly confess inability to suggest measures which will protect the Nation from the grave dangers described. It is believed, however, that if Congress will enact the measures already recommended, providing for a heavy tax on large inheritances with a rigid limitation on the total amount of the bequest, for the reclamation by the Federal Government of all parts of the public domain (including mineral rights) which have been secured by fraud, and for a tax on non-productive land and natural resources, a great step in the right direction will have been taken.

As regards the "foundations" created for unlimited general purposes and endowed with enormous resources, their ultimate possibilities are so grave a menace, not only as regards their own activities and influence but also the benumbing effect[1] which they have on private citizens and public bodies, that if they could be clearly differentiated from other forms of voluntary altrustic effort it would be desirable to recommend their abolition. It is not possible, however, at this time to devise any clear-cut definition upon which they can be differentiated.

As the basis for effective action, it is suggested that the commission recommend:

1. The enactment by Congress of a statute providing that all incorporated nonprofit-making bodies whose present charters empower them to perform more than a single specific function and whose funds exceed $1,000,000 shall be required to secure a Federal charter.

The Federal charter should contain the following provisions:

(a) Definite limitation of the funds to be held by any organization, at least not to exceed the largest amount held by any at the time of the passage of the act.

(b) Definite and exact specifications of the powers and functions which the organization is empowered to exercise, with provision for heavy penalties if its corporate powers are exceeded.

(c) Specific provision against the accumulation of funds by the compounding of unexpended income and against the expenditure in any one year of more than 10 per cent of the principal.

(d) Rigid inspection of the finances as regards both investment and expenditure of funds.

(e) Complete publicity through open reports to the proper Government officials.

(f) Provision that no line of work which is not specifically and directly mentioned in the articles of incorporation shall be entered upon without the unanimous consent and approval of the board of trustees, nor unless Congress is directly informed of such intention through communication to the Clerk of the House and the Clerk of the Senate, which shall be duly published in the Congressional Record, nor until six months after such intention has been declared.

2. Provision by Congress for the thorough investigation, by a special committee or commission, of all endowed institutions, both secular and religious, whose property holdings or income exceeds a moderate amount. The committee or commission should be given full power to compel the production of books and papers and the attendance and testimony of witnesses. It should be authorized and directed to investigate not only the finances of such institutions but all their activities and affiliations.

---

[1] A striking illustration of the benumbing effect of such foundations was revealed by the almost complete cessation of private activity for the relief of the Belgians as soon as the Rockefeller Foundation issued to the press a statement of its intention to undertake such relief.

3. As the only effective means of counteracting the influence of the foundations, as long as they are permitted to exist, consists in the activities of governmental agencies along similar lines, the appropriations of the Federal Government for education and social service should be correspondingly increased.

VI. THE LAND QUESTION AND THE CONDITION OF AGRICULTURAL LABOR.

It was obviously impossible for the commission to attempt a detailed investigation of agricultural condition, but because of the very immediate bearing of the land question on industrial unrest, it was felt necessary to make as thorough investigation as possible of the phases which seemed to have the most direct bearing on our general problem. The phases selected for discussion were, first, the concentration of land ownership as shown by existing statistics; second, the problem of seasonal and casual agricultural labor; third, the increase and change in the character of farm tenancy; and, fourth, the introduction of industrial methods into agriculture through the development of corporations operating large tracts of land. The findings and recommendations with reference to the concentration of ownership and the problems of seasonal labor are set forth elsewhere. At this point it is desired to present the results of the investigations of tenancy and agricultural corporations.

The investigation of these problems was confined practically to the Southwest, because it is in this region that the systems have become most fully developed and their results in the form of the acute unrest of a militant tenant movement are most easily studied. The investigations in this region, however, were very thorough, consisting of detailed studies and reports by field investigators, which were later confirmed by a public hearing.

As a result of these investigations the following conclusions are fully justified:

1. Tenancy in the Southwestern States is already the prevailing method of cultivation and is increasing at a very rapid rate. In 1880 Texas had 65,468 tenant families, comprising 37.6 per cent of all farms in the State. In 1910 tenant farmers had increased to 219,571 and operated 53 per cent of all farms in the State. Reckoning on the same ratio of increase that was maintained between 1900 and 1910, there should be in Texas in the present year (1915) at least 236,000 tenant farmers. A more intensive study of the field, however, shows that in the 82 counties of the State where tenancy is highest the average percentage of tenants will approximate 60.

For Oklahoma we have not adequate census figures so far back, but at the present time the percentage of farm tenancy in the State is 54.8, and for the 47 counties where the tenancy is highest the percentage of tenancy is 68.13.

2. Tenancy, while inferior in every way to farm ownership from a social standpoint, is not necessarily an evil if conducted under a system which protects the tenants and assures cultivation of the soil under proper and economical methods, but where tenancy exists under such conditions as are prevalent in the Southwest, its increase can be regarded only as a menace to the Nation.

3. The prevailing system of tenancy in the Southwest is share tenancy, under which the tenant furnishes his own seed, tools, and

teams and pays the landlord one-third of the grain and one-fourth of the cotton. There is, however, a constant tendency to increase the landlord's share through the payment either of cash bonuses or of a higher percentage of the product. Under this system tenants as a class earn only a bare living through the work of themselves and their entire families. Few of the tenants ever succeed in laying by a surplus. On the contrary, their experiences are so discouraging that they seldom remain on the same farm for more than a year, and they move from one farm to the next, in the constant hope of being able to better their condition. Without the labor of the entire family the tenant farmer is helpless. As a result, not only is his wife prematurely broken down, but the children remain uneducated and without the hope of any condition better than that of their parents. The tenants having no interest in the results beyond the crops of a single year, the soil is being rapidly exhausted and the conditions, therefore, tend to become steadily worse. Even at present a very large proportion of the tenants' families are insufficiently clothed, badly housed, and underfed. Practically all of the white tenants are native born. As a result of these conditions, however, they are deteriorating rapidly, each generation being less efficient and more hopeless than the one proceeding.

4. A very large proportion of the tenants are hopelessly in debt and are charged exorbitant rates of interest. Over 95 per cent of the tenants borrow from some source, and about 75 per cent borrow regularly year after year. The average interest rate on all farm loans is 10 per cent, while small tenants in Texas pay 15 per cent or more. In Oklahoma the conditions are even worse, in spite of the enactment of laws against usury. Furthermore, over 80 per cent of the tenants are regularly in debt to the stores from which they secure their supplies, and pay exorbitantly for this credit. The average rate of interest on store credit is conservatively put at 20 per cent and in many cases ranges as high as 60 per cent.

5. The leases are largely in the form of oral contracts which run for only one year and which make no provision for compensation to the tenant for any improvements which may be made upon the property. As a result, tenants are restrained from making improvements, and in many cases do not properly provide for the upkeep of the property.

6. Furthermore, the tenants are in some instances the victims of oppression on the part of landlords. This oppression takes the form of dictation of character and amount of crops, eviction without due notice, and discrimination because of personal and political convictions. The existing law provides no recourse against such abuses.

7. As a result both of the evils inherent in the tenant system and of the occasional oppression by landlords, a state of acute unrest is developing among the tenants and there are clear indications of the beginning of organized resistance which may result in civil disturbances of a serious character.

8. The situation is being accentuated by the increasing tendency of the landlords to move to the towns and cities, relieving themselves not only from all productive labor, but from direct responsibility for the conditions which develop. Furthermore, as a result of the increasing expenses incident to urban life there is a marked tendency

to demand from the tenant a greater share of the products of his labor.

9. The responsibility for the existing conditions rests not upon the landlords, but upon the system itself. The principal causes are to be found in the system of short leases, the system of private credit at exorbitant rates, the lack of a proper system of marketing, the absence of educational facilities, and last but not least the prevalence of land speculation.

10. A new factor is being introduced into the agricultural situation through the development of huge estates owned by corporations and operated by salaried managers upon a purely industrial system. The labor conditions on such estates are subject to grave criticism. The wages are extremely low, 80 cents per day being the prevailing rate on one large estate which was thoroughly investigated; arbitrary deductions from wages are made for various purposes; and a considerable part of the wages themselves are paid in the form of coupons, which are in all essential particulars the same as the "scrip" which has been the source of such great abuse. Furthermore, the communities existing on these large estates are subject to the complete control of the land-owning corporation, which may regulate the lives of citizens to almost any extent. There is an apparent tendency toward the increase of these large estates, and the greatest abuses may be expected if they are allowed to develop unchecked.

11. Prompt and effective action on the part of the States and Nation is necessary if any alleviation of the conditions which have been described is to be achieved.

It is suggested that the commission recommend:

1. The development through legislation of longer time farm leases that will make for fair rents, security of tenure, and protection of the interests of the tenant in the matter of such improvements as he may make on a leasehold in his possession. Such legislation should look forward to leasing systems that will increase tillage, improve the yielding powers of the soil and maintain a greater population.

In order to secure this desired end it is suggested that the commission further recommend the creation of:

2. National and State land commissions with powers—

(a) To act as land courts with powers to hear evidence given by landlord and tenants as to questions that have to do with fair rents, fixity of tenure and improvements made by tenants on landlords' property; to gather evidence, independently of both parties, that will the better enable such land courts to arrive at the true facts in each case; and to render judgment that will be mandatory for such time as the contractual relationship may be determined to hold.

(b) To operate farm bureaus for the following purposes:

First. To act as an agent between landlords and tenants in the distribution of tenant labor.

Second. To act as an agent between landlords and tenants in the preparation of equitable contracts.

Third. To act as an information agency to assist home-seeking farmers.

Fourth. To assist in the distribution of seasonal labor.

3. The development of better credit facilities through the assistance of the Government and cooperative organization of farmers and tenants. No single measure can be recommended; the results must be achieved through the development of a sound rural-credit system, the development of land banks, mortgage associations and credit unions. Foreign experience shows that through these means the rate of interest can be greatly reduced and the security of both the borrower and the lender can be increased.

4. The general introduction of modernized rural schools and compulsory education of children. The functions of the school system should extend beyond education to the social service of the entire rural community, assisting in the organization of farmers and tenants for cooperative purposes, and promoting other measures looking to the community's welfare.

5. The revision of the taxation system so as to exempt from taxation all improvements and tax unused land at its full rental value.

VII. JUDICIAL SETTLEMENT OF LABOR CLAIMS AND COMPLAINTS.

The investigations of the commission are the basis for the following statements:

1. Among workers of every class there are constantly arising various questions for judicial settlement which under present conditions can not be speedily or satisfactorily adjusted.

2. These claims are of a very diverse character and include not only cases of actual injustice through the retention of wages, but questions of interpretation of contract and the establishment of justice in cases in which contracts are lacking.

3. The ordinary courts are unfitted to decide such questions, not only because of the method of procedure but because of the unfamiliarity of ordinary magistrates and judges with the conditions involved in such claims.

It is suggested that the commission recommend:

1. The establishment either by the States or by municipalities of industrial courts similar to those which have proved to be successful in European countries. The organization and method of procedure of such courts are described in detail in Bulletin No. 98 of the United States Bureau of Labor and need not be discussed here.

2. The Commissioners of Labor or the industrial commissions of the several States should be authorized and directed, where such powers do not now exist, to receive the legal complaints of all classes of workmen, and, where they are found to have a proper basis, to prosecute such claims vigorously, with a view to securing either a voluntary settlement or the award of adequate recompense by the proper tribunal. The commissioners of labor or the industrial commissions should be given adequate legal assistance to enable them to prosecute such claims promptly and vigorously. Proper steps should be taken to provide for cooperation with the Federal Immigration Bureau, if the recommendation on page 51 is adopted.

3. The States and municipalities should consider the desirability of creating an office similar to that of the public defender in Los Angeles to act in civil claims of small size.

VIII. The Law Relating to Trade-Unions and Industrial Disputes.

The commission has conducted through its agents extensive investigations and has held hearings at which the persons who have devoted great study to the question of trade-union law testified at length. The investigations were directed both to establishing the present status of the law governing trade-unions and industrial disputes and to ascertaining the practical effects of certain classes of laws and court decisions. The results of the investigations are largely embodied in the reports of Mr. J. Wallace Bryan, of the Maryland bar, and Mr. Edwin E. Witte.

Because of the necessity for exactness in dealing with questions which are so involved and which have to so large an extent been clouded by contradictory court decisions, it is impossible to present a satisfactory summary of the conclusions which have been reached upon this subject. It may, however, be said that in substance the situation revealed by these investigations is as follows:

1. The greatest uncertainty exists regarding the legal status of almost every act which may be done in connection with an industrial dispute. In fact, it may be said that it depends almost entirely upon the personal opinion and social ideas of the court in whose jurisdiction the acts may occur.

2. The general effect of the decisions of American courts, however, has been to restrict the activities of labor organizations and deprive them of their most effective weapons, namely, the boycott and the power of picketing, while, on the other hand, the weapons of employers, namely, the power of arbitrary discharge, of blacklisting, and of bringing in strike breakers, have been maintained, and legislative attempts to restrict the employers' powers have generally been declared unconstitutional by the courts. Furthermore, an additional weapon has been placed in the hands of the employers by many courts in the form of sweeping injunctions, which render punishable acts which would otherwise be legal, and also result in effect in depriving the workers of the right to jury trial.

3. Important steps have been taken to deal with this situation by the enactment of the Clayton Act, applying to the Federal jurisdiction, and by the passage of laws in Massachusetts and New York which define the rights of parties engaged in industrial disputes. The actual effect of the Clayton Act can not be ascertained until it has been tested in the courts, but eminent legal authorities have expressed grave doubts that it will accomplish the desired results. At any rate, it does not seem to remove the root of the existing injustice, and, furthermore, in all the States except New York and Massachusetts the grave and uncertain situation already described exists. This situation must be corrected.

4. There are, apparently, only two lines of action possible: First, to restrict the rights and powers of the employers to correspond in substance to the powers and rights now allowed to trade-unions, and second, to remove all restrictions which now prevent the freedom of action of both parties to industrial disputes, retaining only the ordinary civil and criminal restraints for the preservation of life, property, and the public peace. The first method has been tried repeatedly and has failed absolutely, not only because of the interven-

tion of the courts but because the very nature of the acts complained of on the part of employers (blacklisting and arbitrary discharge) makes it impossible to prevent them effectively by any form of legislation or administration. The only method, therefore, seems to be the removal of all restrictions upon both parties, thus legalizing the strike, the lockout, the boycott, the blacklist, the bringing in of strike breakers, and peaceful picketing. This has been most successfully accomplished by the British trades disputes act, which is the result of 50 years of legal evolution, and in its present form seems to work as successfully as could possibly be expected.

It is suggested, therefore, that the commission recommend:

1. The enactment by Congress and the States of legislation embodying the principles contained in the British trades disputes act, the text of which is as follows:

An agreement or combination of two or more persons to do or procure to be done any act in contemplation or furtherance of a trade dispute between employers and workmen shall not be indictable as a conspiracy if such an act committed by one person would not be punishable as a crime. An act done in pursuance of an agreement or combination by two or more persons shall, if done in contemplation or furtherance of a trade dispute, not be actionable unless the act, if done without any such agreement or combination, would be actionable.

An action against a trade-union, whether of workmen or masters, or against any members or officials thereof on behalf of themselves and all other members of the trade-union in respect of any tortious act alleged to have been committed by or on behalf of the trade-union, shall not be entertained by any court.

An act done by a person in contemplation or furtherance of a trade dispute shall not be actionable on the ground only that it induces some other person to break a contract of employment or that it is an interference with the trade, business, or employment of some other person, or with the right of some other person to dispose of his capital or his labor as he wills.

It shall be lawful for one or more persons, acting either on their own behalf or on behalf of a trade-union, or of an individual employer or firm in contemplation or furtherance of a trade dispute to attend at or near a house or place where a person resides or works or carries on business or happens to be, if they so attend merely for the purpose of peacefully obtaining or communicating information, or of peacefully persuading any person to work or abstain from working.

Every person who, with a view to compel any other person to abstain from doing or to do any act which such other person has a legal right to do or abstain from doing, wrongfully and without legal authority—

1. Uses violence to or intimidates such other person or his wife or children, or injures his property; or

2. Persistently follows such other person about from place to place; or

3. Hides any tools, clothes, or other property owned or used by the other person, or deprives him of or hinders him in the use thereof; or

4. Watches or besets the house or other place where such other
person resides or works or carries on business or happens to be,
or the approach to such a house or place; or

5. Follows such other person with two or more other persons in a
disorderly manner in or through any street or road, shall on conviction thereof by a court of summary jurisdiction, or an indictment
as hereinafter mentioned, be liable either to pay a penalty not exceeding £20, or to be imprisoned for a term not exceeding three
months, with or without hard labor.

IX. The Policing of Industry.

The commission has made extensive investigations and has heard
many witnesses upon this subject, and as a result the following conclusions are justified:

1. The problem of policing industry is generally conceived to lie
in the suppression of violence and the protection of life and property; but in reality consists in the more fundamental problem of
protecting the rights of employers and employees as well as preserving the peace.

THE ORIGIN OF INDUSTRIAL VIOLENCE.

2. Violence is seldom, if ever, spontaneous, but arises from a conviction that fundamental rights are denied and that peaceful methods
of adjustment can not be used. The sole exception seems to lie in the
situation where, intoxicated with power, the stronger party to the
dispute relies upon force to suppress the weaker.

3. The arbitrary suppression of violence by force produces only
resentment, which will rekindle into greater violence when opportunity offers. Violence can be prevented only by removing the causes
of violence; industrial peace can rest only upon industrial justice.

4. The origin of violence in connection with industrial disputes
can usually be traced to the conditions prevailing in the particular
industry in times of peace or to arbitrary action on the part of
governmental officials which infringes on what are conceived to be
fundamental rights. Violence and disorder during actual outbreaks
usually result from oppressive conditions that have obtained in a
particular shop or factory or in a particular industry. Throughout
history where a people or a group have been arbitrarily denied rights
which they conceived to be theirs, reaction has been inevitable. Violence is a natural form of protest against injustice.

5. Violence in industrial disputes is not immediately the product
of industrial conditions, but of the attitude of the parties to the dispute after grievances or demands have been presented. The principal sources of an attitude leading to violence are:

(a) Arrogance on the part of the stronger party. This may
result immediately in violence through the use of force for the suppression of the weaker party. The force used may be physical or
industrial. Physical force may be and is used by both employers
and employees, through intimidation, assaults, or attacks on property. Such physical aggression is seldom used by employees, as they
are strategically the weaker party and the results are negative; only

under exceptional circumstances can an employer be coerced by the use of force or intimidation. The exceptions seem to lie in the use of secret means, such as dynamite, with the object of weakening the employer's resistance.

The use of force by workers is normally directed not against the person or property of the employer, but against strike breakers and guards. Many instances of the use of physical force by the agents of employers have, however, come before the commission, indicating a relatively wide use, particularly in isolated communities. Such acts of violence usually take the form of assaults upon the leaders of the workers or upon organizers.

The instruments of industrial force belong chiefly to the employer, because of his control of the job of the worker. Their use is more common and more effective than any other form of violence at the command of the employer. The most powerful weapon is the power of discharge, which may be used indiscriminately upon mere suspicion, which under certain conditions may be almost as potent, either in use or threat, as the power of life and death. It is the avowed policy of many employers to discharge any man who gives any sign of dissatisfaction on the theory that he may become a trouble maker or agitator.

The only corresponding weapon in the hands of the workers is sabotage, in the form either of malicious destruction of property or of interference with production. The field of its use is much more restricted in practice than in theory, and its results at best are negative and produce in the employer only a blind resentment and undiscriminating hate. Sabotage as a policy shows no signs of developing in American industry.

(b) Equally productive of an attitude leading to violence is the denial of the use of peaceful methods of adjusting grievances, or the creation of a situation in which their use becomes impossible.

On the part of the employer the arbitrary acts which may be classed under this general head are: Denial of the right to organize; refusal to consider the complaints of workers; refusal to meet the authorized representatives of workers.

Under modern industrial conditions any one of these acts makes peaceful negotiation and settlement impossible. Without organization of the workers their collective claims can not be considered; without the right to appoint such representatives as they choose, workers are at the mercy of the employer's power of discharge, and are usually unequal to the task of presenting and arguing their claims; while the refusal to consider grievances leaves only the alternative of the strike.

On the part of the workers, the possibility of peaceful settlement may be destroyed by refusal to discuss claims, by internal dissensions which render collective and definite action looking to a settlement impossible, and by the issuance of ultimata which allow no time for consideration and negotiaton. In any one of these situations the employer has only the choice between tame submission or absolute resistance to the demands of the workers.

(c) The immediate cause of violence in connection with industrial disputes is almost without exception the attempt to introduce strike breakers to take the place of the workers who have struck or who are locked out. The entire problem of policing industrial disputes grows out of the problem of the strike breaker and the attitude of the State toward him.

All experience shows that if no attempt is made to operate the plant, violence and disturbances requiring the police are practically unknown, whereas the attempt of strike breakers to reach the plant, particularly where strikers are enjoined or prevented from using reasonable means to inform them of the existence of the strike and to use persuasive methods to keep them from entering the plant, is invariably accompanied by disorder and sometimes by active violence.

The existing attitude of the courts and of governmental officials generally is that the entire machinery of the State should be put behind the strike breaker. This attitude is based upon the theory that two important rights are involved—first, "the right of the strike breaker to work," and, second, "the right of the employer to do business." During earlier years, the right of the strike breaker was stressed by the courts, but since the decision of Vice Chancellor Stevenson in 1902 (Jersey City Ptg. Co. *v.* Cassidy, 53 Atl., 230), in which the doctrine was announced as "recently recognized," the right of the employer to do business has been in favor apparently because of its wider application and the fact that being denominated a property right, injunctions could regularly be issued for its protection. Regardless, however, of their origin, both of these so-called rights seem to have been based upon misconceptions by the courts. The "right to work" guaranteed to the strike breaker seems to be based upon the conception that the strike breaker is normally a workingman, who seeks work and desires to take the place of the striker. The fact is, practically without exception, either that the strike breaker is not a genuine workingman but is a professional who merely fills the place of the worker and is unable or unwilling to do steady work, or, if he is a bona fide workingman, that he is ignorant of conditions or compelled to work under duress. The nonworking character of the strike breaker is shown by the fact that very few are ever retained as workers after the termination of a strike, while the attitude of genuine workingmen toward strike breaking is shown by the significant fact that in the bids of employment agencies and detective agencies to furnish strike breakers it is provided that guards will be furnished with each car "to prevent escape in transit," and by the fact that when men are candidly informed in the public employment offices of the existence of a strike, workers practically never apply for such positions, even though they may be in dire want.

The second misconception is contained in the idea that the "right to do business" is an absolute right. Besides the fact that it has only been insisted upon by the courts within the past 20 years and has no express legislative or constitutional sanction whatever, this right is subject to the most severe limitation and infringement even without due process of law. Not only can the legislature limit the right to do business in almost every conceivable way, but health authorities are given power to suspend it entirely if the public safety demands, as in the case of either a human or an animal epidemic. Furthermore, the courts can not and will not guarantee in any way the "good will" which is supposed to be the property aspect of the right to do business, nor will they assess damages on account of any alleged injury based upon the "probable expectancy" of the business.

The right to do business is in fact permitted only so far as its exercise is in the public interest, and it may be restricted or prohibited through the police power whenever it is dangerous or in any way deleterious to the public. This is the reason underlying not only quarantine but every form of regulation and prohibition.

The plea of the workers for the assumption of a new attitude in relation to strike breakers is, however, based not only upon the negative character of the rights of the employer and the strike breaker, but upon a positive though somewhat undefinable demand for recognition that strikers have a right to the jobs which they have left until their grievances are in some way adjusted. The argument is not only that when workers are willing to strike and sacrifice their livelihood, the conditions against which they protest must be assumed to be socially injurious, but, even more, that the worker who has struck in support of his demand for better conditions has not abandoned his job, but, in fact, has a keener interest in it than when quietly submitting to distasteful conditions.

At the very basis of the workers' contentions, however, lies the realization that working conditions can be improved only by strikes and that no strike can be won if the employer can operate his plant without difficulty. This is becoming increasingly true with every step in the Nation's industrial development. During more primitive periods, if workers struck their places could not be filled except through the existence of a surplus of qualified labor in the community or by enticing workers from other employers. Now, the development of transportation, the establishment of specialized agencies for supplying strikebreakers, and the growth of large corporations, which can shift employees from one plant to another, have given each employer a command of the labor market of the entire country. There are agencies in every large city which will contract to supply any kind of labor on short notice, while almost any of the large industrial corporations can either supply the normal demand with one-half or three-quarters of their plants, or recruit from the surplus labor around their various plants a skeleton organization which can resume operations in a short time.

The respective rights of employer, striker, and strikebreaker are matters which can not be solved by any method of cold reasoning, and should not be solved except by the force of public opinion acting either directly or through the medium of their representatives. In such matters we feel that our action can extend no further than the analysis of the issues, the presentation of the pertinent facts, and the expression of such general opinions as we may have reached.

We are convinced, however, that a modification of the legislative and judicial attitude on this question is necessary, and also that in the minds of the public a more general appreciation of the contentions of the workers is already taking place.

A general exception to this may perhaps exist in the case of public utilities, including not only the services which are commonly included, but the supply of milk, ice, and other similar necessities. The absolute dependence of the population of modern cities upon the noninterruption of such services has created a widespread public demand for action which will insure them under all conditions. The public may good-humoredly walk during a street-car strike, but the interruption of the supply of food, fuel, and ice produces an attitude of public desperation. We confess that, under present conditions, no absolute insurance against its interruption by industrial disputes seems practicable. As long, certainly, as these services are performed by private corporations, the right of employees to strike should not and can not constitutionally be abrogated or abridged. Even under Government ownership and operation the problem is only slightly altered by the removal of the incentive of private profit for the maintenance of improper labor conditions, while cooperative operation is too vague even for analysis. At present proper action seems to consist in providing, first, for the most effective possible means for conciliation, investigation, and arbitration; second, for the use of all the leverage of public opinion to promote reasonableness on the part of those involved in the dispute; and, finally, for the plan as outlined elsewhere for defining clearly the rights of the parties to the dispute and the impartial but firm enforcement of such rights.

(*d*) The greatest disorders and most acute outbreaks of violence in connection with industrial disputes arise from the violation of what are considered to be fundamental rights, and from the perversion or subversion of governmental institutions.

This source of acute unrest has been discussed at length in a preceding section, so that at this point it is necessary only to summarize briefly its commonest manifestations, and to state that even the limited investigations which the commission has been able to make show that practically every industrial State has at some relatively recent time permitted its institutions to be used by one party or the other to an industrial dispute (almost without exception the employers) in such a way that the rights of the other party were either nullified or seriously transgressed.

It may be said that every governmental institution and function has been at some time utilized by the stronger industrial factor for the oppression and suppression of the weaker, but those which are most commonly utilized are, first, the police, including not only the municipal police, the sheriffs and deputies, the State police and constabulary, and the militia, but the private guards, detectives, and vigilante organizations, which usurp and exercise the functions of the police. The biased action of the State and municipal police seldom extends beyond the making of unwarranted arrests, the enforcement of unreasonable rules regarding such matters as picketing and public assemblage, and the use of excessive brutality. The State and municipal police are uniformly paid by the public and such control over their action as exists is generally indirect. In the case of the other bodies mentioned the control is frequently direct and their action frankly and bitterly partisan. The sheriffs in many counties deputize guards in the employment and pay of corporations, without any qualifications and sometimes even without knowing their names. Similarly the militia are at times recruited from the guards and other employees of corporations. The private guards, detectives, and vigilantes are openly partisan and can have no other purpose in connection with a strike than to break it with such means as they can command.

The police would, however, be much less effective if their control in a given locality did not usually imply also control of all or part of the local courts to give a legal sanction to lawlessness, to protect those who are criminally liable, and to exercise their full rigor in the prosecution of the strikers. Such controlled courts have not only found it possible through the use of blanket injunctions to make illegal acts which would otherwise be legal, but, resting upon their protection, the police, the deputies, the militia, and the private guards have in many cases felt free to go to unbelievable lengths in order to carry out their plans.

The subserviency of the courts in many parts of the country can not be more clearly shown than by the fact that they have time and again permitted the militia, under color of so-called martial law, to usurp their functions and to defy their associations who resisted the encroachment. The situation is accentuated also by the fact that the decisions of such corrupt and subservient courts become the basis upon which later honest " record worshipping " judges form their own opinions.[1]

When governmental institutions are thus corrupted and used as instruments of oppression men can only resist with such power as they have, not alone for the protection of themselves and their families but for the preservation of the fundamental rights of themselves and their fellow citizens. Resistance to the usurpers of governmental power and to those who pervert to base uses the official power with which they are clothed was made the keystone of the American Nation, and Abraham Lincoln, on a most solemn occasion, said:

If by the mere force of numbers a majority should deprive a minority of any clearly written constitutional right, it might, in a moral point of view, justify revolution—certainly would if such a right were a vital one.[2]

The grave danger in the United States is that on account of the enormous area and the sense of isolation of each section as regards the others, the encroachment upon fundamental rights and the subversion of local governments will be permitted to gain ground without the effective protest of the entire Nation until the liberties of all citizens are hanging in the balance.

STATE CONSTABULARY.

6. The commission devoted a great deal of attention to the question of a State constabulary as a method of policing industry. Extensive investigations of the organization, personnel, and activities of the Pennsylvania State Constabulary were made and a number of witnesses were heard at length. The findings with regard to this particular police organization may be briefly stated: It is an extremely efficient force for crushing strikes, but it is not successful in preventing violence in connection with strikes, in maintaining the legal and civil rights of the parties to the dispute, nor in protecting the public. On the contrary, violence seems to increase rather than diminish when the constabulary is brought into an industrial dis-

[1] See report of B. F. Moore: Application of Writ of Habeas Corpus in Labor and Nonlabor Cases.
[2] Inaugural address, Mar. 4, 1861.

pute; the legal and civil rights of the workers have on numerous occasions been violated by the constabulary; and citizens not in any way connected with the dispute and innocent of any interference with the constabulary have been brutally treated, and in one case shot down by members of the constabulary, who have escaped punishment for their acts. Organized upon a strictly military basis, it appears to assume in taking the field in connection with a strike that the strikers are its enemies and the enemies of the State, and that a campaign should be waged against them as such.

There are certain features of the State police system, however, which seem to be preferable to the present haphazard methods of policing strikes. It is desirable, first, that all kinds of police should receive their entire compensation from the State; second, an organized force, whose records are known, is preferable both to the private police of corporations and to the deputies ordinarily sworn in by sheriffs; third, it is desirable that the force should be strictly disciplined and subject to definite orders; fourth, it is desirable that those in command of any police force should have a reasonable secure tenure of office and should have had previous experience under similar circumstances, as an inexperienced person is likely to become panic stricken by the mere presence of crowds, regardless of their actions.

If these desirable features could be combined with other features which would insure their impartiality during industrial disputes, and raise their ideals from the present militaristic basis to the police basis of preserving the peace and protecting the rights of both parties and the public, the establishment of State police systems for use in connection with industrial disputes might be recommended. But under present conditions, it seems desirable rather to leave the State policing of industrial disputes to the sheriffs and the militia if the restrictions hereinafter suggested are rigidly enforced so as to protect both the organization and the personnel from partisanship.

FREE SPEECH.

7. One of the greatest sources of social unrest and bitterness has been the attitude of the police toward public speaking. On numerous occasions in every part of the country the police of cities and towns have, either arbitrarily or under the cloak of a traffic ordinance, interfered with or prohibited public speaking, both in the open and in halls, by persons connected with organizations of which the police or those from whom they receive their orders did not approve. In many instances such interference has been carried out with a degree of brutality which would be incredible if it were not vouched for by reliable witnesses. Bloody riots frequently have accompanied such interference, and large numbers of persons have been arrested for acts of which they were innocent or which were committed under the extreme provocation of brutal treatment of police or private citizens.

In some cases this suppression of free speech seems to have been the result of sheer brutality and wanton mischief, but in the majority of cases it undoubtedly is the result of a belief by the police or their superiors that they were "supporting and defending the Government" by such an invasion of personal rights. There could be no greater error. Such action strikes at the very foundation of government. It is axiomatic that a government which can be maintained only by the suppression of criticism should not be maintained. Furthermore, it is the lesson of history that attempts to suppress ideas result only in their more rapid propagation.

Not only should every barrier to the freedom of speech be removed, as long as it is kept within the bounds of decency and as long as the penalties for libel can be invoked, but every reasonable opportunity should be afforded for the expression of ideas and the public criticism of social institutions. The experience of Police Commissioner Woods, of New York City, as contained in his testimony before this commission, is convincing evidence of the good results which follow such a policy. Mr. Woods testified that when he became commissioner of police he found in force a policy of rigid suppression of radical street meetings, with the result that riots were frequent and bitter hatred of the police was widespread. He adopted a policy of not only permitting public meetings at all places where traffic and the public convenience would not be interfered with, but instructing the police to protect speakers from molestation; as a result, the rioting entirely ceased, the street meetings became more orderly, and the speakers were more restrained in their utterances.

It is suggested that the commission recommend as measures designed not only to remove the causes which lead to violence but to promote the impartial and effective action of police during disputes:

1. The enactment by Congress of a statute prohibiting, under severe penalties, the transportation of men from State to State, either under arms or for the purpose of arming them, as guards or as agents either of employers or of employees.

2. The enactment by Congress of a statute prohibiting the shipment in interstate commerce of cannon, gatling guns, and other guns of similar character, which are not capable of personal use, when consigned to anyone except military agencies of the State or Federal Governments.

3. The regulation or prohibition of private detective agencies and private employment agencies as hereinbefore suggested.

4. The strict enforcement in all public and private employment offices of the rules requiring full notice of the existence of a strike.

5. The complete assumption by the States and municipalities of the responsibility for policing, and the prohibition of the maintenance of any private police (except a limited number of watchmen without police power except on premises).

6. The definition by statute, by the States, of the conditions under which sheriffs may deputize, such regulations to include provisions that a deputy must be a bona fide resident of the State, that a sworn statement of the complete activities of each deputy covering a period of 10 years immediately preceding his deputization shall be filed with the secretary of state, that no person who shall have been convicted of any misdemeanor or who shall have been imprisoned in any State shall be deputized, and that no deputy shall receive any money or any other thing of value from any person connected with an industrial dispute during his period of service or in connection therewith.

7. The enactment of statutes, by the States, providing a uniform code governing the militia and embodying the following principles:

(*a*) A proclamation of martial law or a state of war, insurrection, or rebellion, by the governor of a State, as the result of an industrial dispute, shall have no effect upon the continuance of constitutional guaranties of the State and Federal Constitutions, nor upon the law and statutes, nor upon the jurisdiction of the courts, nor upon other civil authorities.

(*b*) The writ of habeas corpus or other process of the courts can not be suspended, interfered with, nor disregarded by the military. It is part of the duty of the military to assist in enforcing the process and decrees of the civil courts.

(*c*) The ordinary courts shall have exclusive jurisdiction for the punishment of crime, and in all cases where the same act constitutes an indictable offense under both military and criminal law, court-martials shall have no jurisdiction nor authority to try officers or soldiers accused thereof, but the offender shall be turned over to the civil magistrate for trial.

(*d*) The military may not hold, detain, nor imprison persons arrested by them any longer than is necessary to hand them over to the civil authorities. No person arrested by the militia shall be detained after noon of the following day without being brought before a committing magistrate.

(*e*) The military may not forcibly enter nor search a private house in order to seize arms or other property concealed therein without a search warrant.

(*f*) The military shall have no authority to establish a censorship over the press nor to interfere with the publication of newspapers, pamphlets, handbills, or the exercise of the right of free speech, except under process of the courts.

(*g*) The military shall not limit, restrict, nor interfere with the freedom of movement of peaceable citizens or the rights of public meeting, assemblage, or parades in streets and public highways or elsewhere, except under due process of law.

(*h*) Every military officer under whose orders a civilian is arrested shall within 24 hours thereafter report in writing to the commanding officer the name of the prisoner, the offense with which he is charged, and what disposition has been made of him. Failing, he shall be liable to such punishment as a court-martial may direct.

(*i*) In times of industrial disputes no private guards, detectives, nor employees of either of the contending parties shall be enlisted or employed as members of the militia, and all persons found by the commanding officer to be in the employment of either party to a dispute or actuated by animosity or personal ill will toward either of the contending parties shall be forthwith released from active service.

(*j*) The governor may, in times of disturbance, by proclamation forbid the sale or transportation of firearms, ammunition, and intoxicating liquors, and may require all firearms and other weapons to be deposited with the military at certain places, receipts being given therefor. Proper search warrants may be issued to discover concealed weapons.

8. That the States and municipalities should provide by law for the fullest use of schools and other public buildings for public meetings and lectures and for other similar purposes.

X. The Conditions and Problems of Migratory Laborers.

It has been found as a result of the commission's investigations, which were made chiefly by Mr. P. A. Speek:

1. There are large numbers of American workers, in all probability several millions, who are not definitely attached either to any particular locality or to any line of industry. These migratory workers are continually moving from one part of the country to another as opportunity for employment is presented.

The great movements of these workers are seasonal in character, as, for example, the movement of harvest hands during the summer and autumn, the movement to the lumber and ice camps in the winter, and the movement to the construction camps in the spring and summer. In addition there are large, irregular movements of laborers which are produced by the depression in different trades and localities, and movements due to false rumors about opportunities and to the men's acquired habits of migration.

2. The number of these migratory workers seems to be increasing not only absolutely but relatively. There are no available figures to show this conclusively, but it is the general opinion of students of the subject and of the migratory workers themselves that a rapid increase in their number is taking place.

3. A considerable proportion of these migratory workers are, unquestionably, led to adopt this kind of a life by reason of personal characteristics or weaknesses, and these personal weaknesses are accentuated rather than diminished by the conditions under which they live and work. Nevertheless, even if the migratory workers were all men of the highest character and reliability, there would still be a demand from our industries for the movement of the population in almost as great numbers as at present, in order to supply seasonal demands and to take care of the fluctuations of business.

4. An increasingly large number of laborers go downward instead of upward. Young men, full of ambition and high hopes for the future, start their life as workers, but meeting failure after failure in establishing themselves in some trade or calling, their ambitions and hopes go to pieces, and they gradually sink into the ranks of migratory and casual workers. Continuing their existence in these ranks, they begin to lose self-respect and become "hoboes." Afterwards, acquiring certain negative habits, as those of drinking and begging, and losing all self-control, self-respect, and desire to work, they become "down-and-outs"—tramps, bums, vagabonds, gamblers, pickpockets, yeggmen, and other petty criminals—in short, public parasites, the number of whom seems to be growing faster than the general population.

5. The movement of these migratory workers, at the present time, is practically unorganized and unregulated. Workmen in large numbers go long distances in the hope of finding employment on the basis of a mere rumor, and frequently find that there is either no work or work for only a few. At the same time the demand for labor in a given locality or industry remains unfilled, because the workers have failed to hear of the opportunity. In fact, a large part of the movement of migratory workers at present is determined not by the demands of industry for labor, but by the necessity to search for work.

To illustrate: A man finds himself out of work in a given locality because of the termination of the busy season, because of business depression, or because of his personal discharge; he is unable to secure employment in the locality, and he has no information regarding opportunity for work elsewhere. If he remains in the locality he is almost certain to be arrested as a vagrant. His only recourse is to start moving, and the direction of the movement is usually determined by chance.

6. The attempts to regulate the movements of migratory workers by local organizations have, without exception, proved failures. This must necessarily be true no matter how well planned or well managed such local organizations may be.

7. The problem can not be handled except on a national scale and by methods and machinery which are proportioned to the enormous size and complexity of the problem.

The basic industries of the country, including agriculture and railroad construction work, are absolutely dependent upon these migratory workers.

8. The conditions under which migratory workers live, both in the cities and at their places of employment, are such as to inevitably weaken their character and physique, to make them carriers of disease, and to create in them a habit of unsteadiness and migration.

The provisions for housing and feeding workers in the labor camps are subject to severe criticism, while the lodging houses in the large cities are even worse, especially from the viewpoint of morals. One season spent in a city lodging house is generally sufficient to weaken the physique and destroy the moral fiber of even the strongest man. Numerous instances of the spread of dangerous diseases by migratory workers also have been brought to the notice of the commission.

9. The available information indicates clearly that even the most perfect distribution of workers, in accordance with the opportunities afforded at present by American industries, will still leave enormous numbers unemployed during certain seasons of the year and during periods of industrial depression.

10. The congregation of large numbers of migratory workers in large cities during the winter should be avoided, if possible, not only because they are an unjust burden upon the cities but because of the degenerating effects of city life during long periods of idleness.

11. The movement of migratory and seasonal workers is caused chiefly by the seasonal demand of industries and by the men's search for work, and, to a degree, by their aimless desire to move about. The conditions of their transportation have become grave. Millions of men annually have to, and are allowed to, resort to such a method of movement as stealing rides on the railways. This method of transportation results in the demoralization and casualization of workers, in their congestion in industrial and railway centers, in waste of their time and energy, in frequent bodily injuries and numerous fatal accidents and homicides annually, while, at the same time, it serves but poorly the industrial demand for help.

12. When the workers return to the city, from labor camps, for instance, either to rest or to spend the time between seasons, they not only meet the unhealthy and demoralizing influence of cheap lodging

houses, saloons, houses of prostitution, and other similar establishments in the slums, but they fall easy prey to gamblers, small private bankers, and all sorts of parasites. As a result, what earnings they have left after deduction of their living expenses at work places rapidly disappear, no matter how large these earnings may be.

The principal recommendations for dealing with the problem of migratory workers are outlined under the head of unemployment. In this immediate connection, however, it seems desirable to suggest three necessary measures:

1. The Interstate Commerce Commission should be directed by Congress to investigate and report the most feasible plan of providing for the transportation of workers at the lowest reasonable rates and, at the same time, measures necessary to eliminate the stealing of rides on railways.

If special transportation rates for workers are provided, tickets may be issued only to those who secure employment through public employment exchanges.

2. The establishment by States, municipalities and, through the Department of Labor, the Federal Government, of sanitary workingmen's hotels in which the prices for accommodation shall be adjusted to the cost of operation. If such workingmen's hotels are established, the Post Office Department should establish branch postal savings banks in connection therewith.

3. The establishment by the municipal, State, and Federal Governments of colonies or farms for "down and outs," in order to rehabilitate them by means of proper food, regular habits of living, and regular work that will train them for lives of usefulness. Such colonies should provide for hospital treatment of cases which require it.

XI. UNEMPLOYMENT.

The extent and character of unemployment has been briefly presented in a previous section, but the discussion there dealt only with the larger aspects of the situation in general terms. It remains to present at this point, in summary fashion, the findings which have resulted from the extensive investigations which have been conducted for the commission, principally under the direction of Dr. William M. Leiserson, together with certain specific recommendations relating to the organization of the labor market and the regularization of employment.

EXTENT AND CHARACTER OF UNEMPLOYMENT.

1. Wage earners in the principal manufacturing and mining industries in the United States lose on the average from one-fifth to one-fourth of the working time during the normal year.

This is the conclusion indicated by an examination of practically all of the published material, and of the hearings of the commission, relating to loss of time, irregularity of employment, and unemployment.

2. Excluding the extremely seasonal industries, such as canning, harvesting, lumber cutting and logging, which operate normally only a part of the year, the amount of lost working time varies

greatly for workers in different industries and in different occupations and trades. Loss of time appears to be greatest in bituminous coal mining, iron and steel manufacturing, leather, woolen and worsted clothing, slaughtering and meat packing, and in other industries where the proportion of unskilled labor is large.

3. It has been found that the lowest-paid worker is subject to the greatest loss in working time, not simply because he is unskilled but also because he is poorly nourished and weakened by the effects of unfavorable conditions of living and, in many instances, by unbearably severe conditions of work.

The tendency in the evolution of modern industry toward the employment of a larger proportion of unskilled labor, as well as the fact that many industries have come into existence because of the availability of a supply of casual laborers and of woman and child workers who are willing to work for less than subsistence wages, points to a greater degree of irregularity of employment, unemployment, and loss of working time, than ever before.

4. The actual number or proportion of workers at any given time who are unable to work can not be estimated, because of the lack of adequate data in this country. Recent investigations by Federal authorities and the statements of competent authorities before the commission, however, prove beyond doubt that the number of unemployed persons even in normal times is appallingly great. The statistics of highly organized trades show that even in times of greatest industrial activity there is a considerable percentage, ranging from 7 to 15 per cent of all of the members of unions in different trades and industries, of workers who are unemployed during the year. In any year the unemployed who congregate in the large cities alone during the winter months number several hundred thousand, while in years of industrial depression the number of unemployed in the entire country is at least three million.

5. The loss in working time is of two principal classes: Lack of work and sickness. Lack of work, which may mean the inability of the worker to find employment as well as the absence of a demand for labor of any particular kind or even of all kinds, either in a locality or section or in the country as a whole, accounts for approximately two-thirds of the average worker's loss of time at work, according to the available data on this point; ill health, according to several intensive investigations of wage workers and their families and the examination of the sick records of nearly a million wage earners in this country, accounts for approximately one-fourth of the loss in working time. Strikes appear to be the cause of less than two per cent of the loss in working time, and accidents are the cause in about the same proportion.

6. In addition to the two basic causes of unemployment—unjust distribution of income and land monopolization—which were analyzed in detail in an earlier section of the report, the following causes demand attention:

(a) Evolutionary changes in industry and in social habits and movements which affect the character and the extent of the demand for labor as well as the character and the quantity of the supply of labor. These include changes in industrial structure and methods— such as the increase or decrease in the demand for labor in certain industries and localities, the introduction of machinery and new

processes, and the changes in the character of the demand for labor—
and changes in the organization of industry. The character and
quantity of the supply of labor have been affected by immigration
and by the entrance into industry of women workers, both of which
factors have caused an increase in the supply of cheap and unskilled
labor. To some extent, however, the labor supply is fluid because
of the ease with which considerable proportions of immigrants can
withdraw from the labor market by returning to their homes in
times of industrial inactivity.

(b) Variations in the demand for labor due to fluctuations and
irregularities in industry. Industrial fluctuations may be classed as
cyclical and seasonal. Cyclical fluctuations result from business depressions and at times double the amount of loss of time during a
year, which is illustrated by the fact that the railroads employed
236,000 fewer men in 1908 than in 1907. Seasonal fluctuations may
either be inappreciable, as in municipal utilities, or may displace
nearly the entire labor force. The seasonal fluctuations in the canning industry in California, for example, involve nearly nine-tenths
of all the workers; in logging camps, which depend upon the snow, .
operations are practically suspended in summer; while in the brick
and tile industry only 36.5 per cent of the total number of employees
are retained during the dull season. Irregularities in the conduct of
industry and in the method of employing labor are evident in dock
work, in the unskilled work in iron and steel, and in slaughtering
and meat packing; in the competitive conditions in industries which
force employers to cut labor cost down to the utmost and to close
down in order to save operating expenses; in speculative practices
which result in the piling up of orders and alternate periods of rush
production and inactivity; in loss of time due to inefficient management within plants. In some cases it has been charged although
without definite proof, that irregularity of employment is due to a
deliberate policy of employers in order to lessen the chance of organized movement, as well as to keep the level of wages down in unskilled occupations by continually hiring new individuals.

(c) Conditions determining the worker's ability to grasp or retain
the opportunity to be employed which industry offers. Among these
conditions are ill health, old age, deficiencies in industrial training,
lack of facilities by which the worker and the job can be brought
together, factors causing immobility in the labor supply and its inability to adjust itself to changes in the character of the demand for
labor, and those personal factors, such as dishonesty, laziness, intem-
perance, irregularity, shiftlessness and stupidity, which are commonly included under the term "deficiencies of character." By no
means are all of these conditions under the control of the worker;
in fact, the further investigation goes the greater appears the responsibility which society and the employer bear for the conditions
that determine the worker's ability to retain whatever employment
industry is able to offer regularly.

7. The effects of the loss in working time and the attendant
irregularity of employment may be summed up in the term "the
workers' economic insecurity." Specifically the effects, as shown by
a study of the results of various investigations and by testimony
before the commission, may be summarized as follows:

(*a*) Actual loss of earnings, which in turn results in the necessity for the supplementing of family income by the earnings of women and children, and by payments from boarders and lodgers whose presence is inimical to family life.

(*b*) The depression of the wage level, in some instances, and the preventing of higher wages.

(*c*) Waste in expenditure, due to irregularity of family income.

(*d*) Deleterious effects upon the worker, such as demoralization, worry, loss of skill, irregularity of habits, etc.

(*e*) The gradual loss of economic status by workers who are thrown out of employment and the inevitable drift of a large proportion into the class ordinarily known as "casual laborers," the constant recruiting of the large army of dependents and delinquents who compose the unemployables, and the general loss of national efficiency that so great a number of incapable citizens must entail.

(*f*) The existence of a supply of casual laborers and irregularly employed women and children, upon which parasitic industries, unable to exist unless they pay wages below the standard of decent subsistence, are called into being.

EXISTING CONDITIONS OF EMPLOYMENT.

8. In addition to the large variations which affect entire industries, there is an ever present and equally difficult problem in the unsteadiness of employment. The existing methods of hiring and discharging employees, and the constant changing of positions by the workers themselves, divide the work among a much larger number of employees than are actually needed. Instead of one person being employed where there is work for but one, several are hired during the course of the year to occupy the same position. Thus an investigation of the cloak and suit industry of New York showed that the maximum number of employees in 16 occupations during any week of the year was 1,952. Actually, however, the pay rolls showed that 4,000 people were employed in these occupations. This "turnover" of the labor force, the constant shifting from job to job, the dropping and hiring of men, is peculiar to no industry. It is found everywhere, among women as well as men, and it is a kind of irregularity of employment that is a constant factor. A large mail-order house which began the year with about 10,500 employees and ended with about the same number, engaged during that year 8,841 people in order to maintain their force. A manufacturing establishment employing in 1913 an average of 7,200 people, hired 6,980 during that year. An automobile factory was reported in 1912 to have hired 21,000 employees in order to maintain an operating force of 10,000. A large steel plant employing about 15,000 men hires normally an equal number to maintain that force. During the years when it wanted to increase the force three and one-half times as many were hired as were actually needed to make up the increase. In some lumber camps and sawmills on the Pacific coast all men are discharged twice a year, in July and December, and complete new forces are hired when work is resumed. In the logging camps it is customary to hire five men in the course of the season to keep one job filled.

A manager of a large electrical works made a study of a group of representative factories (large, small, and medium) in the mechanical industries and found that to increase their working force by 8,128 people in the year 1912, they actually hired 44,365 people; that is to say, five and one-half times the number actually needed to make up the increase were hired and 36,237 were dropped from the rolls for one reason or another.

9. Detailed investigations show that a majority of the employees dropped from the pay rolls leave of their own accord. But there is no doubt that many of them leave because they were hired to do work for which they were unfitted; and many others, without actually being discharged, leave because work is slack or threatens to become slack. In the lower paid and more disagreeable jobs there is almost a constant shifting of employees because no one works at these jobs except during those periods when he is helpless and can get no other work. Whatever the reason is for the men quitting, there is no doubt that conditions of employment and methods of hiring and discharging employees have very much to do with causing a large "turnover" of the labor forces. Those employers who have given attention to this question of hiring and discharge have been able to reduce the "turnover" very greatly, and thus make employment more steady.

10. The problem of unemployment has never received adequate attention, apparently because it has been believed generally that it affected only a small part of the working population. Such a belief is absolutely false. Not only is practically every wage earner in constant dread of unemployment, but there are few who do not suffer bitterly many times in their career because they are unable to get work. Every year from 15,000 to 18,000 business enterprises fail and turn their employees out; every year new machinery and improved processes displace thousands; cold weather and wet weather and hot weather stop operations and force wage-earners into idleness; and where there are not these natural causes there are the customs and habits and holiday rushes which result in overwork followed by underemployment. Employers change the locations of their plants and conditions of credit and currency cause depressions and shutdowns and short-time and part-time work. Constantly the methods of hiring and discharging employees are causing people to be dropped from the pay rolls. All these facts in connection with the conservative figures of fluctuation in the amount of employment prove that "the unemployed" eventually include practically every wage-earner, and not alone a surplus portion.

11. Practically all wage-earners are affected by the fluctuations of industry. To count the number of the unemployed at any given time becomes almost impossible, since the number is changing from day to day. The unemployed of to-day are the workers of to-morrow, and vice versa.

The permanently unemployed are really people who have dropped out of the ranks of industry, broken down by the unsteadiness of employment or other causes. Some are mentally defective or physically incapable or both. Others are "down and outs," who have lost the habit of working. Still others live by their wits, by begging, or by crime. During the most prosperous times, when labor is in great demand, these same people do not work. They are "unemployed" in the same sense that young children, the old, and the sick, and those who live on incomes from investments, are unemployed. No amount of work that might be provided by public or private enterprise would have any appreciable effect on these unemployables. They need hospital or corrective treatment. In prosperous times they are considered the subjects of such treatment, but in every period of industrial depression they stand out as the most conspicuous element in the " army of the unemployed."

The failure to distinguish these unemployables from those who are temporarily out of work on account of a slack season or the failure of a firm and those casual workers who are employed for part of every week or month, leads to hopeless confusion.

12. The fluctuations in business affect capital as well as labor, but the result is entirely different. Capital suffers the same fluctuations and every industry has its "peak loads." The essential differences are, first, that a fair return on investments is estimated by the year, while for labor it has become more and more customary to hire and pay and discharge by the week, day, or hour, or by the piece, and, second, that while capital can offset the fat years against the lean, the human beings who are unemployed can not, but must starve or suffer a rapid physical and moral deterioration. The result is that unless the wage earners are very strongly organized—and the vast majority are not—they must bear the whole burden of the waiting period when they must act as a reserve force ready to meet the maximum demand of the busy season. We do not consider policemen unemployed when they are not arresting violators of the peace, and we do not consider firemen out of work when they sit in the firehouses prepared to do their duty. But for most working people industry is still conducted on a sort of volunteer fire department basis. In the busy seasons and prosperous years all are desirable and useful citizens. At other times they are useless and worthless, so far as our industries are concerned. They are turned adrift to take care of themselves and those dependent on them as best they can.

EXISTING AGENCIES FOR EMPLOYMENT.

13. The first step in any intelligent attempt to deal with the problem is the organization of the labor market on a systematic business-like and efficient basis.

14. Labor exchanges can not create work nor make the existing irregular demand for labor steady the year through, but they can, if properly managed, remove the unnecessary loss of time which workers now suffer in passing from one job to the next; they can eliminate the numberless evils which now characterize private employment offices; and they can provide the information and administrative machinery which is essential to every other step in dealing with the problem.

15. The absurdity and waste which characterizes the existing system of marketing labor can best be appreciated by imagining the condition which would be produced if every manufacturer who needed lathes, drill presses, planers, and milling machines advertised for them in the papers, and many machines were sent to him, out of which he could pick the few he wanted. Yet that is exactly what happens when machine hands, human beings, are wanted;

when the calls go out for harvest hands or when any other class of labor is advertised for. No one knows how many will answer the advertisement. Many more than the number needed respond to the calls. The waste of time, energy, car fare, and railroad fare to get to the places is enormous. Often men quit positions in the hope of getting the alluringly advertised work. Many employers do not even advertise. They simply hang the "Help wanted" sign at the door and depend on people to walk the streets and watch for these signs.

16. Wherever systematic methods and intelligent organization and direction are lacking, there evils creep in to add to the chaos. That is exactly what we find has happened in the labor market. The saloon becomes one of the most important places in the country to get information about jobs. Pool rooms, cafés, grocery stores, lodging houses, even street corners and public parks become improvised labor markets. In these places many and strange abuses are met with. Groundless rumors send people scurrying over the city and the country on a wild-goose chase. One job seeker sells information to another, and quite often it is false or misleading. Foremen sell real or bogus jobs under their control. Fees for jobs are paid by buying drinks, and "man catchers" pick up victims to rob or abuse.

17. Of all the evils, the wild rumors regarding available jobs are the greatest. These evils are increased by fake "want ads" in the newspapers, untruthful or innocently misleading advertisements for help, and new stories intended to boost towns or industries or to attract large supplies of labor. Investigators and men who were sent to answer "want ads" found many of these inserted by employment agents who had no jobs to offer but who wanted to collect registration fees. Other advertisements were pure fakes, inserted by "white slavers," bogus real estate and stock brokers, selling agents of "new propositions," padrones, and other swindlers. A study of newspaper want advertisements made a few years ago revealed that when times are good one-fourth or more are "fake ads," while in hard times more than one-half are in this class.

18. Private enterprise has attempted to deal with the situation through the establishment of employment agencies which gather information regarding opportunities for employment and sell the information to work seekers and, under certain conditions, collect fees also from employers. The number of private employment agents varies greatly from year to year, but there must be from 3,000 to 5,000 of these labor middlemen in the country.

Investigations show, however, that instead of relieving unemployment and reducing irregularity, these employment agencies actually serve to congest the labor market and to increase idleness and irregularity of employment. They are interested primarily in the fees they can earn, and if they can earn more by bringing workers to an already overcrowded city, they do so. Again, it is an almost universal custom among private employment agents to fill vacancies by putting in them people who are working at other places. In this way new vacancies are created and more fees can be earned.

19. They also fail to meet the problem because they are so numerous and are necessarily competitive. With few exceptions, there is no cooperation among them. This difficulty is further emphasized by the necessity of paying the registration fees required by many

agencies; obviously the laborer can not apply to very many if he has to pay a dollar at each one.

20. The fees which private employment offices must charge are barriers which prevent the proper flow of labor into the channels where it is needed and are a direct influence in keeping men idle. In the summer, when employment is plentiful, the fees are as low as 25 cents, and men are even referred to work free of charge. But this must necessarily be made up in the winter, when work is scarce. At such times, when men need work most badly, the private employment offices put up their fees and keep the unemployed from going to work until they can pay $2, $3, $5, and even $10 and more for their jobs. This necessity of paying for the privilege of going to work, and paying more the more urgently the job is needed, not only keeps people unnecessarily unemployed, but seems foreign to the spirit of American freedom and opportunity.

21. An additional injustice inevitably connected with labor agencies which charge fees is that they must place the entire cost of the service upon those least able to bear it. Employment agents say that employers will not pay the fees; hence they must charge the employees. Among the wage earners, too, however, those who are least in need and can wait for work, pay the least for jobs and even get them free, while those who are most in need make up for all the rest and pay the highest fees. The weakest and poorest classes of wage earners are therefore made to pay the largest share for a service rendered to employers, to workers, and to the public as well.

22. The fees paid private employment agents in California in the license year ending March 31, 1912, amounted to $403,000. Using these figures as a rough basis, the fees for the country as a whole amount annually to $15,000,000. This enormous sum of money, which is being paid chiefly out of the meager earnings of domestic servants, clerks, and unskilled laborers, would be enough to support a system of public exchanges which would bring order out of the existing chaos.

23. There are many private employment agents who try to conduct their business honestly, but they are the exception rather than the rule. The business as a whole reeks with fraud, extortion, and flagrant abuses of every kind. The most common evils are as follows:

Fees are often charged out of all proportion to the service rendered. We know of cases where $5, $9, $10, and even $16 apiece has been paid for jobs at common labor. In one city the fees paid by scrubwomen is at the rate of $24 a year for their poorly paid work. Then there is discrimination in the charges made for the same jobs. Often, too, men are sent a long distance, made to pay fees and transportation, only to find that no one at that place ordered men from the employment agent. A most pernicious practice is the collusion with foremen or superintendents by which the employment agent "splits fees" with them. That is, the foreman agrees to hire men of a certain employment agent on condition that one-fourth or one-half of every fee collected from men whom he hires be given to him. This leads the foreman to discharge men constantly in order to have more men hired through the agent and more fees collected. It develops the "three-gang" method so universally complained of by railroad and construction laborers, namely, one gang working, another coming to work from the employment agent, and a third going back to the city.

Finally, there is the most frequent abuse—misrepresentation of terms and condition of employment. Men are told that they will get more wages than are actually paid, or that the work will last longer than it actually will, or that there is a boarding house when there really is an insanitary camp, or that the cost of transportation will be paid, when it is to be deducted from the wages. They are not told of other deductions that will be made from wages; they are not informed about strikes that may be on at the places to which they are sent, nor about other important facts which they ought to know. These misrepresentations, it must be said, are often as much the fault of the employer as of the labor agent. Also the employer will place his call for help with several agents, and each will send enough to fill the whole order, causing many to find no jobs. Labor agents and laborers alike are guilty of the misuse of free transportation furnished by employers to prospective help. And it is true also that many applicants perpetrate frauds on the labor agents themselves, as, for example, causing them to return fees when positions actually were secured. This is the result of the general feeling that the whole system of paying fees for jobs is unjust; and if they must pay in order to get work, then any attempt to get the fee back is justifiable.

24. Attempts to remove these abuses by regulation have been made in 31 States, but with few exceptions they have proved futile, and at most they have served only to promote a higher standard of honesty in the business and have not removed the other abuses which are inherent in the system. Where the States and cities have spent much money for inspectors and complaint adjusters there has been considerable improvement in the methods of private employment agencies, but most of the officers in charge of this regulation testify that the abuses are in "the nature of the business" and never can be entirely eliminated. They therefore favor the total abolition of private labor agencies. This is also the common opinion among working people, and in several States attempts have already been made to accomplish this by law.

25. It is significant that trade union members are practically never found among the applicants for charity during periods of unemployment. They may be unemployed, but they are in some way cared for, either by having work found for them or by systematic or voluntary relief. Within each strongly organized trade, it may be said, the problem of connecting man and job is cared for fairly well. The union headquarters is the most common labor market for organized workers. Ordinarily, no systematic employment business is done, but many unions have out-of-work books in which the unemployed write their names, and it is part of the duties of the business agent of every union to be on the lookout for vacancies and to notify members seeking employment of the opportunities. Many unions also have traveling benefits to assist members in going from place to place. But when it comes to placing men outside of their own trades the unions are not successful as employment offices.

Partly for this reason and partly for the reason that only a small part of the wage earners are in strongly organized trades, the trade unions occupy a minor place in the general labor market.

26. Within recent years associations of employers have established employment offices in all the important cities of the country. The movement is spreading very rapidly, and there is hardly an important industrial center in the country that has not a bureau of this kind. These offices are supported out of the funds of the employers' associations, and their services are free to working people. Most of them, however, do a very small employment business.

Almost all of these offices owe their origin to the movement among employers to establish and maintain the so-called " open shop " or the " antiunion shop." Since their establishment, employers have discovered that such offices are very useful also in creating central clearing houses for labor, " constituting the shortest cut between supply and demand." This, however, is not their primary purpose, for nowhere have they extended their operations to include common laborers, who suffer most from disorganization of the labor market. These bureaus are merely divisions of the regular business of the employers' associations, and one of the main purposes of these associations is to prevent the organization of their shops by trade-unions. The employment bureaus are established and maintained to further this purpose.

The employment bureaus maintained by employers' associations, therefore, not only are of no practical value as a means of solving the problem of unemployment, but, on the contrary, because they are organized primarily to prevent the employment of skilled workmen who are distasteful to their members, are actual barriers to the free movement of labor.

27. In every city there are religious and charitable organizations which attempt to find work for destitute persons. In connection with the charity societies of the larger cities, regular employment agencies are maintained, but very little business, comparatively, is done by these officers. Working people do not go to them, and employers do not call for employees at such offices, except occasionally for men to do odd jobs, or when they agree to place someone as a favor to the charity workers. The main work of the charitable employment offices is to find odd jobs for the unemployed who can not hold ordinary positions. They also help people handicapped by age, illness, or other physical or mental defect. Their primary purpose is charity. They may be said to have no effect whatever on employment conditions for able-bodied workers.

Until the State is ready and able to take proper care of its handicapped, diseased, and subnormal members, the charitable employment agencies and institutions will continue to be necessary, because labor exchanges properly organized on a business basis, whether by public or by private enterprise, can not deal with the handicapped classes of labor. Those who are physically or mentally unfit to hold positions should be sent to the places where they will get the relief they need and not to work which they would quit or from which they would be dismissed in a few days.

PUBLIC EMPLOYMENT AGENCIES.

28. In 1890 Ohio created the first public employment offices in this country. Since that time, such offices have been established in 23 other States, and they are now in operation in about 80 cities. Most

of them were created by State laws; a few are municipal enterprises. They represent an expense to the States and cities of about $300,000 annually, and, according to their reports, they fill about 500,000 positions a year.

29. As a result of a very extensive investigation it has been found that the public employment offices of the United States, as a whole, are issuing inaccurate statistics. They are slipshod in recording information about employers and employees. They cater too much to casual laborers and "down-and-outs," thus driving away the better class of workers. Too many are poorly housed, with insufficient lighting and ventilation. They fail to supplant private agencies or to lessen their exploitation of workers. They do not exchange information even when closely located. They fail to bring themselves to public attention, either by advertising or otherwise, and they have failed to arouse public interest in their work. This is true of public employment offices taken as a whole, but there are some very bright exceptions. During the last few years, also, the labor departments have been devoting more attention to the work of public employment offices, and many improvements have resulted which show that the principles underlying the offices are sound, but that they have not been properly carried out.

30. The reasons for the failure of most of the public employment offices are:

First. The inefficiency and lack of training of the officials and clerks who operate the agencies. A public employment office must build up its work by soliciting business and giving service that is felt to be valuable; otherwise little attention will be paid to it. For this purpose men of judgment and experience are necessary to carry on the work. It is a technical business requiring not a mere shuffling of applications but careful selection of applicants and thorough understanding of the requirements of positions to which they are to be sent.

Second. The offices have generally been regarded as political spoils, with a consequent change of personnel after each election.

Third. The salaries have been inadequate to attract competent men.

Fourth. The public employment offices have been the objects of suspicion, if not of actual opposition, by employers and organized labor as well. Union men have feared that the offices might be used as strike-breaking agencies, or to lower wage rates. Employers, on the other hand, have feared that the offices might be used to fill their shops with union men and labor agitators.

The activities of the Federal Department of Labor in connection with unemployment have been chiefly attempts to utilize the existing machinery of the Bureau of Immigration and the Post Office Department for receiving the applications of men out of work, collecting information regarding opportunities for employment, and as far as possible referring idle men to opportunities for work. For this purpose the country has been divided into 18 zones, with a central office in each, which is in charge of an immigrant inspector. Applications from employers and employees are received either directly or through a special arrangement with the Post Office Department.

The statutory authority for the establishment of the system is contained in the act of 1907, creating a division of information in the Bureau of Immigration, broadened in scope by the act creating the Department of Labor. The opportunity to establish the system arose through the great decrease in immigration, which left a large part of the resources of the Bureau of Immigration available for this purpose. The system was established only in March, 1915, and it can not properly be judged on the results of this very limited experience. The most promising feature of the entire system is the arrangement which has been made for close cooperation with the National Farm Labor Exchange, which has been organized by the labor commissioners of the States in the wheat belt. No such close cooperation has yet been established with any other public employment system and no effort has been made to regulate the abuses of the private exchanges which do business in two or more States.

The following observations regarding the present scheme of the Department of Labor seem to be proper:

(a) The system of zones and central offices is sound and affords a suitable framework for the development of the system.

(b) The operation of the system directly by the Bureau of Immigration is likely to deter a great many workmen from utilizing it, through a belief that it is intended only for immigrants.

(c) The employers have generally assumed an attitude of suspicion toward the Department of Labor, which forms a great handicap.

(d) The system does not yet provide for sufficiently close cooperation with the State and municipal employment offices.

(e) The system of registering applications does not provide for the close personal contact which is necessary to ascertain the requirements of the employer or to select the workman who is capable of filling such requirements. The success of every employment office depends upon this personal contact.

(f) The qualifications demanded in the examination of immigrant inspectors are not designed to secure men who are properly qualified to operate public employment offices.

(g) A national employment system should not have to depend upon the exigencies of the general immigration service.

(h) The system can not attain efficiency until provision is made for the regulation of private agencies which operate in two or more States.

(i) The successful operation of a national employment system can not be attained until provision is made for some form of cheap transportation, which will assure the prompt arrival of workers at points where they are needed and eliminate the present wasteful, dangerous, and demoralizing practice of workers riding on freight trains.

(j) In order to secure the confidence of both capital and labor, the creation of national and local advisory committees consisting of employers and employees is advisable. Such committees would also be of great assistance through their knowledge of the local industrial conditions.

It is suggested that the commission recommend:

1. The enactment of appropriate legislation modifying the title of the Bureau of Immigration to " Bureau of Immigration and Employment " and providing the statutory authority and appropriations necessary for—

(a) The establishment of a national employment system, under the Department of Labor, with a staff of well paid and specially qualified officials in the main offices at least.

(*b*) The licensing, regulation, and supervision of all private employment agencies doing an interstate business.

(*c*) The investigation and preparation of plans for the regularization of employment, the decasualization of labor, the utilization of public work to fill in periods of business depression, insurance against unemployment in such trades and industries as may seem desirable, and other measures designed to promote regularity and steadiness of employment.

2. The immediate creation of a special board made up of the properly qualified officials from the Departments of Agriculture, Commerce, Interior, and Labor and from the Board of Army Engineers to prepare plans for performing the largest possible amount of public work during the winter, and to devise a program for the future for performing during periods of depression such public work as road building, construction of public buildings, reforestation, irrigation, and drainage of swamps. The success attending the construction of the Panama Canal indicates the enormous national construction works which might be done to the advantage of the entire Nation during such periods of depression. Similar boards or commissions should be established in the various States and municipalities.

XII. ORGANIZATION, METHODS, AND POLICIES OF TRADE UNIONS.

The investigations of the commission conducted under the direction of Dr. George E. Barnett, are the basis of the following conclusions:

1. The number of trade unionists relative to the working population is steadily increasing, although in certain industries, on account of the opposition of the great corporations and hostile employers' associations, trade unionism is practically nonexistent. At present it may be roughly estimated that in manufacturing, mining, transportation, and the building industries, if the proprietary, supervisory, official, and clerical classes are excluded, 25 per cent of the workers 21 years of age and over are trade unionists.

2. The effects of trade unionism on wages are undoubted. Without some form of combination the wageworkers can not bargain on equal terms with their employers. During the past 15 years, a period of rapidly rising prices, wages in well-organized trades have kept pace with the rising cost of living, in contrast to the relative decline of the purchasing power of the wages received by labor generally.

3. In the well-organized trades the hours of labor have been steadily reduced until at present eight hours is the normal working day for at least one-half of American trade unionists. It is significant of the influence of trade unionism on the length of the working day that it is exactly in those trades in which the trade unionists are a relatively small part of the total working force that they work long hours relatively to other trade unionists.

4. As the unit of industry grows larger and the natural relation which exists between the small employer and his workmen disappears, the opportunity for unjustifiable discharges and petty tyrannies enlarges. The result is distrust and enmity among the employees. The effective remedy is the organization of the workers and the

establishment of a system of trade boards in which the workers are equally represented with power to deal with such questions.

5. By means of mutual insurance in case of death, sickness, accident, old age, and unemployment many trade unions have greatly improved the conditions of their members. The extension of such systems appears to be highly desirable.

6. The trade union is a democratic institution and faces the same problems in securing efficient government that other democratic institutions face. The theory of government which the American trade unions have adopted is the centralization of power in the national trade union as against the local unions. The successful carrying out of this plan of organization will eliminate the chief defects in trade union government. The control by the national union over strikes and the system of mutual insurance is already thoroughly established in the more important unions; it should be established in all other unions.

7. Unwarranted sympathetic strikes have undoubtedly been the cause of great annoyance and considerable economic loss to employers. The annoyance in such cases is particularly great, because no direct action by the employer can be taken; at best he can only use his influence with his associates or competitors. With the increasing control of the national officers over the local unions, this kind of strike seems to be decreasing both in extent and frequency. Such sympathetic action is deep-rooted in the sense of brotherhood which to a greater or less degree pervades and will not be completely eliminated until substantial justice exists throughout industry.

8. A few trade unions exclude qualified persons from membership by high initiation fees or other devices. This policy is condemned by the more important unions and is prohibited by their rules. The evidence presented to the commission shows clearly that the policy of exclusion is antisocial and monopolistic and should be given up by those unions which practice it.

9. In many trades the efficiency of the union depends upon the maintenance of the rule that all those working at the trade shall become members of the union. Where the union admits all qualified workers to membership, under reasonable conditions, such a rule can not become the basis of monopoly, and neither the rights of the individual nor the public interest are infringed by its enforcement.

10. In some trades there are a considerable number of union rules which restrict the productivity of the worker. Some of these rules can be justified on the ground that they are necessary to the protection of the health of the worker. There are some, however, which can not be defended; these rules are antisocial and should be given up. Experience has shown that where industry is regulated by well-organized systems of joint agreements, such rules either disappear or greatly decrease in number and importance. These limitations of output should not, however, be considered as standing alone. The limitations of output by associations of employers and by individual corporations are equally antisocial and have far greater consequence.

11. Jurisdictional disputes are the occasion of frequent and costly strikes. The disputes of this character which have caused most injury are in the building trades. Up to the present, the efforts to lessen these disputes by action of the national unions involved have

largely failed. It is suggested that the commission recommend to the American Federation of Labor and to the national unions that renewed and more effective efforts be made to prevent such disputes.

12. The essential condition for trade-union graft is the placing of the authority to call strikes or to lévy boycotts in the hands of one person without adequate provision for supervision. This condition does not exist in many unions. There is abundant evidence to show that in very many cases it originates with employers who desire to secure an advantage over their competitors. The reason that graft is more prevalent in the building trades is that power is conferred on the business agent to call strikes without reference either to the rank and file or to the national officers. It has been testified by employers who have given much attention to this problem that any well-organized association of employers can eliminate graft whenever its members desire to do so. As far as the unions are concerned the solution seems to lie in the increased participation of the rank and file in the activities of the organization and increased provisions for fixing responsibility upon their business agents.

XIII. Organization, Methods, and Policies of Employers' Associations.

1. The commission finds that in the past 10 years there has been a rapid growth in employers' associations. These associations, excluding those general associations which have been formed for the purpose of advancing the political, commercial, or legal interests of the employers, may be divided into two classes, bargaining associations and hostile associations. The bargaining associations deal with the unions; the hostile associations oppose collective bargaining.

2. The formation of bargaining associations is essential to the existence of a satisfactory system of joint agreements. A considerable number of employers, although accepting the results of the joint conferences in their trades, do not belong to the associations of employers. It is highly desirable that all employers whose establishments are run in accordance with the terms of a joint agreement should be represented in making that agreement. In many bargaining associations the control over the members is very weak. The association has no power of discipline except expulsion, and where participation in the making of the agreement is regarded as of little importance expulsion is an inadequate remedy.

3. The hostile employers' association is a comparatively recent development. In many cases these associations were formed for the purpose of negotiating joint agreements with the unions, but after the failure of negotiations or the breakdown of an agreement they assumed their present form. In some cases associations which have been hostile have resumed relations with the unions. There is a strong tendency, however, for a hostile association after a few years to develop principles and policies which make any agreement with the unions impossible. The hostile association may be regarded, therefore, as a distinct species with definitely fixed characteristics.

4. In the majority of hostile employers' associations, the basic principle is that the conditions of employment shall be determined solely by the individual employer and the individual workman, but in actual practice this results uniformly in the dictation of conditions

solely by the employer. The "declarations of principles" adopted
by these associations declare, for example, that the "number of
·apprentices, helpers, and handy men to be employed will be determined solely by the employer;" "employees will be paid by the
hourly rate, by premium system, by piecework, or contract, as the
employers may elect;" "since we, as employers, are responsible for
the work turned out by our workmen, we must have full power to
designate the men we consider competent to perform the work and
to determine the conditions under which that work will be prosecuted." Even as to wages these associations are unwilling to bargain
collectively, since they refuse to recognize a minimum wage or any
other standard form of wage, without which a collective agreement
is impossible.

5. In a few of the more highly centralized employers' associations
wage rates are set by the association, although other conditions may
be left to the individual employer. In these associations the principle
of individual bargaining is modified to the extent that certain minimum conditions of employment are set by the association.

6. The prime function of the hostile associations is to aid their
members in opposing the introduction of collective bargaining. The
most important device used by the members of the associations in
resisting the attempts of the union to replace individual bargaining
by joint agreement is discrimination against members of the union.
Many of the associations have in their "declarations of principles"
the statement that no discrimination will be made against any man
because of his membership in any organization, but this rule is not
enforced. Ordinarily members of the union are not discriminated
against, but if the number of unionists increases in any shop until it
becomes large, the employer is advised or decides on his own volition
to hire no more members of the union. Moreover, any workman who
is prominent in urging the others to form a union is likely to be
dismissed. The aim of the association is to prevent in ordinary times
such an increase in the number of unionists as will lead to a collective
demand. The proposition is effective against collective action, as
membership of an individual workman in a union constitutes no
menace to the employer's power to control his business unless the
individual can persuade others to act with him.

7. Nearly all of the important associations maintain employment
agencies. These bureaus enable the members of the association to
select nonunionists for employment.

8. Practically all of the associations maintain a secret-service
department through which they are able to ascertain the increase
in the number of the trade unionists and the feeling of the men.
Through this information the association is able to forestall threatened strikes and any other attempt to secure collective action on the
part of the workers.

9. In some of the associations an attempt is made to induce the
individual employer to change conditions when there is evidence
that dissatisfaction exists among his workmen. Similarly some of
the associations have been active in promoting safety systems and
welfare systems.

10. Inasmuch as the right of workers to organize in any manner
that they see fit is fully recognized by society and has repeatedly

been given a legal status in the decisions of even the most conservative courts, there is strong reason for holding that these hostile employers' associations, which are organized primarily for the prevention of organization, are not only antisocial but even perhaps illegal.

It is suggested that the commission strongly recommend:

1. The formation of strong and stable associations of employers for the purpose of negotiating joint agreements and otherwise determining, upon a democratic and equitable basis, the fundamental problems of the trade.

XIV. Joint Agreements.

The investigations of the commission, conducted under the direction of Dr. George E. Barnett, as well as the evidence presented at the public hearings, warrant the following conclusions:

1. The conditions of employment can be most satisfactorily fixed by joint agreements between associations of employers and trade unions.

2. Where the association of employers and the union participating in the joint agreement cover the entire competitive district, it becomes possible to regulate the trade or the industry, not merely with reference to wages and hours, but with reference to unemployment, the recruiting of the trade, and the introduction of machinery and new processes. The method of regulation by joint agreement is superior to the method of legislative enactment, since it is more comprehensive, is more elastic, and more nearly achieves the ideal of fundamental democracy that government should to the greatest possible extent consist of agreements and understandings voluntarily made. The method of legislative enactment is inapplicable to many trade problems, and even where it is supplemented by administrative regulation it is cumbersome.

3. The essential element in a system of joint agreements is that all action shall be preceded by discussion and deliberation. If either party through lack of organization is unable to participate effectively in the discussion and deliberation, to that extent the system falls short of the ideal. Where a union or an employers' association delivers its demands in the form of an ultimatum and denies the other party an opportunity collectively to discuss the demands, a fundamental condition of the joint agreement is lacking.

4. The thorough and effective organization of the employers is lacking in many trades in which the workmen are well organized. It is highly desirable that such organization should be brought about.

5. In a few trades agreements have been made which provide that the members of the union will not be allowed to work for any employers who are not members of the employers' association. The usual result is that the employers' association restricts its membership or in some other manner artificially raises prices to the consumer. Such agreements are against the public interest and should not be tolerated.

6. Joint agreements, on the whole, are well kept. There is a constant increase in the sense of moral obligation on the part of both employers and unions. Violations of agreements on the part of a

small number of men or of a single employer occasionally occur. It is found that the unions tend more and more to punish by fines or other disciplinary measure such infraction on the part of their members. The great difficulty in the rapid solution of this problem is that even graver evils than contract breaking are apt to result from giving officials the power which they must have in order to punish properly individuals or local unions for illegal strikes. The employers' associations, from the nature of the case, have less power over their members, but in practically all cases they exercise in good faith what power they have. Furthermore, since the employer in the first instance has the power to interpret the contract, which he may do unjustly, he may actually be guilty of the breach of contract when the employees who strike against such unjust interpretation are apparently the guilty parties.

7. In certain agreements a specified money guaranty is made by each party, and in any breach of the agreement the guaranty is forfeited to the other side. On the whole, such guaranties do not serve a desirable purpose, since there is danger that the parties may come to regard the forfeiture of the guaranty as a compensation for the breach of the agreement.[1] The sense of moral obligation is thus seriously impaired.

8. It does not seem, nor has it been urged by any careful student of the problem, whether employer or worker, that any good end would be served by giving legal validity to joint agreements. The agreements are formulated by parties acting without legal advice, and it not infrequently happens that the form of words adopted is capable of several constructions. In some cases the language is intentionally general, though its purpose may be fully understood by the different parties. It is not desirable that such agreements, the only ones possible under the circumstances, should be construed by the rigid rules customarily used in the courts.

9. Every joint agreement should contain a clause providing for arbitration in the event that the interpretation of the agreement is in dispute. Under such provision the arbitrator would approach the question unhampered by strict rules of construction. The responsibility for breaking an agreement would under such a plan be definitely located.

It is suggested that the commission recommend:

1. The extension of joint agreements as regards not only the field of industry which they cover and the class of labor included but the subjects which are taken up for negotiation and settlement. Greater responsibility for the character, skill, and conduct of their members should accompany the greater participation of trade-unions in the governing of industry.

XV. AGENCIES OF MEDIATION, INVESTIGATION, AND ARBITRATION.

The result of the very extensive investigations which have been made regarding the agencies for mediation and arbitration in this country and abroad have been embodied in the plan for legislation, which is attached hereto. The plan as presented is limited to a national system, but it is recommended that the State legislatures

---

[1] This statement is not in accordance with the finding of Dr. Barnett, but is formed after consideration of the evidence and opinion of the British Industrial Council.

should enact legislation along the same general lines. The general principles which have governed in drawing up this plan may be stated as follows:

1. The Mediation Commission should be independent of and definitely divorced from every other department of the State or Federal Government. Its only power grows out of its impartiality, and this can not be secured if it is subordinate to any other body whose sympathies either with labor or with capital can be questioned.

2. Mediation should be entrusted to a person as far as possible distinct from those who act as arbitrators or appoint arbitrators.

3. The office of mediator should be placed beyond the suspicion that the office is being used as a reward for party services.

4. The mediator should appoint his own subordinates.

5. It is desirable in the event of the failure of mediation by an official mediator that the parties should be asked to consent to the appointment of a board of mediation and investigation consisting of three persons, one selected by each party and the third by these two. Such a board, it appears, would be able to secure an agreement in many cases where the mediator fails. These boards should have power to summon witnesses and compel the production of papers. In the event that the board could not secure an agreement during the investigation, it should be empowered to make a public report stating the terms on which, in its judgment, the parties should settle.

6. In those cases in which the parties are unable to agree on the third member of the board of mediation and investigation, he should be appointed in the State systems by the State board of arbitration, and in the national system by the mediators, from a list prepared in advance by an advisory board consisting of 10 representatives of employers' associations and 10 representatives of trade unions.

7. National boards of mediation and investigation are to be formed only in disputes involving interstate commerce and in those cases in which the legislature or the executive of a State has requested the intervention of the Federal Government.

8. The Secretary of Labor, or in the States the official bureau or commission, which is created for the protection of the workers, should be employed to appear before the board of mediation and investigation, when it is holding public hearings, either at the request of the board as amicus curiae in the ascertainment of facts regarding labor conditions, or, if appealed to, as the spokesman for the employees in the presentation of their case.

PROPOSED PLAN OF A NATIONAL SYSTEM OF MEDIATION, INVESTIGATION, AND ARBITRATION.

ORGANIZATION.

1. *Scope of authority.*—The National Mediation Commission should be given exclusive authority to intervene, under the conditions hereinafter defined, in all industrial disputes involving any corporation, firm, or establishment, except public service establishments, which is engaged in interstate commerce or whose products enter into interstate or foreign commerce.

This provision differentiates its functions from those of the mediation commission existing at present under the Newlands Act. It is considered desirable for the present to provide for the existence of the two commissions, at least until the proposed commission has been thoroughly tested. It is believed to be wise, however, to provide for their close cooperation from the very beginning, with the idea that they will ultimately be consolidated.

It will be noted that this provision also will have the effect of supplanting the mediation powers which are now vested in the Department of Labor. There is no desire to criticise or belittle the past activities of the mediators operating under the Department of Labor, for such criticism is absolutely unwarranted. It is also freely admitted that the Department of Labor has not had either the time or the resources necessary for the proper development of this function. The proposal is made, however, primarily upon three grounds which seem to be sound and, in fact, compelling: First, the function of mediation depends absolutely upon. the permanent assurance of impartiality. The Department of Labor was created to represent the interests of labor, and it seems not only inevitable but desirable and proper that the Secretary of Labor should always be drawn from the ranks of organized labor. The function of mediation may be administered with absolute impartiality under any particular Secretary, or even under every Secretary, and yet it seems impossible, even under such conditions, to create that absolute assurance of impartiality which is the prime essential. Second, it is the prerogative and duty of the Department of Labor to act, aggressively if need be, for the protection of the workers at all times, and to utilize every resource at its command to give them that protection. The Department must necessarily be greatly impeded in such frankly partisan action, it would seem, if it must at the same time preserve either the substance or the shadow of impartiality in carrying out its function of mediation. Third, in the bitterest disputes, where the public interest most strongly demands intervention, mediation is seldom successful, and a stage is quickly reached where the most vital necessity is for the full and exact facts regarding the dispute, in order that public opinion may be intelligently formed and directed. Experience has shown that such facts can best be secured fully, quickly, and effectively through the medium of public inquiry. This means that the inquiring body must have power to summon witnesses, compel the production of books and papers, and compel testimony, or the proceeding is worse than a farce. It may be regarded as certain that such powers will never be entrusted to the Department of Labor.

2. *Membership.*—The members of the Mediation Commission should be appointed by the President, with the advice and consent of the Senate. The members should represent in proper balance the interests of employers, employees, and the public. The members should serve for terms of six years.

3. *Advisory board.*—The President of the United States should designate an equal number of leading organizations of employers and leading organizations of employees to appoint representatives to act as an advisory body to the President, to Congress, and to the Mediation Commission. This body, designated hereinafter the advisory board, should give advice regarding the duties of the commission, the administration of its affairs and the selection of mediators,

and be empowered to make recommendations regarding legislation. The advisory board should also prepare lists of persons who may be called upon to serve on boards of arbitration and on boards of mediation and investigation. The advisory board should be called together at least once a year by the chairman of the Mediation Commission; it should have an organization independent of the commission and elect its own chairman and secretary.

The members of the advisory board should be paid traveling and other necessary expenses and such compensation as may be determined upon. Provision should be made for the removal of members by the organizations which they represent.

4. *Subordinate officers and assistants.*—The Mediation Commission should have power to appoint, remove at pleasure, and fix the compensation of a secretary (and a limited number of clerks). The appointment of other officers and assistants, such as mediators, examiners, investigators, technical assessors, experts, disbursing officer, clerks, and other employees, should be subject to the civil-service rules. But arrangements should be made to have the examination include experience and other proper qualifications, and to give the Mediation Commission power to examine all candidates orally.

POWERS, DUTIES AND JURISDICTION.

5. *In interstate commerce.*—(*a*) Mediation: Whenever a controversy concerning conditions of employment arises between employer and employees engaged in interstate commerce other than public service corporations, either party should be able to apply to the chairman of the Mediation Commission for its services in the bringing about of an amicable adjustment of the controversy. Or, the chairman of the commission should be authorized to offer, on his own initiative, the services of the mediators of the commission. If efforts to bring about an amicable adjustment through mediation should be unsuccessful, the commission should at once, if possible, induce the parties to submit their differences to arbitration.

(*b*) Arbitration: Procedure should be similar to that outlined in the Newlands Act. If it is necessary for the Mediation Commission to appoint arbitrators, they should be taken from a list prepared by the advisory board.

(*c*) Boards of mediation and investigation: If the parties to the controversy can not be induced to arbitrate, and if the controversy should threaten to interrupt the business of employers and employees to the detriment of the public interest, the commission should be authorized to request the two parties to consent to the creation of a board of mediation and investigation. If the consent of the parties to the controversy is secured, the commission shall form such a board. Of the three members of the board, one should be selected by the employers, one by the employees and a third on the recommendation of the members so chosen. If either side fails to recommend a member, he should be appointed by the commission. If after a stated time the third member is not recommended, the commission should select him. Appointments to boards of mediation and investigation shall be made by the commission from a list prepared for this purpose by the advisory board. The board of mediation and investigation should offer its friendly offices in bringing about a settlement of the dispute through mediation. If mediation should not be success-ful and if the parties to the controversy refuse to arbitrate, this board should have power to make an investigation of the contro-versy, and should be required to submit to the commission a full report thereon, including recommendations for its settlement. The commission should be empowered to give this report and recommen-dations adequate publicity.

(d) Powers to secure evidence: A board of mediation and inves-tigation should have power to administer oaths, to subpoena and compel the attendance and testimony of witnesses and the produc-tion of books, papers, documents, etc., and to conduct hearings and investigations, and to exercise such other similar powers as might be necessary. It should not have power to prohibit or to impose pen-alties for strikes or lockouts.

6. *Not in interstate commerce.*—It should be provided that the commission, or a board of mediation and investigation created by it, may exercise the foregoing powers except the compulsory powers under subdivision " d " of proposal 5, for settling industrial con-troversies between parties not engaged in interstate commerce, if they are requested to do so by the governor or legislature of a State, or by the mayor, council, or commission of a municipality.

7. The Secretary of Labor and the Secretary of Commerce should be authorized to bring to the attention of the commission any dispute in which the intervention of the commission seems desirable. The Secretary of Labor, or such officer as he may designate, should also be authorized to appear before any board of mediation and investi-gation, either at the request of the board as amicus curiae for the ascertainment of facts regarding labor conditions, or, if appealed to, as a spokesman for the employees in the presentation of their case.

COOPERATION.

8. *Cooperation with State and local authorities.*—The commission should be authorized and directed to cooperate with State, local and territorial authorities and similar departments of foreign countries which deal with the adjustment of industrial disputes.

9. *Cooperation with other Federal agencies.*—The commission should, as far as practicable, coordinate its activities and cooperate with other Federal departments in the performance of their duties.

XVI. INDUSTRIAL CONDITIONS AND THE PUBLIC HEALTH—SICKNESS INSURANCE.

The investigations which have been conducted by the commission under the direction of Dr. B. S. Warren, of the Public Health Service, are the basis for the following conclusions:

1. Each of the thirty-odd million wage earners in the United States loses an average of nine days a year through sickness. At an average of $2 per day, the wage loss from this source is over $500,000,000. At the average cost of medical expenses ($6 per capita per year) there is added to this at the very least $180,000,000.

2. Much attention is now given to accident prevention, yet acci-dents cause only one-seventh as much destitution as does sickness and one-fifteenth as much as does unemployment. A great deal of unemployment is directly due to sickness, and sickness, in turn, fol-

lows unemployment. The commission's recent study in Indiana showed that 17.9 per cent of unemployment among women in stores in that State was due to illness. In 1901, a Federal investigation of 25,440 workmen's families showed that 11.2 per cent of heads of families were idle during the year on account of sickness, and that the average period of such unemployment was 7.71 weeks. Other investigations show that 30 to 40 per cent of cases requiring charitable relief are immediately due to sickness.

3. Sickness among wage earners is primarily the direct result of poverty, which manifests itself in insufficient diet, bad housing, inadequate clothing, and generally unfavorable surroundings in the home. The surroundings at the place of work and the personal habits of the worker are important but secondary factors.

4. There are three general groups of disease-causing conditions: (1) Those for which the employer and character of the industry and occupation are responsible; (2) those for which the public, through regulatory and relief agencies, is responsible; and (3) those for which the individual worker and his family are responsible.

5. The employers' responsibility includes, besides conditions causing so-called occupational diseases, low wages, excessive hours, methods causing nervous strain, and general insanitary conditions. Many employers already partly recognize their responsibility; aside from "welfare work," many contribute liberally to employees' sick benefit funds or provide for the entire amount.

6. The public has in part recognized its responsibility in such matters as housing, water supply, foods, drugs, and sanitation. But the recognition of responsibility has not been thoroughgoing, and in the case of local health officers the tendency has been too frequently to provide for the better residential sections and neglect the slums.

7. The greatest share of responsibility rests upon the individual, and under present conditions he is unable to meet it. This inability exists by reason of the fact that the majority of wage earners do not receive sufficient wages to provide for proper living conditions, and because the present methods of disease prevention and cure are expensive and sickness is most prevalent among those who are least able to purchase health. The worker is expected to provide for almost certain contingencies in the future when he lacks means of existing adequately in the present.

8. If we might reasonably expect a rapid increase in the wages of all classes of workers to a standard which would permit proper living conditions and adequate medical attention, it would perhaps be inadvisable to recommend any governmental action. But we feel assured that no such condition is to be expected in the near future and believe that new methods of dealing with the existing evils must be adopted.

9. The remedial measures for existing conditions must be based on the cooperative action of those responsible for conditions; must be democratic in maintenance, control, and administration; must distribute costs practicably and justly; and must provide a powerful incentive for sickness prevention.

10. A system of sickness insurance is the most feasible single measure. This conclusion is based on the following:

(a) The losses occasioned by the wage earner's sickness affect employee, employer, and community, all of whom share in the responsibility. Insurance is the recognized method of distributing loss so as to reduce individual risk to a minimum.

(b) The strongest of incentives—that of lessening cost—is given to efforts to diminish frequency and seriousness of losses; sickness insurance in this respect is a preventive measure of a positive and direct kind. The lower the morbidity and mortality rates, the less the amount necessary for benefits and the lower the insurance rate.

(c) Sickness insurance is no longer experimental, but is rapidly becoming universal. It is not a novelty even in the United States. Although not provided for nor subsidized by Government here, it is most widely used, there being several million workers so insured.

(d) The cost would be no greater than at present. The conclusion appears sound that medical benefits and minimum cash benefits of $7 per week for a period not exceeding 26 weeks in one year, and death benefits of $200, can be provided at a total cost of 50 cents per week per insured person. Budgetary studies of large numbers of workingmen's families show that under present conditions from 25 and 50 cents a week up to 70 cents and even $1.86 is spent for little more than burial insurance. Workers would thus receive immeasurably greater benefits for much less than they now pay.

11. A governmental system of sickness insurance is preferable because—

(a) More democratic; the benefits would be regarded as rights, not charity.

(b) Compulsory features, obnoxious under private insurance, would be no longer objectionable.

(c) On account of the reduction in overhead charges and duplication, higher efficiency in administration would be secured at less cost.

(d) Cooperation with other public agencies is impracticable otherwise.

(e) European experience has proved the superiority of Government systems to private insurance.

(f) Taxation of industry by Federal Government in sickness-insurance system is thoroughly established by the Marine-Hospital Service. Law taxing vessels for such fund was passed in 1798, and its constitutionality has never been questioned.

12. The conclusion seems warranted that a sickness-insurance system for the United States or the several States similar in general principles and methods to the best European systems will be less difficult and radical than has been foreboded. It will not so much introduce new ideas and practices as it will organize existing plans and principles into more effective accomplishment. Existing agencies, in trade-unions, mutual benefit societies, and establishment funds, can be utilized just as they have been in Europe. The real problem becomes one of constructive organization.

It is suggested that the commission recommend a Federal system of sickness insurance, constructed along the lines here briefly summarized.

1. *Membership.*—The membership shall comprise all employees of persons, firms, companies, and corporations engaged in interstate commerce, or whose products are transported in interstate commerce, or which may do business in two or more States. The employees of intrastate establishments to be permitted to be insured, if they so elect, under regulations to be prescribed by the commission.

2. *Fund.*—The fund is to be created by joint contributions by employees, employers, and the Government, the last named sufficient for expenses of administration. Such contributions should probably be in the proportion of 50 per cent from workers, 40 per cent from employers, and 10 per cent from the Government. Individuals or groups desiring larger benefits may arrange to make larger payments, and the rate in any trade, industry, or locality may be reduced where conditions so improve as to make a lower rate adequate. The contributions are to be secured through taxing each interstate employer a certain amount weekly for each employee, the part contributed by workers to be deducted from their wages, thus using the regular revenue machinery of the Government.

3. *Benefits.*—Benefits to be available for a limited period in the form of cash and medical benefits during sickness, nonindustrial accidents, and child bearing; death benefits to be of limited size and payable on presentation of proper evidence.

4. *Administration.*—The administration of the insurance funds is to be carried out by a national sickness insurance commission. The national commission should be composed, by presidential appointment with Senate confirmation, of a director (who would be chairman), representatives of employers and representatives of employees in equal ratio, and, as ex officio nonvoting members, the Federal Commissioner of Labor Statistics and the Surgeon General of the Public Health Service. The commission should be empowered to supervise all funds and determine their character and limits of jurisdiction; promulgate all regulations necessary to enforce the act; establish and maintain hospitals; maintain staffs of medical examiners, specialists, dentists, and visiting nurses; provide for medicines and appliances; make contracts with local physicians; cooperate with local funds and health authorities in disease prevention; and provide for collecting actuarial data.

Correlation of the insurance system with the medical profession, the lack of which has been a serious defect in German and British systems, is absolutely necessary. Contracts with physicians should allow to each a per capita payment for the insured persons under his care, the right of selection of physician to be retained by the insured. For the signing of certificates entitling the insured to benefits, and for treating the insured in hospitals, the Surgeon General should detail physicians from the Public Health Service, their entire time to be given to these and other duties (consulting with local physicians, enforcing Federal laws and regulations, and cooperating with local authorities).

XVII. EDUCATION IN RELATION TO INDUSTRY.

The report dealing with this question has been presented by Commissioner Lennon, and is printed on pages 253–261.

XVIII. SCIENTIFIC MANAGEMENT.

The investigation of scientific management was conducted by Prof. Robert F. Hoxie, with the expert assistance and advice of Mr. Robert G. Valentine, representing the employer's interest in management, and Mr. John P. Frey, representing the interests of labor. The investigation grew out of public hearings held by the commission during the spring of 1914, at which the almost unqualified opposition of labor to scientific management was manifested. The purpose of the investigation was to test by the results of actual practice the claims of scientific management and the charges of the representatives of organized labor.

The investigation, which covered a period of more than a year, was made with the greatest care and thoroughness. Thirty-five shops and systematizing concerns were examined and interviews were had with a large number of scientific management leaders, experts, and employers. The shops visited were, almost without exception, those designated by authorities on scientific management, such as Messrs. Taylor, Gantt, and Emerson, as the best representatives of the actual results of scientific management. In other words, the examination was practically confined to the very best examples of scientific management. The defects and shortcomings pointed out hereinafter are, therefore, characteristic of the system under the most favorable conditions.

As a result of their investigations, Prof. Hoxie, Mr. Valentine, and Mr. Frey submitted a report, agreed upon without exceptions, in which the statements and recommendations which follow are embodied. These statements constitute a very brief summary of the entire report, which should be read as a whole if a complete understanding of their results and findings is desired.

Throughout the report the term " scientific management " is understood to mean the system devised and applied by Frederick W. Taylor, H. L. Gantt, Harrington Emerson and their followers, with the object of promoting efficiency in shop management and operation.

The report, unanimously agreed upon by the commission's investigator and his advisory experts, is the basis for the following statements.

POSSIBLE BENEFITS OF SCIENTIFIC MANAGEMENT TO LABOR AND SOCIETY.

1. As a system, scientific management presents certain possible benefits to labor and to society:

(a) A close casual relation exists between productive efficiency and possible wages. Greater efficiency and output make possible higher wages in general and better conditions of employment and labor.

In so far, then, as scientific management affords opportunities for lower costs and increased production without adding to the burden of the workers in exhaustive effort, long hours, or inferior working conditions, it creates the possibility of very real and substantial benefits to labor and to society.

(b) It is the policy of scientific management, as a preliminary to strictly labor changes, to bring about improvement and standardization of the material equipment and productive organization of the plant, particularly:

Machinery: Installation, repair, operation.

Tools: Storage, care, delivery.

Material equipment: Rearrangement to avoid delays, etc.

Product: Devices for economical and expeditious handling and routing.

Processes and methods: Elimination of waste motions, improvement of accessories, etc.

Reorganization of managerial staff and improvement of managerial efficiency.

Reorganization of sales and purchasing departments with a view to broadening and stabilizing the market.

Improvements in methods of storekeeping and regulation of delivery, surplus stock, etc.

All such improvements are to be commended, and investigation shows that they are not only accepted by labor without opposition but are, in fact, welcomed.

2. Scientific management in its direct relation to labor is not devoid of beneficial aspects, inasmuch as it is to a large extent an attempt at immediate standardization of labor conditions and relations. It may also serve labor by calling the attention of the employer to the fact that there are other and more effective ways to meet severe competition than by "taking it out of labor."

It is true that scientific management and organized labor are not altogether in harmony in their attitude toward standardization of labor conditions and relations. While both seek to have the conditions of work and pay clearly defined and definitely maintained at any given moment, they differ fundamentally as to the circumstances which may justly cause the substitution of new standards for old ones. Trade-unionism tends to hold to the idea that standards must not be changed in any way to the detriment of the workers. Scientific management, on the other hand, regards changes as justified and desirable if they result in increase of efficiency, and has provided methods, such as time study, for the constant suggestion of such changes.

3. The same may be said of many other major claims of scientific management. Whether the ideals advocated are attained or at present attainable, and whether scientific managers are to be found who purposely violate them, scientific management has in these claims and in the methods upon which they are based shown the way along which we may proceed to more advantageous economic results for labor and for society. It may not have succeeded in establishing a practical system of vocational selection and adaptation, but it has emphasized the desirability of it; it may not set the task with due and scientific allowance for fatigue so that the worker is guarded against overspeeding and overexertion, but it has undoubtedly developed methods which make it possible to better prevailing conditions in this respect; it has called attention most forcibly to the evils of favoritism and the rough and arbitrary decisions of foremen and others in authority. If scientific management be shown to have positive objectionable features, from both the standpoint of labor and the welfare of society, this constitutes no denial of these beneficial features, but calls rather for intelligent social action to eliminate that which is detrimental and to supplement and control that which is beneficial to all.

SCIENTIFIC MANAGEMENT IN PRACTICE—ITS DIVERSITIES AND DEFECTS.

4. Conditions in actual shops do not conform to the ideals of the system, and show no general uniformity. Actual field investigations demonstrated beyond reasonable doubt that scientific management in practice is characterized by striking incompleteness and manifold

diversity as compared with the theoretical exposition of its advocates. This incompleteness and diversity in practice apply not only to matters of detail but cover many of the essential features of scientific management even among those shops designated by Taylor, Gantt, and Emerson as representative of their work and influence. The following particular defects were observed:

(a) *Failure to carry into effect with any degree of thoroughness the general elements involved in the system.*—This may take the form of ignoring either the mechanical equipment and managerial organization, adopting simply a few routine features, such as time study and bonus payment, or the adoption of all mechanical features with a complete disregard of the spirit in which they are supposed to be applied.

(b) *Failure to adopt the full system of "functional foremanship."*—The results of prevailing practices do not support the claim that scientific management treats each workman as an independent personality and that it substitutes joint obedience to fact and law for obedience to personal authority.

(c) *Lack of uniformity in the method of selecting and hiring help.*—Upon the whole the range of excellence in methods of selection and hiring in "scientific" shops was the same as in other shops. The workers in scientific-management shops seem to be a select class when compared with the same classes of workers outside, but this result seems to be due to the weeding out of the less satisfactory material rather than to initial methods of selection.

(d) *Failure to substantiate claims of scientific management with reference to the adaptation, instruction, and training of workers.*— Scientific-management shops in general depend upon nothing in the way of occupational adaptation of the workers except the ordinary trial and error method. Investigation reveals little to substantiate the sweeping claims of scientific managers made in this connection, except that in the better scientific-management shops many workmen are receiving more careful instruction and a higher degree of training than is at present possible for them elsewhere. The most that can be said is that scientific management, as such, furthers a tendency to narrow the scope of the workers' industrial activity, and that it falls far short of a compensatory equivalent in its ideals and actual methods of instruction and training.

e) *Lack of scientific accuracy, uniformity, and justice in time study and task setting.*—Far from being the invariable and purely objective matters that they are pictured, the methods and results of time study and task setting are in practice the special sport of individual judgment and opinion, subject to all the possibilities of diversity, inaccuracy, and injustice that arise from human ignorance and prejudice.

The objects of time study are: (1) Improvement and standardization of the methods of doing the work, without reference to a standard time for its accomplishment, and (2) fixing of a definite task time of efficiency scale.

Possibilities of great advantage exist in the use of time study for the first purpose. However, in a large number of shops, time study for this purpose is practically neglected.

In connection with the second purpose, setting of task time or efficiency scale, great variations are noted, and especially the part which fallible individual judgment and individual prejudice may and do play.

Detailed observations of the practice of making time studies and setting tasks showed great variations in methods and results. Seventeen separate sources of variation are pointed out, any one of which is sufficient to and in practice does greatly influence the results of time studies.

In face of such evidence it is obviously absurd to talk of time study as an accurate scientific method in practice or of the tasks set by means of it as objective scientific facts which are not possible or proper subjects of dispute and bargaining.

Furthermore, the time-study men upon whom the entire results depend were found to be prevailingly of the narrow-minded mechanical type, poorly paid, and occupying the lowest positions in the managerial organization, if they could be said to belong at all to the managerial group. Nor does the situation seem to promise much improvement, for the position and pay accorded to time-study men generally are such as to preclude the drawing into this work of really competent men in the broader sense. Aside from a few notable exceptions in the shops and some men who make a general profession of time study in connection with the installation of scientific management, this theoretically important functionary, as a rule, receives little more than good mechanic's wages and has little voice in determining shop policies. In fact, the time-study man, who, if scientific management is to make good the most important of its labor claims, should be among the most highly trained and influential officials in the shop, a scientist in viewpoint, a wise arbitrator between employer and workman, is in general a petty functionary, a specialist workman, a sort of clerk who has no voice in the counsels of the higher officials.

However, the method of time study is not necessarily impracticable or unjust to the workers. Under proper direction time study promises much more equitable results than can be secured by the ordinary methods. The greatest essential is a time-study man of exceptional knowledge, judgment, and tact. The average time-study man does not fulfill these requirements at present.

Finally, it is only in connection with standard products, requiring only moderate skill and judgment in layout and work, that economy seems to allow adequate application of the time-study method. Its natural sphere seems to be routine and repetitive work. As long as industry continues to be as complex and diversified as it is, this element of economy will without doubt continue to operate in a way to limit the legitimate scope of time study and task setting. Task setting as at present conducted is not satisfactory to workmen and creates dissatisfaction and jealousy.

(f) *Failure to substantiate the claim of having established a scientific and equitable method of determining wage rates.*—In analyzing the wage-fixing problem in connection with scientific management two matters are considered: (1) The "base rate," sometimes called the day wage, which constitutes for any group of workers the minimum earnings or indicates the general wage level for that group, and (2) added "efficiency payments," which are supposed to represent special additional rewards for special attainments.

The investigators sought in vain for any scientific methods devised or employed by scientific management for the determination of the base rate, either as a matter of justice between the conflicting claims of capital and labor, or between the relative claims of individuals and occupational groups.

Rates for women with reference to men are, as a rule, on the same basis in scientific-management shops as in other shops. One leader said, "There is to be no nonsense about scientific management. If by better organization and administration what is now regarded as man's work can be done by women, women will be employed and women's wages will be paid."

Scientific-management shops seem as ready as others to raise the rates as the wage level generally advances.

"Bewildering diversity" prevails in relation to the "efficiency payment" or reward for special effort. After a careful and extended analysis and investigation of the different ways of rewarding individual increases in output, it was concluded:

All of these systems definitely belie the claim that scientific management pays workers in proportion to their efficiency. One of them has the obvious intent of weeding out the lower grade of workers, while the other two are so constituted as to make such workers very unprofitable to the employers. Two of them lend themselves easily to the exploitation of mediocre workers—those who can deliver a medium output but can not attain to a standard task set high. All of them furnish a strong stimulus to high efficiency and output, but in themselves furnish no visible check on overspeeding and exhaustion. All of them are capable of being liberally applied, but all can also be used as instruments of oppression through the undue severity of task setting or efficiency rating.

There can be no doubt that under scientific management rates are cut. But to say positively that scientific management, on the whole, furthers the cutting of rates is quite another matter. The fact seems clear that at this point there is a conflict of tendencies within the thing itself. There is a strong inducement for scientific managers to maintain rates strictly, and the honest efforts of those who deserve the name to so maintain them can hardly be impugned. At the same time, however, the greatest advance toward efficiency, for which scientific management stands, is obtained by the constant alteration of conditions and tasks through time study. Such alterations almost of necessity mean constant rate cutting. Were industry once standardized for good and all, scientific management would undoubtedly operate as an unequivocal force tending to the maintenance of rates. As it is with industry in flux, what amounts to rate cutting seems to be almost of necessity an essential part of its very nature.

Finally, all of the systems of payment tend to center the attention of the worker on his individual interest and gain and to repress the development of group consciousness and interest. Where the work of one man is independent of another, the individual has no motive to consider his fellow, since his work and pay in no wise depend on the other man. What either does will not affect the other's task or rates. Where work is independent, the leader can not afford to slow down to accommodate his successor.

It must be admitted that these systems are admirably suited to stimulate the workers, but in so far as there may be virtue in the union principles of group solidarity and uniformity, and in so far as they lay claim to scientific accuracy or a special conformity to justice in reward, they must be judged adversely.

(g) *Failure to protect the workers from overexertion and exhaustion.*—It is claimed by scientific management that protection to workers is afforded by such devices as: Standardization of equipment and performance; substitution of exact knowledge of men and of machines for guesswork in the setting of the task and the determination of the hours and other conditions of work; careful studies of fatigue; elimination of the need for pace setters; transformation of speeders into instructors, and transfer of responsibility from the workers to the management for contriving the best methods of work; maintenance of the best conditions for performing work through furnishing the best tools and materials at the proper time and place; instruction of the workers in the most economical and easiest methods of performing operations; institution of rational rest periods and modes of recreation during working hours; and surrounding the workers with the safest and most sanitary shop conditions.

Investigation indicates that scientific management, in practice, furnishes no reasonable basis for the majority of these specific claims in the present, and little hope for their realization in the near future. In these matters, indeed, the utmost variation prevails in scientific management as in other shops. Several admirable cases were found with respect to all these matters, but shops were not wanting where the management exhibited the utmost suspicion of the workers, referring continually to their disposition to "beat the time-study man," although the time study in such shops was obviously based on the work of speeders and all sorts of inducements were offered for pace setting, where instruction and training of the workers were emphasized by their absence, and where the general conditions of the work were much in need of improvement.

The investigation seems to show clearly that practical scientific management has not materially affected the length of the working day. Aside from shops where the management was evidently imbued with a strong moral sense, the hours of labor in these shops were those common to the industry and the locality.

When we come to the matter of fatigue studies and their connection with speeding and exhaustion, the claims of scientific management seem to break down completely. No actual fatigue studies were found taking place in the shops, and the time-study men, who should be charged with such studies, seemed in general to be quite indifferent or quite ignorant in regard to this whole matter. This does not mean that no attention to fatigue is given in scientific management shops. Cases were found where the health and energy of the workers were carefully observed and attempts were made to adopt the work to their condition, but the methods employed were the rough-and-ready ones of common-sense observation. Rest periods and modes of recreation during the working hours are a regular institution on an extended scale in but one shop visited by the investigators. Isolated instances were encountered elsewhere, but managers in general apparently do not even entertain the idea of their institution.

Scientific management does not always surround the workers with the safest and most sanitary shop conditions. In general, scientific management shops seem to be good shops as shops go. The introduction of the system has the tendency without doubt to clean the shop up and to improve the condition of belting, machinery, and arrangement of material equipment generally. All this is in the direct line of efficiency and safety. Several very notable examples of excellence in safety and sanitation were found. On the other hand, several shops visited were below good standards in these respects, and flagrant specific violations of safety rules were encountered.

As a whole, the facts in nowise justify the assumption that scientific management offers any effective guaranty against overspeeding and exhaustion of workers. The investigation left a strong impression that scientific management workers in general are not overspeeded, but the challenge to show any overspeeded or overworked men in scientific management shops is very easily met. The situation in this respect varies much with the industry. Some instances of undoubted overspeeding were found, particularly in the case of girls and women. But these instances do not warrant a general charge. On the other hand, there appears to be nothing in the special methods of scientific management to prevent speeding up where the technical conditions make it possible and profitable, and there is much in these methods to induce it in the hands of unscrupulous employers.

(h) *Failure to substantiate the claim that scientific management offers exceptional opportunities for advancement and promotion on a basis of individual merit.*—While scientific management undoubtedly separates the efficient from the inefficient more surely and speedily than ordinary methods, it was shown by the investigation that scientific management often fails in the development of functional foremanship and in the elimination of favoritism. It tends to create a multitude of new tasks on which less skill is required and lower rates can be paid. It has developed no efficient system for the placing or adaptation of the workers. It is inclined in practice to regard a worker as adapted to his work and rightly placed when he succeeds in making the task. It tends to confine the mass of workmen to one or two tasks, and offers little opportunity, therefore, for the discovery and development of special aptitudes among the masses. It tends to divide the workers into two unequal classes—the few who rise to managerial positions and the many who seem bound to remain task workers within a narrow field. In the ideal it offers opportunity for promotion from the ranks, and this works out to a certain extent in practice, but not universally.

There is a great deal of exaggeration, too, in statements made concerning special rewards for usable suggestions. Few of the shops make any systematic rewards of this kind, and where this is the case the rewards are usually trivial. In one shop the investigator was shown an automatic machine invented by a workman, which did the work of several hand workers. "Did he receive a reward?" was asked. "Oh, yes," came the answer, "his rate of pay was increased from 17 to 22 cents per hour."

(i) *With reference to the alleged methods and severity of discipline under scientific management the "acrimonious criticism" from trade unions does not seem to be warranted.*—In theory, the scientific managers appear to have the best of the argument, and in practice the investigation showed an agreeable absence of rough and arbitrary disciplinary authority. When the tasks were liberally set, the workers were found generally operating without special supervision except where instructions or assistance were needed. Deductions were indeed made for poor work and destruction of materials, but in the better class of shops apparently with no greater and perhaps with less than ordinary severity.

While it should be remembered that the shops selected represented probably the best of the shops operating under this system, in general, it would seem that scientific management does lessen the rigors of discipline as compared with other shops where the management is autocratic and the workers have no organization.

(*j*) *Failure to substantiate the claim that workers are discharged only on just grounds and have an effective appeal to the highest managerial authority.*—This whole matter is one in which neither management claims nor union complaints seem susceptible of proof, but the investigation indicates that the unions have legitimate basis for charging that discharge is generally a matter of arbitrary managerial authority.

(*k*) *Lack of democracy under scientific management.*—As a result of the investigation, there can be little doubt that scientific management tends in practice to weaken the power of the individual worker as against the employer, setting aside all questions of personal attitude and the particular opportunities and methods for voicing complaints and enforcing demands. It gathers up and transfers to the management the traditional craft knowledge and transmits this again to the workers only piecemeal as it is needed in the performance of the particular job or task. It tends in practice to confine each worker to a particular task or small cycle of tasks. It thus narrows his outlook and skill to the experience and training which are necessary to do the work. He is therefore easier of displacement. Moreover, the changing of methods and conditions of work and the setting of tasks by time study with its assumption always of scientific accuracy puts the individual worker at a disadvantage in any attempt to question the justice of the demands made upon him. The onus of proof is upon him and the standards of judgment are set up by the employer, covered by the mantle of scientific accuracy.

It would seem also that scientific management tends, on the whole, to prevent the formation of groups of workers within the shop with recognized common interests, and to weaken the solidarity of those which exist. Almost everything points to the strengthening of the individualistic motive and the weakening of group solidarity. Each worker is bent on the attainment of his individual task. He can not combine with his fellows to determine how much that task shall be. If the individual slows down he merely lessens his wages and prejudices his standing without helping his neighbor. If he can beat the other fellow, he helps himself without directly affecting the other's task or pay. Assistance, unless the man is a paid instructor, is at personal cost. Special rewards, where offered, are for the individual. Rules of seniority are not recognized. Sometimes personal rivalry is stimulated by the posting of individual records or classification of the workers by name into "excellent," "good," "poor," etc. Potential groups are broken up by the constant changes in methods and reclassification of workers which are the mission of time study.

The whole gospel of scientific management to the worker is to the individual, telling him how, by special efficiency, he can cut loose from the mass, and rise in wages or position.

With the power of the individual weakened and the chances lessened for the development of groups and group solidarity, the democratic possibility of scientific management, barring the presence of unionism, would seem to be scant. The individual is manifestly in no position to cope with the employer on a basis of equality. The claim to democracy based on the close association of the management and the men and the opportunities allowed for the voicing of complaints is not borne out by the facts; and in the general run of scientific-management shops, barring the presence of unionism and collective bargaining, the unionists are justified in the charge that the workers have no real voice in hiring and discharging, the setting of the task, the determination of the wage rates, or the general conditions of employment. This charge is true even where the employers have no special autocratic tendencies, much more so therefore where, as in many cases, they are thoroughly imbued with the autocratic spirit. With rare exceptions, then, democracy under scientific management can not and does not exist apart from unionism and collective bargaining.

Does the scientific manager, as a matter of fact, welcome the cooperation of unionism? Here, again, the facts should decide the contention. The fact is that while in numbers of scientific-management shops some unionists are employed, they are not generally employed as union men, and the union is rarely recognized and dealt with as such. The fact is that those who declare the willingness of scientific management to welcome the cooperation of unionism in general either know nothing about unionism and its rules and regulations or are thinking of a different kind of unionism from that to which the American Federation of Labor stands committed and a kind of cooperation foreign to its ideals and practices.

To sum up, scientific management in practice generally tends to weaken the competitive power of the individual worker and thwarts the formation of shop groups and weakens group solidarity; moreover, generally scientific management is lacking in the arrangements and machinery necessary for the actual voicing of the workers' ideas and complaints and for the democratic consideration and adjustment of grievances. Collective bargaining has ordinarily no place in the determination of matters vital to the workers, and the attitude toward it is usually tolerant only when it is not understood. Finally unionism, where it means a vigorous attempt to enforce the viewpoint and claims of the workers, is in general looked upon with abhorrence, and unions which are looked upon with complacency are not the kind which organized labor in general wants, while the union cooperation which is invited is altogether different from that which they stand ready to give. In practice scientific management must, therefore be declared autocratic in tendency—a reversion to industrial autocracy, which forces the workers to depend on the employers' conception of fairness and limits the democratic safeguards of the workers.

5. Scientific management is still in its infancy or early trial stages, and immaturity and failure to attain ideals in practice are necessary accompaniments to the development of any new industrial or social

movement. Doubtless many of its diversities and shortcomings will, therefore, be cured by time.

Before this can be brought about, however, certain potent causes of present evil must be eradicated:

(a) The first of these is a persistent attempt on the part of experts and managers to apply scientific management and its methods outside their natural sphere.

(b) A second chief source of danger and evil to labor in the application of scientific management is that it offers its wares in the open market, but it has developed no means by which it can control the use of these by the purchaser. In large part the practical departure of scientific management from its ideals is the result of special managerial or proprietorial aims and impatience of delay in their fulfillment. The expert is frequently called in because the establishment is in financial or industrial straits, and the chief concern of the management is quick increase of production and profits. It must meet its competitors here and now, and can not afford to expend more than is necessary to do this, or to forego immediate returns while the foundations are being laid for a larger but later success, and with careful regard to immediate justice and the long-time welfare of its working force. The outcome frequently is conflict between the systematizer and the management, resulting in the abandonment of the scheme only partially worked out on the retirement of the expert, leaving the management to apply crudely the methods partially installed, sometimes to the detriment of the workers and their interests.

It is true that the situation thus outlined is not of universal application. But bitter complaints were frequently heard from members of the small group of experts who represent the highest ideals and intelligence of the movement, in regard to the managerial opposition which they have encountered, and frequent apologies were offered for the conditions and results of their work, accompanied by the statement that they could go no further than the management would allow, or that things had been done by the management against their judgment and for which they could not stand. Moreover, scientific management is closely interlocked with the mechanism of production for profit and the law of economy rules. Many things which would be desirable from the ideal standpoint, and which are a practical necessity if the interests of the workers are to be fully protected, are not always or usually economical. This is specially true of time study, task setting, and rate making.

The arbitrary will of the employer and the law of economy are two potent special forces which contribute to the existing diversity, incompleteness, and crudity of scientific management as it is practiced, even where the systematizer is possessed of the highest intelligence and imbued with the best motives of his group.

(c) But to explain the situation as it exists at present, two other important factors must be taken into consideration. The first of these is the existence and practice of self-styled scientific management systematizers and time study experts who lack in most respects the ideals and the training essential to fit them for the work which they claim to be able to do. Scientific management as a movement is cursed with fakirs. The great rewards which a few leaders in the movement have secured for their services have brought into the field a crowd of industrial "patent medicine men." The way is open to all. No standards or requirements, private or public, have been developed by the application of which the goats can be separated from the sheep. Employers have thus far proved credulous. Almost anyone can show the average manufacturing concern where it can make some improvements in its methods. So the scientific management shingles have gone up all over the country, the fakirs have gone into the shops, and in the name of scientific management have reaped temporary gains to the detriment of both the employers and the workers.

(*d*) Fake scientific management experts, however, are not alone responsible for the lack of training and intelligence which contributes to the diversity and immaturity of scientific management in practice and its failure to make good the labor claims of its most distinguished leaders. The fact is that on the whole, and barring some notable exceptions, the sponsors and adherents of scientific management— experts and employers alike—are profundly ignorant of very much that concerns the broader humanitarian and social problems which it creates and involves, especially as these touch the character and welfare of labor.

It is because of this ignorance and unwarranted assurance that there is a strong tendency on the part of scientific management experts to look upon the labor end of their work as the least difficult and requiring the least careful consideration. To their minds the delicate and difficult part of the task of installation is the solution of the material, mechanical, and organic problems involved. They tend to look upon the labor end of their work as a simple technical matter of so setting tasks and making rates that the workers will give the fullest productive cooperation. They tend naively to assume that when the productivity of the concern is increased and the laborers are induced to do their full part toward this end, the labor problem in connection with scientific management is satisfactorily solved. In short, in the majority of cases the labor problem appears to be looked at as one aspect of the general problem of production in the shop, and it is truthfully assumed that if it is solved with reference to this problem it must also be solved with due regard to labor's well-being and its just demands. This seems to have been the characteristic attitude of scientific management from the beginning. Labor was simply looked upon as one of the factors entering into production, like machinery, tools, stores, and other elements of equipment. The problem was simply how to secure an efficient coordination and functioning of these elements. It was only after the opposition of labor had been expressed that scientific management began to be conscious of any other aspect of the labor matter. And with some notable exceptions scientific management experts and employers still look upon the labor matter almost solely as an aspect of the general production problem, and have little positive interest or concern in regard to it otherwise.

It is probable that scientific managers will object to these statements, pleading that they are mainly variations and conditions due to the time element or to the necessity imposed by the law of costs. They will say, for example, that when a new and unusual job comes in, neither time nor economy will allow of careful time studies, and if careful studies were made of all the variations of a complicated task, the expense of such studies would wipe out the profit; that, in general, they are proceeding toward the full realization of the ideal of scientific management as fast as economy will allow.   But such pleas would serve only to confirm the main contention that scientific managers and scientific management employers generally are necessarily ruled, like all members of the employing group, by the forces of cost and profits; that to them the labor problem is primarily an aspect of the problem of production, and that in the ends the needs and welfare of labor must be subordinated to these things.   Beneath all other causes or shortcomings of scientific management, therefore, in its relation to labor, there seems to be the practical fact of an opposition of interests between the profit-taking and the labor group, which makes extremely doubtful the possibility that its shortcomings from the standpoint of labor are capable of elimination.

GENERAL LABOR PROBLEMS.

6. (a) Scientific management at its best furthers the modern tendency toward the specialization of the workers.   Its most essential features—functional foremanship, time study, task setting, and efficiency payment—all have this inherent effect.

Under the scientific management system fully developed, the ordinary mechanic is intended to be and is, in fact, a machine feeder and a machine feeder only, with the possibility of auxiliary operations clearly cut off and with means applied to discourage experimentation. And what applies to the machine feeder applies with more or less thoroughness to machine and hand operatives generally.

But it is not merely in stripping from the job its auxiliary operations that scientific management tends to specialize the work and the workmen.   Time study, the chief cornerstone of all systems of scientific management, tends inherently to the narrowing of the job or task itself.   As the final object of time study, so far as it directly touches the workers, is to make possible the setting of tasks so simple and uniform and so free from possible causes of interruption and variation that definite and invariable time limits can be placed upon them, and that the worker may be unimpeded in his efficient performance of them by the necessity for questioning and deliberation, the preponderating tendency of time study is to split up the work into smaller and simpler operations and tasks.   Decidedly, then, time study tends to further the modern tendency toward specialization of the job and the task.

With functional foremanship lopping off from the job auxiliary operations, and time study tending to a narrowing of the task itself, task setting and efficiency methods of payment come into play as forces tending to confine the worker to a single task or a narrow range of operations.   The worker is put upon the special task for which he seems best adapted, and he is stimulated by the methods of payment employed to make himself as proficient as possible at it. When he succeeds in this, to shift him to another task ordinarily involves an immediate and distinct loss to the employer, and the worker himself naturally resents being shifted to a new task since this involves an immediate loss in his earnings.   Here worker and employer are as one in their immediate interest to have the job so simple that the operation can be quickly learned, and the task made, and that shifting of tasks be eliminated as far as possible. The employer besides has another motive for this, in that the shifting of the workers multiplies the records and renders more complex the system of wage accounting. It is true that the scientific management employer, like any other, must have a certain number of workers in the shop who are capable of performing a plurality of tasks. But the tendency is to have as few all-round workers as are necessary to meet these emergencies. The methods of scientific management operate most effectively when they break up and narrow the work of the individual, and the ends of scientific management are best served when the rank and file of the workers are specialists.

This inherent tendency of scientific management to specialization is buttressed, broadened in its scope and perpetuated by the progressive gathering up and systematizing in the hands of the employers of all the traditional craft knowledge in the possession of the workers. With this information in hand and functional foremanship to direct its use, scientific management claims to have no need of craftsmen, in the old sense of the term, and, therefore, no need for an apprenticeship system except for the training of functional foremen. It therefore tends to neglect apprenticeship except for the training of the few. And as this body of systematized knowledge in the hands of the employer grows, it is enabled to broaden the scope of its operation, to attack and specialize new operations, new crafts and new industries, so that the tendency is to reduce more and more to simple, specialized operations, and more and more workers to the positions of narrow specialists. Nor does scientific management afford anything in itself to check or offset this specialization tendency. The instruction and training offered is for specialist workmen. Selection and adaptation are specializing in their tendencies. Promotion is for the relatively few. The whole system, in its conception and operation, is pointed toward a universally specialized industrial régime.

(b) But scientific management is not only inherently specializing; it also tends to break down existing standards and uniformities set up by the workmen, and to prevent the establishment of stable conditions of work and pay. Time study means constant and endless change in the method of operation. No sooner is a new and better method discovered and established and the condition of work and pay adapted to it than an improvement is discovered involving perhaps new machinery, new tools and materials, a new way of doing things, and a consequent alteration of the essential conditions of work and pay, and perhaps a reclassification of the workers.

(c) Ample evidence to support this analysis was afforded by the investigation. Where the system was found relatively completely applied, the mass of the workers were engaged in specialized tasks, there was little variation in the operations except in emergencies, apprenticeship for the many was abandoned or was looked upon as an investment which brought no adequate returns and was slated for abandonment; almost everywhere scientific management employers expressed a strong preference for specialist workmen, old crafts were being broken up and the craftsmen given the choice of retirement or of entering the ranks of specialized workmen; in the most progressive shops, the time study men were preparing the way for a broader application of the system by the analytical study of the operations and crafts not yet systematized. Changes in methods and classification of workers were seen even during the short course of the investigation.

(d) What does this mean from the standpoint of labor and labor welfare? Certain conclusions are inevitable. Scientific management, fully and properly applied, inevitably tends to the constant breakdown of the established crafts and craftsmanship and the constant elimination of skill in the sense of narrowing craft knowledge and workmanship except for the lower orders of workmen. Some scientific management employers have asserted belief in their ability to get on a paying basis within three months, should they lose their whole working force except the managerial staff and enough others to maintain the organization, if they had to begin all over again with green hands. What this means in increased competition of workmen with workmen can be imagined. Were the scientific management ideal fully realized, any man who walks the street would be a practical competitor for almost any workman's job.

Such a situation would inevitably break down the basis of present-day unionism and render collective bargaining impossible in any effective sense in regard to the matters considered by the unions most essential. It has been proved by experience that unskilled workers generally find it most difficult to maintain effective and continuous organization for dealing with complicated industrial situations. Effective collective bargaining can not exist without effective organization. Moreover, we have already seen how scientific management, apart from the matter of skill, tends to prevent the formation and weakens the solidarity of groups within the shops.

But, beyond all this, time study strikes at the heart and core of the principles and conditions which make effective unionism and collective bargaining possible with respect to certain most essential matters. When the employer can constantly initiate new methods and conditions and reclassify the work and the workmen, he can evade all efforts of the union to establish and maintain definite and continuous standards of work and pay. Time study is in definite opposition to uniformity and stable classification. It enables the employer constantly to lop off portions of the work from a certain class and then to create new classifications of workers, with new conditions of work and pay. Add to all of this the advantage gained by the employers in the progressive gathering up and systematization of craft knowledge for their own uses, and the destruction of apprenticeship, which cuts the workers off from the perpetuation among them of craftsmanship, and the destructive tendencies of scientific management as far as present-day unionism and collective bargaining are concerned, seems inevitable.

(e) Under these circumstances the progressive degeneration of craftsmanship and the progressive degradation of skilled craftsmen also seems inevitable.

(f) The ultimate effects of scientific management, should it become universal, upon wages, employment, and industrial peace, are matters of pure speculation. During the period of transition, however, there can be little doubt of the results. The tendency will be first toward a realignment of wage rates. The craftsmen, the highly trained workers, can not hope to maintain their wage advantage over the semiskilled and less skilled workers. There will be a leveling tendency. Whether this leveling will be up or down, it is impossible to say. At present scientific management seems to be making the relatively unskilled more efficient than ever before, and they are in general receiving under it greater earnings than ever before. It is evident, however, that the native efficiency of the working class must suffer from the neglect of apprenticeship. Scientific managers have themselves complained bitterly of the poor material from which they must recruit their workers, compared with the efficient and self-respecting craftsman who applied for employment 20 years ago.

Moreover, it must not be overlooked that the whole scheme of scientific management, and especially the gathering up and systematizing of the knowledge formerly the possession of the workmen, tends enormously to add to the strength of capitalism. This fact, together with the greater ease of displacement shown above, must make the security and continuity of employment inherently more uncertain.

If generally increased efficiency is the result of scientific management, unemployment would in the end seem to become less of a menace. But during the period of transition its increase should be expected. Not only must the old craftsmen suffer as the result of the destruction of their crafts, but until scientific management finds itself able to control markets its increased efficiency must result in gluts in special lines, with resulting unemployment in particular trades and occupations. A leading scientific-management expert has stated that one shop of six in a certain industry systematized by him could turn out all the product that the market would carry. The result to the workers, if the statement be true, needs no explanation. Scientific management would seem to offer possibilities ultimately of better market control or better adaptation to market conditions, but the experience of the past year of depression indicates that at present no such possibilities generally exist.

Finally, until unionism as it exists has been done away with or has undergone essential modification, scientific management can not be said to make for the avoidance of strikes and the establishment of industrial peace. The investigation has shown several well-authenticated cases of strikes which have occurred in scientific-management shops. They are perhaps less frequent in this class of shop than elsewhere in similar establishments, owing largely to the fact that organized workmen are on the whole little employed. In its extension, however, it is certain that scientific management is a constant menace to industrial peace. So long as present-day unionism exists and unionists continue to believe, as they seem warranted in doing, that scientific management means the destruction of their organizations or their present rules and regulations, unionism will continue to oppose it energetically and whenever and wherever opportunity affords.

It has been said with much truth that scientific management is like the invention of machinery in its effect upon workers and social conditions and welfare generally—that it gives a new impulse to the industrial revolution which characterized the latter part of the eighteenth and nineteenth centuries and strengthens its general effects and tendencies. A chief characterization of this revolution has been the breakdown of craftsmanship, the destruction of crafts, and the carrying of the modern industrial world toward an era of specialized workmanship and generally semiskilled or unskilled workmen. Scientific management seems to be another force urging us forward toward this era.

CONCLUSIONS.

7. Our industries should adopt all methods which replace inaccuracy with accurate knowledge and which systematically operate to eliminate economic waste. Scientific management at its best has succeeded in creating an organic whole of the several departments of an institution, establishing a coordination of their functions which has previously been impossible, and, in this respect, it has conferred great benefits on industry.

The social problem created by scientific management, however, does not lie in this field. As regards its social consequences neither organized nor unorganized labor finds in scientific management any adequate protection to its standards of living, any progressive means for industrial education, any opportunity for industrial democracy by which labor may create for itself a progressively efficient share in management. Therefore, as unorganized labor is totally unequipped to work for these human rights, it becomes doubly the duty of organized labor to work unceasingly and unswervingly for them, and, if necessary, to combat an industrial development which not only does not contain conditions favorable to their growth, but, in many respects, is hostile soil.

XIX. PRISON LABOR.

The evidence which has come before the commission is the basis for the following statements:

1. The practice of using convicts in penitentiaries and prisons generally for the manufacture of articles for general commerce has been productive of evil results as regards not only the convicts but the general public.

2. The competition of prison-made articles has resulted in the existence of a low wage scale in many industries and has subjected the manufacturers to a kind of competition which should not exist in any civilized community.

3. The only beneficiaries of the convict labor system are the contractors who are permitted by the State to exploit the inmates of prisons.

4. The individual States are powerless to deal adequately with this situation because of the interstate shipment of convict-made goods.

It is suggested that the commission recommend:

1. The abolition as far as possible of indoor manufacture, and the substitution of such outdoor work as that upon State farms and State roads, providing that where prisoners are employed they should be compensated and that the products which they manufacture should not be sold in competition with the products of free labor.

2. The enactment by Congress of a bill providing that all convict-made goods when transported into any State or Territory of the United States shall be subject to the operation of the laws of such.

State or Territory to the same extent and in the same manner as though such goods had been produced therein.

XX. IMMIGRATION.

The evidence presented to the commission is the basis for the following statements:

1. The immigration policy of the United States has created a number of our most difficult and serious industrial problems and has been responsible in a considerable measure for the existing state of industrial unrest.

2. The enormous influx of immigrants during the past 25 years has already undermined the American standard of living for all workmen except those in the skilled trades, and has been the largest single factor in preventing the wage scale from rising as rapidly as food prices.

3. The great mass of non-English-speaking workers, who form about one-half of the labor force in the basic industries, has done much to prevent the development of better relations between employers and employees.

4. The presence of such a large proportion of immigrants has greatly hampered the formation of trade-unions and has tremendously increased the problem of securing effective and responsible organizations.

5. The unreasonable prejudice of almost every class of Americans toward the immigrants, who form such a large proportion of the labor force of our industries, has been largely responsible for the failure of our Nation to reach a correct understanding of the labor problem and has promoted the harshness and brutality which has so often been manifested in connection with industrial disturbances. It has been and to a large measure still is felt possible to dismiss the most revolting working conditions, the most brutal treatment, or the most criminal invasions of personal rights, by saying, " Oh, well, they are just ignorant foreigners."

6. If immigration had continued at the average rate of the past 10 years it would have proved almost, if not quite, impossible to have brought industrial conditions and relations to any proper basis, in spite of the most extreme efforts of civic organizations, trades-unions, and governmental machinery. The great diminution of immigration as a result of the European war has already begun to show its salutary effects.

It is suggested that the commission recommend:

1. The enactment of legislation providing for the restriction of immigration based upon the general provisions contained in the so-called Burnett-Dillingham bill, which has received the approval of two successive Congresses. With a full realization of the many theoretical objections which have been urged against the literacy test, the consensus of evidence is so strong that its practical workings would be to restrict immigration to those who are likely to make the most desirable citizens, to regulate immigration in some degree in proportion to the actual needs of American industry, and finally to promote education in Europe, that it seems necessary at least to urge that this plan be given a practical test.

2. The enactment of legislation providing that within six months from the time of entry all immigrants shall be required, under penalty of deportation, either to declare their intention to become citizens by taking out their first papers or to definitely register themselves with the proper authority as alien tourists, and further providing that all immigrants who have failed to take out their first papers at the end of two years shall be deported, as shall all who fail to take out their second papers when they become eligible, deportation in each case to act as a bar to future entry.

3. The provision by the States and municipalities, with the assistance of the Federal Government, if necessary, for the education of all adult persons who are unable to speak, read, or write the English language. In order to accomplish this it may be necessary to provide that employers shall grant certain definite periods of leisure for such instruction.

XXI. Labor Conditions in American Colonial Possessions.

The attention of the commission was directed to the labor conditions in American colonies by the strike of some 20,000 agricultural laborers in the island of Porto Rico, and by the appeal of the representatives of the Free Federation of Labor of Porto Rico for a hearing at which they might present their statement of the labor conditions, relations between laborers and employers, and the attitude assumed by the local Government during the strike. The commission granted the hearing and, in order that a full and fair presentation of the conditions should be made, invited the Government of Porto Rico to appoint representatives who were fully acquainted with the situation. As a result of the hearing of the testimony of these witnesses, a situation was found which demands immediate attention in order that widespread and deep-rooted evils should be eliminated. These conditions are in large measure an inheritance from centuries of despotic Spanish rule, and it is undeniable that great improvements in certain lines have been accomplished under American administration. Nevertheless, a peculiar responsibility rests upon the American Nation for the conditions of the people in our colonial possessions who occupy the position morally and legally of wards of the Nation.

The investigations were confined to the conditions in Porto Rico, but through the petitions filed with the commission by the inhabitants of other islands and through the information contained in reports of governmental officials, it seems certain that the labor conditions in all American colonies are generally similar to those in Porto Rico, and demand the attention of Congress.

As a result of the investigations and a careful analysis of the extensive documentary evidence filed, the following statements with regard to industrial and social conditions in Porto Rico are warranted:

1. Laborers in Porto Rico, including men, women, and children, are employed at wages which are inadequate to furnish proper food and clothing. The wages of men in agricultural districts range from 35 to 60 cents a day, when employed, and those of the women and children are about one-half this amount.

2. As a result largely of the low-wage standard, the diet of the laborers, consisting chiefly of rice, beans, codfish, and plantains, is so miserably inadequate that the worker not only is rendered inefficient but is to a large extent undernourished.

3. The laborers are further exploited on the large plantations, according to the testimony of the Government representatives, by exorbitant prices for food and other supplies, by deliberate cheating as regards weights and measures, and by unwarranted deductions from their wages for goods that were never purchased.

4. The educational facilities of Porto Rico are so totally inadequate that there are nearly 200,000 children for whose education no provision has been made.

The representatives of the colonial Government give a lack of ability to finance the educational system as the reason for the present conditions.

5. Many thousand people yearly, located in the rural districts, far from medical attendance and unable to afford the high charges of the physicians, die without medical attendance.

6. The labor laws of Porto Rico are inadequate, and the Bureau of Labor is not provided with sufficient funds to enforce the existing laws. The laws supposed to regulate the labor of women and children are generally violated. The provisions of the law restraining child labor are largely nullified by the insertion of a clause which permits this labor if the child is accompanied by a parent or other relative.

The employers' liability law of the island has the archaic fellow-servant clause in it and therefore is noneffective.

7. The great majority of the Porto Ricans are landless, the land of Porto Rico being largely owned by the corporations, wealthy landlords, and the colonial Government and municipalities. Very little land is for sale.

8. As a result, the land rents are inordinately high and tend very strongly to retard the development of a middle class.

9. The housing conditions of the workers are extremely bad. The majority of the rural workers live in huts which do not cost more than $10 to build, and these huts are occupied, on an average, by five people each, although at best there are only semipartitions dividing the huts into two rooms. The existing conditions are a menace not only to health but to morality and every sense of decency.

10. The laborers may be ejected from the huts provided by the employers at any time that the owner sees fit, and, while they pay no rent, they must and do work for the owner at his pleasure.

11. In the cities the conditions are almost equally bad. The city laborers rent apartments or build little houses on rented land. As an illustration of this condition: There were, in 1912, 10,936 people in Puerto de Tierra. These people lived in 1,144 houses, and practically 98 per cent of them were renters, as the occupants of only 30 houses owned both house and land. The land of one owner, which was assessed at $6,340, brought in a total rent of $2,580, or 37.4 per cent. That of another, assessed at $29,460, yielded $7,821 in rent, or 23.9 per cent.

12. Unemployment is very prevalent in the island, and it has been testified that, largely as the result of stimulated immigration, there are between 200,000 and 300,000 more workers than jobs.

13. The immigrants from the English-speaking islands or from the mainland are given preference over the native Porto Ricans, who speak Spanish. This has resulted in much hardship to the natives.

14. The strike of agricultural laborers and other workers which began in January, 1915, was not only justified but was in the interests of the progress of the island. The long hours, low wages, and exploitation of the laborers could not have been relieved except by their organized action. This is in accord with the testimony of the Government representatives.

15. These laborers, hitherto unorganized, excitable, and filled with a sense of the grievous wrongs which they and their families had suffered, were poorly disciplined and may have been guilty of excesses of speech and action, although there is much evidence to indicate that they were peaceful and law-abiding until provoked by the agents of the employers or by the police.

16. Whatever may have been the actions of the strikers, however, there can be no excuse for the actions of the police and municipal authorities, who violated the personal rights of the strikers, treated them in many cases with wanton brutality, resulting in the death of large numbers, held them in excessive bail, denied them access to the ordinary processes of the courts, and inflicted excessive and unwarranted punishments upon them.

17. The blame for such conditions appears to rest primarily upon the rural police and local magistrates.

18. The demands for legislation made by the representatives of the Free Federation of Labor of Porto Rico appear to be wise and reasonable, but without an opportunity for full local investigation it is impossible to fully indorse them.

It is suggested that the commission recommend provision by Congress for early and thorough investigation of the industrial and social conditions in Porto Rico and all other American colonies.

XXII. CHINESE EXCLUSION.

The investigations with reference to that section of the act which directed the commission to inquire " into the question of smuggling or other illegal entry of Asiatics into the United States or its insular possessions " were made largely under the direction of Mr. E. A. Fitzpatrick and Mr. E. H. Busiek. The extensive evidence collected regarding this entire question is contained in the report of Mr. Fitzpatrick, which is submitted herewith.

The constructive suggestions and recommendations which have been approved by the special subcommittee on Chinese exclusion, consisting of Chairman Frank P. Walsh and Commissioners Harris Weinstock and James O'Connell, and accepted by the entire commission, with reservations as to the agency of administration, are as follows:

CONSTRUCTIVE SUGGESTIONS.

CHANGES IN THE LAW.

The following changes should be made in the law in the interest of administrative efficiency:

1. That the many laws relating to the exclusion of Chinese be codified into a comprehensive statute.

2. That Chinese alleged to have entered the United States surreptitiously shall be tried by administrative process, i. e., on Secretary of Labor's warrant—in all cases irrespective of time of entry or defense of citizenship.[1] At the present time only Chinese alleged to have entered within three years may be tried on Secretary's warrant.

3. That immigration officers be specifically given the power of arrest or taking into custody.

4. That immigration officers be given the right to administer binding oaths in all cases arising under the immigration law.

5. That immigration officials be given the power to compel attendance of witnesses and the production of documentary or other evidence in all cases providing for punishment for contempt.

6. That the attacking of an immigration official or interference with him in the performance of his duties, or any maltreatment of him growing out of the performance of his duties, should be made a penal offense.

7. That the place of deportation to which contraband Chinamen shall be sent may be, in the discretion of the Secretary of Labor, the country whence he came, or the country of his citizenship, or the trans-Atlantic or trans-Pacific port from which he embarked for this continent.

8. That there be a clearer and more definite legislative definition of the exempt and of the admitted classes.

9. That there be a clearer definition of legislative policy as to the status under the immigration and Chinese-exclusion law of Chinamen admitted as exempts and subsequently assuming a nonexempt status.

10. That the pecuniary and family conditions for the return of Chinese laborers in the United States to China be repealed.

11. That the recommendation of a new registration because it is needed to enforce the present law be rejected. This must not be understood to mean a rejection of a new registration law as a part of legislative policy, but solely when it is urged for administrative reasons.

12. That masters of vessels be responsible for every Chinese member of their crew who was on board the vessel when it enters and is not on board when it is ready for clearance.

---

[1] *The anomalous citizenship situation.*—A Chinese person can not become a citizen by naturalization. The child of a Chinese alien man and woman, who themselves could never become citizens, would be, if born in the United States, an American citizen. The fact that the parents never intend that the child should be an American citizen, and the child itself even when grown up never regards himself as an American citizen except for purposes of the Chinese exclusion law, does not enter into the matter. The child of an American citizen born on foreign soil—China or elsewhere—is an American citizen.

Chinese arrested for being unlawfully in the United States set up the claim of nativity. This claim is in many cases fraudulent. The matter is easy. A Chinaman, when arrested, is told to stand mute, or, if the story has been concocted, he tells a story like this: " I was born in San Francisco [or in some rural place, where there are no records of birth]. My father and mother returned to China when I was four years old. I remained with my clansman, Mr. Y-M-G, who has since returned to China or died. For the past four years I have remained with my uncle, who was at the baptismal—shaving—feast, and can testify to these facts." Uncle testifies. United States commissioner discharges the Chinaman, and if nativity was the defense the citizenship of the Chinaman is res judicata. Thus are citizens made.

A rather dangerous situation is developing in this connection. In one large city of the country definite efforts are being made to vote the Chinaman and have his citizenship established that way. This of necessity brings the question into local politics and complicates further an already awkward situation. This situation ought to be cleared up. The fundamental change required is an amendment to the Constitution.

UNITED STATES COMMISSIONERS.

1. That the jurisdiction of United States commissioners in Chinese-exclusion cases be abolished, or, what is less desirable.[1]

2. That the following changes in the system be made: United States commissioners should receive adequate compensation for the service rendered. United States commissioners should be made courts of record and stenographic and other expenses provided for. The Government should be given right of appeal in Chinese cases.

THE JUDICIAL SYSTEM.

1. That the handling of cases of contraband Chinamen should be handled by administrative rather than by judicial procedure.

2. That the present administrative procedure be continued practically without modification, except for the improved handling of appeals as recommended elsewhere in these suggestions.

3. That writs of habeas corpus should be issued only on the basis of a prima facie case.

4. That in criminal cases (smuggling) full sentences should be imposed instead of light sentences as at present.

5. That, if advisable, the cases of contraband Chinamen might be held under the board of special inquiry procedure provided for in cases of immigrants not passed upon primary inspection for admission. The adoption of this suggestion would necessitate the employment of a considerable number of additional men, and for this reason ought not to be adopted immediately.

GENERAL ADMINISTRATION.

1. Definitely withdraw the order of 1905.

2. By conference with Treasury Department provide for more careful sealing and supervision of sealed freight cars crossing the border—

(a) By placing seal number and place of each car on the manifest.

(b) By taking number and place of each seal of each car independently and testing seal.

(c) By comparing local record with manifest immediately.

(d) By examination of contents of each car where there is the least discrepancy or suspicion.

THE SELECTION OF INSPECTORS.

1. That the position of Chinese inspector be revived.

2. That the selection of Chinese inspectors by civil-service examination for general immigrant inspectors be continued.

3. That the present examination be changed in scope as follows:

(a) That all papers now required be omitted except "practical questions."

---

[1] All interests would be best served by an administrative rather than a judicial procedure in cases of contraband Chinese. As usual, writs of habeas corpus would be issued by the courts in case of arbitrary action or of jurisdiction in these cases.

(*b*) That greater credit—larger proportion of examination—be given for practical experience in handling the public.

(*o*) That new examination in report writing be given to include a practical test in condensation—material to relate to immigration, formulation of a report on a given statement of fact, letter writing.

(*d*) That the examination include a test on Canadian immigration laws.

(*e*) That it include a test of knowledge of our National Government, particularly of those departments that are related to the work of immigration—

Treasury Department.

Congress.

The judicial system.

Department of State.

(*f*) That, if possible, an oral examination be included.

(*g*) That the examination include somewhere questions on the relation of immigration and emigration to a national policy, on immigration as an internal policy, and a general history of immigration.

4. That the examination have specific reference in its questions to immigration work and not be mere general tests.

5. That Chinese inspectors be selected from the more experienced immigrant inspectors who show an inclination and ability in the special requirements of this end of the service.

6. That the probationary period of an immigrant inspector be one year.

CHINESE INTERPRETERS.

1. That in the selection of interpreters the present examination be continued except that, in testing ability to translate or interpret, actual cases be taken in course of routine work rather than the present moot examination.

2. That in securing candidates for positions as interpreters the Immigration Service should look to the large number of Chinese students in our universities, particularly those who are here at the expense of the United States Government (the Boxer indemnity money).

3. That the position of Chinese interpreter be graded into two grades at least, as follows:

(*a*) Those who can interpret the spoken Chinese of one or more dialects.

(*b*) Those who can in addition read the written language.

4. That the salary program outlined for inspectors be adapted to the interpreters.

5. That a conference be arranged by the various departments of Government who use interpreters of Chinese to work out some plan of securing honest, capable interpreters—perhaps in cooperation with the universities.

A STAFF ORGANIZATION AT WASHINGTON.

1. That there be established at Washington a staff organization including at least—

(*a*) Another Assistant Secretary of Labor to handle Chinese appeal cases, etc.

(*b*) A central law organization providing for the continuous study of the legal aspects of immigration.

(*c*) A central Chinese smuggling bureau, reenforcing district administration in its attempt to deal with smuggling gangs and other organized smuggling.

(*d*) A central agency of training and inspection, providing for the continuous supervision and training of the men in the service.

(*e*) A central clearing house of information and records.

2. That it be specifically made a function of the division of supervision and training to keep district officers informed as to—

(*a*) Significant court decisions in all districts.

(*b*) Significant discoveries of district offices, e. g., the Japanese (Korean) passport case.

(*c*) Effective methods of handling particular situations, e. g., of commissioner who refuses to give full credence to preliminary hearings before immigrant inspectors by bringing contraband Chinamen immediately before commissioner.

(*d*) Chinese refused papers in any place.

3. That this organization should keep field officers informed as to forward steps and other significant developments.

SALARY PLAN.

1. That the service be regarded for salary purposes as a unit rather than as 23 individual units.

2. That the administrative officers work out a detailed plan of graded salary increases.

3. That there be an annual increase in salary of a definite amount for a definite number of years of service upon certification of meritorious service during the preceding year. On the basis of an initial salary of $1,380, it seems to us there ought to be an annual increase of at least $36 per year for 15 years, making a maximum salary of $1,920. The specific amounts named are offered as suggestions.

4. That positions in the service ought to be graded and correspondingly higher initial salaries provided for the higher grades. The system of annual increases, perhaps of the same amount, ought to be provided here. A larger increase for a less number of years might be advisable. It should be provided in this connection that a man promoted from a lower to a higher position, if he is receiving a higher salary than the initial salary of the higher position, should receive the next higher salary to the salary he is receiving in the lower position. A person standing in a little house watching those who come across an international bridge in Suspension Falls, another doing primary inspection work or board of inquiry work at Ellis Island, another working " under cover " among the thugs of Buffalo and being beaten into insensibility, another doing train inspection work—would receive no pay because of differences of duties. It is submitted that some recognition of this difference in duties ought to find expression in the salary schedule.

5. Superior service should be rewarded both by formal commendation and by salary increases. Two provisions might be included:

(*a*) The reward for a single brilliant piece of work, such as working under cover with smugglers, risking one's life, and landing the gang in jail.

(*b*) The provision of a higher annual increase for men giving continuous superior service.

REDISTRICTING.

1. That there be a redistricting of the United States for immigration purposes with more regard to geographical facts and to the efficiency of the service.

2. That district offices take a periodic census in cooperation with the State or National Census or both, or, if necessary, independent of each. (This would help local offices to really see their problems. It would acquaint them with their constituency.)

3. That this census be kept up to date and supplemented by cooperation with municipal and State boards of health and bureaus of vital statistics by recording currently—
    (*a*) Chinese births.
    (*b*) Chinese deaths.
    (*c*) Chinese marriages.

4. That this census be kept up to date and supplemented by making part of the record all the examinations of Chinese in connection with routine and other investigations. A system of cross reference cards should be on file in Washington. It should be kept up to date and supplemented by listing removals and advising as far as possible the district to which the Chinaman moved.

5. That the force should be increased and the whole group of inspectors be organized for regular field work. This should take the place of any system of national arrest crews.

6. That the system of rewards of conductors, trainmen, and policemen who supply information leading to arrests of contraband Chinese or smugglers, which seems now in abeyance, be revived and be provided for in an emergency fund for each district. (Approval of Washington perhaps should be required in each case.)

7. That a business and occupation census of each district accompany the census of persons.

8. That the force of immigrant inspectors assigned to Chinese work be increased.

9. That the equipment to be used in the work of administering the Chinese exclusion law be adequate to cope with the smugglers.

FRANK P. WALSH.[1]
JOHN B. LENNON.[1]
JAMES O'CONNELL.[1]
AUSTIN B. GARRETSON.[1]

---

[1] See supplemental statement.

SUPPLEMENTAL STATEMENT OF CHAIRMAN FRANK P. WALSH.

Charged by your honorable body with an investigation to discover the underlying causes of dissatisfaction in the industrial situation, we herewith present the following findings and conclusions, and we urge for them the most earnest consideration, not only by the Congress, but by the people of the Nation, to the end that evils which threaten to defeat American ideals and to destroy the well-being of the Nation may be generally recognized and effectively attacked.

WE FIND THE BASIC CAUSE OF INDUSTRIAL DISSATISFACTION TO BE LOW WAGES; OR, STATED IN ANOTHER WAY, THE FACT THAT THE WORKERS OF THE NATION, THROUGH COMPULSORY AND OPPRESSIVE METHODS, LEGAL AND ILLEGAL, ARE DENIED THE FULL PRODUCT OF THEIR TOIL.

We further find that unrest among the workers in industry has grown to proportions that already menace the social good will and the peace of the Nation. Citizens numbering millions smart under a sense of injustice and of oppression, born of the conviction that the opportunity is denied them to acquire for themselves and their families that degree of economic well-being necessary for the enjoyment of those material and spiritual satisfactions which alone make life worth living.

Bitterness, bred of unfilled need for sufficient food, clothing, and shelter for themselves and their wives and children, has been further nourished in the hearts of these millions by resentment against the arbitrary power that enables the employer, under our present industrial system, to control not only the workman's opportunity to earn his bread, but ofttimes, through the exercise of this power, to dictate his social, political, and moral environment. By thwarting the human passion for liberty and the solicitude of the husband and father for his own, modern industry has kindled a spirit in these dissatisfied millions that lies deeper and springs from nobler impulses than physical need and human selfishness.

Among these millions and their leaders we have encountered a spirit religious in its fervor and in its willingness to sacrifice for a cause held sacred. And we earnestly submit that only in the light of this spirit can the aggressive propaganda of the discontented be understood and judged.

The extent and depth of industrial unrest can hardly be exaggerated. State and national conventions of labor organizations, numbering many thousands of members, have cheered the names of leaders imprisoned for participation in a campaign of violence, conducted as one phase of a conflict with organized employers. Thirty thousand workers in a single strike have followed the leadership of men who denounced government and called for relentless warfare on organized society. Employers from coast to coast have created and maintained small private armies of armed men and have used these forces to intimidate and suppress their striking employees by

158

deporting, imprisoning, assaulting, or killing their leaders. Elaborate spy systems are maintained to discover and forestall the movements of the enemy. The use of State troops in policing strikes has bred a bitter hostility to the militia system among members of labor organizations, and States have been unable to enlist wage earners for this second line of the Nation's defense. Courts, legislatures, and governors have been rightfully accused of serving employers to the defeat of justice, and, while counter charges come from employers and their agents, with almost negligible exceptions it is the wage earners who believe, assert, and prove that the very institutions of their country have been perverted by the power of the employer. Prison records for labor leaders have become badges of honor in the eyes of many of their people, and great mass meetings throughout the Nation cheer denunciations of courts and court decisions.

To the support of the militant and aggressive propaganda of organized labor has come, within recent years, a small but rapidly increasing host of ministers of the gospel, college professors, writers, journalists, and others of the professional classes, distinguished in many instances by exceptional talent which they devote to agitation, with no hope of material reward, and a devotion that can be explained only in the light of the fervid religious spirit which animates the organized industrial unrest.

We find the unrest here described to be but the latest manifestation of the age-long struggle of the race for freedom of opportunity for every individual to live his life to its highest ends. As the nobles of England wrung their independence from King John, and as the tradesmen of France broke through the ring of privilege inclosing the Three Estates, so to-day the millions who serve society in arduous labor on the highways, and aloft on scaffoldings, and by the sides of whirring machines, are demanding that they, too, and their children shall enjoy all of the blessings that justify and make beautiful this life.

The unrest of the wage earners has been augmented by recent changes and developments in industry. Chief of these are the rapid and universal introduction and extension of machinery of production, by which unskilled workers may be substituted for the skilled, and an equally rapid development of means of rapid transportation and communication, by which private capital has been enabled to organize in great corporations possessing enormous economic power. This tendency toward huge corporations and large factories has been furthered by the necessity of employing large sums of capital in order to purchase and install expensive machinery, the use of which is practicable only when production is conducted on a large scale. Work formerly done at home or in small neighborhood shops has been transferred to great factories where the individual worker becomes an impersonal element under the control of impersonal corporations, without voice in determining the conditions under which he works, and largely without interest in the success of the enterprise or the disposal of the product. Women in increasing numbers have followed their work from the home to the factory, and even children have been enlisted.

Now, more than ever, the profits of great industries under centralized control pour into the coffers of stockholders and directors who never have so much as visited the plants, and who perform no service in return. And while vast inherited fortunes, representing zero in social service to the credit of their possessors, automatically treble and multiply in volume, two-thirds of those who toil from 8 to 12 hours a day receive less than enough to support themselves and their families in decency and comfort. From childhood to the grave they dwell in the shadow of a fear that their only resource—their opportunity to toil—will be taken from them, through accident, illness, the caprice of a foreman, or the fortunes of industry. The lives of their babies are snuffed out by bad air in cheap lodgings, and the lack of nourishment and care which they can not buy. Fathers and husbands die or are maimed in accidents, and their families receive a pittance, or succumb in mid-life and they receive nothing.

And when these unfortunates seek, by the only means within reach, to better their lot by organizing to lift themselves from helplessness to some measure of collective power, with which to wring living wages from their employers, they find too often arrayed against them not only the massed power of capital, but every arm of the Government that was created to enforce guaranties of equality and justice.

We find that many entire communities exist under the arbitrary economic control of corporation officials charged with the management of an industry or group of industries, and we find that in such communities political liberty does not exist, and its forms are hollow mockeries. Give to the employer power to discharge without cause, to grant to or withhold from thousands the opportunity to earn bread, and the liberties of such a community lie in the hollow of the employer's hand. Free speech, free assembly, and a free press may be denied, as they have been denied time and again, and the employer's agents may be placed in public office to do his bidding.

In larger communities where espionage becomes impossible the wage earner who is unsupported by a collective organization may enjoy freedom of expression outside the workshop, but there his freedom ends. And it is a freedom more apparent than real. For the house he lives in, the food he eats, the clothing he wears, the environment of his wife and children, and his own health and safety are in the hands of the employer, through the arbitrary power which he exercises in fixing his wages and working conditions.

The social responsibility for these unfortunate conditions may be fixed with reasonable certainty. The responsibility, and such blame as attaches thereto, can not be held to rest upon employers, since in the maintenance of the evils of low wages, long hours, and bad factory conditions, and in their attempts to gain control of economic and political advantages which would promote their interests, they have merely followed the natural bent of men involved in the struggle of competitive industry. The responsibility for the conditions which have been described above we declare rests primarily upon the workers who, blind to their collective strength and oftentimes deaf to the cries of their fellows, have suffered exploitation and the invasion of their most sacred rights without resistance. A large measure of responsibility must, however, attach to the great mass of citizens who, though not directly involved in the struggle between capital and labor, have failed to realize that their own prosperity is dependent upon the welfare of all classes of the community, and that their rights are bound up with the rights of every other individual. But, until the workers themselves realize their responsibility and utilize to the full their collective power, no action, whether governmental or altruistic, can work any genuine and lasting improvement.

Fourteen years before Abraham Lincoln was called to the high office where he immortalized his name, he uttered these great truths:

Inasmuch as most good things are produced by labor, it follows that all such things of right belong to those whose labor has produced them. But it has so happened in all ages of the world that some have labored and others have without labor enjoyed a large proportion of the fruits. This is wrong and should not continue. To secure to each laborer the whole product of his labor, or as nearly as possible, is a worthy subject of any good Government.

With this lofty ideal for a goal, under the sublime leadership of the deathless Lincoln, we call upon our citizenship, regardless of politics or economic conditions, to use every means of agitation, all avenues of education, and every department and function of the Government, to eliminate the injustices exposed by this commission, to the end that each laborer may " secure the whole product of his labor."

FRANK P. WALSH.

NOTE.—Chairman Frank P. Walsh also presented the following dissenting opinion:

Although I have signed the report prepared by Mr. Basil M. Manly, director of research and investigation, because I believe it represents an unassailable statement of the existing industrial situation, because it fully complies with the requirements of the act of Congress creating the commission, and because the recommendations are as a whole wise and necessary for the welfare of the Nation, I, nevertheless, desire to record my dissent on the following points:

1. The recommendation for new administrative machinery for mediation and arbitration in the form of a special commission. I believe that the commission created by the Newlands Act, and the Department of Labor, if their powers are enlarged and they are adequately supported, will be fully able to deal with the situation.

2. The recommendations for a literacy test as a method of restricting immigration. I wish to record my opposition, as a matter of principle, to all restrictions upon immigration.

3. The recommendations regarding civil government in such isolated communities as coal camps, which I believe can not be adequately dealt with except by the Government taking over all coal lands and leasing them upon terms which will make possible their operation upon a cooperative basis by the workers.

Notwithstanding many meritorious statements contained in the report of Commissioners John R. Commons and Florence J. Harriman, I feel it my duty to dissent from the same in toto, for the reasons following:

1. It wholly fails to comply with the law creating the commission, in that it does not set forth the facts regarding the condition of labor in the leading industries of the United States and the underlying causes of industrial dissatisfaction.

2. The whole scheme of the control of labor, and the laws governing the same, is undemocratic and not in accord with the established principles of representative government.

3. The entire plan suggested is opposed to the habits, customs, and traditions of the American people.

4. The suggestions in the main are impractical and impossible of performance.

5. It opens up unlimited opportunities for graft and corruption.

6. If the ponderous legal machinery provided for in this report could be put in operation throughout our Nation, it would mean— (a) that the economic condition of the workers of the country would be absolutely subjected to the whim or caprice of an army of officials, deputies, and Government employees, and (b) the establishment of an autocratic control over the business operations of manufacturers, merchants, and other employers, repugnant to American standards of freedom in manufacture and commerce.

SUPPLEMENTAL STATEMENT OF COMMISSIONER AUSTIN B. GARRETSON.

My signature is appended to the report of Mr. Basil M. Manly, director of research and investigation of the United States Commission on Industrial Relations, submitted to the commission and transmitted herewith, as to the findings of fact contained therein.

I am in general agreement with the recommendations contained in that report except as to the formation of the system of State and Federal commissions and a Federal industrial council.

On this recommendation I neither approve nor condemn. But out of regard for the opinion of the great body of intrastate labor most directly affected, I dissent.

I am also in accord with the statement of fact contained in the report of George P. West on the Colorado situation.

I am favorable to the extension of the provisions of the Newlands Act to all classes of interstate employees who can constitutionally be brought under its provisions and would favor the enlargement of the body administering it to meet the added responsibilities which would thereby be placed upon it, but limiting the powers thereof to the settlement of industrial disagreements and to the gathering of information germane to their mission.

I favor the creation of State commissions, similarly constituted and acting in corelation and understanding with the Federal board.

I heartily concur with the report of Commissioners Lennon and O'Connell except on those points where disagreement is herein noted. I dissent in whole from report rendered by Commissioner J. R. Commons. I render individual opinion and suggestion only on—

CAUSES UNDERLYING INDUSTRIAL UNREST.

Any student who accepts and applies the belief that the "proper study of mankind is man" can not fail to trace certain fundamental causes, general in their character, which underlie industrial unrest which will continue to grow until either the causes are peacefully removed or revolution ensues.

To me there appear to be four of these basic causes.

The first lies in the inequitable distribution of the fruits of industry.

Our industrial system makes it possible for one man, in only a portion of the span of human productive life, to take unto himself and claim as his own a fortune of a hundred millon dollars or more, while millions of deserving men, availing themselves of every opportunity for unremitting toil, are only able to secure a grave in the potters' field or else burden their families with an installment debt for the cost of interment.

158

The creation of such colossal fortune naturally breeds in the mind of the possessor the sentiment, belief, and practice that he is superior to society and not subject to the law. The possession thereof makes him unregardful of the opinions of society or of the mandates of the law, incites him to disregard and hold himself independent of the moral precepts and beliefs of society and tends toward the effort to prostitute the administration of justice, and under the present system renders him practically immune from the penalties prescribed by the law.

The transmission to heirs or trustees, degenerate or otherwise, of fortunes so vast or of business interests so far-reaching makes them the virtual arbiters of the destiny of hundreds of thousands of their fellow beings in regard to whom they have neither sympathetic feeling, intelligent interest, nor humanitarian desire, and the testimony before this commission has made it evident that in some instances these heirs or representatives even resent the imputation that any obligation whatever can rest upon them for the welfare of the said fellow beings or that even intelligent knowledge as to what would constitute well-being should be required of them.

Second, the methods of the formation and administration of law would in themselves justify undying, righteous unrest from the fact that they create, encourage, and demonstrate knowledge and belief that there is no equality before the law as between the man who has and the man who has not.

Primarily there is the trend through legislation to exalt the property right at the expense of the personal right. Next, the tendency of a great majority of our courts to extend and amplify this trend. This appears in the declaring unconstitutional of a great portion of the legislation that in later years is appearing if it in any way restricts the rights of property, while at the same time any legislative act which tends to make effective the constitutional, personal right of the individual is nullified upon the same ground.

In other words, to exalt money above man.

The tendency also of a large number of the same tribunals is to legalize the maintenance of armed forces, either by the corporation or the large individual employer, and the virtual levying of war through the use of the State militia as a private guard for property interests, or as an economic weapon for the purpose of prejudicing the interests of the worker, is abetted and approved, while at the same time rigorously prosecuting and punishing the individual for taking any similar action, individually or collectively, in defense of his person or his family.

Thus the man who uses a deadly weapon to protect himself or his home against the aggression of hired thugs has set in motion against him the whole machinery of the State, while the corporation which enlisted, equipped, and paid a private armed force, formed and used not for the maintenance of peace or the protection of property but solely as an economic weapon, is lauded as a conservator of peace, law, and order.

Our laws deal strictly and effectively with those who contribute to the delinquency of an individual, but the hirelings of a corporation may debauch a State for their own economic gain and receive only laudation from those who " sit in the seats of the mighty."

The man who, on account of hunger of himself or family, steals a loaf is held up to public view as a " horrible example " of the increase of crime and decadence of the moral sense, while he who exploits the public or by dishonest or fraudulent representation or manipulation secures millions of their money is by the same agencies held up to the youth of the land as an example of what intelligent effort and devotion to business may accomplish.

The system of wholesale arrests during industrial disturbances for acts which, committed under ordinary conditions and when no industrial disturbances prevailed, would not constitute ground for arrest, is one of the significant indications of the use of governmental agencies, not as a preserver of peace but as a purely economic weapon.

The intrusion of what has been aptly described as "invisible government" into all the chanels of life—the educational system, primary, secondary, and higher, the church, the press, the legislative branch, and the judicial system—and the recognized potency of its meretricious efforts contributes its elements to the whole.

Third, irregularity of employment, with the consequent restriction of opportunity and with its consequent extension of belief that unremitting toil under present conditions can bring no fair recompense, thus stifling healthy incentive to labor, is creating an army of unemployed that must, in the last analysis, be reckoned with, and unless remedy is found whereby incentive may be restored and recompense be made apparent, society itself must pay the forfeit.

Fourth, land monopoly with resulting prohibitive price, the greatest influence in creating congestion in the cities, bears its own share of the responsibility for unrest.

Tracing the history of every vanished civilization makes apparent the fact that in every instance decadence was preceded by urban congestion and by immense land holdings by the aristocrat or the capitalist.

As to the remedy for these evils, an income and inheritance tax that would be, above a certain figure, absolutely confiscatory would make impossible, first, the creation, and, second, the transmission of the dominating accumulation of wealth in the hands of any individual, group, or family. When the unlimited power of reward or purchase had ceased to exist, the subconscious tendency of legislatures and of those who interpret and administer the law to be subservient to property interests would of necessity disappear.

It is worth consideration as to whether or not a limitation can properly be set upon profit in a business enterprise.

Every code, ancient and modern, prescribes penalties for usury, and modern codes define the rate of interest permitted. Therefore, if a man loans money, he can only demand what is described as the legal rate for the use thereof.

Is it, or is not, equally consistent for the Government to prescribe a rate beyond which profit shall not extend?

In the question of dealing with land, should not the same doctrine be applied to land that in the arid States is applied to water, i. e., that no more land can be held by an individual than he can put to productive " use," thus making unused land revert to the State and acquirable by those who would utilize it?

A. B. GARRETSON.

SUPPLEMENTAL STATEMENT OF COMMISSIONERS JOHN B. LENNON AND JAMES O'CONNELL.

Our signatures are appended to the report of Mr. Basil M. Manly, director of research and investigation of the United States Commission on Industrial Relations, submitted to the commission at its session held in Chicago during the months of July and August, 1915, except that portion of the report recommending a system of mediation, conciliation, investigation, and arbitration, applicable to both State and Nation, which proposes to create a commission of three members, together with an advisory council of 20 members, 10 representing employers and 10 representing employees. The entire plan is set forth in the report of the staff as submitted to the Commission on Industrial Relations; also in a report to the commission by Prof. George E. Barnett, and also in the report of Commissioner John R. Commons. From these recommendations we dissent for reasons assigned in this statement.

The evidence submitted to the commission at public hearings, together with the evidence secured by special investigators, has been fairly set forth in Mr. Manly's report and with even justice to all, whether employers, employees, or the public.

CRITICISMS NOT JUSTIFIED.

Our fellow commissioners who are representatives of the employers contend in their statement that the report of Mr. Basil M. Manly for the staff is deficient in that it does not properly present an indictment against labor on the grounds of fostering and promoting violence in trade disputes, jurisdictional disputes accompanied by strikes, limitation of output, sympathetic strikes, contract breaking, apprenticeship rules, refusal to use nonunion materials, alleged graft, and so forth, and that it does not include these things among the fundamental causes of industrial unrest. All the evidence submitted to the commission, as we understand and interpret it, proves that these things, in so far as they do exist, are in no sense causes of industrial unrest but, on the contrary, are evidences of existing industrial unrest and are evils that are incidental to a situation wherein labor has at times been forced to fight with such weapons as it could command for advantages and rights that in justice should be freely accorded to the wage earners. So long as labor organizations are forced by employers to fight for the mere right to exist, and so long as wages paid to labor are so low that the unorganized wage earner often sees no choice except that between resorting to such weapons or seeing himself and his family sink below the poverty line, just so long will these evils at times manifest themselves as symptoms of the worker's desperation. The union, fighting for its right to live, is sometimes forced to tolerate

acts that would not be countenanced if its entity were secure and its
energies were not absorbed in fighting for existence.

STRONG ORGANIZATIONS THE CURE.

Experience shows that the evils complained of rapidly disappear
in labor organizations as soon as the organization prevails over the
opposition of the employers and establishes its right to organize.
Strong unions mean decent wages, and decent wages raise wage
earners to a plane of thought and action where all their acts and
mental processes must no longer be directed toward a desperate
struggle for the very right of themselves and families to live.

Organized labor fully realizes how unfortunate it is that labor in
its struggle for existence has occasionally been driven to consider its
immediate advantage at the expense of the true economic principles
that must govern in the long run. All the energies of organized
labor's representatives have been exerted to minimize or eliminate
any tendency toward limitation of output or jurisdictional disputes,
but, at the same time, organized labor insists that these tendencies
where they exist are the logical and inevitable outgrowth of evils in
industry that can be removed only by trade-union action by the
wage earners. We could cite evidence at great length to show that
the tendencies complained of, so far as they exist at all, have grown
out of the hard necessities with which labor has been confronted.
It is enough here to quote briefly from the testimony of the distinguished economist, Prof. Jacob H. Hollander, of Johns Hopkins
University, given before this commission in New York City on
January 20, 1915. Prof. Hollander in discussing the limitation of
output said:

We lose sight of the fact that trade-unions and unionists are not soldiering
in the matter, but they are animated by a very high degree of fraternity
in the matter, that they are willing to adopt the same principle if it is a matter
of piecework instead of time work; that the endeavor of society should be to
bring back industrial conditions from that unwholesome mess into which they
have slumped from this abnormal disproportionate allotment of workers to
particular fields in excess of the requirements in those fields. We must without
deviating one iota from the proposition which you have stated that it is socially
unsound that workmen should do less than they properly could—society should
seek to bring about conditions where they will do what they can without involving displacement and unemployment on the part of their fellow workmen.

We hold that the report of Mr. Manly contains no statement that
is unworthy of credence, and that will not bear careful investigation.
The conclusions and recommendations are warranted by the statement of facts and the accumulated evidence in the hands of the
commission.

THE EVIDENCE.

All evidence accumulated, whether by special investigators or at
public hearings, will be submitted to Congress, and we trust the people of our country will demand that it be published in full, particularly the following, which are well worth the most careful study by
all persons interested in human welfare. The reports cited below
have been prepared by competent investigators and were submitted
to the commission after careful investigation and verification by

Director Basil M. Manly and by members of the commission, and are the latest information upon the various subjects covered by them.[1]

Evidence Taken at All Public Hearings.

Causes of Industrial Unrest, by Mr. W. J. Lauck.

Violence in Labor Disputes, by Mr. Luke Grant.

Structural Iron Workers, by Mr. Luke Grant.

Sickness Prevention and Insurance, by Dr. B. S. Warren.

Mediation, Arbitration, and Investigation, by Prof. Geo. E. Barnett.

Conditions of Labor in Principal Industries, by Mr. Edgar Sydenstricker.

Efficiency Systems in Industry, by Prof. Robert F. Hoxie, Mr. John P. Frey, and Mr. Robert G. Valentine.

Industrial Education, by Commissioner John B. Lennon.

Labor Complaints and Claims, by Mr. P. A. Speek.

Trade-Union Law, by Mr. J. W. Bryan.

Colorado Situation, by Mr. George P. West.

The Telephone and Telegraph Industry, by Mr. Christopher T. Chenery.

Labor Conditions in Porto Rico, by Mr. Christopher T. Chenery.

Labor Conditions in the Black Hills, by Mr. William P. Harvey.

Labor Conditions in Los Angeles, by Mr. William P. Harvey.

Preliminary Report on the Land Question, by Mr. Charles W, Holman.

Agricultural Labor and Tenancy, by Mr. John L. Coulter.

Unemployment, by Mr. William M. Leiserson.

Extent and Growth of Labor Organizations, by Mr. Lee Wolman.

Injunctions in Labor Disputes, by Mr. Edwin E. Witte.

The Inferior Courts and Police of Paterson, N. J., by Mr. Redmond S. Brennan and Mr. Patrick F. Gill.

Chinese Exclusion, by Mr. Edward A. Fitzpatrick.

EXTENT OF UNREST.

The principal duty imposed, under the law creating the commission, was to seek to ascertain the causes of industrial unrest and offer such recommendations as we believe might alleviate that unrest. There can be no question but that unrest exists, in some instances, to an alarming extent. Thousands and tens of thousands of our people feel that they are deprived, under existing conditions in industry, of an opportunity to secure for themselves and their families a standard of living commensurate with the best ideals of manhood, womanhood, and childhood. They resent the fact that the existing system of the distribution of wealth creates at one end of our industrial scale a few multi-millionaires and at the other end thousands and tens of thousands of men, women, and children who are at all times in a situation where they are uncertain as to where their next meal will come from. Hungry, poorly clothed, and without the opportunities that a fully rounded life requires, they become filled with a sullen resentment that bodes no good for the future of our Republic.

We have found men and women who are inclined to ascribe this condition to the fact that the Government exercises no power of mandatory character to prevent strikes and lockouts. Many have

---

[1] These reports have not been printed with this document, on the recommendation of Chairman Frank P. Walsh, as stated in his letter in Senate Report No. 143, Sixty-fourth Congress. The reports on Structural Iron Workers and the Colorado Situation were printed by the commission itself in 1915.

been the propositions submitted to us for compulsory arbitration or, at least, compulsory investigation with power to recommend a settlement. Some have proposed an elaborate machinery, to be set up by the General Government, and of a similar character by the States, providing for conciliation, mediation, arbitration, and investigation, all of which, while without definite compulsory features, establishes a legal machinery that must of necessity exercise an influence in that direction.

The plan for the creation of an industrial commission, both national and State, proposes to assign to a commission of three members the administration of all labor laws of either State or Nation, giving to them powers far in excess of those exercised by the President of the United States or the governor of any State. This we believe to be bureaucracy run mad, and a subversion of democracy dangerous to the civil and social liberty of all citizens. We hold that all power should be, in the final analysis, with the people, and we, therefore, dissent from any such plan.

NEW GOVERNMENTAL MACHINERY UNWISE.

The activities of such a commission, supplemented by the proposed advisory committees of employers and labor representatives, would be so balanced as to prevent substantial progress and tend to perpetuate present conditions. Such a plan conceives of labor and capital as static forces and of the relations between them as always to remain unchanging.

We believe that the work now being done by the Department of Labor in industry generally, and by the Board of Mediation and Conciliation, dealing with interstate public utilities, is better than any that could be expected of any additional board that has been suggested to this commission. We believe that the Department of Labor, with further experience and larger appropriations, will develop a high state of efficiency in adjusting labor disputes that are capable of being adjusted by anyone other than the parties directly interested and will adequately carry on the work provided by the law creating the Department of Labor, to wit:

SECTION 1. The purpose of the Department of Labor shall be to foster, promote, and develop the welfare of the wage earners in the United States, to improve their working conditions, and to advance their opportunities for profitable employment.

SEC. 8. The Secretary of Labor shall have power to act as mediator and to appoint commissioners of conciliation in labor disputes whenever in his judgment the interests of industrial peace require it to be done.

We favor the extension of the Newlands Act to cover all employees engaged in interstate commerce, such as the railroad telegraphers, the shop and track men employed by railroads, the employees of express companies, of the Pullman Co., of commercial telegraph and telephone companies, and other public utilities performing interstate service that, in the interest of the Nation, must be continuous.

The evidence submitted to this commission is substantially to the effect that where trade-union organization exists among the workers, there, at the same time, exists the least amount of industrial unrest of a character that is dangerous to the peace and welfare of our Nation. It is true that the union men and women are not satisfied with their conditions; they are not, however, despondent as to the possibility of securing better conditions; they know what the unions have accomplished, and they have an abiding faith that their further desires can be attained.

Instead of any elaborate machinery for the prevention of strikes or lockouts we are convinced, from the testimony gathered by this commission, that the most effectual course that can be pursued to bring about general contentment among our people, based upon a humane standard of living, is the promotion of labor organization. The most casual investigator will soon discover that in those lines of industry where organization of labor is the strongest, there is the least danger of industrial revolt that would endanger the fundamental principles of our Government and the maintenance of a nation with respect for law and order. Where organization is lacking dangerous discontent is found on every hand; low wages and long hours prevail; exploitation in every direction is practiced; the people become sullen, have no regard for law or government, and are, in reality, a latent volcano, as dangerous to society as are the volcanoes of nature to the landscape surrounding them.

THE ONE TRUE REMEDY.

We therefore urge as the great remedy for such unnecessary industrial unrest as we have found more, and more, and still more organization of labor and of the employers in each industry as well. The education of the trade unions has been conducive to a higher and better citizenship. In recent years there have come to our assistance scores and hundreds and thousands of people outside the ranks of unionists—ministers, professors, journalists, professional men of all kinds—who have reached the conclusion that is herein stated, that the most efficient cure for such industrial unrest as should be cured, is union organization.

We hold that efforts to stay the organization of labor or to restrict the right of employees to organize should not be tolerated, but that the opposite policy should prevail, and the organization of the trade unions and of the employers' organizations should be promoted, not, however, for the sole purpose of fighting each other, but for the commendable purpose of collective bargaining and the establishing of industrial good will. Organizations of employers that have no object in view except to prevent labor having a voice in fixing the conditions of industry under which it is employed have no excuse for existence, as they are a bar to social tranquillity and a detriment to the economic progress of our country. The evidence before the commission shows that organized labor has no desire, nor has it attempted, to control the business of the employer. It insists that it has a right to a voice, and a potent voice, in determining the conditions under which it shall work. This attitude, we are sure, will be continued in spite of the opposition of any so-called employers' organizations. This country is no longer a field for slavery, and where men and women are compelled, in order that they may live, to work under conditions in determining which they have no voice, they are not far removed from a condition existing under feudalism or slavery.

In emphasizing with all the force at our command the necessity of collective action by wage earners through strong organizations, if the problem of industrial unrest is to be solved, we wish again to quote from testimony of Prof. Hollander. He undertook to sum up for this commission those conclusions regarding the solution of this problem that have been reached not only by himself, but by the great body of economists in this country and abroad. He said:

The opinion of political economists in so far as I can voice it is that social unrest, which is manifest not only in this country but in every industrial country, is due to the existence of economic want or poverty, if by that we understand not on the one hand pauperism or on the other economic inequality. By poverty I mean the existence of large areas of industrial society in receipt of incomes less than enough to maintain themselves and those dependent upon them in decent existence. We believe that is the consequence, not of any absolute dearth—that the world produces enough to go around; that it is, therefore, not a question of insufficient production, but of defects in distribution. * * * There is a view among economists that there is nothing in any current theory of wages that precludes the laborer from obtaining a sufficient wage, and that if he fails it must be in consequence of the fact that he enters into the wage contract on a plane of inequality. The wage contract, in short, is the result of a bargain between the employer and the employee, and if the employer is in a superior competitive position by reason of combination and the laborer is unorganized he is at a bargaining disadvantage which is certain to redound to his hurt.

I think political economists accordingly then are in agreement that trade unionism is essential as a means of bringing the workmen into industrial bargaining on a plane of equality.

*   *   *   *   *

You have asked specifically what the remedy [for poverty] is. It means a very decided revulsion of opinion as to trade unionism. The general attitude among employers of labor is often open and decided opposition to organized labor. Until society recognizes the unwisdom of that attitude and demands that the laborer must enter into his wage bargain on a plane of competitive equality, society has not lifted its finger to remedy that evil.

THE PUBLIC'S DUTY.

We submit the report of Mr. Basil M. Manly as our report, asking for it the fullest possible consideration by the men and women of our country who are interested in the social and moral uplift of humanity.

Labor must work out its own salvation. Wageworkers can attain that degree of well-being to which they are entitled only by their own efforts. The general public can not be expected to do for them what they fail to do for themselves, nor would it be desirable that those rights and benefits to which they are entitled should be handed down to them by the Government or by organized society as grace from above. But the general public is vitally interested in the efforts of wageworkers to win for themselves equal justice and such a degree of material well-being as will enable them to maintain themselves and their families in comfort, security, and health. Society's interest in the triumph of labor's cause should spring not only from the love of justice and the human sympathy that animates every good citizen, but from a realization that industrial and social evils menacing large groups of the population can not continue without eventually bringing disaster to society as a whole. While inviting the aid of every good citizen, we, as representatives of organized labor, urge that this aid be directed not solely to seeking new legislation or new governmental machinery designed as a cure-all, but to giving moral support to labor's own efforts, and insisting that trade unions be fostered and encouraged as the most effective agencies making for the wage-workers' progress.

We concur in, and adopt as a part of our report, the statement under the heading "Supplemental statement of Chairman Frank P. Walsh."

We concur in the dissenting opinion of Chairman Frank P. Walsh from the report of Commissioners John R. Commons and Florence J. Harriman.

We concur in that part of the report of Commissioner Austin B. Garretson under the heading "Causes underlying industrial unrest."

We concur in the history and statement of facts regarding the Colorado strike, as written by Mr. George P. West, which is printed as an addendum to this report.[1]

JOHN B. LENNON.
JAMES O'CONNELL.

---

[1] The report by Mr. George P. West has not been printed with this document, on the recommendation of Chairman Frank P. Walsh, as it was printed by the commission itself in 1915. See his letter in Senate Report No. 143, Sixty-fourth Congress.

II.

Report of Commissioners John R. Commons and Florence J. Harriman

SIGNED BY

Commissioners Commons, Harriman, Weinstock, Ballard, and Aishton

TOGETHER WITH

The Dissenting Opinion of Commissioner Weinstock, the Report of Commissioners Weinstock, Ballard, and Aishton, and the Supplemental Statement of Commissioner Thurston

REPORT OF COMMISSIONERS JOHN R. COMMONS AND FLORENCE J. HARRIMAN.

ENACTMENT, INTERPRETATION, AND ENFORCEMENT OF LABOR LAW.

We can not find ourselves able to agree to any of the findings or recommendations of the staff or any resolutions based upon them, because they have not the criticism of employers, employees, and others affected by them, which we consider indispensable in order that we might have before us assurance that they were accurate and not chargeable with important omissions. These reasons are stated more fully in paragraph 4 following, and are equally appropriate for those who refuse to sign this report. We find ourselves unable to agree with other recommendations and resolutions for legislation, because they contain few or no practicable suggestions for legislation that would be enforceable, or because they are directed to making a few individuals scapegoats, where what is needed is serious attention to the system that produces the demand for scapegoats, and with it the breakdown of labor legislation in this country. In this way we interpret the act of Congress which requires us to inquire "into the scope, methods, and resources of existing bureaus of labor and into possible ways of increasing their usefulness." From our personal experience we agree with many of the alleged findings and with the objects intended to be accomplished by the enactment of proposed laws, but we consider that it is not worth while to propose any more laws until we have provided methods of investigation, legislation, and administration which can make laws enforceable. A law is really a law only to the extent that it is enforced, and our statute books are encumbered by laws that are conflicting, ambiguous, and unenforceable, or partly enforced. Here is probably the greatest cause of industrial unrest, for as soon as people lose confidence in the making of laws by the legislature, in their interpretation by the courts, and in their administration by officials, they take the law into their own hands. This is now being done by both employers and employees. Before recommending any additional much-needed laws affecting wages, hours, child and woman labor, unemployment, or other substantive laws to improve industrial conditions, we must call attention to the widespread breakdown of existing laws and must devise methods of revising them and enacting and enforcing new laws so that they will fit actual conditions and be enforceable and enforced. With the widespread demand for more laws to remedy widespread and well-recognized causes of industrial unrest, there is a curious feeling that, if only more laws are placed on the statute books, they will, in some unexplained way, get themselves enforced.

While recognizing the justice of much of this demand for new laws, we are not placing them first in our report, but rather the methods of investigating conditions, of enacting legislation, of judicial interpretation, and administrative enforcement necessary to make them worth while as a real remedy.

Other industrial nations have gone far ahead of the United States in adopting labor legislation, much of which is also needed here; but their laws are drawn up so as to be enforceable, and their machinery of enforcement is such that the people are willing to entrust new laws to their officials for enforcement. Our Government is different from theirs and requires different methods, but, if our methods and officials can not be made as effective and trustworthy as theirs, then we can not trust more laws than we now have to their hands.

One of the most important facts to be recognized is that governments, whether State or Federal, can not be looked to alone for remedying evil conditions. As soon as people come to look upon the coercive power of government as the only means of remedying abuses, then the struggle for control of government is substituted for the private initiative through private associations, from which the real substantial improvements must come. We must look for the greatest improvement to come through the cooperation with government of the many voluntary organizations that have sprung up to promote their own private interests. The most important ones, for our purposes, are employers' associations, labor unions, and farmers' organizations. These are directly affected by most labor legislation, and they have much more powerful influence than have unorganized interests upon legislatures and administrative officials.

Furthermore, the struggle between capital and labor must be looked upon, so far as we can now see, as a permanent struggle no matter what legislation is adopted. If this is not recognized, proposed remedies will miss the actual facts. But there are certain points where the interests of capital and labor are harmonious or can be made more harmonious. In fact, this field where there is no real conflict between employers and employees is much wider than at first might be imagined. By recognizing these two facts of permanent opposition and progressive cooperation, it may be possible to devise methods of legislation, court interpretation, and administration which will reduce antagonism and promote cooperation. For, while we can not look to government alone for remedying abuses, it is only by legislation that we can give voluntary organizations a greater share in working out their own remedies and in cooperating with government toward increasing the points of harmony.

Some progress has been made in this direction in the past few years in some States, through the enactment of laws creating industrial commissions, but none of these laws go to the full extent required in order to carry out the foregoing principles. By observing the strong and weak points of these laws, as well as those of other States and the Federal Government which have not adopted similar laws, we can draw certain conclusions, which we do in the form of recommendations. A draft of a bill embodying most of these recommendations was submitted to the legislatures of Colorado and New York during the legislative sessions of 1915 and was adopted with more or less serious modifications and additions by those legislatures. The recommendations below contain most of the terms of the foregoing draft and also of improvements which seem essential to be made in the industrial commission laws of the States and of proposed laws for State or Federal Governments. Some of the recommendations are based on personal experience in the administration of labor laws.

INDUSTRIAL COMMISSIONS.

1. State and Federal industrial commissions to be created for the administration of all labor laws. All bureaus or divisions dealing with conditions of labor, including industrial safety and sanitation, workmen's compensation, employment offices, child labor, industrial education, statistics, immigration, and so on, to be placed under the direction of the commission. Each commission to consist of three commissioners to be appointed by the governor or President, as the case may be, with the consent of the Senate. Members to be appointed with the advice of the advisory representative council. (See par. 2.) The term of each commissioner to be six years, except that the terms of the commissioners first appointed shall be so arranged that no two shall expire at the same time. The Federal Department of Labor to be retained for educational and political purposes, and a similar department might be created in large industrial States, such as New York and Pennsylvania.

The tendency of labor legislation in the States which have given attention to this matter has been toward a complete centralization of the administration of the labor laws in the hands of a single department. Wisconsin in 1911 established an industrial commission for the administration of all labor laws, and Ohio, after one year of separate administration of the compensation law, created in 1913 a similar commission, and incorporated the compensation commission into an industrial commission. In New York and Pennsylvania the responsibility for the administration of labor laws has been divided between a commissioner of labor, who is responsible for their enforcement, and an industrial board of five members, the sole duty of which is to make necessary rules and regulations having the force of law. In New York there has also been a separate commission for the administration of the compensation act. The tendency, however, is strongly toward the industrial commission plan, as the New York plan, which was devised at the time of the reorganization of the labor department of that State in 1913 and adopted in the same year by Pennsylvania in an act largely copied from the New York law, has already (1915) been given up in the State of its origin. The New York commission under the law of 1915 consists of five members, and is charged with the administration of all labor laws and the workmen's compensation law, and also with the duty of making the rules and regulations for carrying these laws into effect. In Pennsylvania a compensation act has this year (1915) been enacted, and, while no change has been made in the organization of the labor department, the administration of the compensation act has been intrusted to that department.

During the present year (1915) at least five States have enacted legislation for a closer union of the administration of their labor and compensation laws. Colorado, with serious modifications, and Indiana have enacted laws creating industrial commissions similar to those of Wisconsin and Ohio. Nevada has created an industrial commission of three members for the administration of its compensation act and has conferred upon one of the commissioners, to be designated as commissioner of labor, the duty of enforcing all laws of the State for the protection of the working classes. In New Jersey, after an unsuccessful attempt to create an industrial commission, provision has been made for two additional employees in the department of labor for the purpose of correlating the work of that department with the administration of the compensation act.

In California the industrial accident commission administers the compensation act and also laws dealing with safety in places of employment, although the labor bureau also has the latter authority; and in Massachusetts, while there are still separate boards in charge of the labor department and of the administration of the compensation law, the two boards sit jointly for the purpose of making rules and regulations for the prevention of industrial accidents and occupational diseases.

In several States bills have been introduced for the creation of an industrial commission for the administration of all such laws. In New Jersey such a bill was introduced by the president of the State Federation of Labor, who is also a member of the assembly, and in Maryland such a bill was prepared and introduced at the instance of the State labor department. In Illinois the report of the efficiency and economy committee recommended the consolidation of the various departments dealing with labor laws, including the board administering the compensation act, and in Missouri a legislative committee, after a careful study of the subject, reported in December, 1914, in favor of the enactment of a compensation law and the creation of an industrial commission to administer both it and the other labor laws of the State. This latter report is particularly important, because it represents the result of a recent official study of the problem and consideration of the experience of the States which have advanced labor laws.

As already explained, the fundamental principle of these recommendations is that the administration of all the labor laws of a State shall be centralized. An illustration of the advantages is found in uniting the administration of the labor laws relating to safe and sanitary conditions of employment with the administration of the workmen's compensation laws.

It is probably unnecessary at this stage of the development of workmen's compensation legislation to consider the question whether there should be a responsible officer or officers charged with the administration of such laws, or whether their administration should be left to individual initiative and the final determination of courts of law, already burdened with many other and equally important responsibilities. That question is settled, and the only point is as to the character of the administrative agency. Both the nature of the compensation laws and the experience which has been gained during their operation in many States point to a board or commission, instead of the courts, as the best form of administration. Economy of administration then is secured if the administration of safety laws is placed in the hands of the compensation commission. Fewer highly paid executive officers and other employees are required, and there is secured avoidance of duplication in the work itself. For example, it is essential to the administration of both these laws that employers should be required to make reports of accidents. On the one hand they furnish necessary information respecting the nature of accidents and the possibilities of prevention; on the other, they are necessary in the actuarial work involved in the administration of compensation. The same is true of the inspections which are frequently necessary in the course of the administration of both laws and in most instances one inspection would serve both purposes. Furthermore, the information derived from hearings in compensation is of great assistance to the commissioners, who are also charged with responsibility of the labor laws generally, in giving them a broader view of the problems with which they are dealing.

The same kind of events that have led up to the State industrial commission are taking place in Federal legislation. Already two bills on workmen's compensation have been well advanced and one of them creates a commission separate from the Department of Labor. The bill for compensation of employees of the Government (63d Cong., 2d sess., H. R. 15222) takes the place of the present law administered by the Department of Labor, and provides for a "United States Employees' Compensation Commission" consisting of three commissioners, no one of whom shall hold any other Federal office or position. The other (63d Cong., 1st sess., S. 959), providing for employees of private employers in interstate commerce, leaves the administration of the law to the courts, a method that has been effectually discredited. Whether either or both bills on workmen's compensation are adopted, they should be united, as already shown in the case of the States, under a commission that administers the safety laws.

When the Department of Labor was created the important work of safety for mine workers was left in the Department of Interior under the Bureau of Mines. Safety on railroads is in the hands of the Interstate Commerce Commission. The Bureau of Standards, of the Department of Commerce, develops safety standards for electric and other equipment. The Public Health Service, of the Treasury Department, investigates industrial diseases and factory sanitation. The Bureau of Labor Statistics, of the Department of Labor, investigates and publishes bulletins on accidents and diseases in various industries. Lately a bill has passed the House providing for a safety bureau in the Department of Labor, with power to investigate any or all of the matters of safety now carried on either in that department or in any other department. The seamen's law recently enacted is in the hands of the Department of Commerce, assisted by the Department of Labor. The Department of Agriculture has a division on rural housing and social conditions.

This overlapping of jurisdiction in matters of industrial safety and sanitation has grown up without any plan, according to the accident of such such officials as happened to be on the ground or to get a hearing in Congress; or on account of objection to placing authority in one department or another. And now, with the prospect of Federal legislation for compensation for accidents and occupational diseases, one or two more bureaus are likely to be created, with their most important object the prevention of accidents.

At the same time three great private associations have sprung up which are doing as much or more for safety than all the State and Federal Governments combined. The Conference Board of National Allied Safety Organizations, composed of representatives from the National Association of Manufacturers, the National Founders' Association, the National Metal Trades Association, and the National Electric Light Association, has begun the standardization of safety devices for millions of employees, regardless of any standards which State or Government officials may set up.

The National Council of Safety, composed of the safety experts of most of the large corporations of the country and of representatives of labor, has developed an extensive campaign of accident prevention. The Workmen's Compensation Service Bureau, supported by the liability-insurance companies, is doing expert work of the highest order in safety devices and processes for the assistance of such employers as are policy holders in those companies.

With these three national organizations representing the employing interests, with at least five, and the prospect of seven, bureaus representing the Federal Government, and with similar agencies more or less developed in the States, all of them working on the same problem of compensation for accidents and prevention of accidents, the time is ripening for some kind of correlation and uniformity. It can not be expected that Congress and the people will long be satisfied with this expensive and wasteful disorganization of the national energies that are directed to the great work of safety and compensation. Just as the States are moving toward centralization under industrial commissions, so the same problem must force the Federal Government toward not only centralization of its own work but correlation with the States and with private organizations.

It does not follow that all of the Federal bureaus dealing with safety and health should be bodily taken from their several departments and transferred to an industrial commission. There may be cases where their work on industrial safety and health is tied up with their other work. It is only necessary that the several departments should be required by law to discontinue any overlapping or conflict of jurisdiction, and that an industrial commission should have authority to bring them all together into a national council of industrial safety and health and require them to agree on a definite plan of dividing up the work and cooperating with each other and with private associations organized for similar work. Other comments will be found under paragraph 3.

ADVISORY REPRESENTATIVE COUNCIL.

2. An advisory representative council consisting of the Secretary of Commerce and the Secretary of Labor and of, say, 10 employers (including farmers) and 10 representatives of labor unions (including women). The representatives on the council to be selected from lists, not including lawyers, submitted by recognized employers' associations in the State or in the Nation, as the case may be, such, for example, as State associations of manufacturers, the National Metal Trades Association, the National Founders' Association, associations of coal operators, of railroad presidents, of brewers, of farmers'

organizations, etc. The representatives of employees to be selected from lists submitted by the American Federation of Labor, the railroad brotherhood, the Women's Trade Union League, and independent organizations. In all cases either the associations entitled to representation should be named in the law, or provision should be made whereby the governor or President, upon investigation, shall name organizations which are considered representative by organized employers and organized employees themselves and permit them to name their representatives. Similar provision in case an organization ceases to exist or to be representative. Any organization to be entitled to recall its representative on notice. The representative council to be appointed by the governor or the President before the appointment of the commission and the governor or the President to call it together and to consult with it regarding the names proposed to be nominated for commissioners. The Industrial Commission to invite also a limited number, say, 10, of individuals or representatives of organizations including persons especially interested in unorganized labor and representatives of such organizations as the International Association for Labor Legislation, the National Child Labor Committee, and the Consumers' League and individual employers and employees, as may be advisable for their assistance, to be members of the advisory council. The council to take no vote on any subject except procedure and to have no veto on any act of the Industrial Commission. Nominal compensation or no compensation to members, with necessary expenses. The representative council to effect its own organization and call meetings independent of the commission, to be provided with a secretary and needed clerical assistance, to hold meetings perhaps quarterly and on call, to keep and publish records of its proceedings. The Industrial Commission to be required to submit all proposed rules, regulations, and publications to the representative council, allowing sufficient time for examination and discussion, and to publish any protest or criticism filed by any member of the council, along with the commission's own publication.

This recommendation is an extension of a principle which is left optional in several State commission laws, but the mandatory feature has been partially adopted by law in New York. The recommendation creates a body similar to the Superior-Councils of Labor in France, Belgium, and Italy, the Industrial Council in England, and many councils of private representative citizens who assist Government officials in Germany. In Wisconsin the appointment of a council is optional with the commission, but it has been appointed for several purposes, and this policy has been demonstrated to be the most effective of all that the commission has adopted. The omission by that commission to adopt it at times has been a source of severe and just criticism, and accounts for the granting of permits against which objections are rightly made. In New York the representative council is mandatory, but the selections are made by the governor, and are therefore liable to be political and nonrepresentative. For these reasons it is recommended that the council not only be mandatory, as in New York, but that no action of the commission, except in case of specified emergencies, shall be valid and no publication shall be issued unless previously submitted to the representative council. In this respect the advisory representative council would have powers in excess of those of similar councils, except perhaps the Superior Council of Belgium.

Appointment by the governor, President, or Industrial Commission is required in order that members may receive necessary expenses. Lawyers are excluded because the council should be composed of persons with practical experience in industry.

The history of governmental commissions and departments has often been the appointment of men on the recommendation of politicians or special interests or the accident of personal acquaintance. An executive, in looking around for competent appointees, is often at a disadvantage because he can not get impartial and disinterested men to accept, or because he does not have impartial and competent advice in his selections. To the proposed Industrial Commissions is given the most serious problem before the American people. Almost everything turns on the kind of men appointed. They must be men not only competent but having the respect of the great opposing interests. Their position is that of a kind of mediator as well as of administrator. Such appointments should not be made in haste, nor in the secret of the executive's accidental advisors. They should be considered publicly, and especially by the opposing interests whose fortunes will be committed in great part to their hands. The governor or President can not, of course, be bound by the action of the council, but he can be required to get their advice on names proposed.

It is intended that the members of the commission itself should not be representative of either employers or employees, but that they should have the confidence of both sides. This is expected to follow from the requirement that the governor or President should consult the council before making his nominations of commissioners. In this way, what is known as "the public" would be represented in part by the commission, while capital and labor would be represented in the council.

By this method it can be expected that capable men may be attracted from their private occupations into public service as members of the commission. Usually the kind of men required for such positions dread the political and personal attacks that are connected with public office. But it would be difficult for an eminent man to resist the call to public office when he has the united invitation of the President, the employers, and the labor unions of the country.

The representative council has no veto power, but is intended merely as a cooperative body representing employers, employees, the public as it is represented by the Secretaries of Commerce and Labor, and individuals selected by the commission. Its duties are purely advisory. Its purpose is not only to give the governor or President and the commission the benefit of advice and to bring together for conference representative labor men and employees, but to guarantee as far as possible that all appointments (par. 3), all investigations and publications (par. 4), all rules and regulations (par. 5), and other acts of the commission, shall, before they are published or become valid, be under the continuous supervision of the recognized leaders of organized capital and organized labor, and public representatives.

No requirement is made for the appointment of advisory experts, such as lawyers, engineers, and physicians. These may be appointed by the Industrial Commission as members of the third interest on the council, but it is found in practice that the services of consulting experts are secured without expense to the State if representative employers and employees have a part in the advisory council. This is attended to because the employer and employee representatives themselves have not the technical knowledge and can not give the time necessary to consider all details, but must consult experts in whom they have confidence. This they do, and are thereby prepared to discuss intelligently the acts of the commission. The council and the commission can, of course, call in such experts to their conferences at any time.

The employer and employee members of the advisory council should be strictly representative and responsible to the organizations represented. For this reason the organizations and not the Government should pay the salaries of the members. The result as shown in Wisconsin, where not even expenses are paid, is that the representatives are usually business agents of the unions and large employers selected by the employers' associations.

The council should organize with its own officers, independent of the commission, but should hold its conferences with members of the commission or with members of the staff. It should appoint expert advisory committees as needed for different subjects, such as safety, employment offices, etc. It should be provided with clerical and other help from the staff of the commission.

Since the powers of the council are only advisory it is not essential that it should vote on any questions except procedure. Hence it is not necessary to have equal representation of any interests or full attendance at all meetings. Each member should be furnished by mail with all proposals and proposed publications of the industrial commission.

For the reasons just cited it is not necessary that the commission itself should consist of more than three members. They are not expected in the larger States or in the Federal Government to attend to details of administration. Their duties will be mainly those of consultation and conferences with the council, supervision of the executive heads of divisions (par. 3), and public hearings.

This advisory council provides effective publicity for every act of the commission. The ordinary publicity required by law is that of a public hearing, and is limited to rules and regulations which are to have the effect of law. Such public hearings have become mere legal formalities, at which usually lawyers appear for each side and little or no opportunity is given for the two sides to get together on points where they can agree. The commission then retires and issues such rules and regulations as it may choose. These formal public hearings are not even required by law in some cases, but (par. 5) the recommendation provides that before the public hearing the employers and employees, with the commission and its staff, shall have considered and drafted the proposed rules so that when it comes to the public hearing they are present to explain and defend them. If objections are raised at the public hearing the proposed rules are referred back to the advisory council and the staff of the commission for reconsideration before being finally approved and issued as the legal act of the commission. If no public hearing is required by law, rules can not be issued except on advice of the representative council.

In this way an effective publicity is secured by a thorough consideration of the rules, because both those who are to be compelled by law to obey the rules and those in whose interest they are issued have assisted in drafting them.

Additional comments will be found under paragraph 3.

CIVIL SERVICE AND COMMENTS ON PRECEDING PARAGRAPHS.

3. The commission to appoint a secretary, bureau chiefs, or chiefs of divisions, and such other employees as may be necessary, all of them to be under civil-service rules. Provision to be made for the advisory representative council or a committee named by it, representing both employers and employees, to assist the civil service commission in conducting examinations, except for clerical positions, and making it mandatory on the civil service commission to appoint these representatives on its examining boards. Members of advisory council while serving on such boards to receive extra compensation. If there is no civil service commission in the State, then the advisory council shall cooperate with the industrial commission in the examinations. The commission afterwards to make its appointments from the eligible list of those who pass the examinations. A graded system of salaries and promotions to be adopted, by which the members of the staff may rise to the position of heads of bureaus or divisions, where they would receive salaries equivalent, if necessary, to those received by the commissioners. Any proposed removal of subordinates to be brought before the advisory council before action.

Many of the features of this section are adopted in the New York act, but the examination by employers and employees is not mandatory on the Civil Service Commission, and a few of the chief positions are exempt from civil-service rules. The Civil Service and Industrial Commissions of Wisconsin have practiced this method of examination and appointment for employment offices and for chiefs of divisions, although not required by law.

Objection sometimes is made to civil-service examinations as being impractical and theoretical. Indeed, civil-service examinations are likely to be impractical if conducted by experts. These objections can be avoided in the examinations for these positions by requiring that the Civil Service Commission, if there is one, shall cooperate with the representative council. The examinations would thus be conducted with the aid of men thoroughly acquainted with all the practical difficulties involved in the duties of the positions to be filled. By making use of oral or written, assembled or nonassembled, competitive or noncompetitive examinations, as best suited to the particular purposes, it should be possible to obtain all the advantages of the civil-service system with few of its disadvantages.

Furthermore, it is not enough that examinations for positions under the Industrial Commission should secure efficiency and permanency; it is even more important that they should secure impartiality. The Industrial Commission itself and its entire staff are looked upon as mediators in adjusting the administration of labor laws to the actual conditions of industry. It is essential that both sides should have confidence in the staff of the commission, and therefore that both sides should have a voice in its selection.

This provision for representatives of employers and employees on examining boards should not be left optional with Civil Service Commissions or the Industrial Commission, but should be mandatory. It has been found that several Civil Service Commissions object to this provision, because they wish to retain unqualified authority for conducting examinations and making up eligible lists. This is one of the features of bureaucracy which should not be permitted where such vital issues as the contest between capital and labor are at stake. The provision in the recommendation does not prevent Civil Service Commissions from appointing experts on their examining boards; it merely requires them also to appoint, in addition, the recognized representatives of the interests who have previously been nominated by the interests themselves.

At the present time secretaries and bureau chiefs in the Federal Government are exempt from civil-service rules, and are usually appointed by the President and confirmed by the Senate. This is a serious discouragement to competent subordinates, who are thereby prevented from rising by promotion to the higher positions in their bureaus, and who see less competent political appointees brought in over their heads as well as frequently changed.

These recommendations are intended to place the highest positions under the Industrial Commission on an equivalent with the commissioners themselves. It would be unfortunate and impracticable, except in smaller States, if the commissioners were required to give their entire time to the details of administration. This is the case where a commission must perform as many functions as are required in the large State and Federal Government commissions. This they would be compelled to do if their chiefs of divisions were frequently changed, as under the present system. The chiefs of divisions and bureaus, both under Federal and under State commissions, should be as competent as the commissioners to deal with employers and employees, and much more competent in dealing with subordinates. In foreign countries the office of factory inspector, as well as all other offices dealing with the relations of employers and employees, are considered as professions. In some of those countries the universities provide training courses and lectures on the subjects for which the officials are preparing, and these are required to be taken as a part of the civil-service rules. The appointee then serves as an apprentice in the department and by promotion may reach the highest position. As a result a high grade of inspector is obtained. Only when the officers and employees of the commissions have such opportunities as these for a life work, provided they are impartial as between employers and employees, can officials be interested in preparing themselves for the work, or academies like those at West Point and Annapolis be adopted for the training of civil servants.

The advisory representative council, proposed in paragraph 2, also protects the administration of labor laws from the just fear of government by a bureaucracy. There must be officials if labor laws are to be enforced. The courts can not be relied upon alone, because prosecution can be begun only by private individuals. Consequently administrative officers and inspectors have been provided to initiate prosecutions. These officials constitute a necessary bureaucracy, if the laws are enforced. But it can not be asserted that the present system of political appointments of inspectors avoids the evil of bureaucracy. The essential evil of bureaucracy is not so-called permanency of tenure, but the refusal of the official to take advice from laymen. The loudest agitator against bureaucracy becomes at once the most confirmed bureaucrat when he gets into office, because he determines to run his office in his own way, regardless of the advice of those who are compelled to obey his orders. In this sense the American officeholder is much more of a bureaucrat than are the European officials, who are compelled to consult the superior councils of labor or industrial councils of representatives of interests. It is for this reason that the legislatures and Congress should make it mandatory that the representative advisory councils should be created and that the industrial commissions and their staffs should confer with them before any act of the commission can have the validity of law. It is also necessary that the Civil Service Commission should appoint representatives from the council on its examining boards before any valid eligible list for appointment of subordinates can be made.

Another charge against civil-service rules is the objection to permanency of tenure and the inability to get rid of an official who adheres to outworn methods. This objection often has force, but the remedy is not that of returning to political and partisan appointments or frequent removals when changes occur in the political branch of Government. Officials, under most civil-service laws, can be removed at any time, provided reasons be given and no civil service commission should have authority to reinstate any official, as is the mistaken policy of some States. Permanency of tenure means only permanency on "good behavior." The principal reason why officials adhere to old methods is because there is no continuous supervising authority in a position to force them into new and better methods. The provision for an advisory council with which the officials are compelled to confer has been found to be the most effective method of compelling such officials to keep up with the changing conditions that require new methods. If, then, they are obstructive or incompetent to do this, there is good cause for removal.

COMMISSIONS AND CLASS CONFLICTS.

There are, of course, criticisms and objections raised against industrial and other commissions. It is not claimed here that they always work well. But they work better than the system they have displaced, and they have been found to be the only alternative where legislation attempts to regulate the relations of great conflicting and hostile interests. Many States and Congress have been forced by actual conditions to create railroad and interstate commerce commissions in order to take the details of the contest between railroads and shippers as far as possible out of the legislatures and the courts. Congress has been compelled, after 25 years of futile antitrust legislation, to turn over the contest between trusts and their competitors or customers, to a Federal trade commission. The contest between bankers and the commercial and business classes that depend on credit for their existence has been turned over to the Federal Reserve Board.

The contest between capital and labor is more serious than any of the other contests. Since the year 1877 it has frequently resulted practically in civil war, with the army or militia called in to suppress one side or the other, according to the will of the executive. It is claimed by some that this contest is irrepressible and will end in revolution, and at least it is plain, when the military power is called upon to decide a contest, that the ordinary machinery of government, which is fairly successful in other contests, has broken down.

It is not a solution of the contest to claim that these outbreaks are caused solely by agitators and have no foundation in conditions that need remedying. Such a solution, carried to its limit, means the suppression of free speech, free press, and free assembly, which can be accomplished only by military power. That there are conditions which need remedying is shown by the enormous amount of labor legislation of the past three decades, and the enormous amount of new legislation proposed. This legislation has come from the free discussion and investigation of actual labor conditions, and if there is no effective way for this discussion to be carried on and the alleged facts to be verified or disproved, then the result must be an excess of unfounded and impractical agitation mixed up with real grievances. There are unbridled agitators of this kind on both sides of the contest, and it is only when the two sides are brought together, and their charges, countercharges, and alleged grievances are boiled down by investigation to the residuum of facts, that mere unfounded agitation can be expected to give way to deliberations on remedies for recognized evils.

This does not mean that both sides can be made to agree on remedies for all evils and grievances, even after they have agreed on the facts. It means only that there is found to be a much larger field than was supposed where they can agree, and it is worth while for legislation to provide the means for bringing both sides together for a continuous search after the common points of agreement. When they have agreed upon and disposed of less disputatious points, they are in a position to go on to those disputed points which had been thought irreconcilable. This is the main reason for creating Industrial Commissions with adequate powers of impartial investigation, with conferences and discussions by both sides, and with power to decide on regulations and then to enforce them. (Par. 5.)

While some of the functions outlined for the proposed Industrial Commission are now being performed by the Department of Labor through its bureaus, it is not proposed that the department be abolished. (Par. 1.) It is even proposed that in large industrial States a similar department might be created in addition to the Industrial Commission. In nonindustrial States, where the labor department is mainly educational and not administrative, there would, of course, be no occasion for an Industrial Commission. Such occasion would usually first arise in case a workmen's compensation law were enacted.

We take it to be commonly accepted that a department, with its head having a seat in the Cabinet, is chiefly designed to advise and aid the administration in formulating its policy toward the interests in charge of that department, and to foster and promote the welfare of those interests. To be sure, other responsibilities are intrusted to the department, but the foregoing are its prime duties.

That Congress intended it to be so is manifested in the statutes creating the different departments. Thus the law establishing the Department of Commerce declares that it should foster, promote, and develop the foreign and domestic commerce, the mining, manufacturing, shipping, and fishery industries, and the transportation facilities of the United States. Likewise in creating the Department of Labor in 1885, Congress stated its purpose to be the diffusion of "useful information on subjects connected with labor, in the most general and comprehensive sense of that word, and especially upon its relation to capital, the hours of labor, the earnings of laboring men and women, and the means of promoting their material, social, intellectual, and moral prosperity." Congress reiterated its position when it raised the Department of Labor to Cabinet rank in declaring that its purpose should be "to foster, promote, and develop the welfare of the wage earners of the United States, to improve their working conditions, and to advance their opportunities for profitable employment." It is also mandatory upon the Secretary "to make such special investigations and reports as he may be required to do by the President, or by Congress, or which he himself may deem necessary."

Congress has not only declared that it regards Cabinet officers or department heads as the personal choice of the President, whom they are to assist in formulating his executive policy, but it has also accepted it in practice. This is illustrated by the fact that the Senate, even when controlled by an opposition party, usually ratifies the President's nominations promptly and without objections.

When influential economic groups feel that the Government can be of assistance in promoting their interests, they set about to bring political pressure to bear upon Congress to create a department that will concern itself with their welfare. Thus the Department of Agriculture was created in 1889, largely through the efforts of the National Grange and other farmers' organizations. In the same way the Department of Commerce was created on the petition of the business and manufacturing interests.

Of course, the different departments have also been intrusted with administrative duties. The Department of Agriculture administers the meat-inspection service, the Department of Commerce the steamship-inspection service, the Department of Labor the immigration service, and so on. However, whenever an acute administrative problem arises, owing to an intense conflict between two opposing economic interests, and requiring a disinterested enforcement of law, it has usually not been intrusted to one of these political departments. Hence, when Congress turned its attention to the dispute between the railroads and the great majority of shippers, it did not create a Department of Commerce to administer the law, but instead intrusted it to the Interstate Commerce Commission, a disinterested and nonpolitical body. Again, when Congress determined upon legislation to deal with "the new economic problem involved in the increased tendency toward concentrated ownership of the large industries of the country," no one even thought of suggesting that this matter be turned over to the Department of Commerce. On the contrary, without a single objection, an independent administrative commission, the Federal Trade Commission, was created to enforce the legislation. The same is true with the Federal Reserve Board. Congress has also applied this policy to the labor problem. The first important administrative act directly affecting capital and labor was not assigned to the Department of Labor for execution, but to a disinterested and nonpolitical board. We refer to the Newlands Act of 1913, and preceding acts relating to arbitration of labor disputes on railroads. When an effort was made to place the administration of this act under the Department of Labor, both the railroad companies and the railroad brotherhoods opposed and prevented the change.

We are of the opinion that if, in dealing with the labor problem, this policy is carried out consistently, considerable of the industrial unrest will be allayed. We believe that it should be the conscious policy of Congress to separate the policy-determining functions from the administrative functions. The Department of Labor should be intrusted with investigaitons that would aid the President and his administration in determining upon a labor policy. It should also be the educational medium through which the country is to be informed on the various labor issues that need solution or have not yet been legislated upon. As a matter of fact, this has been the department's chief and most effective activity. A glance at the list of publications of the department shows the influence it has had as a pioneer in labor legislation in this country. The present unanimity of opinion in favor of workmen's compensation, safety and sanitation, vocational training and employment bureaus, is largely due to its having concentrated upon educating the public to the need of such legislation. And the department wisely continues to fulfill its chief mission by pointing the way to future improvement of the conditions of labor. Its recent publications aim to enlighten and crystallize public opinion on such mooted but vital questions as sickness and unemployment insurance, old-age pensions, housing of workingmen, cooperation, employers' welfare work, home and factory conditions of women and children. To make its work still more effective the department has begun issuing a monthly review which will supply information on all questions affecting labor. We have no doubt that with the aid of the Department of Labor, legislation upon these subjects will be secured sooner than otherwise.

On the other hand, when public opinion, through legislation, has determined upon a policy, it is vital to its success that it be administered by disinterested persons not connected with a political department. This is necessary in order to obtain the mutual and voluntary cooperation of employers and employees, and, unless they are assured of a disinterested administration of the law, they will be reluctant to assist in its successful enforcement. Naturally a department which initiates and advocates new legislation is bound to antagonize those who are not in accord with its views. It is futile to expect the Department of Labor to get the good will and cooperation of those whom it successfully defeated in the legislative battle. We must remember that the department is constantly advocating new legislation, even while it is administering that which has been enacted. Thus the bitter feeling against it is bound to be permanently at high pitch, and those who differ from it would likely have no confidence in its being able to administer the law disinterestedly. Then, too, as we shall show, if a law is administered through a political department,

its efficient administration may be subordinated to political expediency.

It is in order to avoid these difficulties that we recommend the
method already adopted in several States. We believe-that an
Industrial Commission, removed from the heat of political controversy, created with the safeguards proposed herein, would have
the confidence of employers and employees. Although employers
and employees may have hopelessly divergent opinions on policy, yet
when the policy is once determined upon by Congress they are equally
concerned in its efficient and disinterested administration. If assured
of this, they cooperate in its successful enforcement.

Furthermore, much opposition to labor legislation, both by capital
and labor, is based upon the fear that its administration will be
partial. And even when such legislation is enacted, unless both sides
have confidence in the disinterestedness of the administrators, it is
doomed to remain a dead letter on the statute books.

In recommending that the policy-determining function be separated from the administrative function, we wish to separate, as much
as possible, the problems upon which capital and labor disagree from
those in which they have a common interest. Legislation is a matter
of opinion. Men may honestly differ as to the wisdom of a certain
law. Difference of opinion when strongly contested invariably en-
genders suspicion and distrust. Hence, if an Industrial Commission
were called upon to initiate and advocate new legislation it would
be forced to antagonize and lose the good will of either capital or
labor, or of both. Such an outcome must inevitably hamper its administrative duties, which it can not carry out successfully unless it
has the confidence of both sides.

But it is highly essential that the conditions of labor be constantly
improved and adjusted to new industrial developments. This function of studying and promulgating the best policies for promoting
the welfare of labor should be left to the Department of Labor, as
originally intended when created. The future interest of our country
demands that a department devote itself exclusively to the furtherance of the welfare of labor. New problems must constantly be
studied, information furnished, and remedies suggested. Considering that in the final analysis public opinion, as expressed through
legislation, determines the nature of the remedy, it is proper that a
political department be intrusted with the duty of aiding in determining that policy. It is with this idea in mind that we make the
distinction between the enactment of law which is political in its
nature and must be fought out in the Congress and in the Cabinet
and the administration law which is nonpolitical and should be administered by disinterested parties in cooperation with representatives of capital and labor.

The conclusion is that all subjects upon which Congress has not
legislated so as to require an administrative department should be in
the hands of the Department of Labor. Among these are the important subjects of sickness insurance, invalidity insurance, unemployment insurance, old-age pensions, occupational disease, child and
woman labor, and so on. The department should make studies of
comparative administration of labor law and the administration of
laws in the States. Other subjects might be mentioned. In fact
there should be no limitation on its field of investigation and the

education of the public to the evils which labor suffers and the remedies that should be adopted.

The Industrial Commission is purely an administrative body not intended to promote new legislation, except where it is needed in connection with its administration of existing laws. Other new legislation gets its initiative elsewhere. The proper place for opposing interests to make their fight on new laws is in the State legislatures and in Congress. Each side necessarily endeavors to elect its representatives, to employ its lobby, and to use every honorable method in its power to defeat the other side. The outcome is usually a compromise not wholly satisfactory to either. But it does not follow that the fight should be kept up in the administration of the laws that are enacted. Whatever they are, they should be enforced exactly as they stand, and neither side should control the executive and administrative officers. These should be impartial. It is because executive officials are mainly partisans that the administration of labor laws in this country has broken down. They may be appointed by political parties, but back of the politicians are the employers or the trade-unions that make secret or open deals with the politicians in order to control the offices. It can not be expected that employers will readily accept investigation or obey the orders of officials whom they know or suspect to be agents of unions or of politicians, intent on strengthening unionism or making political capital out of their positions. It is natural that employers should protect themselves either by getting their own agents into the positions or by getting a weak and inefficient trade-unionist appointed. In any case the laws are not enforced, and the laboring classes in turn become desperate and defiant of Government. An illustration is found in the recent industrial troubles in Colorado. Probably no State of its size in the Union has had upon its statute books more labor laws than Colorado, nor more trade-union representatives in office to enforce them, yet the nonenforcement of the labor laws was undoubtedly one of the contributing causes of the recent troubles. The history of many other States is similar, so far as nonenforcement is concerned. Labor representatives alternate with employer representatives or with labor politicians, who make a show of enforcing the laws while the masses of labor get no substantial benefit.

American experience has shown that this situation can be met only by a nonpartisan commission, removed as far as possible from politics. In other countries, and in British colonies having parliamentary forms of government, this kind of separate commission is not required, for the good reason that the Cabinet officer who enforces the labor laws is a member of Parliament, and Parliament must be dissolved and a new election ordered if the Cabinet loses control. Having a seat on the floor of the legislature he must answer questions put by the opposition. If one of his subordinates is inefficient or takes sides against employers or unions, some one in Parliament is liable to rise and demand explanations, and the Cabinet minister is compelled to explain and to stand by the subordinate or to repudiate him. The opposition may even be able to defeat the ministry and get a new election. Consequently, Cabinet officers are responsible to Parliament, and, although they are partisans and politicians, they are careful that their subordinates, who actually administer the laws, shall be impartial and efficient. In no other country, governed by a parliament, would such important boards as the Interstate Commerce Commission, the Federal Trade Commission, the Federal Reserve Board, or the State railroad and public utility commissions, be taken out from under the jurisdiction of a responsible cabinet minister. In this country it is found necessary to make them wholly or partly independent, because there is no officer directly responsible to the legislature or the people who can be given control over them.

The same is true of the labor departments of parliamentary countries compared with such departments in the American State and Federal Governments. The issues in this country are too vital and menacing, they are too easily turned into political capital, and, at the same time, the politicians in charge are too little responsible to the legislatures, to Congress, and to the voters, for the American people to leave them in the hands of partisan or political officials. The plan of an industrial commission with a representative council as herein recommended, is based on American experience and fitted to American conditions in dealing with such issues of opposing interests.

But the commissions created to deal with the relations between other opposing interests can not be accepted as models for dealing with the opposing interests of capital and labor. The Interstate Commerce Commission was designed to reconcile the opposing interests of railroads and shippers, the Federal Trade Commission of monopolies and competitors, the Federal Reserve Board of bankers and borrowers, but in none of these cases were the opposing interests strongly organized for aggression and occasional paralysis of business verging on civil war. It was not so necessary then that the opposing sides should be strongly represented, as is recommended in the creation of the Advisory Representative Council. This council is a kind of parliament designed to hold the commission continuously to the impartial performance of its duties and the accuracy of investigations upon which the impartial performance of duties depends.

The Industrial Commission, as here proposed, adopts methods in the field of labor laws similar to those that collective bargaining between unions and employers adopts in drawing up voluntary joint agreements. Modern trade agreements are, in fact, almost complete codes of labor law for a particular industry, and, if voluntary collective bargaining could become universal and effective for all employers and employees, then the State or Government might not need to enact many labor laws. Something like this is actually attempted in those countries having compulsory arbitration. They provide easy methods for organizing and perpetuating unions of employers and unions of employees. They try to induce the representatives of these unions voluntarily to recognize each other, to get together to investigate grievances and demands, to confer and to draw up and enforce a joint agreement covering all alleged evils and grievances. If they can not succeed in doing this they provide a court of arbitration with substantially all the powers that the conferees of the unions and employers would have if they acted without compulsion.

But compulsory arbitration is too remote to be considered, or even anything which would logically lead to compulsory arbitration. In paragraph 14 we recommend voluntary collective bargaining with the Government acting only as mediator without any compulsory powers. Our alternative proposed for compulsory arbitration is in part an industrial commission with a council of employers and employees.

The need of an industrial commission becomes more pressing in proportion as new laws are enacted and new executive duties are added. It was the introduction of workmen's compensation that forced attention to the situation. Here is a new type of legislation which is so evidently a matter in which employers are as much concerned as employees that it was not considered proper to intrust its administration to a department controlled solely in the interests of labor. Consequently separate commissions were created independent of the labor bureau, or else the compensation law was put in charge of the courts.

But the most important effect of the compensation laws is not the compensation to workmen, for no law pretends to pay the workman anything for his suffering nor even to pay him his total loss in wages. The most important effect is the universal pressure on employers to prevent accidents and to heal the injury as soon as possible.

Wherever this object of the law was understood either the work of factory inspection for accident prevention was taken from the labor bureau or the compensation commission and the labor bureau were consolidated. One reason for doing this is that employers have become as much interested in accident prevention as have workmen, for it becomes a matter of business and profits. Another reason is that the compensation commission itself may not be tempted to exalt the less important object of compensation over the more important one of accident prevention and speedy cure.

The employers now become just as much concerned as the employees in having an efficient factory inspection. They must do their own inspection, anyhow, for the sake of reducing the costs of compensation, and they do not need to be prosecuted as they did before. What they need in factory inspection is the help of inspectors who are expert in showing them how to prevent accidents and how to organize safety committees and to get the "safety habit" into their employees. Whatever reason may formerly have existed for trade-unions to get their members appointed as factory inspectors in order to drive home prosecutions no longer exists. Neither do employers any longer have reason for using political or underhanded methods in order to get weak and inefficient inspectors appointed. Employers now wish to cooperate with factory inspectors, and the only kind they can cooperate with are those who are impartial and efficient. The fact that employers have taken the lead in their three great safety organizations mentioned under paragraph 1, instead of being led by State and Federal labor officials, shows unmistakably the need of enlisting employers in at least this branch of labor law.

Another subject, unemployment, the most serious and distressing of all, is almost universally agreed as needing a comprehensive plan of employment offices. It is now generally admitted that it must be dealt with by the Federal Government. Both England and Germany have national systems of public employment offices. The English system is operated directly by the National Government; the German system is operated by the city and State governments correlated and supervised by the Federal Government. A combination of both methods will, perhaps, be necessary in this country. Bills have already been introduced in Congress, and the Department of Labor has begun the establishment of offices. But, in the contest between employers and trade-unions, the control of employment offices is essential to either side. The antiunion employers' associations already have sufficient employment offices, and many local trade-unions have employment agencies of their own.

Employers control the jobs. They hire whom they please. Surely they can not be expected to hire workmen sent to them by trade-unionists or politicians who happen to run the public employment offices. This accounts for the inefficiency of the offices in almost every place where they have been tried. They sink to the level of charity, finding occasional short jobs for casuals, but do not become the great labor exchanges which they should be as the first step in dealing with the most serious of all problems, unemployment. Experience shows that employers must have confidence in the ability and impartiality of the officials who run the employment offices or they will not patronize them. On the other hand, trade-unionists must have confidence that the offices will not be used to furnish strike breakers. The only effective solution of this predicament is the management of these offices by joint committees of organized employers and organized employees and their joint civil-service examination of the officials who run the offices. Under the Industrial Commission plan there are not only representative councils at the national headquarters, but similar councils for each State and for each local office.

Furthermore, no Federal legislation is more urgent than the supervision of private commercial offices doing an interstate business. If this country expects to promote public offices and to regulate private offices, the only effective way is through joint control by the acknowledged representatives of organized employers and employees, cooperating with a Federal commission that is impartial and nonpolitical.

The subject of industrial education is vital to the Nation as a whole and immediately critical for both employers and employees. Yet, when a bill is introduced in Congress for national aid to industrial education, the administration is not placed under the Department of Labor, where it would naturally belong and where more has been done than in all other departments in the investigation of the subject. It is proposed to place the administration under an ex officio board of cabinet officers with an officer of the Bureau of Education acting as executive. Furthermore, no standards of efficiency are imposed upon the States as a condition of receiving the funds appropriated out of the Federal Treasury. (Par. 17.) This bill combines the features of political control, "pork-barrel" finance, and exclusion of the two great interests of employers and employees who are most directly concerned. The reasons for such recommendations are the popular demand for industrial education, and the lack of any effective method of bringing together the representatives of employers (including farmers) and employees. Such representatives are the ones who know the needs of industry and agriculture and are competent, with the aid of qualified educators, provided neither side dominates the other, to set up the standards of efficient industrial training which should be made the essential condition of receiving Federal aid. For this purpose the Industrial Commission should add to its advisory council representatives of organizations of educators, such as the National Education Association, and the National Society for Promotion of Industrial Education. The Federal Industrial Commission, upon the advice of such a council, including employers, employees, farmers, and educators, could then determine the standards as a basis for receiving subsidies, which should probably require the States to provide governing boards of employers, employees, farmers, and educators, continuation day schools with compulsory attendance on the employer's time, adequate training of teachers with practical industrial experience, and so on.

In making the preceding three recommendations no reflection is intended on any particular State or Federal official now charged with the administration of labor laws. It is conceded that many of them may be doing the best work possible under existing laws. But it is recognized that the conditions under which they work make it impossible either to administer existing laws effectively or to assume the administration of additional laws urgently required to meet the increasingly difficult and complex problems of capital and labor.

Instead of interfering with the commendable work of trade-unions the recommendations are intended to strengthen unionism at its weakest point. One of the most serious obstacles in the way of a harmonious labor movement is the struggle of ambitious unionists to get the indorsement and control of their unions for political positions. The conflicts within unions for such indorsement and support are notorious in weakening the unions. Furthermore, in order to get and hold a political position the unionist must make alliance or connivance with and concessions to the leaders of political parties, and therefore is not free to support consistently the demands of labor. He must also often support or even appoint other politicians whose influence is used against the unions. This unquestionably weakens or destroys the confidence of laborers generally in the integrity and faithfulness of all their leaders who accept political positions, or are suspected of trying to get such positions. It is only when the union representative is paid from his union treasury instead of the public treasury, and is recalled by his union, that he is truly representative and the union itself has a sound basis for permanency and growth.

Our recommendations adopt this principle and counteract this weakness of unionism by making their representatives on the advisory council dependent solely on the unions. They receive no salaries from the public treasury, and can be recalled at any time when they cease to be representative. The result is that the unions usually nominate for such positions their regular officers or business agents who receive salaries from the union treasury for other purposes. Under such circumstances there can ordinarily be no question of the union representatives " selling out " to employers or politicians.

INVESTIGATIONS.

4. The Industrial Commissions to make and publish investigations and recommendations on all subjects whose administration is intrusted to them. Investigations and recommendations on other subjects to be made only on the request of the legislature, Congress, or the court. (Pars. 12, 13.) Since it is provided (par. 14) that the

Federal and State commissions shall cooperate in the mediation of labor disputes, the Federal commission should be the agency to which the States should look for continuous investigations and publications for the entire country of wages, hours of labor, cost of living, joint trade agreements, and all subjects involved in labor disputes, but the names of establishments or individuals should be kept confidential. It should publish, at least annually, a report on all strikes, lockouts, boycotts, blacklists, that have terminated during the year, but should not make such investigations during an industrial dispute unless consented to by both parties in the manner elsewhere provided. (Par. 14.) In making such reports it should give all material facts, including demands, negotiations, picketing, strike-breakers, conciliation, the acts of State or Federal authorities, as well as joint agreements reached with or without cessation of business. In preparing these reports the commission should not call upon any mediator, but should, if necessary, use its powers of compulsory testimony.

In order to assist State minimum-wage commissions in the most difficult part of their work the Federal commission should also investigate and report upon interstate competition and the effect of minimum-wage laws. Such investigations are of assistance' also in determining other questions. State commissions should make reports on safety, compensation for accidents, minimum-wage investigations, employment offices, child labor, etc.

No publication of any investigations to be made or any rules (par. 5) to be issued without previously submitting them to all members of the representative advisory council, with opportunity for criticism, the latter to be published by the commission with its own report. All forms, schedules, and instructions for investigators likewise to be submitted to the advisory council.

These recommendations regarding investigations are the most important of all the recommendations regarding the Industrial Commission. All of the other recommendations culminate in the validity of its investigations. Investigations furnish the basis for drafting laws by the legislature, for formulating rules and regulations by the commission (par. 5), for interpretation of laws and rules by the courts, and for prosecutions in enforcing the laws. The recommendations for an industrial commission, for an advisory council, for civil-service appointments, for subsidies (par. 17), and for court procedure (par. 7) are all directed toward securing reliability and confidence in the investigations and conclusions of the commission.

It is required that all investigations and proposed publications shall be submitted to the representative council before they are issued and time enough given for consideration and criticism. If, then, any rules are issued (par. 5) or investigations published without the approval of either side, their validity and accuracy are at once condemned and the commission is discredited. Under a partisan or political department of labor, it is unlikely that statistics and investigations are accepted, either by the public or by both employers and employees, at their face value. Nothing more serious can exist, in a country which depends so much on public opinion, than this distrust of official publications and statistics which purport to give all the facts upon which public opinion forms its conclusions. Employers, employees, and the general public should be able to rely implicitly for their conclusions on official statistics on wages, hours of labor, health, safety, cost of living, unemployment, costs of production, distribution of wealth, strikes, boycotts, and all other material facts bearing on the relations of capital and labor. All labor legislation, all administration of labor laws, all efforts at mediation and arbitration, all recommendations of public bodies, go back for their justification to statistics and investigations. The money of the Government is worse than wasted, and the officials are discredited if there remains any interested body of citizens who do not place confidence in these official statistics and investigations. The temptation is so great, in view of the struggle between capital and labor, to distort or suppress or obliterate facts that no precautions too great can be taken to secure thorough criticism, verification, and filling in of omissions before the facts are published. No matter whatever else may be recommended, no recommendation can be depended upon that does not provide fully for the integrity, reliability, and complete inclusion of all material facts in every publication of official statistics and investigations. There is no certain method of doing this except in the recommendation that all alleged facts of statistics and investigations be submitted to the parties directly interested and affected by the conclusions. The proposed advisory council, composed of acknowledged representatives of these parties, acting independently, without intimidation or connivance, and watchful against any advantage attempted by the opposing yet cooperating interest, consulting their constituents on any matter, can be trusted to see to it that no material facts or conclusions are published without conclusive proof and none suppressed without disproof. If any member of the council objects to any final statement or conclusion, he is entitled within limits to have his protest published along with the report of the commission. In fact, the entire spirit of these recommendations is the utilization by Government of the organizations that have both common and hostile interests, in order to protect the Government itself against partisanship and partiality in dealing with the serious conflict between those interests. It is because the reports, findings, and recommendations of the present commission were not submitted to parties affected thereby or to an advisory committee similar to the one proposed for a permanent commission that we can not accept them as verified or criticized, so that we could have before us when finally acting upon them any criticisms or assurance that their statements were accurate or that important omissions had not been made. An advisory committee to this commission, similar to the one proposed, was approved for a short time and, after making changes in the proposals of the staff having the measures in charge, made certain unanimous recommendations as bills to this commission, but the committee was discontinued before it could complete its work. No staff of investigators, however careful, can be expected to have such complete knowledge of their subject as to be trusted without the scrutiny and criticism of the interests or persons affected by their reports. Whenever a permanent industrial commission is created there can be no provision more essential than that of providing the representative machinery for reliable investigations, findings, and publicity.

An illustration of the method of supervision of investigation here advocated is afforded by the Interstate Commerce Commission. The statistics of wages and hours collected by that commission are of importance in matters of mediation. They were so collected and arranged that they could not be relied upon for that purpose. Consequently a conference was called, consisting of the railway accountants, the railroad brotherhoods and other labor organizations, the statisticians of the commission and of the Department of Labor, to consider the statistics. After the discussion, which failed in some respects to reach agreement, the Interstate Commerce Commission issued new rules changing several features of the statistics in order to avoid the criticisms advanced, the changes to go into effect in 1915. It is this method of statistical investigation that is recommended to be made mandatory on Industrial Commissions.

The Industrial Commissions herein recommended are modeled in part upon the example of the railroad and public utilities commissions, the Interstate Commerce Commission, the Federal Trade Commission, and the Federal Reserve Board. Their powers are partly legislative, partly judicial, and partly executive. That which is most important is their power of making investigations of facts and conditions and then issuing orders (par. 5) based on such investigations. The legislature or Congress lays down a general policy or standard, but does not go into all of the minor details and variations that are needed to fit the policy to actual conditions. In the case of railroads it gives up the attempt to enact a schedule of freight and passenger rates and merely requires of railroad corporations that all rates and services shall be reasonable, that there shall be no discriminations, and so on. The commission then investigates each case as it comes up and issues a detailed order intended to carry out the policy and enforce the standard laid down by the legislature or Congress. In the case of labor law the legislative standards differ according to the object of the law. In matters of safety the legislature requires employers to keep their work places safe, and leaves to the commission the investigation of conditions and of safety devices necessary to be installed in each industry or shop, with power to order them installed. In compensation for accidents the legislature requires the employer to pay 50 per cent or more of the wages lost for a certain time, and then gives the commission power to investigate each case if necessary, and to determine exactly the amount and all details, and to order the employer to pay that amount. Other standards may be set up by the legislature, if it wishes to do so, for hours of labor, minimum wages, exclusion of women and children from dangerous employment, regulation of private employment offices, and so on, covering the entire field of labor legislation.

It is evident that the legislature can not itself make all of these investigations. It must depend upon others. In practice, too, the legislature and Congress are not willing to delegate to a single executive official the power of issuing rules and orders. This power is quasi judicial. Consequently the legislature and Congress create commissions with three or more members, in order to require deliberation and a fair representation and hearing for all interests that are benefited by or compelled to obey the rules. A single executive official is liable to be one-sided and partisan, or to act without deliberation, or to be frequently changed, but a commission can be organized so as to be impartial, deliberative, and continuous.

In the administration of all other labor laws, such as those on industrial education, child labor, hours of labor, minimum wage, and so on, there are points of antagonism and points of harmony between capital and labor. The points of antagonism are enlarged and exaggerated when one side or the other, through practical politicians, controls the offices. The points of harmony can only be discovered by investigation, and the investigations must be cooperative between employers and unions, else neither side will have confidence in the results. The Industrial Commission and its subordinate officials, of course, have to be depended on to make the actual investigations, but the provision in the foregoing recommendation, that all matters and all proposed publications shall be submitted to the advisory council, representing the opposing interests, for their advice and criticism but not their veto, goes as far as practicable toward securing that the investigations, conclusions, and rules of the commission and its subordinates will have the confidence of both sides.

The particular recommendation regarding investigations of labor disputes is associated with a later recommendation regarding mediation. (Par. 14.) While recommending voluntary mediation, it is recognized that strikes and lockouts are of such public importance that the public is entitled to accurate information regarding their causes and continuance. In connection with its other investigations the investigation of strikes and lockouts shows underlying causes of industrial unrest and the failure of legislation or administration to remedy them. Official investigations and reports on those subjects have not as a rule been accepted, because they have been colorless for fear of giving offense, or because they are conducted under the direction of partisans of one side or the other. It is expected that investigations conducted under the supervision of the advisory council will avoid the defects of many official investigations.

All investigations of a general character, such as those on safety devices, wages, hours, conditions of labor, and interstate competition, should be made by the Federal commission, relieving the State commissions or bureaus for their work of local investigations, administration, and inspection, the Federal commission to be the central standardizing agency, leaving the State free to adopt or reject the standards. (Par. 17.) The investigation of interstate competition and the effect of minimum wage laws will be of use in the most difficult part of the work of State minimum wage commissions, which we indorse in so far as women and children are concerned.

5. The commission to make rules and regulations for carrying into effect the provisions of the labor laws which it enforces. This may be done by providing, in the industrial commission law or otherwise, for certain brief standards as may be determined by the legislature, for example, that all places of employment shall be safe and sanitary, as the nature of the industry will reasonably permit, that no person shall be allowed to work for such hours of labor or at such times as

are dangerous to his or her life, health, safety, or welfare, that employment offices shall give correct information, shall not split fees, and so on. Or, less preferably, the existing labor laws may be retained or new ones enacted in minute detail, and the Industrial Commission may be given power merely to make such additional rules and regulations or variations from the laws as are necessary to give them full effect. Rules to be submitted to the advisory council before issuing.

The method of brief legislative standards above mentioned is adopted by most of the States having Industrial Commissions and it is here recommended, but the latter is the method adopted in New York. The original policy of American labor legislation involved an attempt to cover in detail every contingency which might arise. This method has proved itself impractical. It is impossible for a legislature charged with so many other duties and having but little time for attention to any of them, to intelligently provide in detail for such matters as the safeguarding of machinery or the regulation of hours of labor and periods of rest in hundreds of different employments and under hundreds of different circumstances. Legislation upon these subjects has to-day reached the stage long ago reached by legislation relating to public health and public utilities. The legislature can provide only the general standards and must leave to administrative officers the duty of "filling in details."

Whether the labor laws of a State consist only of a few sections, as in Wisconsin, or are a bulky law, as in New York, there still exists the necessity for the further filling in of details, and if the labor laws enacted by the legislature are at all lengthy, as in New York, there exists the additional necessity of some means for variations in deserving cases, either by express provision of the law or, in the absence thereof, by the tacit overlooking of violations by the officials charged with the administration. This latter practice is an opportunity for graft or favoritism. A factory inspector goes into an establishment and has the power to order changes amounting to several thousand dollars. He finds many points where the strict letter of the law does not apply. Since he is the only person who actually interprets the law on the ground he can readily overlook violations. But where the laws do not go into details, but an Industrial Commission determines the details in the form of rules fitted to conditions, the inspector no longer has discretion in overlooking violations. He must report all the violations, and the employer has another remedy besides influencing the inspector. He can go to the commission with a petition that a different rule be made to apply to his case, and the commission, after a public hearing, may grant or reject the petition, or modify its rule for that particular establishment. Variations must be made in any case. The difference is, that where there is no commission with power to make rules, the variations are made in secret by the different inspectors, while where the commission has this power they are made in public. (Par. 6.)

In the recommendations above, the briefest kind of a legislative standard is indicated. Whatever its length, however, the best method of filling in the details is the same. It is not unconstitutional to delegate such power to a single individual, but it is undesirable and, as already pointed out, impracticable to confer it upon one person. The alternative is to confer it upon a board or commission. The chief question arising here is whether a board shall be created especially for this purpose or whether one board shall perform this duty together with that of administering the laws and the rules and regulations made by it. The latter is the Industrial Commission recommended. The other method has been tried in the two greatest industrial States in the Union, New York and Pennsylvania, but the former State abandoned it after a two-years' trial. In New York it was adopted two years ago when the factory investigating commission declined to take the administration of the labor department away from a single executive, but adopted a compromise through establishing an industrial board of four members, together with the labor commissioner as chairman, to perform the rule-making function whether in the form of general rules or variations. While the board has done much good work, there remains little doubt that the same work can be performed even more intelligently and effectively by a commission which is also actively engaged in administrative work. In both cases, the aid of committees representing particular industries or interests has been and must be largely relied upon. On the other hand, an industrial board such as formerly existed in New York, and still exists in Pennsylvania, the rule-making duties of which are solely legislative in their nature, without power of enforcement, is not much better equipped to make such rules and regulations than the legislature, except that its number is smaller and its personnel chosen particularly for this one duty.

The recommendations provide different methods of securing uniformity of State and Federal legislation on various subjects (pars. 17, 18). This uniformity has been secured in the case of railroads by exactly the same method as the one here proposed to be made mandatory. When Congress enacted a law requiring safety couplings there were a large number of manufacturers of couplings in the market. Congress gave authority to the Interstate Commerce Commission to decide on the kind of couplings that would accomplish the object of securing safety. The commission called in the representatives of the railroads and of the railroad brotherhoods, with the manufacturers of couplings, and after several conferences the present standards were adopted. Other standards applying to railroad cars were also adopted in this way. .

At the present time there is urgent need for Federal aid in securing uniformity of safety devices. This can be done to a certain extent through voluntary cooperation with the States. Various States with industrial commissions are going ahead with their own standards, and there is apparently no means of securing uniformity until a Federal commission is given power to act. This could be done if the Federal commission brought together representatives of State factory inspectors, along with its advisory council of employers and employees, and the private national safety organizations mentioned under paragraph 2. By agreeing on standards, these could be adopted by every State commission which has power to make rules. And the Federal commission would be merely a central standardizing agency, leaving to the States the voluntary adoption of the standards. If it were desired to go further, a Federal law granting to the Federal Industrial Commission power to set standards for interstate shipment of machinery not equipped with the standard safety devices might be adopted. Each method would require a Federal commission to set standards.

The illustration regarding safety is taken not because that is the most important problem, but as furnishing an illustration of possible methods applicable in other lines. Similar uniformity might be secured in the regulation of private employment offices and other lines of labor legislation, as the States or Congress may determine. Of course, if the Congress enacted legislation similar to the Palmer-Owen child-labor bill, the extreme step would be taken of attempting to force States to come up to Federal standards. This may be necessary in some cases, but the Federal Industrial Commission affords methods of securing uniformity in some branches of legislation by less extreme measures.

The courts have generally denied the contention that this delegation of power to make rules and issue orders is unconstitutional as a delegation of legislative or judicial power, and the Supreme Court of the United States has used the term "administrative" to describe those powers which are partly legislative or judicial, but are not so exclusively one or the other that they may not be properly conferred upon an executive or administrative body. (See Interstate Commerce Commission v. Humboldt S. S. Co., 224 U. S., 474; Pennsylvania Railway Co. v. International Coal Mining Co., 230 U. S., 184; Mitchell Coal & Coke Co. v. Pennsylvania Railway Co., 230 U. S., 274.)

REVIEW BY COMMISSION.

6. Any person in interest to be entitled to petition the commission for a hearing on the legality or reasonableness of any rule or regulation or of any order directing compliance with any provisions of law or other rule or regulation or for a special order applicable to a single establishment. The commission may change its rule or regulation before final decision by a court on its legality.

This recommendation is embodied in one form or another in all of the State commission laws. Under the prevailing system of administering labor laws a person affected by an order enforcing an act of the legislature has no opportunity to object to its constitutionality, reasonableness, or validity except by awaiting prosecution and submitting his objection as a matter of defense. Not only is this cumbersome and undesirable as a matter of procedure, but it is open to a very serious objection that it brings this matter up often for final decision by a petty court, or even before a local magistrate or justice of the peace.

Not only does a provision of the sort here recommended give the person affected opportunity to make proper objections, but it gives the commission an opportunity to reconsider its rules and orders from the point of view of their actual application in concrete cases before they are subjected to tests in the courts. Questions arising in the application of rules and orders to concrete cases frequently depend upon facts and conditions which are difficult to bring out accurately and thoroughly in the courts. The proceedings before the commission will develop the facts and conditions which are alleged to justify the provision and those which the employer depends upon to defeat it better than could be done in any court. It is frequently necessary for the court to have such facts available in order to arrive at a proper decision upon the constitutionality of such a rule or order, and in the absence of such a proceeding as this, an appellate court has practically no means of obtaining such information. This could not be better illustrated than in the recent decision of the New York Court of Appeals (People *v.* Schweinler Press, 214 N. Y., 395), upholding the constitutionality of the section of the labor law prohibiting night work for women, and, in effect, overruling its own decision of eight years previous, holding a similar provision unconstitutional. In the opinion of the recent case the court frankly says that its previous decision was due to a lack of proof at that time that the prohibition bore some direct relation to the public health and welfare, and that subsequently such proof had been gathered and was of such a nature as to warrant a different decision. In this case the evidence had been gathered largely through the efforts of a special factory investigating commission, but the whole incident illustrates the necessity for a thorough consideration of all facts involved before the matter is taken into the courts, and making the results of such consideration available for the use of the courts.

The special order applicable to a single establishment is necessary in order to take into account peculiar conditions, which, if rigidly applied, might render the entire law or general rule unconstitutional.

COURT REVIEW.

7. Any person in interest to be entitled to bring a special action in court to test the legality and reasonableness of any provision of the labor laws, of any rules and regulations made thereunder, or of any order directing compliance therewith. (It is probably advisable, in the case of State commissions, to limit the jurisdiction of such cases to a court sitting at the State capitol.)   Actions involving rules and regulations and orders not to be brought until final determination of the petitions for review (par. 6) by the commission.   Provision also to be made for suspending prosecutions pending determination of petitions or actions for review in court. Matters of fact which had not been before the commission to be referred back to the commission and opportunity given for the commission to change its rules or regulations before final decision by the court. Rules and regulations of the commission to be made prima facie reasonable in all court proceedings.

This recommendation is provided for in different ways in the different State commission laws. The purpose of these provisions, together with those relating to review by the commission (par. 6), is to secure a uniform interpretation of the labor laws and the rules and regulations for carrying them into effect; to prevent their being held unconstitutional by petty courts (which often results, on account of the impossibility of appealing such a decision, in an absolute bar to further enforcement of such provisions in that locality, even though the provisions may eventually be upheld by a higher court); and to protect the commission from ill-considered action by higher courts not having before them sufficient information to enable them to arrive at an intelligent decision.

8. The commission to have the incidental powers such as those of subpœnaing and examining witnesses and administering oaths, and so on, necessary for the full performance of duties imposed upon it. These powers, however, to be strictly limited to those branches in which the commission, on the basis of experience or the constitutional rules regarding evidence, finds them indispensable. In all other work the commission to have no powers of compulsory examination, and so on.

The powers of compulsory investigation and public hearings are liable to serious abuse in order to gain some temporary publicity or personal advantage, but in practice it is found that competent investigators and informal conferences, such as those of the proposed advisory councils, can secure more valuable and reliable information than when individuals are placed on the stand and required to talk to the stenographer.

CONTINUOUS INDUSTRY, EMPLOYMENT, AND INSURANCE.

9. In all industries or occupations operating continuously day and night and seven days a week the legislatures or Congress should enact laws requiring three shifts of eight hours each and one day of rest in seven, or their equivalent, administered under rules of an industrial commission laid down for each industry or establishment as may be required.

This class of legislation has been widely adopted in European countries, but has been found unenforceable without the aid of an administrative body competent to take into account the many differences of different establishments. In those countries hundreds of different rules are issued for different industries. For example, the rules for Pullman employees would differ materially from those for steel mills or hotels. We consider such laws unenforceable without this provision, and their enforcement can not be secured without a commission under the supervision of a representative council such as we recommend.

The Industrial Commission, with its advisory council, in its administration of employment bureaus is evidently the body to work out improvements not only in the bureaus themselves but in measures designed to provide for the unemployed or to regularize employment, such as workmen's hotels, or advice to Federal, State, and municipal authorities for shifting their work to the winter months or to periods of depression. These matters have been remarkably provided for in Germany, where the employment bureaus, with their advisory councils, have become the most effective of those in any country.

Such measures as sickness insurance, invalidity insurance, and unemployment insurance evidently require a large amount of investigation before they can be recommended. Their principal object should be the cooperation of employers and employees in the prevention of sickness, invalidity, and unemployment. Their administration and the drafting of laws and rules will evidently have to be intrusted to a commission with such an advisory council as is proposed.

POLICE AND MILITARY.

10. That such detective agencies may operate in more than one State, or be employed by industrial corporations engaged in interstate commerce, or which may use the mails shall be compelled to take out a Federal license, under the Industrial Commission, with regulations that will insure the character of their employees and the limitation of their activities to the bona fide business of detecting crime. Similar license and regulation for all private employment offices engaged in interstate business.

That all enterprises shall be forbidden the right to employ private armed guards, except as watchmen on the premises, or to have such watchmen deputized as police except where such is found necessary by the State or Federal Industrial Commission. That rules adapted to the differences required by various industries should be made by the Industrial Commission, in order to carry these laws into effect.

That such enterprises shall exercise their right to call upon the constituted authorities to furnish them with the necessary protection to their property, and to the lives of their workers, against the threatened attack of rioters or strikers; and that it shall be incumbent upon the constituted authorities to furnish such protection in the way of police or deputy sheriffs, and that a failure on their part to do this shall lay the political subdivision in which such damage to life or property may take place liable to damages. That all individuals denied their constitutional rights of habeas corpus, free access to public highways, free speech, etc., shall have similar power of action in damages against the political division in which such denial takes place. That all highways now claimed as private property shall be made public.

That the militia of the several States being subject to regulation by Congress, carefully drawn rules for their personal organization and conduct in the field shall be drawn up by the War Department, after conference with the Industrial Commission and advisory council, and that all parties arrested by the militia during the time of troubles shall be turned over for trial to the civil authorities. Similar rules should be drawn up by State authorities, with the cooperation of the State industrial commission and its advisory council, for the regulation of State constabulary. The War Department, with the aid of the Industrial Commission and advisory council, should investigate and recommend legislation regarding the shipment of arms and guards in interstate commerce.

One of the principal reasons why corporations are compelled to employ private guards is the failure of the taxpayers to provide them. This is also one of the principal reasons why laborers and labor organizers are denied their constitutional rights. Taxpayers take little part in the elections or otherwise to provide officials competent to and willing to protect the rights both of capital and labor, because the invasion of these rights does not affect them. This would be changed if the political subdivision were made liable in damages. Yet it is not proper, as has been done in some States, to provide for protection of property in this way without providing also for protection of labor in the same way. Laws designed to regulate deputy sheriffs or the police force can not be made effective under our system of local government without liability of taxpayers for violation.

The drafting of rules for the conduct of militia or State constabulary should not be left entirely to military authorities but should be drafted with the joint discussion and advice of employers and employees, who are more directly affected than other classes in the community. It is not intended that the Industrial Commission or advisory council shall have a veto on any regulations issued by the military or police authorities, but they should have opportunity for criticism and advice. The entire subject of policing industry has not been sufficiently investigated from all points of view, and more specific recommendations than these can not now be indorsed. It is therefore recommended above that further investigations from all points of view should be referred to the proper Federal and State authorities, assisted by the representatives of all interests affected.

LEGAL AID.

11. State commissions (and perhaps the Federal Commission) should render aid and assistance to deserving workmen in the adjustment of disputes other than collective disputes, and the recovery of claims arising out of their relations with their employers, and generally take such action as may be necessary for the protection of employees from fraud, extortion, exploitation, and other improper practices. For this purpose the commission to be authorized to assign members of its staff to appear in justice and other courts which adjudicate such claims, and to create local advisory committees of employers and employees to pass upon all such claims in cooperation with the deputy of the commission and in advance of court procedure.

This recommendation has been partly adopted in the New York act. An examination of the reports of existing public agencies of this sort and of the legal aid societies of the large cities of this country shows that by far the largest single class of cases with which they are called upon to deal is the adjustment of small wage claims. In some communities there already exist municipal and other so-called "poor men's courts" and "small debtors' courts," intended especially for the speedy settlement of small claims and disputes; but even the best of these courts are scarcely sufficient in themselves to meet the situation which confronts many employees. In some of them a very large proportion of disputes over small wage claims, in some instances as high as 90 per cent, can be settled if the two parties can only be brought together under conditions which make it certain that if a settlement is not made there is some one standing back of deserving claimants ready to push their cases.

Then, too, these cases frequently involve a general practice from which many individuals suffer, and yet it is impractical for any one of them to take the necessary action to secure redress or put an end to the practice. Members of a given class are often made the victims of exploitation or improper practices under conditions where it is not practical nor worth while for any individual to fight the matter out, and yet where the aggregate loss to the class is considerable. The ordinary shipper is generally able to pay for necessary legal services, and still Congress and a number of the State legislatures have required the Interstate Commerce Commission and the State commissions to render just such aid to shippers having claims against railroads, because of the economic disadvantage in which an individual shipper is placed in a contest with the railroads. That employees stand in need of such protection from the State is evidenced by the mass of labor legislation which has been enacted and the agencies which have been created for its administration.

Nor does such provision lack precedents other than the railroad legislation already referred to. For some years the bureau of industry and immigration of the New York Labor Department has, in cooperation with the New York Legal Aid Society, extended just such assistance to immigrants, and almost the exact provision here recommended has been included in the industrial commission law just enacted in New York.

Kansas City maintains its own legal aid bureau as part of the city government, and of the five or six thousand cases a year handled by it, almost half are wage claims. The largest class of cases handled by the public defender of Los Angeles is wage claims.

The above recommendation is intended to establish in the United States a system analogous to the industrial courts of France, Germany, and other European countries. But it can not be expected that many localities will initiate this class of courts, and it will require a State commission to make them general. If municipalities were given authority and then actually established such courts, the State commission would withdraw.

LEGISLATION.

12. The Industrial Commission, upon request of the legislature or Congress, or the committee on relations between capital and labor, to investigate a subject and draft bills. The commission to make recommendations regarding legislation affecting subjects under its jurisdiction.

It is not proposed that the Industrial Commission shall initiate legislation or make recommendations, except on laws previously assigned to it for administration. Matters outside its jurisdiction would bring it into the political and controversial field. Yet when Congress or the legislature is considering new legislation, such as sickness insurance, unemployment insurance, and so on, it might refer the matter, in its own discretion, for further investigation and recommendation. Advanced legislation is fought out by lobbies and in committees, and the advantage of reference to the Industrial Commission would be the cooperation of its advisory council in drafting a workable law, eliminating "jokers," and carrying out the intent of the legislature. At present there is no definite means provided whereby lobbyists can be required to come together and confer regarding measures. They appear usually as antagonists or lawyers before legislative committees, and not as the conferees of an advisory representative council. This proposition is by no means a novel or untried one. After fruitless administration of the impractical coal-mining laws, which had been placed on the statute books mainly by the labor unions of Illinois and Colorado, the legislature turned the matter of revising the mining code over to a joint committee selected by the coal operators and the mine workers' union, and then enacted into law, without amendment, the code which the two opposing interests, in conference with the legislative committee, jointly recommended.   The advisory committee on apprenticeship of the Wisconsin commission has recently agreed upon an apprenticeship law satisfactory to employers, trade unions, and the commission, and this was adopted by the legislature without change.   This method of legislation can be indefinitely extended to all matters, with the result. that, while both sides protect their own interests, they often eventually reach agreement on points where their interests and those of the public are common.

This, of course, does not do away with the final authority of Congress or the legislature, nor with the battle of opposing interests in the legislative branch of government where they have not been able to agree, nor where other interests are affected.   Here is the proper place for the lobbyists of both sides to endeavor to get the support of representatives of the people, and to override the other side. There could not be much of the advanced legislation required to meet the problems of capital and labor without a struggle in the legislature or Congress on new issues.   But when the legislature is ready to take an advanced step, it is an advantage to require the combatants to confer on the details and to subject their differences to investigation by an impartial body on which they have representation.   This advantage is intended in the above recommendation.

SUPREME COURTS.

13. At the request of the Supreme Court (State or Federal) the Industrial Commission shall investigate and report upon any questions of fact referred to it by the court and bearing upon the constitutionality or reasonableness of any Federal or State statute or administrative rule on the relations of employer and employee. Amendment of the judicature act so as to permit a State to appeal from its own supreme court to the Federal Supreme Court on a decision against a State based on conflict with the Federal Constitution.

While the principles of law are held to be settled and unchangeable, their applications change when conditions change.   Decisions of the courts on the constitutionality of labor laws often turn on the information which is placed before the court as to the necessity of the law.   The Supreme Court declared an eight-hour law for miners constitutional and a ten-hour law for bakers unconstitutional largely because it was furnished with conclusive information on conditions in the mines.but not in the bakeries.   (Holden v. Hardy, 1898, 169 U. S. 366; Lochner v. New York, 1907, 198 U. S. 45.)   The court of New York in 1907 declared (People v. Williams, 189 N. Y. 131) a law prohibiting night work for women unconstitutional, but held a similar law constitutional in 1915 (People v. Schweinler Press, 214 N. Y. 395), and gave as the reason for its change of opinion the evidence placed before it in the second case.   The court said in 1915:

1. It is urged that whatever might be our original views concerning this statute, our decision in People v. Williams (1907) is an adjudication which ought to bind us to the conclusion that it is unconstitutional.   While it may be that this argument is not without an apparent and superficial foundation and ought to be fairly met, I think that a full consideration of the Williams case and of the present one will show that they may be really and substantially differentiated, and that we should not be and are not committed by what was

said and decided in the former to the view that the legislature had no power
to adopt the present statute. * * *

While theoretically we may have been able to take judicial notice of some
of the facts and some of the legislation now called to our attention as sustain-
ing the belief and opinion that night work in factories is widely and substantially injurious to the health of women, actually very few of these facts were
called to our attention, and the argument to uphold the law on that ground was
brief and inconsequential.

Especially and necessarily was there lacking evidence of the extent to which
during the intervening years the opinion and belief have spread and strengthened that such night work is injurious to women; of the laws, as indicating
such belief, since adopted by several of our own States and by large European
countries, and the report made to the legislature by its own agency, the factory
investigating commission, based on investigation of actual conditions and study
of scientific and medical opinion that night work by women in factories is generally injurious and ought to be prohibited.

Other illustrations might be given showing the way in which
courts respond to the needs of progressive legislation when once they
have before them ascertained facts. Investigations by attorneys or
interested parties may have a certain weight in court, but the weight
can not be as great as the investigations and findings of an impartial
commission, supervised by representatives of the interests affected
by the decision. Criticism of the courts for decisions overturning
laws designed to protect labor, and the demands for constitutional
amendments depriving the court of power to declare laws unconstitutional, or providing for recall of decisions or recall of judges, often
fail to reach the real difficulty. The difficulty is that bureaus or
departments of labor and statistics have been so incompetently managed or their investigations so remote from the concrete facts that
need to be established that the courts have had no reliable information and have been compelled to fall back on their own meager
information or "common knowledge." If the court had at hand a
reliable and well-equipped referee with power to get the facts, as in
the Industrial Commission, it is probable that it would call upon
such referee instead of basing its judgment on the doubtful claims
and technical arguments of attorneys.

It will be noted, however, that this recommendation is merely supplementary to those in paragraphs 6 and 7. In those paragraphs
the rules and regulations of the commission itself dealing with labor
conditions are tested before the court, and they are made prima facie
valid and reasonable as based on adequate investigation. The present
recommendation is optional with the court and may pertain to an
act of the legislature or the rule of an administrative body upon
which the court is not reliably informed as to the facts.

A provision similar to this is included in the recent Federal Trade
Commission act (sec. 7).

The recommendation for amendment by Congress of the judicature
act is based on the fact that private individuals or corporations can
now appeal to the Federal courts if the decision of the State court is
against them, on the ground of conflict with the Federal Constitution, but the State itself can not appeal if its own State court has
decided against the State on the ground that the State law conflicts
with the Federal Constitution. It is sufficient that a State court
should decide issues under the State Constitution, but the Federal
Supreme Court alone should decide finally all issues under the Federal Constitution. With the provision that the Supreme Court

should require the Industrial Commission to investigate and report upon the facts which are alleged to justify the State legislation in question, the way is prepared for the Supreme Court to have before it the economic and social facts necessary to pass intelligently upon these questions of constitutionality.

MEDIATION AND MINIMUM WAGE.

14. The Industrial Commission (State or Federal) shall appoint, remove, and fix the compensation of a chief mediator of industrial disputes, the chief mediator to hold his position until removed by the Industrial Commission and to appoint such assistants as may be needed, and to fix their compensation with the approval of the Industrial Commission. He should appoint temporary mediators for special cases, without requiring them to give up their private business or offices.

The chief mediator and all assistant mediators to be selected from an eligible list prepared by the Civil Service Commission on a nonassembled examination, with the assistance of the Industrial Commission and the advisory council.

The chief mediator and his staff to have no powers whatever of compulsory testimony and to be prohibited from arbitrating any dispute, from making any public recommendation, or from revealing in any way, directly or indirectly, any information which they may have secured from any parties relative to an industrial dispute. Any violation to be sufficient ground for immediate removal by the Industrial Commission. The powers of the mediators to be those solely of voluntary mediation or conciliation, but the chief mediator shall offer his services in confidence to both sides of a dispute which, in his judgment, is of public importance.

The chief mediator and his staff to be wholly independent of the Industrial Commission, except as to appointment and removal, to the extent that they be prohibited from reporting any facts or recommendations whatever to the Industrial Commission or any other authority relative to the merits of any industrial dispute.

In case the mediator is unable to secure an agreement through conciliation, he shall recommend arbitration to both parties, and if both consent to abide by the decision of arbitrators he shall proceed to assist them in selecting a board of arbitration in any way and consisting of any number of members that both sides may agree upon. If agreement is not reached within a specified time on the third party to the board of mediation, the chief mediator shall appoint the same.

In case both parties do not consent to arbitration the mediator shall recommend the appointment of a board of mediation and investigation, which shall have power to make public its findings and recommendations, but such recommendations shall not be binding on any person. If both parties shall consent to such a board, the mediator shall assist them in creating the same and shall appoint the third member, if the parties can not agree on the same within a specified number of days.

In case both parties accept either a board of arbitration or a board of mediation and investigation, such board, as the case may be, shall have power of compelling testimony. The Newlands Act and the Department of Labor act should be so amended that all mediation and conciliation, whether on railways or in other industries, shall be consolidated under the mediator of the Federal Industrial Commission.   The Federal commission should cooperate with State mediators.

In the case of women and children, minimum wage boards should be created by the State industrial commissions.

The foregoing recommendation is intended to provide for strictly " voluntary " methods of mediation and arbitration. When engaged in this branch of its work the commission is not only prohibited from using its compulsory powers, but its mediation work is so rigidly separated from its other work that it can not even be suspected of using the coercive power of Government to favor either side. The mediator and his staff are to be strictly confidential advisors to the opposing interests, without the power of Government, or even the threat of using that power, to coerce either side of a collective dispute. If coercion is used in the form of " compulsory testimony " it is only with the previous voluntary consent of both sides.

The reasons for reaching this conclusion, and for recommending that in other branches of its work the proposed commission shall have the ordinary coercive powers of Government, are based on the fundamental distinction between collective bargaining and the individual labor contract. The principle in general is, that Government should not employ its coercive powers to regulate collective bargaining, but should, in certain matters, employ the force of law and administration to regulate the individual labor contract. It does the latter through laws on child labor, hours of labor, safety and health, workmen's compensation, sickness insurance, minimum wage, and so on.

Collective bargaining, in its last analysis, is based upon the coercive power of antagonistic classes organized for aggression and defense. The bargaining power of either side is the power to use the strike against the lockout, the boycott against the blacklist, the picket against the strikebreaker, the closed union shop against the closed nonunion shop, and so on. These are essential weapons, and no plausible verbiage or double meaning of words should blind us to the fact that these weapons are coercive, and are intended to be coercive, and, in the last analysis, will be used, secretly or openly, as coercive, by either side. Their object is similar to legislation regulating the individual labor contract except that they regulate it through joint agreement backed by their coercive weapons, instead of fines and imprisonment.

The question then is, Shall the coercive power of Government be used to deprive one side or the other, or both sides, of any or all of their coercive weapons designed to control the individual labor contract?

The most extreme use of this power is known as compulsory arbitration. Here the Government attempts to deprive both sides of all coercive weapons by completely prohibiting strikes, lockouts, boycotts, blacklists, picketing, and strikebreaking, and by preventing either side from using its methods of strategy designed to overcome the other side.

But the Government may use its coercive power to deprive either side of only a part of its weapons or strategies. Arbitration, or a joint agreement, consists of several steps, and at each step each side either employs its weapons or else resorts to strategy in order to play for position and to gain an advantage when it comes to using the weapons.

The first step in strategy of collective bargaining is recognition of the union; that is, recognition by the employer of the representatives of the union by consenting to confer with them. How important this preliminary step is considered by both sides is shown by the meaning which they give to the term "recognition." To "recognize a union" is considered to be not to merely hold a conference with its agents, but also to investigate grievances and demands, to negotiate concerning the terms of a collective agreement, and even to employ union men on terms consented to by the union. Strictly speaking, these are not "recognition," but are steps in collective bargaining that follow recognition. Recognition in the ordinary use of the term (the one here used) would be merely a conference in which the employer meets certain individuals, not as individuals but as recognized agents of the union authorized to speak on behalf of his employees. But it is so well understood that recognition, even in this limited sense, will be followed by other steps, that the decisive battle is often fought out at this point. The employer knows that, if he meets the leaders, the union has gained an advantage. He has acknowledged to all nonunionists and timid unionists in his shop that the union is something he can not ignore, and this is a flag of truce and a concession for his employees to join the union or come out openly on its side. By just so much he has weakened his bargaining power against the union. Consequently, if he has decided not to have a certain union in his shop he must refuse at the very beginning to confer with its agents.

If, then, the Government steps in and compels both sides to confer, it may take the first step in the name of "compulsory investigation" or "compulsory testimony," without power to prevent a strike or lockout. If the Government is given power to step in and compel the employer and employee to testify, to produce papers and records, it is attempting to substitute compulsion for voluntary consent at two important steps of collective bargaining. It introduces compulsory recognition and compulsory negotiation[1] under the guise of "compulsory testimony." The mere compulsion on employers, through prosecutions, as proposed by our colleagues, to compel employers to confer with unions, can have no result, unless it be accompanied by compulsion to investigate, as in the Canadian and Colorado acts, or to arbitrate, as in Australia. If employers are compelled merely to confer they can, of course, reject all propositions, and the nominal recognition of the union thereby secured would only be a further opportunity for declaring their determination not to

---

[1] These terms may appear ridiculous, but they are not more ridiculous than the term "compulsory arbitration." Arbitration, strictly speaking, is the voluntary consent of both parties to refer a dispute to a third person and to accept and carry out his decision. It is no longer "arbitration" if the Government coerces the parties by constituting itself the third party and compelling them to accept and carry out the decision. But if, in common usage, we have agreed to forget the absurdity of compulsory arbitration, we can also forget the same absurdity in the terms "compulsory recognition" and "compulsory negotiation."

recognize the union. If such a law is intended to accomplish anything it should go further and compel the employers to submit to compulsory investigation or compulsory arbitration, and this would mean compulsion also on the unions to confer and testify or to arbitrate.

In our hearings in San Francisco we found unions that refused to meet the employers for a joint agreement, but required them to sign up individually the demands which the unions had already decided upon. This can not properly be called collective bargaining or recognition of an employers' association any more than the decision of employers not to deal collectively but to deal with their employees individually. A law requiring employers to confer with and recognize unions should also require unions to confer with and recognize employers, and if this is made effective it would result in something like the Canadian or Colorado acts, described below. Employers who are strongly fortified against unions object to compulsory testimony because it weakens their bargaining power, but employers dealing with strong unions desire it because by recognizing the union they have already consented to investigation. Their next step is to compel the unions to wait for the investigation before striking.

This next step in collective bargaining is usually a provision that both sides shall continue at work or return to work while investigation and determination is in progress. This is, of course, the great object of arbitration, and practically all voluntary methods provide that work shall continue while arbitration is going on. This provision is recognized in the Canadian industrial disputes investigation act, latterly adopted by New Zealand and Colorado. The Government prohibits either side from a strike or lockout for 30 days, pending compulsory testimony and recommendation, but the parties are not compelled to accept the recommendation. After the 30 days have expired they may start their strike or lockout without any legal penalty. The Government meanwhile invites each side to appoint its representatives on a board of investigation and mediation and the two to select a third member. If either side refuses to appoint its representative the Government steps in and names the representative. If both sides are unable to agree on the third member the Government again steps in and names the third member. In other words, the Government coerces each side to go through the same forms that they would do if they agreed voluntarily to refer a dispute to arbitration, and it prohibits them from strike or lockout pending a finding and recommendation. This is compulsory recognition, compulsory negotiation, compulsory testimony, and compulsory labor pending investigation, but without compulsion after investigation.

On the other hand, the weak union favors compulsory conference and recognition because it seems to give it an advantage in bargaining. Both strong and weak unions are opposed to compulsory testimony because they get the equivalent by recognition, and they fear that it will lead to the compulsory waiting of the Canadian act. For these reasons the Canadian system should be put in the same class as compulsory arbitration, since the Government interferes to weaken or strengthen the collective bargaining power of either side. This is the essential point of Government intervention. The term "arbitration" is misleading because it signifies the voluntary agreement on an umpire and the voluntary acceptance of his award. But arbitration can not be voluntary when the Government throws its coercive power to one side or the other by appointing a representative of either side, or an umpire, on the arbitration board without the consent of both sides. This is coercive interference with collective bargaining power, which is the essential element in compulsory arbitration.

For this reason it can not be claimed that the Canadian system is "voluntary arbitration." This term is also misleading. Collective bargaining is not voluntary in the same sense that individual bargaining is voluntary, since it depends on certain coercive weapons such as strikes, boycotts, blacklists, and so on, together with strategy in using these weapons, and these are not instruments in individual bargaining. All that is meant by voluntary arbitration is that the Government does not use its coercive power to weaken or strengthen the collective coercion of either side.

The first object of the Canadian law is the commendable one of bringing both parties together for investigation of the demands and grievances, with the hope that, by delaying hostilities for 30 days, time will be given for mediation, conciliation, and a voluntary agreement. For this reason the boards created are properly called boards of "mediation and investigation." It often occurs that within the 30 days both sides reach such a voluntary agreement and, if so, the board is dissolved after approving the agreement.

The second object is, in case a voluntary agreement is not reached by this kind of mediation within 30 days, that the publication of a set of recommendations by the board will bring to bear the pressure of public opinion on both sides so that they will feel obliged to accept the recommendations and continue at work. Compulsory recognition, negotiation, and testimony are used as the means of coercion through the support that public opinion may give to the Government.

But mere public opinion is not enough to accomplish this object. The next step is the compulsory arbitration of Australasia, which brings the power of fine and imprisonment to enforce an award made by a public official.

It is believed that any of these compulsory methods are unsuited to American conditions, and that the foregoing recommendation for a voluntary board of investigation, adapted from the Canadian act but without its compulsory features, will prove a valuable addition to the present Newlands Act, which goes only as far as voluntary arbitration in interstate railroad disputes. If one party or the other refuses to accept a board of arbitration with power to make a binding award, it is proposed that the mediator shall invite both to create a board of investigation with power to take testimony and to make recommendations which are not binding as an award. The jurisdiction of the Newlands Act is proposed to be extended under the Federal Commission to all labor disputes in all industries engaged in interstate commerce. It is believed that in many cases of serious public concern neither side can afford to reject an offer on the part of the Government to use its powers of compulsory testimony to ascertain the facts and to make recommendations, provided the parties retain their liberty to reject the recommendations. The value of this proposal consists in the probability that a thorough investigation, participated in by both sides, may lead to agreement, as it has often under the Canadian act. But this should be brought about by consent of both parties and not by compulsory representation of either side, nor compulsory postponement of hostilities, as provided in the Canadian act.

The intent of the foregoing recommendation is that the mediator shall use all of the powers of persuasion that he can summon but is not to use, nor to be in a position to threaten or even to suggest the use of, any powers of coercion. Even compulsory testimony is to be used only in case he can persuade both parties to consent to its use. The mediator is not even permitted to make public any information he may acquire regarding a dispute, or to give that information to the Industrial Commission or to any other public authority that has the power of governmental coercion. Mediation and arbitration are to be voluntary throughout, as far as government is concerned.

The case is different with individual bargaining. Here it is recognized that the individual worker is at a disadvantage with the employer. In fact, he usually makes no bargain at all. He merely accepts or rejects the terms offered by the employer. Where this is so, and there is a public interest to be gained, Congress or the legislatures and the industrial commissions should exercise adequate compulsory powers to equalize and protect the bargaining power of individual employees.

It should be remembered that in the eyes of the law the labor contract is an individual contract—a contract between an individual workman and an individual employer. Even if the employer is a corporation of thousands of stockholders and bondholders, they are treated as a single individual for the purposes of a contract. But the law does not usually recognize a collective or joint agreement between a union and an employer or employers' association as a contract. The courts will not usually enforce it as they enforce individual contracts. Such a contract, so called, will not bind anybody by the force of law. A contract with a trade-union is not a contract in law; it is merely an understanding, or a usage, or a joint agreement that, when the real labor contract is made between individual employer and employee, it will be made according to the terms of the joint agreement. If an individual employer breaks the agreement by hiring a workman on different terms, the only means that the union has of enforcing the agreement is that of a strike. It is not a breach of contract. The union can not usually get an injunction or damages in court on account of the violation. In the same way the employer's only practicable remedy is the lockout. He probably can not bring a suit for damages, because the union agreement was not a contract. The legislature might, of course, change the law and provide for the legal enforcement of the collective bargain. This would be compulsory arbitration. But as it now stands a joint trade agreement is a kind of usage or understanding agreed to by two opposing interests and generally enforced on individuals by the coercive weapons of strike, lockout, boycott, or blacklist. It differs from a statute in the fact that its enforcement is left to private organizations or individuals while the enforcement of a statute

or order of a commission is effected by the penalties of imprisonment,
fines, or damages. A minimum wage law, for example, may differ in
no respect from a joint agreement with a union, except that the one
is enforced by legal penalties or the threat of penalties, and the other
by a strike or the threat of a strike.

The practical conclusion to be drawn from this distinction is that,
since a State industrial commission may be both a mediator and a
minimum wage commission, it should act only as a voluntary mediator where a union is actually in operation and securing agreements.
But where there is no effective union there the minimum wage should
apply. This is the condition of women and child workers, and for
them the State, but not the Federal commission, should create advisory minimum wage boards, which, acting with the women inspectors of the commission, should make investigation and recommend
the minimum wage and other conditions to the industrial commission. The last named would then hold public hearings and the rules
of law would apply as already outlined in preceding paragraphs.

The same principle applies to other labor legislation which regu-
lates the individual labor contract, such as child labor laws, workmen's compensation, safety, health, employment offices, legal aid,
mechanics' liens, and so on. These are matters which are not usually
an issue in collective bargaining even of unions composed of men,
and do not usually lead to strikes or lockouts. Neither is the individual workman, in making his contract of employment, able to
protect himself in these matters. When government here comes to
the aid of the weaker party to the wage bargain, it is not usually intervening in the field of collective bargaining. The situation is different
in matters of wages, hours of labor, and shop rules which govern the
manner of work, dismissals, promotions, and so on. Where unions
show themselves strong enough to protect individuals in these matters
the function of government should, as far as possible, be limited to
voluntary mediation.

It doubtless has appealed to some people who consider the employer's position more powerful than that of the union, that the
employer should be compelled in some way to deal with unions, or at
least to confer with their representatives. But, if the State recognizes any particular union by requiring the employer to recognize it,
the State must necessarily guarantee the union to the extent that it
must strip it of any abuses that it may practice. The State might
be compelled to regulate its initiation fees and dues, its apprenticeship ratio, its violation of agreements, and all of the other abuses on
account of which the employer refuses to deal with it. This is exactly
what is done through compulsory arbitration, and there is no place
where the State can stop if it brings compulsion to bear on the employers without also regulating by compulsion the unions. If so,
the whole question is transferred to politics, and the unions which
attempt to use a friendly party to regulate the employer may find a
hostile party regulating them. We believe that collective bargaining
and joint agreements are preferable to individual bargaining, and
we believe that the general public should support the unions in their
efforts to secure collective agreements. But this can only be done
through the influence of public opinion without the force of law.
It is based on the conclusion that two opposing organizations, equally
strong, are able to drive out abuses practiced by the other. This is

very different from recommending that the Government should step in and drive out the abuses.

This conclusion and recommendation in favor of voluntary mediation is based also, in part, as already stated, on the distinction between collective bargaining and the individual labor contract. While Government for the past 80 years has been wisely interfering more and more with the individual labor contract, through child labor laws, wage payment laws, mechanics' liens, workmen's compensation, and so on, for the benefit of the weaker party, yet in matters of governmental interference with collective bargaining, we have to deal with great organized, hostile interests that are capable of using their power in the politics of the country, in the administration of labor laws, and even in the courts of justice. Any interference with their collective bargaining power forces them to get control, if possible, of the political parties or the executive and administrative officials, or the courts, that interfere. The result is more far-reaching and destructive than the mere decision one way or another in a particular dispute. It tends to corrupt or to discredit or to make inefficient the Government itself. This country is so large, with such extremes of sectional interests, with industrial and class interests, with nationality and race interests, and with such extremes of wages and costs of living, that it is an easy matter for these powerful organized interests to make alliances with others for the appointment or control of officials. When this is done, neither side can have confidence in the mediators or arbitrators who are chosen without their consent. A system, even though compulsory only in part, is likely to break down after a few decisions which are resented by either side. The department or commission responsible for the decision loses confidence and therefore usefulness. For this reason the weakest part of our recommendation is that the mediator shall appoint the third party to a voluntary board of arbitration or a voluntay board of investigation in case the two parties can not agree. It seems necessary that some authority be given that power. But the mediator is likely to lose the confidence of the side that loses in an arbitration, since he will be held responsible for the arbitrator whom he appointed. This might incapacitate him for future mediation. But we can think of no other agency that would be acceptable to both sides. If the mayor, or the governor or the President appoints the third man, employers would object. If the courts were to appoint him the unions would object. We are forced to recommend that this authority be given to the mediator, but we propose that he should not be tied down to any procedure that would prevent him from devising any system that his ingenuity might suggest rather than fall back on his precarious power of appointing the odd man.

After considering all forms of governmental compulsion in collective disputes and even admitting their partial success in other countries, we conclude that, on the whole, in this country as much can be accomplished in the long run by strictly voluntary methods as by compulsory methods of avoiding strikes and lockouts. It can not be expected that strikes and lockouts can be abolished altogether. Even countries with compulsory systems have not succeeded in preventing all of them. In our country, the voluntary method in collective bargaining avoids the much more serious evil of discrediting the agencies of Government which must be looked to for impartial enforcement of

laws affecting the individual labor contract. It is to the enactment
and enforcement of laws protecting laborers as individuals that we
must look for the removal of underlying causes of industrial unrest
and for the eventual reduction of strikes that now spring from the
cumulative abuses that individuals suffer without other effective
remedies. But the removal of these abuses can not be accomplished
without the efficient and nonpartisan administration of laws, and this
is the main purport of our recommendation for industrial commissions to regulate the individual labor contract.

TRADE DISPUTES.

15. Congress and the State legislatures to enact laws similar to the
British trades disputes act of 1906, relieving employers' associations
and labor unions, as well as their members, officers, or agents, when
acting in their behalf, of criminal suits, damage suits, and injunctions
on account solely of combination or conspiracy connected with a labor
dispute, when the act would be lawful if done by one person. Such
laws would permit the use by either side without legal penalty of
its weapons of closed union shop and closed nonunion shop, of strike
and lockout, boycott and blacklist, peaceful picketing and strike-
breaking, peaceful inducement to break a contract to work or to break
off allegiance with a union, in pursuance of an effort to win a labor
dispute. The law would not prevent prosecutions for conspiracy
where the act if done by one person would be a crime. We copy
below sections of the British trades disputes act as indicating the
kind of legislation which with modifications to suit American laws
would probably reach these objects:

Conspiracy.—An agreement or combination by two or more persons to do or
procure to be done any act in contemplation or furtherance of a trade dispute
between employers and workmen shall not be indictable as a conspiracy if such
an act committed by one person would not be punishable as a crime. * * *
An act done in pursuance of an agreement or combination by two or more persons shall, if done in contemplation or furtherance of a trade dispute, not be
actionable unless the act, if done without any such agreement or combination,
would be actionable.

Damages.—An action against a trade-union, whether of workmen or masters,
or against any members or officials thereof on behalf of themselves and all other
members of the trade-union, in respect of any tortious act alleged to have been
committed by or on behalf of the trade-union, shall not be entertained by any
court.

Breach of contract and interference with business.—An act done by a person
in contemplation or furtherance of a trade dispute shall not be actionable on the
ground only that it induces some other person to break a contract of employment, or that it is an interference with the trade, business, or employment of
some other person or with the right of some other person to dispose of his
capital or his labor as he wills.

Picketing and sabotage.—It shall be lawful for one or more persons, acting
either on their own behalf or on behalf of a trade-union or of an individual
employer or firm in contemplation or furtherance of a trade dispute, to attend
at or near a house or place where a person resides or works or carries on business or happens to be, if they so attend merely for the purpose of peacefully
obtaining or communicating information or of peacefully persuading any person
to work or abstain from working.

Every person who, with a view to compel any other person to abstain from
doing or to do any act which such other person has a legal right to do or abstain
from doing, wrongfully and without legal authority—

1. Uses violence to or intimidates such other person or his wife or children
or injures his property ; or,

2. Persistently follows such other person about from place to place ; or,

3. Hides any tools, clothes, or other property owned or used by the other person or deprives him of or hinders him in the use thereof; or,

4. Watches or besets the house or other place where such person resides, or works, or carries on business, or happens to be, or the approach to such house or place; or,

5. Follows such other person with two or more other persons in a disorderly manner in or through any street or road,

shall, on conviction thereof by a court of summary jurisdiction, or an indictment as hereinafter mentioned, be liable either to pay a penalty not exceeding £20, or to be imprisoned for a term not exceeding three months, with or without hard labor.

It is apparent from all the preceding recommendations that the creation of industrial commissions with advisory councils, depends for its success on the permanency of organizations of employers and organizations of laborers. It is only as we have organizations that we can have real representation. The preceding recommendations are designed, through salaried positions for civil service appointees and unsalaried positions for the representatives of organizations, to keep the latter continuously responsible to the organizations that elect and recall them. For this reason any policy of Government that tends to destroy the organizations or to compel them to hide their operations in secrecy tends to weaken the basis upon which improvement in the enactment and administration of labor law must be based. Such a policy is that which permits employers to collect damages, and in a lesser degree to secure injunctions against unions without at the same time effectually permitting unions to bring similar proceedings against employers' associations. The decision in the case of the hatters' union (208 U. S., 274) awarding heavy damages for boycotting against practically all members of the local union, will make it possible to collect damages in all cases where an unlawful conspiracy is shown. Since damages arise from all strikes and boycotts, there is no conceivable limit to which suits for damages can be brought. The result must be the weakening or destruction of unions or driving them into secrecy and a more generally avowed policy of violence.

This policy also brings the courts into the field of collective bargaining, and necessarily leads, sooner or later, to the efforts of both sides to control the judicial as well as the administrative and legislative branches of Government. Just as our earlier recommendations were intended, in part, to take the administration of labor law out of the hands of either side and to make it a joint affair, so this recommendation is intended, in part, to relieve the courts of similar partisanship in matters of collective bargaining. It is believed that strong organizations of employers and employees are much more capable than the courts of holding each other in check and preventing abuses on either side. The recommendation is intended to recognize the collective weapons of both sides as the means of securing this result, and yet, through the Industrial Commission and its advisory council, including mediators and the efficient enforcement of labor laws, to minimize the necessity of resorting to these weapons.

The so-called Clayton Act of 1913 was supposed by some lawyers to accomplish the result intended in the foregoing recommendation, but other lawyers contend that the law of conspiracy has not been changed by the act. At any rate, the law does not apply to the States, only one of which, California, has adopted a similar law, and another, Massachusetts, has withheld adoption owing to an unfavorable reply by the Supreme Court on the question propounded by the legislature. It is admitted that the British act accomplishes the intended purpose, and consequently we take it as the model in case these other acts are found, under court decisions, not to do so.

The recommendation is, as already said, intended to prevent the courts from interfering with the collective weapons, provided they are peaceful, that either side uses to defeat the other side. It is recognized, of course, that these weapons are coercive and are intended to be coercive, but they are not coercive in the sense of physical violence. They are coercive only in the sense that numbers of people acting together to do an act lawful for each separately have more power over individuals than a single individual acting by himself would ordinarily have. But even an individual acting alone may have the same kind of coercive power, which in his case would be lawful, as, for example, when an employer compels a union man to give up his membership in a union by threatening to discharge him if he does not. This kind of individual coercion is held to be entirely lawful, and any State or Federal statute which prevents the employer from using such coercion is unconstitutional. This is so even if the employer is a corporation with thousands of stockholders and bondholders, for the corporation is held to be, for that purpose, not a conspiracy, but a single person. By declaring laws unconstitutional which attempt to deprive the employer or corporation of the right to discharge a man on account of his unionism, the court steps in to prohibit the State from depriving the employer of a coercive weapon used to defeat the union. It prohibits a State from depriving an employer of the closed nonunion shop as a coercive weapon against unions.

A counterweapon which the union has is the closed union shop. If the employer discharges or threatens to discharge one of his employees on account of his membership in a union, the only effective weapon that the employee may have, in order to retain his membership, may be a strike or the threat of a strike by his union to compel the employer to discharge all nonunion men. In some States a strike for such a purpose, under the decisions of the courts, is unlawful, on the ground that it is a conspiracy to compel the employer to give up his right to employ whom he pleases, or a conspiracy to deprive the nonunion man of his right to work for whom he pleases. The foregoing recommendation is intended to make it plain that no employer or union of employers shall be prevented by law or by a court from running a closed nonunion shop if he can, and no union shall be prevented from compelling him to run a closed union shop if it can, so long as the method would be lawful for a person not backed by a union.

In a similar way it is lawful for an employer to furnish other employers, whether members of his association or not, with information as to whether an employee is a member of a union or a union agitator, and to file such information in the employment bureau of an employers' association. If the workman can not prevent his employer by law from discharging him on account of unionism, much less can he require another employer to hire him. It is lawful also for an employers' association to expel a member who refuses to comply with a nonunion rule, and, except in case of a public utility, to refuse to deal with him or to discriminate against him. Furthermore, since other employers' rights of furnishing information to fellow employers are so great, it is practically impossible to get proof that they contain the malicious purpose which constitutes a blacklist, and statutes preventing employers from using some of these legal rights have been held unconstitutional. But, as a rule, the employers' blacklist does not need to go to these extreme measures permitted by law, because it is effective short of these measures.

The case is different with the union's weapon, the boycott. To carry out a boycott the union must circulate " unfair lists " and must induce as many persons as possible to withdraw their patronage. The courts distinguish between the primary boycott and the secondary boycott. The former is perhaps legal in some cases, just as a strike is legal, for it is merely the refusal to patronize an employer on the part of the same persons, or their fellow unionists, who have struck against the employer, or who are locked out or blacklisted by him or his association. It is doubtful, though, whether this primary boycott is legal if it extends to members of unions other than the one directly injured. The American Federation of Labor, for example, can not carry out a primary boycott on goods which the hatters' union has boycotted, since it is prohibited from publishing the information. And even the strike and the primary boycott are sometimes unlawful if the court holds that the purpose or the means are unlawful. The courts will not directly enjoin either a strike or a primary boycott. They can not compel a man to work or to purchase. But they can make the unlawful strike or primary boycott ineffective by enjoining even peaceful picketing or persuasion, or the circulation of "unfair lists" designed to notify others that the boycott is on.

But the secondary boycott is generally held illegal because it is an additional boycott placed upon a third party, usually a merchant, who continues to sell the goods of the boycotted employer. As to this third party the boycott is primary, and he can secure an injunction or damages on the ground of conspiracy to injure him without just cause, or to compel him to break a contract, if he considers the damage to himself worth while. But boycott suits are not often brought by third parties, either because the damage to them is usually slight, since they only need to patronize other manufacturers whose goods the boycotters are willing to buy, or because the courts protect them through suits brought by the party originally boycotted. The employer originally boycotted would not secure protection if he depended on a hundred or a thousand boycotted merchants not seriously concerned to bring separate suits. Consequently the vast majority of boycott cases are brought by the person primarily boycotted, in order to prevent the spread of boycotts to other persons who deal with him; in other words, to prevent a secondary boycott against himself. The boycotted employer hides behind the alleged injury done to third parties in order to get damages, not for them, but for himself, as in the case of the Loewe Co. against the hatters' union. The ground of action is not injury to third parties, but interference with the employers' right to have free and uninterrupted business dealings with all who wish to deal with him. This does not seem to be equal treatment of the employers' blacklist which interferes with the unionists' right to have uninterrupted access to all employers, and the employees' boycott which interferes with the employers' right of access to the commodity market.

The arguments now used to declare the secondary boycott illegal are those formerly used to declare the strike and the primary boycott illegal. Our recommendation simply carries forward another step the effort to secure equality between organized capital and organized labor.

Of the other weapons, the strike and lockout, the employers' association does not usually employ its weapon, because it can force the union to strike or yield, but the strike is illegal if the purpose is illegal, such as the purpose in some States of securing a closed union shop. The recommendation is intended to remove all illegality from the strike.

This recommendation is intended to do away with the doctrine of conspiracy for both employers' associations and labor unions, except in so far as the conspiracy is one to commit what would be a crime for one person, and to do away with all suits for damages, including injunctions to prevent damage, against a union or against its members when acting for the union, except suits for damages against conspirators to commit a crime.

The doctrine of conspiracy is based on the undoubted fact that, while a lawful act done by only one person may be coercive and cause damage, or be intended to cause damage, yet the coercion and damage are ordinarily so small, compared with the social advantage of liberty to do as one pleases, that, except in breach of contract, the court does not entertain a suit at law for damages or for prevention of the coercion that causes damages. Yet the same lawful act, if done by agreement between two or more persons, may reach a point of coercion where the damage, compared with the social advantage of liberty to combine with others, is so serious that the agreement becomes unlawful. Therefore, those who enter into an agreement to do an act which would be lawful without the agreement, or their agents, may be prosecuted for damages or may be prevented by injunction from using the coercive power of numbers to cause the damage. It is this doctrine of conspiracy, or coercion through mere numbers, that is sought to be removed by the recommendation. Individuals and the individual members of unions who conspire with them would continue to be arrested, prosecuted, and punished as individuals or conspirators for all acts which are criminal for them as individuals, but no suit for damages could be brought against the union for acts committed by or on behalf of the union.

In other words, the recommendation removes completely the doctrine of civil conspiracy according to which damages may be collected or injunctions issued. It, however, retains the doctrine that all conspirators who join in procuring an act that is criminal for one person to do are likewise guilty with the person who does it. This might include all the members of a union if all were proven actualy to have joined in such a conspiracy. Those who conspired could still be prosecuted and sent to prison, as was done in the case of the officers and members of the structural iron workers for transporting dynamite. The recommendation is not intended to change the law in this respect. It would change the law in the hatters' case.

Employers are already learning the ineffectiveness of the injunction and the danger to themselves of throwing on the courts the burden of protection which they can as readily secure through their own organizations. With their advantages of position, both as owners of the means of livelihood and the possessors of the power of discharge and of blacklist of union members which goes with the ownership of property, they have a superior power over unions. Our recommendations do not grant employers' associations rights additional to those which they now enjoy in fact; they merely grant the unions corresponding rights.

The British act also defines the kind of picketing that is criminal in that it is not peaceful, and thereby defines what is peaceful picketing. In these cases of illegal or criminal picketing and in the destruction or damage to physical property those who have done the criminal acts and those who have conspired to have them done may be fined and imprisoned, but the union funds or the property of its members not proven to have joined in the criminal conspiracy could not be taken for damages.

Without entering into further details, the object of the recommendation is to place unions and employers' associations upon an equal basis in the use of their competitive weapons.

Regarding the constitutionality of this recommendation it should be noted that it takes both employers' associations and unions from under the operation of the antitrust laws. This differs from the Clayton and other acts which take only unions from under the antitrust laws or common law and might be good ground for declaring these laws unconstitutional. The British act does this by distinguishing between employers as merchants or associations of manufacturers, who sell commodities to the public, and whose bargain may be called the "price bargain," and the same employers in the different function of dealing with labor, and whose bargain is the "wage bargain." The employers, in their function of merchants and manufacturers, or sellers of products or commodities to consumers or the public, continue to come under the antitrust laws, and the Interstate Commerce Commission, the Federal Trade Commission, and the State public utility commissions have been created for the purpose of protecting the public against them as such. These commissions regulate price bargains for commodities or products, between corporations and consumers.

But it does not follow that even the same employers when organized to regulate the wage bargain with employees should be treated as a conspiracy or trust. They perform a very different function and public policy is very different. In the case of the price bargain the public is interested in securing low prices, but in the case of wage bargain it is interested in permitting high wages. Yet the public needs protection against abuses of labor unions as it does against the abuses of trusts. The employers' association stands between organized labor and the public just as the railroad and public utility commissions and the trade commission stand between merchants' or manufacturers' associations and the unorganized public. But the employers' associations are a better protection to the public against the abuses of unions than are the courts. Labor leaders who wish to keep discipline in their unions and the observance of joint agreements realize that they can not do so unless confronted by a strong employers' association. They realize that continued abuses lead eventually to the destruction of their unions. An employer who stays out of his organization is as culpable as a laborer who stays out of his union. Employers should organize 100 per cent just as the unions endeavor to reach that mark.

It would, therefore, seem to be proper and constitutional classification in the interest of public policy to treat manufacturers under a law prohibiting or regulating trusts and public utilities and to treat the same persons as employers under different laws, like those of mediation and trade disputes, where both employers' associations and trade-unions are given immunities for the use of peaceful coercive weapons which they do not possess under the antitrust laws.

FOUNDATIONS.

16. Considerable attention has been given by this commission to the largest foundations or endowments now in the hands of private trustees. Any proposed legislation on this subject should be preceded by a complete investigation of all foundations and endowments, else the law would have effects not contemplated by the legislature or Congress. Such an investigation would include all endowed charities, endowments of religious organizations and universities and colleges. We are informed that such investigations have been made in England and France, resulting in legislation. The investigation should be complete, covering all aspects of the question and bringing out both the advantages and the disadvantages of such foundations and endowments. The legislature could then act intelligently on the subject.

We are convinced that many of these endowments in private hands have a beneficial effect on the work of State and governmental institutions. Large private universities have set the example and stimulated the States to support and enlarge their State universities. Some of the investigations and reforms started by recent large foundations have already induced Congress and administrative departments to enter the same field and to extend it. In fact, almost everything that Government now does was done at first through private initiative, and it would be a misfortune if private endowments, unless plainly shown to have committed abuses, should be prohibited. Even their abuses can be rectified by the legislature through its control over charters, if reasonable ground can be shown. But it is better, for the most part, that they should go on at their own initiative in order that the people through their Government may see the value of their work and then take it up and extend it more widely than the private foundations are able to do. It is largely for this reason that we recommend a " Federal fund for social welfare " (par. 18), in order that the Nation may compete with or displace private foundations in this vital matter.

However, experience has abundantly shown that there should be no alliance between these private foundations or endowments and the Government. The State or Government should neither subsidize them nor be subsidized by them, nor cooperate with them. Such cooperation has often led to public scandal. Instead of subsidizing private charity the State should use its money to displace it by better and more universal charity. Instead of calling upon private foundations for help, the Government should treat them as competitors.

No effort on the part of Government officials to secure financial assistance from them should be allowed.

17. The Federal commission to have charge of all subsidies granted to the States for the promotion of industrial education, safety, employment offices, and other matters, as Congress may determine. The commission to meet the expenses of State officials when called together for conferences on standards and uniformity. Subsidies to be granted on condition that the standards are maintained.

The Public Health Service now has authority to call conferences of State health officials and to meet their expenses. The same power should be given to the proposed industrial commission. A large part of the work of the commission will be the field work of advising State officials as to the best methods of administration. This kind of work is now done by the Department of Agriculture and the Public Health Service.

Subsidies are recommended in certain cases because the State governments are not in position to secure adequate funds and as an inducement to bring their standards up to the standards formulated by the Federal commission.

(Funds for this purpose are recommended in paragraph 18.)

FEDERAL FUND FOR SOCIAL WELFARE.

18. A Federal inheritance tax on all estates above $25,000, beginning at 1 per cent on the excess above $25,000 and rising to 15 per cent on the excess above $1,000,000 for the class of direct heirs, such as wife, children, and parents. Higher rates for more remote relatives and strangers. The Federal inheritance tax to be a supertax, added upon the existing rates assessed by the States. Provision, however, to be made that any State which repeals all inheritance tax laws, or refrains from enacting them, shall receive from the Federal Government, say, 50 cents per capita of its population per year. The administration and collection of this tax to be placed in charge of present assessors and collectors of income taxes, who already collect income taxes on estates in the hands of executors. Revenues derived from inheritance taxes to be placed in trust with the Federal Reserve Board for investment in securities approved by Congress. The fund to be known as "Federal fund for social welfare." Expenditures of income derived from such securities to be made under the direction of the Federal industrial commission for such purposes of industrial and social welfare as Congress may authorize. Should the income from investments not be adequate to meet the authorized expenditures, further investments to be withheld and the principal to be expended. Revenues derived from activities of the commission, such as head tax on immigrants, etc., to belong to the fund. Also unexpended balance to be held in the fund for disposition by Congress.

A similar fund collected from immigrants in excess of the expenses of the service is held with accruals for disposition by Congress.

We have previously shown the need of improved administration in providing for any future program of social legislation. We have held that it is useless to undertake any additional labor legislation if effective, nonpartisan machinery of administration is not provided, but even with such machinery it can not be expected that the expense of government will be reduced. In fact, the expenses will be increased, and no legislation should be attempted unless the possibility of getting these revenues is fully considered.

Moreover, these revenues must be continuous, else the whole program will be liable to sudden breakdown through failure of funds. Hostility to labor laws is just as effective when it succeeds in killing appropriations, on the ground of economy, as when it defeats the law itself.

Already the increased expense of administration of labor laws is bringing active and effective protest. The greatest leap in this expense has come with workmen's compensation. So far as this increase is due to inefficiency of the existing political and partisan methods of administration the protest is valid. The remedy consists in improving the efficiency and eliminating the partisanship, and this is the purport of what we have previously said. So far, also, as the increase places excessive burdens of taxation on the already burdensome taxes of the people, the protest also is valid. But here the remedy consists in discovering new sources of revenue that will not be burdensome.

A Federal inheritance tax, partly distributed to the States, seems to be the most appropriate method of securing these new sources of revenue. The principal underlying cause of social unrest is the uncertainty of income of wage earners and small producers. A steady, continuous income, even though it be small in amount, is of more importance than high wages or earnings at certain times and no earnings at other times. This uncertainty of income is the main cause of the dependence, inequality, and oppression which produce conflicts between capital and labor.

The great majority of wage earners can not provide in advance for future contingencies when they will get no income. These contingencies come from accidents, sickness, invalidity, old age, death, unemployment, and the lack of industrial education.

There are two main reasons for this inability to provide for contingencies: (1) Inability in bargaining for wages to take into account future contingencies and future cost of living. The wage earner may be able when bargaining to get enough wages for current cost of living, but he does not include insurance premiums in his notion of current cost, except so-called "industrial insurance" to provide for funeral expense. (2) Lack of thrift and habits of saving, owing in part to their own fault and in part to the contingencies which eat up their savings and bring discouragement. In either case, under competitive industry, the condition may be accepted as permanent.

On the other hand, employers and investors are much more able to provide in advance for a future continuous income against contingencies. All investments are made with reference to equalizing the flow of income over a future period of time in the form of interest or dividends.

Inheritances are the principal means by which owners, without effort or thrift on their part, secure titles to wealth and its future continuous income. Consequently, for the Government to take a part of large inheritances which provide continuous incomes and to devote the proceeds to the purpose of making incomes more nearly continuous for those who are not able, under existing conditions, to do it for themselves appeals to the sense of justice. It may be accepted in advance that men of wealth will approve of an inheritance tax on two conditions, namely, that the tax will be devoted to a great public purpose, and that the funds will be administered economically and efficiently without partisanship or practical politics. These two conditions are essential and are contemplated in our recommendations for a Federal industrial commission and a Federal fund for social welfare.

Some of the purposes for which this fund might be used, in order to meet the object of social welfare, are, in addition to the overhead expenses of the commission, the safety and health agencies of the Federal Government and, perhaps, subsidies to States conforming to standards; industrial education and subsidies to States; Federal employment offices and subsidies to States which adopt an approved plan coordinating with the Federal plan; Federal supervision of private employment offices doing interstate business; investigation and statistics of labor conditions; mediation; administration of immigration laws; workmen's compensation and subsidies to systems of sickness, unemployment, and other forms of social insurance as may be approved by Congress. Opportunities for investment should be considered, such as workmen's houses, workmen's hotels, hospitals, rural-credit associations, and similar investments made by Germany in respect of its various insurance funds.

It is impossible to estimate at this time the revenue that would be derived from such a tax. We have estimated the amounts now collected by the States from inheritance taxes at $25,000,000, as against the $50,000,000 that they would receive at 50 cents per capita. The present systems in vogue in 32 States yield revenues from $1,096 in Wyoming to $11,162,478 in New York. The amount per capita of population ranges from 1 cent per capita in Texas and Wyoming to 59 cents in Connecticut, 66 cents in Illinois, 68 cents in Massachusetts, and $1.28 in New York. The latter four States would lose if they abolished their inheritance tax and accepted the Federal distribution of 50 cents per capita. Other States would gain. Yet this can not be considered a just criticism of the proposal, for the States which lose are those in which wealthy people choose to reside and yet their fortunes arise from ownership of property scattered throughout the country. The present system of State inheritance taxes practically permits a few States to collect taxes on property whose value is created by many of the States. A Federal inheritance tax is the only method by which the entire Nation, which contributes to the value of estates, can secure revenues from the values which it creates.

The recommendation of returning 50 cents per capita to the States is designed to induce them to turn over to the Federal Government the sole right of imposing inheritance taxes and yet to preserve to the States at least a part of such preempted claims as they may have acquired by getting into the field first.

The Federal machinery is already in existence for collecting income taxes, and the same officials, without any appreciable increase in the number, can assess and collect inheritance taxes. Executors of estates whose annual incomes amount to $2,500 or more per year are now required to make returns to collectors of internal revenue, and the only addition required for an inheritance tax is that executors of estates of $25,000 should make returns of the total value of the estates. This can, of course, be done at the same time when they fill out the blanks which show net incomes. Internal-revenue officials also investigate all cases where it is suspected that full returns of income are not made. No additional officials are therefore required for these purposes. The only addition would be such number of officials as are required for general supervision. The machinery is already in existence, and no tax can be so cheaply administered as a Federal inheritance tax.

The significant feature of the proposed inheritance tax is the high rates on direct heirs, as compared with the very low rates imposed in the States. The estates going to wife and lineal heirs include probably 80 per cent to 90 per cent of all estates, and it is therefore from such estates that the largest revenues are expected. Such estates are scarcely touched by American inheritance tax laws. The sensationally high rates imposed in some States on estates going to strangers and remote heirs are something of a delusion, for scarcely 5 per cent of the estates go to such beneficiaries. The rates on estates going to strangers reach their highest figure at 35 per cent in California on the excess over $1,000,000 and fall as low as 5 per cent in Pennsylvania and other States. But the rates on the excess over $1,000,000 going to direct heirs is only 10 per cent in California and falls to 1, 2, or 3 per cent in most of the States. Our recommendation affects mainly these estates going to direct heirs, which are 80 to 90 per cent of all estates, and the highest rate on such estates is 15 per cent on the excess over $1,000,000. This conforms more nearly to the inheritance taxes of leading European countries which would yield according to various estimates over $200,000,000 if adopted by the Federal Government of this country.

The following administrative reasons for making the inheritance tax a Federal tax are submitted by Prof. T. S. Adams, of the Wisconsin tax commission, who also suggests the repayment to States as a method of inducing them to yield to the Federal tax. He says:

1. The present system gives rise to a large amount of double or multiple taxation and if the existing laws were enforced, the situation would be unbearable. Most State laws tax the transfer of all securities owned by resident decedents and yet attempt to tax the transfer of some securities owned by nonresident decedents when they represent property in the State passing the law. I have known one block of railroad stock to be assessed in Wisconsin (residence of decedent), in Illinois (where the stock was deposited in a trust company), and in Utah, where the railroad was incorporated, and it is not unlikely that other States through which the railroad passed imposed a tax before the estate was finally settled. Four different and conflicting taxes are thus in use at the present time.

2. At present administration of such laws is costly, ineffective, unjust, and capricious. Wisconsin attempts to tax the transfer of all securities representing, however indirectly, property in Wisconsin. It is impossible where holding companies hold the stock in the companies immediately owning the Wisconsin property. To enforce it, particularly where bonds are concerned, agents must be employed outside the State. We keep two—in New York and Chicago. We should have an agent in every place in the country where estates are probated. To enforce the Wisconsin interpretation would cost an enormous sum.

3. Yet the Western States are insisting on the Wisconsin idea in inheritance taxation. As they do so, double taxation and cost of administration must increase greatly. Cost of administration has not been excessive in the past, merely because the laws have not been enforced.

4. Except in a few States the yield of the inheritance tax is very irregular. The proposed commutation payment by the Federal Government would substitute a regular for an irregular State revenue, besides greatly decreasing cost of collection—or prospective cost of collection.

5. Rich men change their rendezvous very easily. Rhode Island and a few other States do not tax inheritances at present. They do and can prevent the proper development of inheritance taxes in other States. It is the compulsion of the "twentieth man."

6. A number of States can not employ progressive rating in inheritance taxation—an essential attribute of sound inheritance taxation.

IMMIGRATION.

19. Underlying the entire problem of self-government in this country, and placing a limit on the ability to remedy abuses either through politics or labor unions, is the great variety of races, nationalities, and languages. We know how the Southern States have dealt with the problem and how constitutional amendments forced upon them by the Northern States have been treated. Considering this outcome, it is doubtful whether the additional proposed amendments designed to protect rights of individuals in those or other States would accomplish the ends intended.

A similar problem is forced upon us by the large immigration of backward races or of classes from other countries with no experience in self-government. One of these races, the Chinese, has been actually excluded from immigration. Others less competent are admitted. The doctrine of a haven for the oppressed has been rejected in the case of the Chinese and can not consistently be raised against restriction on immigration designed to accomplish a similar purpose of protection to Americans. Especially is the problem of the Americanized element in the labor unions in maintaining discipline almost insoluble when it comes to dealing with 10, 20, or 30 races or languages. The right of employers to bring aliens into their establishments is the same as their right to bring in naturalized or native Americans. The resulting situation is the great strikes recently entered upon without previous organizations or discipline by nationalities that have suddenly come together, notwithstanding their racial antipathies and language impediments, on account of a united antagonism against their employers. Such strikes receive but little consideration from American police, sheriffs, and militia and are usually defeated. On account of their incapacity for self-government, it might perhaps be shown that in isolated communities the paternal despotism of a corporation is preferable to unionism or political control by these backward nationalities. The violation of contracts and inability of their leaders to maintain discipline and observe contracts, which make some American employers so determined against recognizing unions, may often be traced back to the unruly mixture of races and nationalities whom they have employed. Other problems, such as those of the political franchise, must be taken into account in any measure designed to further restrict immigration, but we are convinced that very substantial restrictions on immigration, in addition to the present restrictions, should be adopted, and that comprehensive measures should be taken to teach the English language and otherwise "Americanize" the immigrants. One of the principal services of American trade-unions is their work in teaching immigrants the practice of democratic government. They might almost be named as the principal Americanizing agency. Another promising measure is the so-called social center, designed to use the schoolhouses and public buildings for instruction and discussion outside school hours. Such a measure, if adopted by all States, as has been done by some, would be of advantage also to native Americans in the free discussion of public questions.

Since immigration is one of the principal issues between capital and labor, its administration should be turned over to the proposed Federal industrial commission, where capital and labor will have an equal voice. This would place all administrative positions in the service, up to and including the Commissioner General, under the civil-service rules proposed in paragraph 3. In 1905, when a trade-union man was Commissioner General, he was required by the administration to give written or oral instructions to inspectors not to make any arrests of Chinese for deportation as required by law. (Washington file, 15427 1 C.) Instead of resigning and making public protest he yielded and gave the required instructions, which practically nullified the law by preventing the deportation of smuggled Chinese. Had such orders been required to be submitted to the advisory council, as proposed in these recommendations, a public protest would have been made by the labor members of the council, since they would be responsible to their unions and not to the Government for their salaries. Even now, with the many charges of Chinese smuggling, the presence of unsalaried labor representatives on an advisory council, with the right to have access to all the records and to have all orders submitted to them before issuing, would place them in a position to prevent such secret violations of the law. In addition they would receive through their fellow-unionists throughout the country complaints or evidence against inspectors supposed to be in conspiracy with Chinese smugglers and would be in position to present their charges and to require investigation and removal if necessary. Various outside commissions, including this commission, have been required to investigate the matter of Chinese smuggling, but they are baffled. The advisory council proposed would be a continuous commission not terrified by any political administration and having a voice in the appointment and removal of inspectors under civil-service rules. (See par. 3.) Doubtless appeals from the commission to the Department of State and the President should be allowed in cases involving political refugees and the interpretation of treaties with foreign countries. These are substantially our conclusions derived from the attempted investigation of Asiatic smuggling.

FARMERS AND FARM LABORERS.

20. One of the growing evils to be feared is the increasing congestion of populated centers at the expense of the rural districts. This is true not only of America but also of Europe. The allurements of the city tend to draw annually thousands from the country to the city. Congested cities, especially in hard times, mean enlarged ranks of the unemployed.

This tendency is strengthened where the struggle of the small farmer not only to hold on to his land but to make a living becomes hopeless and where the conditions are such that the farm laborer or the farm tenant sees little or no possibility of becoming a future landowner.

Not least among the causes of higher cost of living has been the tendency to increase city populations at the expense of agricultural populations, thus decreasing relatively the supply and increasing the demand and thereby inevitably raising the cost of food.

The last census shows that we are becoming the victims of increasing absentee landlordism and farm tenancy. It points out that while the number of farm owners during the preceding decade increased 8 per cent, the number of farm tenants increased 16 per cent. If this ratio should continue for a few more decades, many parts of our Republic will find themselves in the condition from which Ireland has so recently emerged.

For many generations Ireland was one of the most distressed countries in the world. All of its evils were due primarily to absentee landlords and farm tenants. But within the last decade a wonderful change has taken place in the social and economic condition of the Irish peasant, brought about by the enactment by Parliament of what has since become known as the Irish land bill. This act created a royal commission, with power to appraise the large Irish land estates owned by absentee landlords, at their real and not at their speculative value, to buy them in the name of the Government at the appraised value, plus 12 per cent bonus, to cut them up into small parcels, to sell them to worthy farm tenants, giving some 70 years' time in which to make small annual payments on the amortization plan, the deferred payments bearing but 3 per cent interest. In addition to this, the Government made personal loans to peasants sufficient to cover the cost of stock and farm implements, also payable in small annual installments bearing a minimum rate of interest. The Government further furnished the various farm districts with farm advisors, trained graduates from agricultural colleges, who act as friend, adviser, and scientific farm instructor to the peasants. Within a decade the wretched and more or less law-breaking farm tenant has been converted into an industrious, progressive, and law-abiding landed proprietor; in fact, he has become so law-abiding that many jails in the farming districts, formerly filled with agrarian criminals, have been converted into public schools.

In Texas this commission found a condition of farm tenancy like that of Ireland and seemingly typical of growing conditions in various parts of the country. We therefore recommend to Congress and to the various States that steps shall be taken to lighten the burdens of the small farmer, and make it more possible to encourage the tenant, farm laborer, and city dweller to become land proprietors.

Not least among the burdens of the small farmer is the great difficulty, as a rule, on his part in obtaining the necessary credit with which to better and to improve his land, at a low rate of interest and under terms that will permit him to make payments spread over a long term of years.

Under the rural credits system of Germany a small farmer can borrow his money as cheaply as can a great banker. Not only can he do this, but he can spread the payments over a period of 30 or more years. It is this system of rural credits, among other things, that has made it possible for the German farmer, despite the high price of his land, his heavy taxes, and his small acreage, not only to successfully compete with the American farmer, but to enjoy a fair degree of prosperity; so much so that in more recent times there have been comparatively few German agriculturists who have emigrated to this country.

We therefore recommend that Congress and the various States pass rural credit acts that will give to the small American farmer the same privileges and benefits that for so long a time have been enjoyed by the small farmers in Germany and other European countries, which, following Germany, have adopted rural credit systems. We recommend serious consideration to adapting the Irish land bill and the Australian system of State colonization to our American conditions. It is not our intention in this report to enter into minute details as to how this should be carried out. In a general way, however, we believe it not only desirable but practicable for the Federal Government, through its Department of Agriculture, and the various States, through their departments of agriculture, to secure large bodies of land at appraised actual values, that have been thoroughly tested by experts for their quality, issuing bonds for the payment for same, if need be, and to cut them up into small parcels, making the necessary improvements and selling them to qualified colonists with small first payments, making the balance payable in, say, 30 years on the amortization plan, the deferred payments bearing only the same rate of interest that the Government itself is called upon to pay, plus a small addition to cover the cost of Government administration. We believe in this way the most effective check can be created, on the one hand, to minimize farm tenancy and, on the other hand, to make it possible for the farm laborer and the farm tenant to become land proprietors. We believe that this, if carried out wisely and intelligently, will have a large share in minimizing industrial unrest and in adding to the wealth of the Nation, both materially and in the quality of its citizenship.

CORPORATION CONTROL.

21. Corporation control over politics and labor has for a long time been a well-known matter of serious concern in all American States. This commission has held hearings on the subject of such control in isolated communities at Lead, S. Dak., Butte, Mont., and in Colorado, and other communities were partly investigated by a member of the staff.

In Lead we found a strong union had recently been driven out on account of its sudden demand for the closed shop, and this was followed by a paternal absolutism that controlled labor, business, and politics. In Butte we found a strong union split into factions and destroying its own property, followed by refusal of the corporation to deal with either faction. In Colorado we found a long history of refusals to deal with unions, accompanied by strikes at intervals of 9 or 10 years. In each of these cases the ownership and control of the property was in the hands of absentees, who left the operating management to executives on the ground.

We condemn the conditions found in Colorado which show the control of corporations over labor and politics, and we find there a system that has taken hold throughout the country. Here the serious problem is not the personality of any individual who may or may not be responsible, but the correction of a system which has grown up mainly under absentee ownership and which determines the acts of individuals according to their self-interest within the terms prescribed by the system.   Immediate and public action is necessary to see that courts of justice are not prostituted to the service of one class against another, but the huge system of corporate control requires more far-reaching remedies before attainment. Absentee ownership can not be brought to the sense of its responsibility without the enactment and adequate enforcement of workmen's compensation for accidents and occupational diseases, sickness, invalidity, and old-age insurance. Meanwhile a partial method of meeting its responsibility is a staff of safety, health, and labor commissioners, independent of the local executive staff, to report directly to the board of directors. The work of such a staff is directly in conflict with that of the executive staff, for the latter must get out " production " while the other must acquaint the directors and company with the oppression of labor which increased production and lower costs often bring. The labor department can not be made subordinate to the executive department if the corporation really intends to safeguard its employees.

We are not in favor of public ownership as solely a matter of improving labor conditions, and before such can be recommended there should be a more complete investigation and regulation and a clearing up of the values that will be paid and the administrative control that will follow. More immediate and necessary is a series of laws that will take the control of politics out of the hands of corporations and place it in the hands of the people. Several of our previous recommendations are intended to accomplish this purpose in so far as labor and capital are concerned, but we should add effective corrupt practices acts, designed to protect the secret ballot, to limit the amount of money and number of paid electioneerers in elections, to prevent intimidation, and so on, as far as elections are menaced by political machines and wealth. Direct primaries for the nomination of candidates, protected by corrupt practices acts. Constitutional and legislative initiative for State and Federal Governments. The initiative would permit the people to change the Constitution at any point where the courts had depended upon it for a decision, and would make unnecessary any provision for recall of Supreme Court judges or of their decisions, or of taking from higher courts their power to declare laws unconstitutional. The recall of elected officials, including executives and judges of the lower courts, but not judges of the supreme courts or members of the legislature. Proportional representation, as adopted in Belgium, South Africa, Australia, and the Irish parliament, by which all parties or factions would be able to elect their own representatives in the legislatures or Congress in proportion to their numbers and without making deals with other parties. This would permit a labor party to have its representatives, as well as other minor parties, and would permit women, who we consider should have the suffrage, and other minor parties to elect their own representatives without making compromises in order to get the votes of the major parties. These minor parties, containing as they do the advanced views on labor and social problems, are entitled to their proportionate share of influence in the legislatures or Congress. It can be seen that such a measure would take away from corporations much of their present inducement to control the great parties. It would furnish a legislature which would be a true reflection of the wishes of all the people. This recommendation applies to the legislature the principle of representation of interests, which we advance in the case of the advisory council to the Industrial Commission.

JOHN R. COMMONS.
FLORENCE J. HARRIMAN.
HARRIS WEINSTOCK.[1]
S. THRUSTON BALLARD.[1]
RICHARD H. AISHTON.[2]

NOTE.—Commissioner Weinstock also presented the following dissenting opinion:

I dissent from the report prepared by Commissioner Commons on the question of immigration. That report says:

We are convinced that very substantial restrictions on immigration, in addition to the present restrictions, should be adopted.

I am of the opinion that we have abundant immigration laws already on our statute books which, if enforced, will keep out of the country unfit immigrants. In normal times this country can profitably employ all the desirable and fit occidental immigrants that knock at our door, thereby adding greatly to the wealth and the strength of the Nation.

HARRIS WEINSTOCK.

[1] See supplementary reports.
[2] See supplementary report. Appointed commissioner Mar. 17, 1915, to serve the unexpired term of Hon. F. A. Delano, resigned.

REPORT OF COMMISSIONERS WEINSTOCK, BALLARD, AND AISHTON.

We concur in the report prepared by Commissioner Commons, dissenting, however, on the two following points, and supplementing it by certain other findings and recommendations following herewith.

First. We dissent from the recommendation that the secondary boycott should be legalized. We regard the secondary boycott as unjust, inequitable, and vicious, in that it subjects third and innocent parties to injury and, at times, to great loss if not ruin. We are, therefore, as much opposed to it as we are to the blacklist. There have been instances where, for example, a strike would occur on a newspaper. The strikers would demand, for example, that a certain business house advertising in such paper should, despite the fact that it was under contract, withdraw its patronage, and on refusal of the advertiser to violate its contract with the newspaper, it became the victim of boycotts at the hands of the strikers more or less injurious, if not disastrous, in their results to such advertiser. The Supreme Court of the United States has, in our opinion, wisely and justly declared the secondary boycott illegal, and we regard it as an injury to society to legalize a system so vicious.

It has been pointed out that—

* * * the boycott is the chief weapon of modern unionism, and also characteristic generally of its spirit and methods. A discussion of a boycott as a mere withdrawal of patronage is idle and academic. When that is the extent of the boycott in any particular case, the patronage is simply withdrawn, and nothing more is heard about it. From that simple procedure the modern boycott has been developed into a very different thing, and what has become known as the secondary boycott, dragging in third parties to the dispute and penalizing them for patronizing one of the parties to the dispute, has played an important part.

Dealing with this phase of the question, Judge William H. Taft, in an early case (1893), said:

The boycott is a combination of many to cause a loss to one person by coercing others against their will to withdraw from him beneficial business intercourse by threats that unless those others do so, the many will cause serious loss to them.

In the case of Moore v. The Bricklayers' Union, Judge William H. Taft says:

The conflict was brought about by the effort of defendants to use plaintiff's right of trade to injure Parker Bros., and, upon failure of this, to use plaintiff's customers' rights of trade to injure the plaintiff. Such effort can not be in the bona fide exercise of trade, is without just cause, and is therefore malicious. The immediate motive of defendants here was to show to the building world what punishment and disaster necessarily follows a defiance of their demands. The remote motive of wishing to better their condition by the power so acquired will not, as we think we have shown, make any legal justification for defendants' acts. We are of the opinion that even if acts of the character and with the intent shown in this case are not actionable when done by individuals, they become so when they are the result of combination, because it is clear that the terrorizing of a community by threats of exclusive dealing in order to deprive one obnoxious member of means of sustenance, will become both dangerous and oppressive.

231

The Anthracite Coal Strike Commission, in its report in touching upon secondary boycotts, says:

It was attempted to define the boycott by calling the contest between employers and employees a war between capital and labor, and pursuing the analogies of the word, to justify thereby the cruelty and illegality of conduct on the part of those conducting the strike. The analogy is not apt, and the argument founded upon it is fallacious.

There is only one war-making power recognized by our institutions, and that is the Government of the United States and of the States in subordination thereto, when repelling invasion or domestic violence. War between citizens is not to be tolerated, and can not in the proper sense, exist. If attempted it is unlawful, and is to be put down by the sovereign power of the State and Nation. The practices which we are condemning would be outside the pale of civilized warfare. In civilized warfare, women and children, and the defenseless are safe from attack, and a code of honor controls the parties to such warfare, which cries out against the boycott we have in view. Cruel and cowardly are terms not too severe by which to characterize it.

Second. We further dissent from said report in its limitation of public inquiry in labor disputes only to cases where both sides invite such inquiry. We believe that in the public interest there are times when compulsion in labor disputes is thoroughly justified. We feel, with organized labor, that there should be no restriction put upon the right to strike, realizing as we do, that the strike is the only weapon which, in the interest of labor, can be effectively and legally used to aid in bettering its conditions. We feel, also, that there should be no restriction placed upon the employer in his right to declare a lockout in order better to protect what he regards as his interest, and we therefore would not favor any plan that would inflict penalties upon the worker or upon the employer for declaring a strike or lockout.

Where the two sides to a labor controversy are fairly well balanced in strength, the winning side must depend, in the last analysis upon the support of public opinion. Public opinion, therefore, becomes a most important factor in the interest of industrial peace. Such public opinion, however, to be of value, must be enlightened. Under prevailing conditions this is almost impossible. All that the public is now able to get, as a rule, are garbled and ex parte statements, more or less misleading and unreliable, which simply tend to confuse the public mind.

Where strikes and lockouts take place on a large scale, and more especially in connection with public utilities, the public inevitably becomes a third party to the issue, in that it has more at stake than both parties to the dispute combined. For example, if the street railways of a large city are tied up, the loss to the railway companies in the way of revenue, and to the workers in the way of wages, is great, but this loss becomes insignificant compared with the loss inflicted upon the rest of the community, to say nothing of the annoyance, inconvenience, and menace to life and property, which not infrequently occur in such industrial disputes. The public, therefore, as the third party to the issue, is justified in demanding that an investigation take place, and that the facts be ascertained and presented in an impartial spirit to the general public, so that ways and means may be found of adjudicating the dispute or of throwing the influence of a properly informed public opinion on the side which has the right in its favor.

We, therefore, earnestly recommend that in the case of public utilities, the proposed industrial commission shall not only have power to mediate and conciliate, but also, at the request of either side to a dispute, or upon the initiative of the commission itself, should have the power, all voluntary methods having failed, to undertake a compulsory public inquiry when, in the discretion of the commission, public interest demands it; that it be given the fullest powers to summon witnesses, place them under oath, demand books and documents, all with a view of ascertaining the underlying causes of the dispute and the issues involved, to the end of making recommendations that, in the judgment of the board of inquiry, consisting of three members, one to be chosen by each side and the third to be chosen by these two, would be a fair and reasonable settlement of the points in dispute. It being understood, however, that neither side is obliged to accept such recommendations, but may continue to strike or lockout, as the case may be. Meanwhile, however, the public will have ascertained in the most reliable way the issues involved, the facts as they have been found by the board of inquiry, and the basis upon which a fair settlement can be established, thus enabling the public more intelligently to throw its support where it rightfully belongs.

With the two foregoing modifications, we heartily concur in the report prepared by Commissioner Commons. We desire, however, additionally, to report as follows:

We find that the alleged findings of fact and, in a general way, the comments thereon made in the report of the staff of this commission, under the direction of Mr. Basil M. Manly, which has been made a part of the records of this commission, without the indorsement, however, of the commission, so manifestly partisan and unfair that we can not give them our indorsement. What we regard as the desirable recommendations in the report of Mr. Manly are dealt with to our satisfaction in the Commons report, which has our approval.

We find that Mr. Manly's report places practically all the responsibility for the causes of industrial unrest at the doors of one side, forgetting that both sides to the issues are human, and, being human, are guilty of their fullest share of wrongdoing, and are alike responsible in greater or lesser degree, for the causes of industrial unrest.

We are, therefore, prompted, in the interest of fairness and justice, to present herewith some of the additional causes of industrial unrest that, in the course of the investigations and public hearings of the commission, have forced themselves upon our attention.

Despite the fact that we have been appointed to represent, on this commission, the employers of the Nation, we are free to admit that the investigations made by the commission, and the testimony brought forth at our public hearings, have made it plain that employers, some of them, have been guilty of much wrongdoing, and have caused the workers to have their fullest shart of grievances against many employers. There has been an abundance of testimony submitted to prove to our satisfaction that some employers have resorted to questionable methods to prevent their workers from organizing in their own self-interest; that they have attempted to defeat democracy by more or less successfully controlling courts and legislatures; that some of them have exploited women and children and unorganized workers; that some have resorted to all sorts of methods to prevent the enactment of remedial industrial legislation; that some have employed gunmen in strikes, who were disreputable characters, and who assaulted innocent people and committed other crimes most reprehensible in character; that some have paid lower wages than competitive conditions warranted, worked their people long hours and under insanitary and dangerous conditions; that some have exploited prison labor at the expense of free labor; that some have been contract breakers with labor; that some have at times attempted, through the authorities, to suppress free speech and the right of peaceful assembly; and that some have deliberately, for selfish ends, bribed representatives of labor. All these things, we find, tend to produce industrial unrest, with all its consequent and far-reaching ills.

There is, therefore, no gainsaying the fact that labor has had many grievances, and that it is thoroughly justified in organizing and in spreading organization in order better to protect itself against exploitation and oppression.

On the other hand, in justice to employers generally, it must be said that there has been much evidence to show that there is an awakening among the enlightened employers of the Nation, who have taken a deeper personal interest in the welfare of their workers than ever before in industrial history; that such enlightened employers are growing in number and are more and more realizing that, if for no other reason, it is in their own self-interest to seek the welfare of their workers and earnestly to strive to better their conditions. Employers, on their own initiative, have created sick funds and pension funds; have expended vast sums of money to insure greater safety to their workers; have, as compared with conditions of the past, greatly improved their methods of sanitation; have done much to regularize employment; have increased wages; and in every way have endeavored to lighten the burdens of their workers.

While there are many deplorable conditions yet remaining to be rectified, and while the condition of the worker is still far from ideal, we believe that, on the whole, the impartial investigator must find that, in normal times, on the average, the hours of the American worker are the shortest, his wages the highest, his working conditions the most favorable, his standard of living the highest, and his general well-being the best in the world's industrial history.

Industrial Commissioner John B. Lennon, who is also a member of the executive council of the American Federation of Labor, in the absence of official figures has estimated that there are at this time about 20,000,000 wage earners in the United States, and that about 3,250,000 of these are members of various labor unions. In other words, as a liberal approximation, about 16 per cent of the wage earners of America are members of trade unions.

Considering that the American Federation of Labor came into life in 1881, some 34 years ago, and considering the earnest and zealous efforts that have been made by its representatives and the representatives of other labor organizations to agitate, educate, and organize, and considering still further the highly commendable objects professed by organized labor, the membership results are disappointingly small.

One reason given for the comparatively small percentage of unionists in the ranks of labor is the hostility against unionism on the part of many employers. Organized labor points out that there are many employers' associations that are organized not to deal with, but to fight, unionism, and that this, in many instances, and more especially in the larger industrial enterprises, presents a very serious obstacle for organized labor to meet and to overcome.

Representing as we do on this commission the employers' side, we are at one with the other members of our Federal commission who represent the general public, and also with those representing organized labor, in believing that, under modern industrial conditions, collective bargaining, when fairly and properly conducted, is conducive to the best good of the employer, the worker, and society. We find that there are many enlightened employers who concur in this view, who in the past recognized and dealt with organized labor, but who now refuse to do so, and who, under proper conditions, would willingly continue to engage in collective bargaining. With good cause, in our opinion, however, they place the responsibility for their refusing to do so at the door of organized labor. There is an abundance of available testimony in our records to show that many employers are frightened off from recognizing or dealing with organized labor for fear that to do so means to put their heads in the noose and to invite the probability of seriously injuring, if not ruining, their business.

The prime objection that such employers have to recognizing and dealing with organized labor is the fear of (a) sympathetic strikes, (b) jurisdictional disputes, (c) labor union politics, (d) contract breaking, (e) restriction of output, (f) prohibition of the use of non-union-made tools and materials, (g) closed shop, (h) contests for supremacy between rival unions, (i) acts of violence against non-union workers and the properties of employers, (j) apprenticeship rules.

While we have found many sinners among the ranks of the employers, the result of our investigation and inquiries forces upon us the fact that unionists also can not come into court with clean hands; that this is not a case where the saints are all on one side and the sinners all on the other. We find saints and sinners, many of them, on both sides.

The hope of future industrial peace must lie in both sides using their best endeavors to minimize the causes that lead to the growth of sins and sinners on each side of the question.

SYMPATHETIC STRIKES.

Taking up seriatim the objections offered by many employers to recognizing and dealing with organized labor, we come first to that of the sympathetic strike. The employer contends, and we find ourselves in sympathy with his contention, that it is a rank injustice to subject him to a strike of his employees who have absolutely no grievances, to stop work because some other group of workers, possibly at a remote point, have a real or fancied grievance against their own employer, especially when such stoppage of work may not only inflict a very serious loss, but may mean ruin to the enterprise of the innocent employer, thus making it, in violation of all the equities, a clear case of punishing the many innocent for the one or the few who may be guilty, who were party to the original dispute.

JURISDICTIONAL DISPUTES.

The employer further points out that not only is his business liable to be ruined by the sympathetic strike, but, more especially in the building trades, is he likely to become an innocent victim of jurisdictional disputes for which he is in no wise responsible and over which he has absolutely no control.

Sidney and Beatrice Webb point out that—

It is no exaggeration to say that to the competition between overlapping unions is to be attributed about nine-tenths of the ineffectiveness of the trade-union world.[1]

Innumerable instances have occurred where jurisdictional strikes have lasted for months and sometimes for years.[2]

The elevator constructors had a serious and costly dispute with the machinists in Chicago over the installation of pumps connected with hydraulic elevators. A strike resulted for more than two years, during which most of the elevator men in the city were out of work while members of the machinists and other unions supplied their places with the Otis Elevator Co.[3]

In 1910 the secretary of the bricklayers said:

Our disputes with the operative plasters' union during the past year have taken thousands of dollars out of our international treasury for the purpose of protecting our interest. The loss in wages to our members has amounted to at least $300,000. The loss to our employers has been up in the thousands, also.[3]

Prof. Commons, in his studies of the New York building trades, comments on the jurisdictional disputes as follows:

Building construction was continuously interrupted, not on account of lockouts, low wages, or even employment of nonunion men, but on account of fights between the unions. A friendly employer who hired only union men, along with the unfriendly employer, was used as a club to hit the opposing union, and the friendly employer suffered more than the other.[3]

The Chicago machinery movers caused considerable delay in the construction of the Harris Trust Building, and in a period of less than a year were responsible for no less than 50 separate strikes, during which the work of the employers was delayed.[4]

Jurisdictional disputes waste both labor and capital. They make it impracticable in many cases to use improved appliances and cheaper materials. They are responsible for hesitancy in undertaking and increasing expense in prosecuting buildings, to the detriment of the building industry.[4]

Finally, where the disputes are long continued, they are responsible for that whole train of evil results which follows upon idleness and poverty.[5]

Sidney and Beatrice Webb again point out that in the industries of Tyneside, within a space of 35 months, there were 35 weeks in which one or the other of the four most important sections of workmen in the staple industry of the district absolutely refused to work. This meant compulsory idleness of tens of thousands of men, the selling out of households, and the semistarvation of whole families totally unconcerned with the disputes, while it left the unions in a state of weakness from which it will take years to recover.[6]

That wise and far-seeing labor leaders keenly appreciate the great wrongs inflicted not only upon the employers, but upon the workers themselves, by virtue of cessation of work in jurisdictional disputes, is emphasized by the following extracts from the report of Mr.

[1] Industrial Democracy, vol. 1, p. 121.
[2] The Bricklayer and Mason, February, 1911, p. 127.
[3] Trade-Unionism and Labor Problems.
[4] Interview, secretary of Building Employers' Association, Chicago, July, 1912.
[5] Industrial Democracy, vol. 1, p. 121.
[6] Ibid., vol. 2, p. 513.

Samuel·Gompers, president of the American Federation of Labor, at its convention in 1902:

. Beyond doubt, the greatest problem, the danger which above all others is threatening not only the success but the very existence of the American Federation of Labor, is the question of jurisdiction. Unless our affiliated national and international unions radically and soon change their course, we shall, at no distant date, be in the midst of an internecine contest unparalleled in any era of the industrial world, aye, not even when workmen of different trades were arrayed against each other behind barricades over the question of trade against trade. They naturally regard each other with hatred, and treat each other as mortal enemies.

There is scarcely an affiliated organization which is not engaged in a dispute with another organization (and in some cases, with several organizations) upon the question of jurisdiction. It is not an uncommon occurrence for an organization, and several have done so quite recently, to so change their laws and claims to jurisdiction as to cover trades never contemplated by the organizers, officers, or members; never comprehended by their titles, trades of which there is already in existence a national union. And this without a word of advice, counsel, or warning.

I submit that it is untenable and intolerable for an organization to attempt to ride roughshod over and trample under foot rights and jurisdiction of a trade, the jurisdiction of which is already covered by an existing organization. This contention for jurisdiction has grown into such proportions and is fought with such an intensity as to arouse many bitter feuds and trade wars. In many instances employers fairly inclined for organized labor are made innocently to suffer from causes entirely beyond their control.

As proof of the prophetic and far-sighted utterances of President Gompers, it has been pointed out that "in 1911, in Chicago, his grim prophecy was actually fulfilled in the bitter jurisdictional wars fought by rival unions in that city in which paid thugs and gunmen turned the streets of Chicago into a condition of anarchy, and in which, as a mere incident from the union standpoint, millions of dollars of construction work remained idle, with a resultant loss to owners, contractors, and the business interest of the city beyond possibility of calculation."

We ask, what sane or thoughtful employer would willingly put his head in a noose such as this by recognizing and dealing with unions, and thus invite possible ruin?

LABOR UNION POLITICS.

The third objection of employers to recognizing and dealing with organized labor is the risk they run, especially in the building trades, where power to declare a strike is concentrated in the hands of a business agent, of finding themselves at the mercy of either a corrupt business agent or one who, for the sake of union politics, is endeavoring, in order to perpetuate himself in office, to make capital at the expense of the innocent employer by making unwarranted and unreasonable demands against the employer.

CONTRACT BREAKING.

The fourth reason offered by the employers for refusing to recognize or to deal with organized labor, is its increasing unreliability in keeping trade agreements. To give one case in point, our record gives the story in undisputed statement published in the United Mine Workers' Journal, which is the official organ of the United Mine Workers of America, written by Mr. W. O. Smith, ex-chairman of the executive committee of the Kentucky District of United

Mine Workers of America, in which Mr. Smith, among other things, says:

> Because of the indifference of the conservative members of our unions, and the activity of the radical element which is responsible for the greatest menace which has ever threatened the United Mine Workers of America, the local strike, during the past two or three years the international, as well as the district and subdistrict officials, have been confronted with many perplexing problems, some of which seem to threaten the very life of the organization. But I believe I am safe in saying that no problem has given them so much concern as the problem of local strikes in violation of agreements.
>
> Thousands of dollars are expended every year in an effort to organize the 250,000 nonunion miners in the United States, while hundreds of our members go on strike almost every day in absolute, unexcusable violation of existing agreements.[1]

This criticism comes not from an employer, but from an ardent, earnest unionist, in high standing in his organization.

Corroborating the statement of Mr. Smith, comes a statement published in Coal Age of December 20, 1913, issued by the Association of Bituminous Coal Operators of Central Pennsylvania, addressed to Mr. Patrick Gilday, president of District No. 2, U. M. W. of A., Morrisville mines, Pennsylvania, dated Philadelphia, December 12, 1913, in which, among other things, the following appears:

> Whereas, Rules 12 and 13 of said agreement provide, " that should differences arise between the operators and mine workers as to the meaning of the provisions of this agreement or about matters not specifically mentioned in this agreement, there shall be no suspension of work on account of such difference, but an earnest effort be made to settle such differences immediately." Whereas, notwithstanding the fact that Rule 15 provides the right to hire and discharge, the management of the mine and the direction of the working forces are vested exclusively in the operator, the United Mine Workers of America have absolutely disregarded this rule, in that they have at numerous times served notices on substantially every operator belonging to our association, that unless all the employees working for such operators should become members of the union on or before certain dates mentioned in said notices, that they, the Mine Workers, would close or shut down the operators' respective mines, and in many instances did close the mines for this reason, and refused to return to work unless such nonunion employees were discharged. This conduct is in direct violation of the contract, and specifically interferes with and abridges the right of the operator to hire and discharge; of the management of the mine, and of the direction of the working forces; this conduct in violation of contract on the part of the Mine Workers, as well as that mentioned in the preceding paragraph, has resulted in more than one hundred strikes during the life of our scale agreement.[2]

Numerous other illustrations could be given from the records of the commission, showing that there are other instances where unions did not observe their contracts, tending to make, in the minds of many employers, a character for all unionism, and thus increasing their hesitancy in recognizing and dealing with unions.

RESTRICTION OF OUTPUT.

Not least among the reasons given by fair-minded employers for refusing to recognize or deal with labor unions, is the fact that many unions stand for a limited output, thus making among their workers for the dead level, and thereby making it impossible for the union employer successfully to compete with the nonunion employer, who is not faced with such handicap.

---

[1] New York hearings, U. S. Commission on Industrial Relations, pp. 2750–2751.
[2] New York hearings, U. S. Commission on Industrial Relations, pp. 2061–2062.

British industrial conditions are cursed with the practice of limited output, as compared with the absence of this practice in industrial Germany. As a consequence, Germany, in time of peace, has industrially outrun Great Britain by leaps and bounds.

The British unionist, by practicing limited output, has thus played directly into the hands of his keenest industrial competitor, the German.

The records of the commission also show that organized labor, almost as a unit, is very strongly opposed to the introduction in industry of what has become known as scientific management, or efficiency methods. In relation to this phase of the problem, we find ourselves at one with the statement made and the opinions expressed by Mr. Louis D. Brandeis before the commission at Washington, in April, 1914, who, when invited to express his opinion on the question of efficiency standards, scientific management, and labor, among other things, said:

My special interest in this subject arises from the conviction that, in the first place, workingmen, and in the second place, members of the community generally, can attain the ideals of our American democracy only through an immediate increase and perhaps a constant increase, in the productivity of man. * * * Our ideals could not be attained unless we succeed in greatly increasing the productivity of man. * * * The progress that we have made in improving the conditions of the workingman during the last century, and particularly during the last 50 years, has been largely due to the fact that intervention or the introduction of machinery has gone so far in increasing the productivity of the individual man. With the advent of the new science of management has come the next great opportunity of increasing labor's share in the production, and it seems to me, therefore, of the utmost importance, not only that the science should be developed and should be applied as far as possible, but that it should be applied in cooperation with the representatives of organized labor, in order that labor may now, in this new movement, get its proper share.

I take it that the whole of this science of management is nothing more than an organized effort, pursued intensively, to eliminate waste. * * * It is in the process of eliminating waste and increasing the productivity of man, to adopt those methods which will insure the social and industrial essentials, fairness in development, fairness in the distribution of the profits, and the encouragement to the workingman which can not come without fairness.

I take it that in order to accomplish this result, it is absolutely essential that the unions should be represented in the process. * * * When labor is given such a representation, I am unable to find anything in scientific management which is not strictly in accord with the interests of labor, because it is nothing more than fair, through the application of these methods which have been pursued in other branches of science, to find out the best and the most effective way of accomplishing the result. It is not making men work harder—the very effort of it is to make them work less hard, to accomplish more by what they do, and to eliminate all unnecessary motion, to give special effort and special assistance to those who, at the time of the commencement of their work, are mostly in need of the assistance because they are less competent.

* * *. As I view the problem, it is only one of making the employer recognize the necessity of the participation of representatives of labor in the introduction and carrying forward of the work, and on the other hand, bringing to the workingman and the representatives of organized labor, the recognition of the fact that there is nothing in scientific management itself which is inimical to the interests of the workingman, but merely perhaps the practices of certain individuals, of certain employers or concerns who have engaged in it.

I feel that this presents a very good opportunity for organized labor. It seems to me absolutely clear, as scientific management rests upon the fundamental principles of advance in man's productivity, of determining what the best way was of doing a thing, instead of the poor way, of a complete coordination and organization of the various departments of business, that the introduction of scientific management in our businesses was certain to come; that those who oppose the introduction altogether are undertaking a perfectly impossible task; and that if organized labor took the position of absolute opposition, instead of taking the position of insisting upon their proper part in the introduction of this system, and the conduct of the business under it, organized labor would lose its greatest opportunity, and would be defeating the very purpose for which it exists.

On being asked the question what, in his opinion, would be the status of unionism in the event of scientific management becoming a common industrial condition, Mr. Brandeis said:

I think there would be a great deal left for unionism to do, and do not think the time will come when there will not be, as long as there is a wage system in existence. * * * I do not feel that we have reached the limit of the shorter day, certainly not in some employments, nor do I think we have reached the limit of the higher wage; certainly we have not reached the limit of the best conditions of employment in many industries.

All of these subjects are subjects which must be taken up, and should be taken up by the representatives of the men and women who are particularly interested. There will be work for unions to do as long as there is a wage system.

Mr. Brandeis further stated that he saw no menace to unionism in scientific management, and that he favored labor having a voice in determining all the factors involved in scientific management.

In answer to the question if he thought the fears groundless on the part of organized labor in looking upon scientific management as a menace to unionism, he answered, saying:

Yes; groundless except for this—I think, for instance, that the existence of the system of scientific management, unless the unions choose to cooperate with the effort to install it, may menace unionism, because the most efficient and advanced employers may adopt it, whether the unions like it or not, and in that way these establishments may become successful, and be so buttressed by their success as to be able to exclude unions from their business. That is the menace, if they do not take part, but if they cooperate it seems to me it simply advances unionism.

Mr. Brandeis confirmed the thought that if unionism is wise it will make the most of its opportunity by enlisting its cooperation in the movement, and will endeavor to bring scientific management to its highest possibility at the earliest day, in order that it may better share the increased surplus created by such scientific management, and that for unions to work against it is in the nature of a colossal error. The testimony of Miss Ida Tarbell on this point was in full accord with that of Mr. Brandeis.

PROHIBITION OF USE OF NONUNION-MADE TOOLS AND MATERIAL.

The sixth reason offered by employers for refusing to recognize or to deal with organized labor is that when they do so they are often not permitted to use nonunion-made tools or materials, thus placing upon themselves a burden and a hardship from which nonunion employers are free, and thus also laying themselves liable to get into all sorts of controversies with the union, which are vexatious, annoying, time-losing, and, frequently, most costly, as they sometimes lead to grave and serious strikes.

CLOSED SHOP.

The seventh reason why many employers refuse to recognize or to deal with organized labor (and among these may be mentioned the employers of large bodies of workers who have previously had trade agreements with organized labor) is the matter of the closed shop.

Many such employers are quite willing to recognize and to deal with unions upon a tacit or written open-shop agreement, but they have no confidence, based on their previous experience, that an open-shop agreement will be respected by the unions. Such employers labor under the fear that, despite an open-shop agreement or understanding, the union, at its first opportunity, will force them to compel the nonunion worker to join the union. Employers such as these are unwilling to place themselves in the position where the union can control them despite an open-shop agreement or understanding and, so to speak, put a pistol to their heads and command them in turn to command a nonunion worker on pain of dismissal to join the union. Such employers feel that, having an open-shop agreement or understanding, if for any reason a worker does not choose to join the union, they as employers should no more compel him to do so than they would compel him to join any particular fraternal society or religious body. They feel that if they are working under an open-shop agreement or understanding and such nonunion worker is capable, efficient, and has rendered long and faithful service, that they are doing him and themselves a great injustice either to force him into a union or to discharge him because he will not join a union.

Where an employer enters into an agreement with a union which does not stipulate that only union men shall be employed but leaves the employer free to employ exclusively union men or some union and some nonunion men as he may prefer, so long as he maintains for all men union conditions, that in such an event the union has no right to demand that the nonunionist should be compelled by the employer to join the union or a strike will follow. For the union, under such conditions, to strike, as it has done, notably in the Pennsylvania coal fields, and as pointed out also by W. O. Smith, ex-chairman of the executive committee of the Kentucky district of the United Mine Workers of America, whose statements have been quoted herein, is a violation, on the part of the union, of its contract.

It may be held that unionists working under an open-shop agreement or understanding always reserve to themselves the right, for any reason or for no reason, to cease to work alongside of nonunion men, and that they further reserve the right to determine the psychological moment at which it is in their interest to cease work or to go on a strike because they will not work alongside of nonunion men. It is the fear of the likelihood of their doing this that frightens off many employers from recognizing or dealing with organized labor. They feel that even when they are operating under an open-shop agreement or understanding which does not deny them the right to employ nonunion men so long as they work under union conditions, they are working with a sword suspended over their heads by a slender thread, which may break at any moment, and are liable to have a strike on their hands at the most critical time, which may spell ruin for their business. Employers, as a rule, do not deem it a good business policy to invite such risks.

An impressive example of this policy on the part of organized labor was brought out in the testimony taken by the commission at Lead, S. Dak. Supt. Grier, of the Homestake Mining Co., Lead, S. Dak., at the hearing held by the commission at that point in August, 1914, stated that he had recognized and dealt with the Lead City Miners'

Union from 1877 to 1909, with the understanding that they were at liberty to employ union or nonunion men as they preferred. Late in October, 1909, a resolution was published in the daily papers that on and after the 25th of November, 1909, members of the federation would not work with those working for the Homestake Mining Co. who failed and neglected to become members of the union in good standing; and in consequence, on the 25th of November, the mine was closed down, and from that day on the company has not recognized nor dealt with organized labor.

We are, however, of the opinion that where an employer enters into an agreement with a union which stipulates that only union men shall be employed, a thing which he has both a moral and a legal right to do, the nonunion worker, in that event, can have no more reason to find fault with the employer in declining to employ him than a certain manufacturer would have if the employer, for reasons satisfactory to himself, should confine his purchases to the product of some other manufacturer.

CONTESTS FOR SUPREMACY BETWEEN RIVAL UNIONS.

Testimony has been given before this commission indicating, in more than one instance, that contests between rival unions, or factions of the same union, have led to strikes causing industrial unrest from which the worker as well as the employer, has suffered harm and loss.

ACTS OF VIOLENCE AGAINST NONUNION WORKERS AND THE PROPERTIES OF EMPLOYERS.

The ninth objection raised on the part of the employers against unionism, which has been substantiated abundantly by investigation and by testimony taken by the commission, is the resort on the part of unionists to violence in labor troubles, and to the fact that unionists condone such violence when committed in the alleged interest of labor.

The most notable case, of course, in modern industrial history, is that of the structual iron workers, which resulted in the plea of guilty on the part of the McNamara brothers, for the blowing up of the Los Angeles Times Building, killing over 20 innocent people, and which further resulted in Frank Ryan, the president of the Structural Iron Workers' National Union, and a group of other labor union officials, being convicted and sentenced to prison.

As a matter of fact, the bringing into life of this United States Commission on Industrial Relations was due primarily to the long series of crimes committed at the instance of the structural iron workers' union, which culminated in the blowing up of the Los Angeles Times Building, with its attendant loss of life of innocent citizens, and which aroused a state of public sentiment demanding that an investigation be made by an impartial Federal body, to inquire into the underlying causes of industrial unrest, the existence of which seemed to be evidenced by the violent activities on the part of labor in various parts of the country.

Vincent St. John, secretary of the Industrial Workers of the World, in his testimony before the Commission on Industrial Relations at a public hearing in New York, said that he believed in violence when it was necessary to win. He said that if the destruction of property seemed necessary to bring results, then he believed in the destruction of property.

A. Johannsen, of California, State organizer for the building trades of California, and general organizer for the United Brotherhood of Carpenters, in his testimony before the United States Commission on Industrial Relations at Washington in May, 1915, in speaking of the reelection of Frank Ryan, president of the National Structural Iron Workers' Union, among other things thanked the Lord that the union had the courage to reelect him president after he had been convicted as a participant in the dynamiting crimes of the structural iron workers. He further expressed the hope that it was true that the convicted dynamiters, after being reelected to office by the iron workers, were met by a procession of applause at Fort Leavenworth while on their way to prison, and that President Ryan performed his official duties while there, and rendered his official reports as president of a union of 10,000 members and a part of the American Federation of Labor.

In contradistinction to the opinion of Mr. Johannsen, to the effect that he thanked the Lord that the union had the courage to reelect Frank Ryan president after he had been convicted as a participant in the dynamiting crimes of the structural iron workers, we have the opinion of Dr. Charles W. Eliot, president emeritus of Harvard University, who, in his testimony before the United States Commission on Industrial Relations at New York, January 29, 1915, in referring to this very instance, said, in answer to the question as to how he regarded the action of the structural iron workers' union in reelecting Frank Ryan president after his conviction of crime, "As a serious moral offense against the community as a whole." [1]

Speaking about respecting court labor injunctions, Witness Johannsen said:

I don't think the power of an injunction goes much beyond the courage of those who are enjoined. I think that if a person is convinced in his own mind and his own feelings that his case is just, that his demands for an increase of wages, or whatever the fight may be—if you think and feel you are right, why, then go ahead. Never mind about those pieces of paper. [2]

On being asked whether he (Johannsen) believed that Frank Ryan, president of the Structural Iron Workers' National Union, and his associates, were innocent men railroaded to prison, he said that he did, and that he was satisfied they never committed any crime against labor or a better society, and were therefore unjustly convicted. This was his attitude, despite his attention having been called to the opinion and decision rendered by the circuit court of appeals, including Judges Baker, Seaman, and Kohlsaat, against whose integrity and fairness no whisper had ever been heard, and who seemingly went into the evidence in the dynamiting cases most exhaustively and carefully, and who, among other things, in their decision, said—

The facts thus recited, as proven by the Government on the trial, may be mentioned in part as follows: Almost 100 explosions thus occurred, damaging and destroying buildings and bridges in process of erection where the work

[1] New York hearings, U. S. Commission on Industrial Relations, p. 1907.
[2] Washington hearings, May, 1915, U. S. Commission on Industrial Relations, p. 958.

was being done by open-shop concerns, and no explosions took place in connection with work of a similar character, where the work was done by closed-shop concerns. * * * In connection with this work of destruction, dynamite and nitroglycerine was purchased and stolen, and various storage places arranged to conveniently store such explosives which were to be used in the destruction of property in the various States referred to. * * * Large quantities of dynamite and nitroglycerine were at various times stored in the vaults of the association at Indianapolis, and also in the basement of the building. * * * Four explosions occurred in one night at the same hour in Indianapolis, and explosions were planned to take place on the same night, two hours apart, at Omaha, Nebr., and Columbus, Ind., and the explosions so planned did occur on the same night, at about the same time, instead of two hours apart, owing to the fact that one clock was defective. * * * All the dynamite and nitroglycerine * * * including the expenses incident to the stealing of the dynamite, were paid out of the funds of the international association, and these funds were drawn from the association upon checks signed by the secretary-treasurer, John J. McNamara, and the president, Frank M. Ryan, plaintiff in error.

The written correspondence on the part of many of the plaintiffs in error * * * furnish manifold evidence not only of understanding between the correspondents of the purposes of the primary conspiracy, but many thereof convey information or direction for the use of the explosives, while others advise of the destruction which has occurred, and each points unerringly not only to the understanding that the agency therein was that of the conspirators, but as well to the necessary steps in its performance of transporting the explosives held for such use. This line of evidence clearly tends to prove, and may well be deemed convincing of the fact on the part of many, if not all, of the correspondents.

Plaintiff Frank M. Ryan was president of the association and of its executive board, and was active manager and leader of the contest, and policies carried on throughout the years of the strike and destructive explosions in evidence. Letters written and received by him at various stages of the contest clearly tend to prove his familiarity with and management of the long course of destroying open-shop structures, however guarded in expression. He was at the headquarters of the association for the supervision of operations periodically, usually two or three days each month, uniformly attended the meetings there of the executive board, and made frequent visits to the field of activities. * * * He signed all of the checks in evidence for payments for expenditures for purchase, storage, and conveyance of explosives. * * * Many other letters in evidence, both from and to him, however disguised in terms, may well authorize an inference of his complete understanding of, and complicity for, the explosions, both in plans and execution.[1]

Masses of testimony were filed with the commission to prove that organized labor at times resorted to a policy of lawlessness. Among other documents may be cited a magazine under the title of A Policy of Lawlessness, a partial record of riot, assault, murder, and intimidation, occurring in strikes of the iron molders' union, during 1904, 1905, 1906, 1907, published by the National Founders' Association, in which are given, as a partial list taken from court records, a great number of instances of violence on the part of labor unionists in labor disputes; and also a document published as a report, submitted by the committee on labor disputes of the Cleveland Chamber of Commerce, entitled "Violence in Labor Disputes," giving hundreds of instances where unionists had resorted to violence in labor troubles in that community alone.

Mr. Luke Grant, special investigator for the United States Commission on Industrial Relations, in his report to the commission on

---

[1] Washington hearings, May, 1915, U. S. Commission on Industrial Relations, pp. 1004–1013.

the National Erectors' Association and the International Association of Bridge and Structural Iron Workers, says:

Do they [the unions] believe in violence? They did not destroy property and they don't know who did. They probably adopted resolutions denouncing the unknown perpetrators, and offering a reward for their arrest and conviction. The Western Federation of Miners, in convention, offered a reward for the arrest of the men who blew up the Independence depot in June, 1904, killing 14 men. Harry Orchard afterwards confessed that he and Steve Adams did it, acting as agents for the officers of the union.

In this way do union men collectively approve of violence, that few if any of them would individually permit (p. 148).

Referring to the industrial war between the National Erectors' Association and the structural iron workers' union, Mr. Grant continues to say:

When the hopelessness of the situation became apparent to the union officials, resort was made to the destruction of property. Diplomacy was out of the question, so dynamite was tried (p. 150).

The report of Luke Grant brings out the fact that the structural iron workers had no grievances against their employers in the matter of wages, hours, or working conditions. The only question at issue was that of the closed shop. To enforce the closed shop, the structural iron workers seemed to feel themselves justified in dynamiting over 100 properties and destroying many innocent lives.

Police Commissioner Arthur Woods, of the city of New York, in his testimony before the United States Commission on Industrial Relations in May, 1915, at Washington, D. C., speaking of violence by labor unions, among other things, said:

The result of our investigation shows a course of procedure like this: There would be a strike and the strikers would retain some gunmen to do whatever forcible or violent work they needed. The employer, to meet this violence, would in a comparatively small percentage of cases, and not as many cases as the gunmen were employed on the other side, hire a private detective agency. The function that the gunmen were to perform was to intimidate the workers that were hired to take the place of the strikers. * * * There were three indictments for murder in the first degree.

The question was asked Police Commissioner Woods in how far his investigations had warranted the statement that appeared in the New York Herald of May 14, 1915, reading as follows:

Several of the indictments mentioned assault upon members of the union, and in this connection District Attorney Perkins said last night that the reign of lawlessness was caused by union leaders who wished to perpetuate themselves in power, who hired assailants to assault contenders in their own unions for their places, and who used their union offices to extort blackmail under threats from employers. Seven men are indicted for assault in a riot for control of the union. Four men are indicted for hiring Dopey Benny's men to go to a nonunion factory and rough-house the employees as they left, and wreck the plant. A dozen workers were wounded in that fight.

Six union men are accused of extortion and assault in using violence to collect a fine of $100 upon an employer. Four others are accused of hiring the Dopey Benny band to shoot up a nonunion factory. Many shops were fired. The factory suffered a damage of $1,000 and several persons were injured. Other indictments mentioned cases where the band was employed by union leaders to attack nonunion workers, to wreck factories, and even to assault nonunion men who opposed the leaders (pp. 964–5).

To all of the foregoing, Police Commissioner Woods replied, "That is the general line of things that we found."

One of the ablest and clearest-headed exponents of the cause of labor that testified before this commission was Morris Hillquit, of New York. In speaking of violence in labor troubles, he is quoted as saying,[1] that the resort to violence and lawbreaking was "ethically unjustifiable and tactically suicidal." Mr. Hillquit pointed out that wherever any group or section of the labor movement "has embarked upon a policy of 'breaking the law' or using 'any weapon which will win a fight,' whether such policy was styled 'terrorism,' 'propaganda' of the deed, 'direct action,' 'sabotage,' or 'anarchism,' it has invariably served to destroy the movement by attracting to it professional criminals, infesting it with spies, leading the workers to needless and senseless slaughter, and ultimately engendering a spirit of disgust and reaction."

Robert Hunter, commenting on the foregoing statement made by Morris Hillquit, says (p. viii):

It will, I think, be clear to the reader that the history of the labor movement during the last half century fully sustains Mr. Hillquit's position.

APPRENTICESHIP RULES.

The question of apprenticeships has led to much industrial strife and consequent industrial unrest, where unions have arbitrarily determined the number of apprentices that the employer may take on. Where this practice has prevailed the union employer has, in competition with the nonunion employer, been seriously handicapped. The remedy for this evil lies obviously in a joint agreement under the direction of the proposed State industrial commissions, in which each side has an equal voice in determining the proper quota of apprentices to be employed.

In conclusion, it is our desire to point out that organized labor is chargeable with its fullest share of creating causes of industrial unrest, because of its sympathetic strikes, its jurisdictional disputes, its labor union politics, its contract breaking, its resort to violence in time of trouble, its policy of limited output, and its closed shop policy. There is an abundance of evidence in the records of the commission to show that organized labor is also guilty of intimidating courts, more especially the lower criminal courts, to deal lightly with labor offenders charged with criminal assaults in labor troubles; and that some judges, more especially in the lower courts, toady to organized labor for vote-getting purposes, and dismiss union labor men guilty of lawbreaking, or impose on them nominal penalties out of all proportion to the crimes committed.

These various policies have brought about their fullest share among the workers, to say nothing of the injury inflicted on employers and on society, of poverty, suffering, wretchedness, misery, discontent, and crime. Organized labor will never come into its own, and will indefinitely postpone the day when its many commendable objects will be achieved in the broadest sense, until it will cut out of its program sympathetic strikes, until it can prevent cessation of work in jurisdictional disputes, until it can more successfully prevent labor union politics, until it can teach many in its rank and file to regard more sacredly their trade agreements, until it can penalize its members for

---

[1] Robert Hunter, Violence and the Labor Movement, p. viii.

resorting to violence in labor disputes, and until it can make it a labor union offense to limit output.

Organized labor may ask, "If we cut out the evil policies complained of from our program, what offensive and defensive weapons will be left us with which to protect ourselves against the unfair employer?"

The answer is that when labor is effectively organized it has two most powerful weapons at its command that the employer, as a rule, dreads and fears because of the great damage these weapons can inflict on him, namely, the strike and the primary boycott, both of which are within the moral and legal rights of the worker to use.

Generally speaking, the evils complained of have been eliminated from the program of the railway brotherhoods. As a consequence, railway managers do not hesitate to recognize and to deal with the railway unions, to their mutual advantage and satisfaction, with the result that collective bargaining has become the common condition in the railway world. Railway strikes and lockouts have now become most infrequent, and industrial unrest due to these causes in this sphere of activity has become greatly minimized.

If these evils are eliminated by organized labor from its program, much will have been done to stimulate collective bargaining and to minimize the existing causes of industrial unrest. The remedies for all these evils do not lie with the employer; they rest wholly and solely with unionists. The responsibility for the growth of these evils, in our opinion, rests primarily with unionists who neglect their union duties and who are as unmindful of their duties as union men as are many voters of their civic duty who remain at home on election day.

We have faith in the honesty of purpose, in the fairness of spirit, and in the law-abiding character of the American worker, and we do not believe that the rank and file of American wage earners are in favor of many of the practices of some unions which have subjected unionism to so much severe, but just, criticism. We believe it is the duty of each unionist regularly to attend the meetings of his union in order that democracy shall prevail in trade-unions instead of an autocracy or despotism, which inevitably follows where the best membership fails to attend union meetings and thus permits the affairs of the organization to get into the hands of incompetent, ill-judging, or dishonest officials, who, for their selfish ends, abuse the power and authority vested in them.

Wherever there are found honest, high-minded, clear-headed labor leaders—and in the course of our investigations and hearings we have come into close personal touch with many such as these, who have commanded our esteem and respect—it will be found that, as a rule, they represent unions where the better membership takes a lively and active interest in the welfare of the association, and regards it as a sacred duty to regularly attend its meetings.

We say frankly that if we were wage earners we would be unionists, and as unionists we should feel the keen responsibility of giving the same attention to our trade-union duties as to our civic duties.

The ideal day in the industrial world will be reached when all labor disputes will be settled as a result of reason and not as a result of force. This ideal day can be hastened if the employers, on the one hand, will earnestly strive to place themselves in the position of the worker and look at the conditions not only through the eye of the employer but through the eye of the worker; and if the worker will strive to place himself in the position of the employer, and look at the conditions not only through the eye of the worker but through the eye of the employer.

This, of course, means the strongest kind of organization on both sides. It means that employers must drive out of the ranks of their associations the law breaker, the labor-contract breaker, and the exploiter of labor. It also means that, in the interests of fairness, every board of directors of an industrial enterprise should have within its organization a committee for the special purpose of keeping the board of directors advised as to the condition of their workers. And it finally means that trade-unions must, in order to minimize the causes of industrial unrest, among other things remove the weak spots in unionism set forth herein, thereby hastening the day when employers will no longer fear to recognize and deal with unions, and when collective bargaining shall thus become the common conditior.

Finally, we feel that employers, individually and through their associations, in common with thoughtful representatives of labor, should give their fullest share of thought and lend their heartiest cooperation in aiding to solve, through constructive legislation and other ways, the great problems of vocational education, continuation schools, woman and child labor, apprenticeship, hours of labor, housing, sickness insurance, workmen's compensation, safety measures, old-age pensions, and unemployment. The hope is therefore expressed that employers will strive to work with rather than against intelligent labor representatives in aiding, through these various movements, to lessen industrial unrest and to still further improve the condition of wage earners and their dependents.

HARRIS WEINSTOCK.
S. THRUSTON BALLARD.
RICHARD H. AISHTON.[1]

[1] Appointed commissioner Mar. 17, 1915, to serve unexpired term of Hon. F. A. Delano, resigned.

SUPPLEMENTAL STATEMENT OF COMMISSIONER S. THRUSTON BALLARD.

The law creating the United States Commission on Industrial Relations, in additon to other things, says: "The commission shall seek to discover the underlying causes of dissatisfaction in the industrial situation and report its conclusions thereon."

The causes of industrial unrest may be put under five main groups:

First. Low wages.

Second. Unemployment, through seasonal occupations, periods of depression, accidents, and sickness.

Third. The development of large industries.

Fourth. Long working hours and insanitary conditions.

Fifth. Unsatisfactory rural conditions.

I will analyze each of these groups separately.

First. Low wages, with all the attendant evils, I consider the prime cause for industrial unrest.

One of the chief factors in wage depression is undoubtedly the encouraged, stimulated, and probably assisted immigration which has brought to our shores millions of unskilled workers in the last few years. These immigrants, coming from those countries where vastly lower wage rates prevail, develop in America a wage competition of whch the employer naturally takes advantage.

The European war will probably relieve this immigration situation for the next few years, but it is a question to which our Government must give serious consideration in the near future.

Inefficency of the unskilled worker is also a contributory cause of low wages. The average applicant for work is irresponsible and untrained.

With all our vaunted free-school system, our industrial education is deplorable. In our large cities they are beginning to consider the question seriously, but our rural schools are lamentably deficient. This inefficiency, which tends to lower the whole standard, can be corrected only through improved educational facilities.

Government assistance should be given to aid in the establishment of vocational, trade, and continuation schools as a part of our public-school system.

The gravitation of industries into large units has caused the skilled worker to be supplanted by the unskilled, who becomes merely a cog in the wheel of the great machine, performing the monotonous duties that anyone could easily do after a few weeks' practice.

The wages of the unskilled laborer are so pitifully small that it is almost impossible for him to maintain a family, even with the most rigid economy.

I suggest as the only remedy for low wages, due to these conditions, the enactment of a national minimum wage law.

Second. Under the second cause of industrial unrest—unemployment—we have seasonal occupations, as, for example, ice cutting and logging in winter, harvesting and fruit-picking in summer.

This problem will always be with us, and should be dealt with through an efficient system of national employment agencies, to be administered by the Federal Government.

Private employment agencies have proved inadequate; have even in many cases been used to exploit the worker. I therefore strongly recommend that all employment agencies be managed by the Government.

We have also unemployment due to periods of depression. The Federal employment agencies would take care of these cases, bringing, when possible, the man and the job together, but in periods of long depression, when no work is to be found, Government, State, and municipal work, which had been held in reserve for this purpose, should then be provided.

Should all these resources be exhausted and there still remain unemployed workers, there should be Government concentration camps where work with a small wage would be provided, supplemented by agricultural and industrial training.

The fear of unemployment because of accident or illness fosters a feeling of discontent which tends to cause industrial unrest.

Workmen's compensation laws and sickness insurance, with proper restrictions, would be the proper correctives here.

Workmen's compensation laws thus far developed protect the man only when accident occurs during working hours, and this is paid for entirely by the employer. If an accident occurs causing injury to a man just before entering his work place, the consequent loss to his family is just as great as though he had been hurt five minutes later within the factory walls, and yet he receives nothing.

I therefore recommend that the workmen's compensation law should provide insurance against accident wherever and whenever caused. This insurance, however, should be paid by the man himself, his employer, and the Government jointly. The same idea should apply also to sickness insurance.

The worker himself should feel these responsibilities and should always share the expense of such insurance.

Third. We have, as the third cause for industrial unrest, the development of large industries with their absentee ownership. Large business, properly controlled, is an economic benefit, but the very size makes coordination between the employers and workers most difficult. There is no personal contact, hence a lack of sympathy and understanding.

Where a few cents per day in the wage of the individual workman means hundreds of thousands of dollars annually to the business, and where there are so many units that one foreman can be pitted against another to maintain the cost of production at the lowest possible point, the natural tendency is to depress the wage.

As to the remedy, I would suggest that all corporations doing interstate business be required to take out a national charter that will entail certain responsibilities and possibly grant certain immunities from State control.

This charter should not allow overcapitalization. Each board of directors, in addition to its other committees, should have a labor committee whose duty it should be to become thoroughly acquainted with the labor conditions of the business, and make regular reports thereon to the board. These reports should be published with the financial and other reports, and thus give the stockholders a thorough understanding of the business.

Fourth. Long working hours and insanitary conditions are additional factors in the problem of industrial unrest. Nothing affects the man's physical well-being, and consequently his earning power, more than these.

The remedy will be found in publicity and legislation, with factory inspection by competent Government officers.

Personal experience for a number of years convinces me that in continuous occupation, workmen will do more work and better work on an 8-hour basis than on 12, and that one day in seven for rest must be allowed if the man is to develop the fullest degree of efficiency.

I therefore favor a national eight-hour law for continuous labor.

Sanitary conditions of work I have found to be a paying proposition to the employer, as well as just and beneficial to the worker.

Fifth. With regard to unsatisfactory rural conditions, I view with real concern the fact that our small landowners are becoming tenants, while the small farms are passing into the hands of a few.

Everything possible should be done to aid and encourage our farmers; the United States Government should adopt a plan for the scientific distribution of our agricultural products, and for a rural-credit system, as it is practiced to-day in some foreign countries.

Unsatisfactory rural conditions which make it difficult for the small farmer to earn a decent livelihood for his family cause many poorly equipped young men and women to flock to the cities. As a rule, they are thoroughly inefficient and lamentably ignorant of the temptations of city life, and are rarely able to earn a living wage.

Life on the farm should be made sufficiently attractive and lucrative to induce these boys and girls to remain there. This can be done only through our rural schools, which are now most inadequate.

The education of country children must fit them for country life. No love of the beautiful, no patriotic gratitude to his country for his education can be felt by the child who spends weary months in uncomfortable hovels, where he receives impractical and frequently useless instruction.

Our Government should aid the States in establishing comfortable rural schools, with longer terms and with better-paid and better-equipped teachers.

In every rural school there should be departments of household arts—that is, cooking, sewing, and millinery—and manual training and agriculture. These schools should be open for agricultural instruction throughout the summer—in fact, each one should become an experiment station for the neighborhood. The schoolhouse should be the social center—the meeting ground for instruction and social pleasures.

In order to satisfactorily carry out the suggestions contained in this report, it would be necessary to have a nonpartisan commission in charge of industrial questions, as suggested by the majority report of this commission.

This would require large additional revenue, which must be derived by some form of taxation.

The fairest of all taxes are the income and inheritance taxes. This question, however, must be carefully studied and weighed, since the tax is paid by one class while the benefits are largely enjoyed by another.

Care should be taken that it does not become confiscatory, and thus stifle individual incentive and effort.

In addition, I believe that every individual should pay his proportion, no matter how small it may be. It will inspire in him a feeling of citizenship and make him an integral part of our Nation.

S. THRUSTON BALLARD.

III

Report of Commissioner John B. Lennon on Industrial Education

SIGNED BY

Commissioners Lennon, O'Connell, Garretson, Ballard, and Walsh

REPORT OF COMMISSIONER JOHN B. LENNON ON INDUSTRIAL EDUCATION.

The Commission on Industrial Relations gave careful study and investigation to the subject of industrial or vocational education. We found the general subject of education, whether academic, cultural or industrial, so exceedingly important and interesting to all classes of citizens as to warrant a brief statement covering especially the subject of the pressing need for industrial education and the bearing that such education would have upon industrial unrest.

The terms "vocational" or "industrial" education are used to indicate the training given in many varieties of schools and by many different modes of teaching. Our attention has been almost entirely confined to a study of that kind of education which has to do with the preparation of boys and girls for useful employment in industry, particularly as applied to mechanical and agricultural employment.

DEMAND FOR INDUSTRIAL EDUCATION.

The great importance of this subject appears to be fairly well appreciated by every class of our citizenship, trade-unions, employers' organizations, educators, merchants, legislators, etc. The universal interest in this subject warrants the conclusion that its proper solution is of paramount importance to the welfare of the Nation, in order to establish that kind of education that will enable the boys and girls of the United States to enter upon their industrial life properly equipped to make their lives a success. Our attention has been forcibly called to the fact that the great mass of the wageworkers are without any accumulated means. Their children are therefore compelled to enter gainful pursuits at an early age. Therefore the great need that our system of education should be so constructed as to equip these boys and girls with vocational and industrial knowledge that would make them, from the beginning, useful workers, enabling them to earn and demand a living wage and treatment that will not be injurious to their future welfare, as well as the opportunity to advance from time to time in their chosen occupations.

Among the tramps and hoboes, also in the ranks of those who are employed only when labor is scarce, we have found thousands of graduates of grammar and high schools, some even having the advantage of a university education, indicating that however cultural their education may have been it was not always of practical value in the mill, in the shop, or on the farm.

Private trade schools can not remedy this. They are operated generally in the interest of employers and do not give the most important element of education—namely, the interest of the workers themselves—the consideration it deserves.

255

The private training school can not cover this problem. All boys and girls require this practical equipment, and it can be secured only through and in connection with our system of public schools. To properly perform this duty, the general responsibility rests on all our people. It is a public and not a private function, and the State and Nation must be held responsible for its early and successful solution.

The needs of modern industry do not seem to be met by any existing scheme of training for general usefulness in the crafts or for the development of all-around mechanics. Therefore, the pressing need is for a general educational policy that will make possible a continuous development of both adults and minors in industry who are over 14 years of age. Boys or girls who go into the shop at 14 or later develop into specialists but not mechanics. If for any reason they lose their job they are no more fit for another place than they were when they first began. The work, therefore, that must be done for those already in industry is to train them to fit into work wherever help is required in the shop.

Our public schools must be prepared and required not only to give some vocational consideration to pupils over 14 years of age who remain in the schools, but to provide for compulsory continuation daytime schools on the time and at the expense of employers, and voluntary night schools for both academic and vocational training for boys and girls who are at work and for adults who desire further knowledge which will be of use in their vocation.

We hold that all experience shows conclusively that public instruction privately controlled or any plan that fails to comprehend the entire number of pupils in the United States is dangerous and unworthy of support.

We hold that the advantages of vocational education should be open to all adults or minors in the public schools if they remain after 14 years of age, and in night schools and continuation schools after they enter industry, and these advantages we believe should be provided entirely at public expense.

There seems to be but slight, if any, advantage to be obtained by undertaking vocational training of pupils before they reach the age of 14. Their entire time prior to that age is required to lay a foundation for what may be termed their general education. This being true beyond any question, the State must provide for education after entrance into industrial life as well as before. Fairness to all classes demands the opportunity for vocational teaching after the boy or girl of 14 or over has entered industry.

The children of the well-to-do parents are continued at school through the several years of high-school work entirely at public expense, in order to fit them for professions and business life. Is it unreasonable that the public should equally provide schooling for those who, because of economic pressure, must enter industry at from 14 to 16 years of age?

This the working class demands for their children, and it must be provided if our public-school system is to continue to hold a high place in the respect and esteem of all classes of our citizens. In a Republic such as the United States, the school system should be adapted to the needs of all classes, rich and poor; those who are to enter professions and those who are to go into the shop, the factory, the mill, or to work upon the land.

We believe it to be assured that if all our schools will extend practical vocational teaching to cover instruction after 14 years of age, a very large number of pupils will remain at school until the age of 16 or even later, if the school is providing for their future usefulness and success as well as or better than can be done in the factory. This is the most important element in the consideration of the subject of industrial training. Keep the children at school as long as possible, extending their vocational knowledge, widening their academic training, teaching them not only their rights but their duties as citizens of our Republic, stirring their ambition for a life worth living, and making of them dear men and women rather than cheap.

It can not be denied that our public schools, as now generally conducted, do not accomplish as much work that is substantially effective in fitting their pupils for productive labor with their hands as should be the case. We must have a plan of education in the school that develops both the power to think and the power to do.

We find that as a rule the first eight years of the school life of a boy or girl must of necessity be very largely, if not entirely, devoted to work of a cultural character, for the reason that up to the age of 14, when the first eight years of school life are completed, neither boys nor girls have developed any clearly defined likes or dislikes as to what their life work shall be, nor can either parents or teachers be considered safe guides as to the careers of children of that age. Justice, as well as the best interest of the pupil, demands that the desires and wishes of the child shall have primary consideration in the determining of his life work, and to assign this work arbitrarily, either by the school board, the teacher, or even the parents, is not much less than criminal.

The schools should provide the greatest possible variety of occupations, making the opportunity of choice as varied as possible. And this vocational training should be in the same building as that where the child spends his first eight years in school, in order that by observation of the vocational work and by contact with the pupils and vocational teaching, he shall have every possible opportunity to determine what he wants to study for a vocation.

Industrial education in the United States is on trial. It will and should be judged by practical men and women, and that course should be pursued which promises the best possible results.

CONTROL OF VOCATIONAL SCHOOLS.

It is believed that all vocational schools should be a part of the public school system; that they should be entirely free, supported by the National, State, county, or city government; that all textbooks and equipment should be furnished to the pupils free; and that a plan of management of such schools should be developed which would give to the workers and employers in each community, in the State, and in the Nation, a potent voice in their entire control, in conjunction with the regular boards of school officials. As to vocational school work, the committee in control should consist of an equal number of members representing organized labor, organized employers, and the regularly constituted school authorities, a majority of whom would be required to finally determine practices and methods. Every vocational teacher should be a practical man or woman from the trades or occupations taught; and the product, if any, of such schools, should not be sold on the market in competition with regular industry. Ample opportunity exists for the use of any possible product of the vocational schools by the city, county or State.

GENERAL RECOMMENDATIONS.

The establishment of vocational schools for all children in school over 14 years of age is advocated, as well as compulsory continuation and night vocational schools, with such academic work as may be advisable for all persons over 14 years of age in industry and agriculture.

Education vitally interests all our people and neither money nor time should be spared to make the education of the United States the most thorough, the most potent for human uplift and progress, of any system of education in the world. To lead in this great work is our proper position, not to follow. Thoroughness should be the aim of our Nation and our States. Poorly trained workers in industry are now entirely too plentiful. This should be overcome by excellent vocational training. We believe there are now too many cheap workmen. This Nation should work for men, women, and children who will not consent to cheapness, either in wages, conditions of labor, or character.

The public schools, whether academic or vocational, should be entirely neutral as to unions and their control, and exactly the same should be true as to the exercise of any control for class interests by employers or employers' organizations. And surely there is no room in our schools to warrant the teaching of any degree of hostility toward trade unions or employers' organizations.

The general recommendations of the special commission on national aid to vocational education have our most hearty approval and we approve of the passage of a law by the Congress of the United States with that end in view. The need of the States for such assistance is clearly set forth.

It is recommended that Congress authorize by law the creation of a Federal board to administer funds appropriated by Congress to the several States for vocational education, the board to consist of three members, one educator, one representative of organized labor, and one representative of organizations of employers, to be appointed by the President with the consent of the Senate, to serve for a term of six years, the first appointments to be for two, four, and six years; with salaries of $8,000 each per annum; the Federal board so constituted to establish rules and standards for expenditure of Government funds awarded to the several States.

The Federal board shall require of each State asking for Government funds the adoption of the following standards before any awards can be made or funds be appropriated by the board:

1. Compulsory daytime continuation schools for all children in industry between the ages of 14 and 18 years, for not less than five hours per week, at the expense of their employers.

2. Night schools for all persons over 18 years of age who are desirous of further educational opportunities, either cultural or vocational.

3. Standards of efficiency for teachers.

4. Joint State control in administration, of vocational education by public-school authorities, organized labor, and organized employers, with equal representation.

5. The Federal board to establish some model schools for industrial training in agriculture and vocations, as examples to the several States.

This problem of vocational education not only is important materially but is intimately a human problem, involving as it does the social welfare and progress of all the people.

The boys and girls of the farm, if assured by proper education of becoming generally successful farmers, will remain farmers, rather than undertake to compete in the industries with properly trained workers of the cities. This will help to solve the problems that are threatening injury to our great agricultural industries, and will eliminate a cause of industrial unrest.

In the farming districts the country school remains practically as it was 50 years ago. Pupils are not taught what is essential to develop them into excellent farmers and farmers' wives, but the cultural education of days gone by is continued, to the considerable exclusion of teaching how to farm and how to manage a farmer's home. Surely the Nation has here a mission of helpfulness to perform that which, as a great nation, it can not longer afford to leave largely neglected. Its prosperity as a nation depends upon the character and efficiency of its men and women much more than upon its geographical position or the quality of its soil, and to build character and effectiveness we must lay the foundations well by a proper education of our boys and girls. We should not strive merely for educating them into correctly working automatic machines. The human side must be uppermost and receive attention of the most careful nature. It is not worth while to make square holes and then try to fit into them round men and women.

Education should take into account, at every stage, manhood and womanhood, and where and how the life is to be surrounded, and what can be done through education to make each life successful and therefore worth while. Dexterity is worth while, but good character is more vital to real service in the world of industry and civilization. At present our schools in city and country do not make good, either in the development of skill, in the duties of service, or in a clear understanding of human rights and consequent human duties toward our fellows. Industrial education can not possibly take the place of industrial experience. All that can be hoped for is that our schools will make their teaching a real preparatory process for entering upon industrial life, with proper conception of life work instead of no conception at all.

CONTINUATION OR PART-TIME SCHOOLS.

All minors entering industry after 14 years of age are entitled to further aid from organized society in order to enable them to complete their vocational and cultural education. This is possible only through the establishment of compulsory day time continuation schools of at least five hours per week, at the expense of employers, and night schools. The eagerness with which minors and adults take advantage of such schools is sufficient evidence to warrant legislation giving these opportunities to all minors and to such adults as may care to take advantage of them. These schools, in order to be of value, must be compulsory upon all minors in industry up to at least 18 years of age. Schools in the United States should meet fully the needs of every class of pupils, those who expect to enter colleges and prepare for the professions as well as the much larger class that is to enter industrial life. The parents of the wageworking class contend, with much reason, that their children are not given the same vocational consideration under our present school systems as are the children of the well to do who expect to become lawyers, doctors, etc.

The State has established schools to train, for a useful industrial life, the mentally, morally, and physically deficient, and this effort has the hearty approval of every good citizen. If this work is worth doing, then it must be of vastly greater importance to establish one general scheme of education so as to make useful men and women out of the normal boy and girl, and neither expense nor investigation should be spared to accomplish this most desirable object.

TEACHERS.

It seems self-evident that no one can successfully teach others that of which he has no knowledge himself. We recommend, therefore, in the selection of teachers to impart trade education that only practical workmen shall be used. They should be selected with care as to character, and, as far as possible, craftsmen should be selected as trade teachers who have a considerable degree of cultural education. The opportunity should be continually extended for the proper education of teachers capable of teaching vocations, and, in so far as it may be advantageous, academic education also. The need of well-developed brain power is not waning in the least. What is demanded is the educated hand to apply in industry the ideas and knowledge of the brain. Our children need to know more as to their economic value and more of their social duties and responsibilities. The schoolhouse is the place where much of this should be taught, in order that the duties of honorable citizenship shall be appreciated. Real social service is the highest attainment the individual can aspire to reach. All education is of value in life, and the State should properly be held responsible for the education of her children, in order that the best possible use shall be made by the greatest possible number of the opportunities of life as they present themselves from year to year.

CONCLUSIONS.

The existing system of public education is inadequate. The present specialization of shop conditions is not favorable to a complete mastery of any trade or calling in the shop, store, or industry. This being admittedly true, it devolves on our public-school system to meet adequately the emergency in conjunction and cooperation with industry. The temperamental difference in children must have consideration in determining their life work and preparation therefor. The boy or girl must not become merely a cog in the great wheel of industry. Therefore the urgent need of vocational education in conjunction with practice in the shop or factory that makes each individual in a few years capable to fit into any place in the industry where help may be required. We now have too many handy men and specialists, who have no place into which they can fit when for any reason their particular work is no longer required.

Vocational education, on account of the wonderful changes in industrial production, must take the place of apprenticeship. To solve this problem right is to find a solution for much of the unnecessary social unrest of our day and generation.

There can be no question that industrial education is coming rapidly. Prejudiced opposition will be futile. The necessity is great and it must and will be met. The National Government should properly perform its full share of the responsibilities of meeting this demand for the best and fullest education of our children.

The entire subject is dealt with exhaustively in the report of the Special Commission on Vocational Education, which submitted its report June 1, 1914.

JOHN B. LENNON.
JAMES O'CONNELL.
AUSTIN B. GARRETSON.
S. THRUSTON BALLARD.
FRANK P. WALSH.

IV

ADDITIONAL FINDINGS OF FACT, CONCLU-
SIONS, AND RECOMMENDATIONS

ADDITIONAL FINDINGS OF FACT, CONCLUSIONS, AND RECOMMENDATIONS.

At regular sessions of the commission with all members present, the following resolutions were offered for adoption as a part of the commission's report to Congress. The members of the commission whose names appear in connection with the various resolutions voted for their adoption and thereby made the resolutions a part of their individual reports to Congress.

ADOPTED BY UNANIMOUS VOTE.

Whereas the commission finds that the terms "open shop" and "closed shop" have each a double meaning, and should never be used without telling which meaning is intended, the double meaning consisting in that they may mean either union or nonunion: Therefore, for the purposes of this report, be it

Resolved, That the Commission on Industrial Relations will not use the terms "open shop" and "closed shop," but in lieu thereof will use "union shop" and "nonunion shop."

The union ship is a shop where the wages, the hours of labor, and the general conditions of employment are fixed by a joint agreement between the employer and the trade-union.

The nonunion shop is one where no joint agreement exists, and where the wages, the hours of labor, and the general conditions of employment are fixed by the employer without cooperation with any trade-union.

Wherever the terms are used in this report, they bear the interpretation as set forth above.

ADOPTED BY MAJORITY VOTE OF COMMISSIONERS WALSH, LENNON, O'CONNELL, GARRETSON, AND WEINSTOCK.

The sources from which industrial unrest springs are, when stated in full detail, almost numberless. But, upon careful analysis of their real character, they will be found to group themselves almost without exception under four main sources which include all the others. These four are:

1. Unjust distribution of wealth and income.
2. Unemployment and denial of an opportunity to earn a living.
3. Denial of justice in the creation, in the adjudication, and in the administration of law.
4. Denial of the right and opportunity to form effective organizations.

We recommend that private ownership of public utilities be abolished and that the States and municipalities take over the same under just terms and conditions, so that they may be operated by the States or municipalities.

RECEIVED APPROVAL OF COMMISSIONERS WALSH, LENNON, O'CONNELL, AND GARRETSON.

We find that the limitation of the right of suffrage to men has been a most serious handicap to women in industry in their long and splendid struggle to secure compensation for their labor, humane working conditions, and protective laws.

We recommend that private ownership of coal mines be abolished; and that the National and State Governments take over the same, under just terms and conditions, and that all coal lands shall thereafter be leased upon such terms that the mines may be cooperatively conducted by the actual workers therein.

All religions, the family life, the physical well-being of the worker, the integrity of the State, and the comfort and happiness of mankind require that no human being shall be permitted to work more than six days in each week. This commission refuses to recognize any claim of so-called business expediency or alleged domestic or public necessity which ignores this elemental and righteous demand. We therefore suggest that stringent laws be passed by State and Nation making it an offense punishable by fine and imprisonment to permit any person to work more than six days in each week.

We find that practically nothing has been done toward the very necessary development of organizations of women engaged in domestic service, and that no standards governing the toil of the thousands thus engaged have been established.

As a necessary step in this direction we recommend that the hours of such workers should be limited to eight hours per day; that no such persons be permitted to work over six days in each week; that a minimum wage be fixed for this class of employees which will insure them a comfortable life without being required to live in the homes of persons employing them, where they may be subjected to objectionable or uncomfortable living conditions.

That all of the improvements and safeguards recommended for adoption in this report as applying to women in other lines of industry shall apply with equal force and effect to women engaged in domestic service.

We find that the direct and proximate cause of the killing of men, women, and children, destruction of property, and looting of the homes of the striking miners in the southern Colorado coal fields during the strike therein was the arbitrary refusal of the coal-mine operators to meet and confer with the representatives of the workers in their several mines. Inasmuch as the officials of the Colorado Fuel & Iron Co. admit that said company fixed the prices and conditions of labor in the State of Colorado at the time in question, after fully considering and weighing all of the testimony advanced at the public hearings, and especially the admissions and declarations of the officers and directors of the Colorado Fuel & Iron Co., including Mr. John D. Rockefeller, jr., we find that the final and full responsibility for the refusal to confer with said representatives, and for all the deplorable results which followed such refusal, must be

placed upon Mr. John D. Rockefeller and Mr. John D. Rocke-
·feller, jr.

We wish to report to your honorable body that Mr. John D. Rockefeller, jr., and Mr. W. L. Mackenzie King, witnesses regularly called
before this commission, refused to answer questions relevant and
material to the inquiries provided for in the act of Congress creating
this commission, as shown by the excerpts from the official transcript
of the testimony filed·herewith and attached hereto, and we therefore
recommend that the said witnesses be summoned by the House of
Representatives, according to its usual procedure, immediately upon
its convening, or as soon thereafter as may be reasonably convenient,
and that said questions again be propounded to said persons, and that
they be compelled to answer the same.

QUESTIONS WHICH MR. W. L. MACKENZIE KING REFUSED TO ANSWER.

Chairman WALSH. What salary do they pay you?

Mr. KING. That is a matter you do not have a right to inquire into. I was
asked if I would undertake this work for a period of years. I said I would
not, that all I would undertake to do was to take it for a year; that I wanted
to be perfectly free at the end of a year to terminate my arrangement with the
Rockefeller Foundation if I did not see it was going to give the opportunity
for the practical results I wanted to get. I made an undertaking with them
on that basis, with that understanding, and they asked me to take it for another
period of time, and I refused, and I made the further stipulation that if by
any chance an election should be brought on in Canada, I should resign before
that time. I think under those circumstances the public would hardly expect
me to answer what particular remuneration I am receiving.

Chairman WALSH. Are you going to make your report to anybody? Are you
going to give anybody these facts that you are collecting, the result of these
interviews?

Mr. KING. No, sir; I have not decided that, but if you mean am I going to
give them to anybody connected with the Foundation or Mr. Rockefeller, I
would say no.

Chairman WALSH. Are you going to give them to the Government?

Mr. KING. No.

Chairman WALSH. Are you going to give them to the organizations of
workers?

Mr. KING. I will give them the results.

Chairman WALSH. But as far as the facts are concerned, your purpose is to
keep them absolutely secret?

Mr. KING. No, sir; I would not be telling the truth to say that.

Chairman WALSH. Who are you going to tell them to?

Mr. KING. On that I shall use my own judgment.

Chairman WALSH. Did you talk to the president or secretary or treasurer
of the United Mine Workers of America in Denver?

Mr. KING. I have said already, Mr. Chairman, that I desired to have regarded as confidential the persons that I saw.

Chairman WALSH. Did you call upon the president, the secretary, or the
treasurer of the State Federation of Labor of Colorado?

Mr. KING. I have already stated that I intend to regard as confidential
the interviews that I had in Colorado. That is my position in regard to
that. * * *

Chairman WALSH. I asked if you saw the president, the secretary, or the
treasurer of the United Mine Workers of America or the president, the secretary, or the treasurer of the State Federation of Labor of the State of Colorado?

Mr. KING. I remain just exactly where I put myself before.

CHAIRMAN WALSH. You refuse to answer that question?

Mr. KING. I refuse to disclose any of the interviews I had in Colorado; and
let me make this perfectly plain, Mr. Chairman. I saw some of the persons you
have mentioned——

Chairman WALSH (interrupting). Name them.

Mr. KING. No; I will not. I do not intend to disclose the names, and I do not intend to let the impression go abroad that I avoided seeing anyone, not for one minute. * * *

Chairman WALSH. Did you find it [industrial unrest] very bitter in Colorado?

Mr. KING. I prefer not to discuss the Colorado situation at all.

Chairman WALSH. Please outline for this commission the policies which you consider should be put into effect in Colorado in the industry of the Colorado Fuel & Iron Co.

Mr. KING. No, Mr. Chairman. I have said I do not desire to discuss the Colorado situation.

Chairman WALSH. Do you consider that the miners in Colorado were justified in demanding a recognition of their national union?

Mr. KING. I have already said I don't care to discuss the merits of that strike one way or the other.

Chairman WALSH. Where do you keep them [referring to notes Mr. King testified he had made in Colorado]?

Mr. KING. I am not going any further in my answer.

Chairman WALSH. Think again, and maybe you will go further?

Mr. KING. No; I won't.

Chairman WALSH. Are they in charge of anyone else or in your possession?

Mr. KING. That is my affair, Mr. Chairman.

Chairman WALSH. Are they kept in New York or Washington or at your home?

Mr. KING. They are not kept either in New York, Colorado, or at my home at this moment.

Chairman WALSH. In Washington?

Mr. KING. I have nothing further to say.

Chairman WALSH. It is a dead secret?

Mr. KING. Yes; a dead secret.

QUESTIONS WHICH MR. JOHN D. ROCKEFELLER, JR., REFUSED TO ANSWER.

Chairman WALSH. It is not in a letter. It was in a newspaper statement. Did you write your own newspaper statements, or were they dictated, or were they written by some one else?

Mr. ROCKEFELLER. I assume the responsibility for everything that was sent out in my name. * * *

Chairman WALSH. Did Mr. Ivy Lee write the newspaper interviews purporting to come from you?

Mr. ROCKEFELLER. I have answered the question.

Chairman WALSH. Do you assume the responsibility for that?

Mr. ROCKEFELLER. For everything that goes out in my name.

Chairman WALSH. I am asking for the fact. Did you write it?

Mr. ROCKEFELLER. I have covered the situation, Mr. Chairman.

Chairman WALSH. You do not care to go any further?

Mr. ROCKEFELLER. I do not. I do not think it necessary.

Chairman WALSH. Did you write that answer? [Referring to the prepared statement which Mr. Rockefeller read upon the stand.]

Mr. ROCKEFELLER. I take the responsibility for that entire answer.

Chairman WALSH. Did you write it or did somebody else write it for you?

Mr. ROCKEFELLER. It is not a matter that I think is material.

Chairman WALSH. Did Mr. Lee write it?

Mr. ROCKEFELLER. I have no further answer to give.

Question. What agreements or understanding, verbal or written, exist between the Foundation and Mr. King, regarding the scope of the work which is to be done under his direction, and the method of investigation which is to be pursued?

(a) By whom was the arrangement with Mr. King made?

Answer. Mr. King was appointed pursuant to a resolution adopted at the meeting of the executive committee of the Rockefeller Foundation held August 13, 1914, of which the following is a copy:

" *Resolved*, That William Lyon Mackenzie King be, and he is hereby, appointed to make a comprehensive study of the problem of industrial relations at a salary of $—— a year from October 1, 1914.

" It was, on motion, further

" *Resolved*, That the secretary be authorized to approve all bills for necessary traveling expenses and all other expenses incurred by Mr. King in the pursuance of his work under the direction of the executive committee. The secretary presented a recommendation from Mr. King for the employment of Robert F. Foerster, Ph. D., to prepare a catalogue, etc."

The amounts of the salaries have been omitted as being information of a confidential nature not material to this inquiry.

RECEIVED APPROVAL OF COMMISSIONERS WALSH, LENNON, AND O'CONNELL.

The money with which the Rockefeller Foundation was created and is maintained consists of the wages of workers in American industries. These wages were withheld by means of economic pressure, violation of law, cunning, and violence practiced over a series of years by the founder and certain of his business associates.

Under the law as it now exists, it is impossible to recover this money and pay it over to the equitable owners. We therefore recommend that appropriate legislation be passed by Congress, putting an end to the activities of this foundation, wherever the Federal law can be made effective, and that the charter granted by the State be revoked, and that if the founders have parted with the title to the money, as they claim they have, and under the law the same would revert to the State, it be taken over and used by the State for the creation and maintenance of public works that will minimize the deplorable evil of unemployment, for the establishment of employment agencies and the distribution of labor, for the creation of sickness and accident funds for workers, and for other legitimate purposes of a social nature, directly beneficial to the laborers who really contributed the funds.

O

Milton Keynes UK
Ingram Content Group UK Ltd.
UKHW022104150124
436101UK00005B/131